FREUD'S FREE CLINICS

Freud's Free Clinics

PSYCHOANALYSIS & SOCIAL JUSTICE, 1918–1938

Elizabeth Ann Danto

We are not the first
Who with best meaning have
incurred the worst.

—WILLIAM SHAKESPEARE, *KING LEAR*

COLUMBIA UNIVERSITY PRESS NEW YORK

COLUMBIA UNIVERSITY PRESS

Publishers Since 1893
New York   Chichester, West Sussex
Copyright © 2005 Elizabeth Ann Danto

Library of Congress Cataloging-in-Publication Data
Danto, Elizabeth Ann.
   Freud's Free Clinics : psychoanalysis and social justice, 1918–1938 /
   Elizabeth Ann Danto
      p.   cm.
   Includes bibliographical references and index.
   ISBN 0–231–13180–1 (alk. paper)
   1. Psychoanalysis—Europe—History—20th century. I. Title.
   BF173.D365 2005
   150.19'5'09409041—dc22
                                                    2004043141

Casebound editions of Columbia University Press books are printed on permanent
   and durable acid-free paper.

Designed by Lisa Hamm
Printed in the United States of America
c 10 9 8 7 6 5 4 3 2 1

TO PAUL

CONTENTS

3 1933–1938: Termination

ACKNOWLEDGMENTS

THE PEOPLE and institutions without whom this book would simply not exist, are a large and generous company. I am deeply thankful.

Dean James Blackburn and President Jennifer Raab have imbued the Hunter College School of Social Work with a wonderful energy. They, and the students and faculty, make Hunter and the City University of New York an exceptional place for teaching and writing.

I am honored to have received research support from the TIAA-CREF (2004), the DAAD/German Academic Exchange Service (2002), the Eugene Lang Junior Faculty Development Award at Hunter College (2000), the Hunter College President's Teaching and Research Incentive Award (1999), the Rockefeller Archive Center Research Award (1999), and the American Psychoanalytic Association Fellowship for 1998–1999. I thank Robert Buckley at Hunter College for his brilliant administration of these awards.

Among the archivists and librarians, the bedrock of this book, I want to thank Nellie Thompson and Matthew von Unwerth at the A. A. Brill Archives of the New York Psychoanalytic Society and Institute; Sanford Gifford of the Boston Psychoanalytic Society and Institute for the papers of Helene and Felix Deutsch and Grete and Eduard Bibring; Thomas Rosenbaum of the Rockefeller Archives Center for assistance with documents from the Rockefeller Brothers Fund, the Laura Spellman Rockefeller papers, the Rockefeller Foundation Archives, and the Commonwealth Fund; Rachel Vigneron for assistance with Otto Fenichel's *Rundbriefe* in the

Library at Austen Riggs Center, Stockbridge, Massachusetts; Marvin Krantz for access to the Sigmund Freud Archives and the papers of Anna Freud, Siegfried Bernfeld, Otto Fenichel, and Muriel Gardiner in the Manuscript Collections, Library of Congress, Washington DC; Eckhardt Fuchs of the German Historical Institute, Washington DC; Stephen Novak for access to Sigmund Freud's personal library, Library of the College of Physicians and Surgeons, Columbia University; also the Otto Rank papers and transcripts of Oral Histories of the Psychoanalytic Movement by Bluma Swerdloff in the Rare Book and Manuscript Collection, Columbia University Libraries; Jerome Kavka of the Chicago Institute for Psychoanalysis for the papers of Therese Benedek and Franz Alexander; Ellen M. Shea for the Edith Banfield Jackson papers at the Schlesinger Library, Radcliffe Institute for Advanced Study, Harvard University; the New York Historical Society for the NY State Board of Charities records; Mary Boyd Higgins at the Wilhelm Reich Infant Trust; Dianne Spielmann at the Leo Baeck Institute in New York City; the Archives of the Sophia Smith Collection, Smith College School of Social Work, Northampton, Mass.; Lesley Hall for the Melanie Klein papers at the Wellcome Institute for the History of Medicine, London; Riccardo Steiner, Polly Rossdale, and the Committee on Archives at the British Psycho-Analytic Society (London) for the papers of Ernest Jones; Michael Molnar at the Freud Museum in London; Tom Roberts of the Sigmund Freud Copyrights/Paterson Marsh Ltd., UK; Robert Elwall for Ernst Freud's archives, Royal Institute of British Architects, London; Winfried Schultze at the Universitätsarchiv of Humboldt University in Berlin; Inge Scholz-Strasser and Christian Huber at the Archives of the Sigmund Freud Foundation, Vienna; Helmut Gröger at the Josephineum Institute for the History of Medicine, Vienna; Gregor Pickro at the Bundesarchive in Koblenz, Germany; Johanna Bleker, Thomas Mueller, and Cornelius Borck at the Center for the Humanities and Health Sciences, Institute for the History of Medicine in Berlin; and Philip Swan, Tanya Manvelidze, and Norman Clarius of the Hunter College Libraries. Many of these kind men and women are also historians, psychoanalysts, social workers, and physicians, and I thank them for their unstinting help and insight.

Martin Bergmann, Jean-Luc Donnet, Judith Dupont, Solange Faladé, Sanford Gifford, Pearl King, Eva Laible, Else Pappenheim, the late George Pollock, the late Helen Schur, Lou T. Seinfeld, Robert Stewart, Bluma Swerdloff, Mary Weigund, and the late Joseph Wortis all graciously agreed to be recorded on tape. Thanks for the memories.

Portions of this book have been presented to meetings of the American Association for the History of Medicine, the Society for the History of Science, the Hagley Museum for the History of Science and Technology, the Council on Social Work Education, the International Association for the History of Psychoanalysis, the Richardson Seminar on the History of Psychiatry, the Ad Hoc Committee on Community Clinics of the American Psychoanalytic Association, and the Austen Riggs Center. Selections have been published in article form in *Psychoanalytic Social Work*, in the *Journal of the American Psychoanalytic Association*, and in the *International Journal of Psychoanalysis*.

My friends have been a supportive, funny, loving team, cheering me on as I labored through draft after draft of manuscript. Among the wonderful people in what we call the People's Republic of Fifth Street, a tree-lined community of small buildings and high stoops in the East Village, some like Lucinda, Steven, Arie, and Ni and LiMing have moved away; others like Heide, Doug, and Zeke, or Tricia and Oscar, or Kathryn and Margaret down the block, or Monica and Abe, the Goyals, Lisa and her family of musicians, Marva, Joseph, AJ, Romy, Hayes, Lydia, Judy, David, Mark are so many I can hardly name but I appreciate them all. I am also indebted to Ruth Sidel, Anne Talpain, Norma Tan, Janet Becker, Eve Golden, Clark Sugg, and Ruby and Kevin Eisenstadt. For assistance with translations and scholarship, I thank Heide Estes, Janna Schaefer, Paul Werner, Louise Crandall, Theresa Aiello, George Franks, Mimi Abramovitz, Barbara Levy Simon, Alain de Mijolla, and Craig Tomlinson. At Columbia University Press I thank John Michel for his courage and kindness and Susan Pensak for her editorial perspicacity. With translations as with the historical material, all errors of fact or interpretation remain my own.

I come from a family of writers and, for this legacy, I would like to thank my father Arthur C. Danto, my mother-in-law Vivian L. Werner, and my late mother Shirley Rovetch Danto. Family and step-family members range across the country and I thank them all.

Paul Werner, my witty, moral, worldly husband, has contributed three full-length critical readings of this book and more, truly making it what it is today. Such love is rare and I am lucky.

"The Conscience of Society" —

INTRODUCTION

IN VIENNA of the 1920s and early 1930s doctors who were very busy, like Sigmund Freud, could issue an *Erlagschein*, or voucher, to a current or prospective patient who would later use it as a form of currency to pay another doctor. The *Erlagscheine* were often elegantly printed on pale orange paper, inscribed in classical scripts, and, lacking any particular sequence, made for an especially versatile combination of bank deposit slip and personal check. The vouchers appealed to practically everyone in the city's psychoanalytic community. Private practitioners could choose to endorse an *Erlagschein* (figure 1) to a clinic as a pledge to redeem (in cash or in time) the treatment hours they would ordinarily donate in person. Sigmund Freud regularly endorsed *Erlagscheine* of two to four hundred shillings to the psychoanalysts' own free clinic in Vienna, known as the Ambulatorium.

1 A voucher for two hundred Austrian shilllings, signed by Freud (Archives of the Boston Psychoanalytic Society and Institute)

In 1918, just two months before the Armistice, Freud had rallied the psychoanalysts assembled in Budapest for their fifth international congress to start these "institutions or out-patient clinics . . . where treatment shall be free. The poor man should have just as much right to assistance for his mind as he now has to the life-saving help offered by surgery," he affirmed, embracing the new rhetoric of Austrian social democracy. "It may be a long time before the State comes to see these duties as urgent. Probably these institutions will be started by private charity."[1]

Behind these declarations, as behind all Freud's psychoanalytic projects, lay an interesting tension between psychological theory and therapeutic practice. Whereas his theory aimed to be ahistorical, a de facto science, Freud's clinical *practice* conformed to the social-democratic political ideology that prevailed in post–World War 1 Vienna. When the psychoanalysts in Freud's circle opened the Ambulatorium for adults, children, and families who sought outpatient mental health treatment in May 1922, the character of social democracy and its social welfare institutions had already so permeated Freud's native city that their clinic was just one of many free services. And Vienna was neither the first nor the only city to house a psychoanalytic clinic. In these years of nascent modernism, Freud's expressions of social conscience inspired the creation of a string of at least twelve other cooperative mental health clinics from Zaghreb to London.[2] As late as 1935 Freud still wrote that "out of their own funds, local [psychoanalytic] societies support . . . outpatient clinics in which experienced analysts as well as students give free treatment to patients of limited means."[3] The intervening decades saw the practice of psychoanalysis unfold in plain offices, case by case, on couches where theory hovered invisibly over clinical encounters. Between 1918 and 1938 psychoanalysis was neither impractical for working people, nor rigidly structured, nor luxurious in length.

At least one fifth of the work of the first and second generation of psychoanalysts went to indigent urban residents. This made psychoanalysis accessible to students, artists, craftsmen, laborers, factory workers, office clerks, unemployed people, farmers, domestic servants, and public school teachers. Freud's idea so influenced trainees and medical students that they sought to subsidize their education by agreeing to treat patients at no cost. Established physicians and intellectuals treated troubled young children and their mothers, delinquent adolescents, and people whose psychosomatic illnesses ranged from asthma to epilepsy who would not otherwise have been able to afford treatment. The relatively easygoing nature of this exchange combined with the broad-mindedness of interwar political culture set a tone that allowed people from frankly opposite social worlds to meet in a psychoanalyst's waiting room. Even among analysts who outwardly avoided politics, a practice at a free clinic implicitly reflected a civic commitment to human welfare. Helene Deutsch, an active member of Freud's inner circle who took charge of the Vienna Psychoanalytic Society's Training Institute after spending 1923 and 1924 in Berlin, spoke for her generation. "Revolutionism," she wrote in her story of the second generation of psychoanalysts, was "a spirit of reform . . . [that] can never be defined simply through its social application; it is an attribute of individuals who are drawn to everything that is newly formed, newly won, newly achieved."[4]

From 1920 until 1938, in ten cities and seven countries, the activist generation of psychoanalysts built free treatment centers. Freud had spoken "half as prophecy and half as challenge," said Max Eitingon, the psychoanalyst whose wealth and administrative talent made possible the first clinic in 1920, the Berlin Poliklinik. The Poliklinik's innovations included length-of-treatment guidelines, fractionary (time-limited) analysis, and, of course, free treatment. Child analysis was first formally debated there and psychoanalytic education was standardized. In Vienna the dilemma of how to open a psychoanalytic clinic without needlessly offending the conservative psychiatric establishment hinged on the diplomatic skills of Freud's friend Eduard Hitschmann who set up the second clinic, Vienna's Ambulatorium, in 1922. In 1926 the British psychoanalysts started a clinic in London under Ernest Jones, Britain's psychoanalytic mastermind and later Freud's first major biographer. Also in 1926 Ernst Simmel, cofounder with Eitingon of the Berlin Poliklinik, opened an inpatient center at Schloss Tegel just outside the city. In 1929 the pioneer Hungarian analyst Sándor Ferenczi founded a free clinic in Budapest. By then, in Vienna Wilhelm Reich, whose fusion of psychoanalysis and left-wing politics remains as controversial today as in the 1920s, had created the Sex-Pol, a network of free health and mental health clinics with a particularly strong liberationist bent.

Eventually other psychoanalytic societies followed with plans, some fulfilled and some not, for free clinics in Zaghreb, Moscow, Frankfurt, New York, Trieste, and Paris. They were free clinics literally and metaphorically: they freed people of their destructive neuroses and, like the municipal schools and universities of Europe, they were free of charge. In the heady climate of progressivism and social movements between the two world wars, psychoanalysis was supposed to share in the transformation of civil society, and these new outpatient treatment centers were to help restore people to their inherently good and productive selves. Psychoanalysts believed they had a social obligation to donate a portion of their time to people who could not otherwise afford psychoanalysis. Most never even considered weighing the effectiveness of treatment against the financial burden imposed on the patient.

Erik Erikson, Erich Fromm, Karen Horney, Bruno Bettelheim, Alfred Adler, Melanie Klein, Anna Freud, Franz Alexander, Annie Reich, Wilhelm Reich, Edith Jacobson, Otto Fenichel, Helene Deutsch, Alice Bálint, Frieda Fromm-Reichmann, Hermann Nunberg, Rudolf Loewenstein, and Martin Grotjahn—these were just some of the free clinic analysts who later fanned out across the Western world, some carrying the torch of progressivism and others burying it. Today they are known for their theoretical revisionism and for the many ways in which they followed, transformed, or broke away from classical Freudian theory. But in the 1920s and early 1930s the same analysts saw themselves as brokers of social change for whom psychoanalysis was a challenge to conventional political codes, a social mission more than a medical discipline. Erich Fromm, in residence at the Frankfurt Institute of Social Research in the late 1920s, and Ernst Simmel, head of the Berlin Association for Socialist Physicians, were Poliklinik analysts who based their practice on a symbiotic relationship with the political values of the Weimar era. Berlin's intellectual freedom afforded Melanie Klein the autonomy to analyze children in depth. Karen Horney, perhaps best known as the psychoanalyst who introduced cultural relativism into Freudian theory, was a founding member of the Poliklinik and the first woman to teach there. For Viennese intellectuals like Bruno Bettelheim, Otto Fenichel, and Siegfried Bernfeld, steeped in the romantic activism of central Europe's left-wing youth movements, psychoanalysis represented human liberation, social empowerment, and freedom from bourgeois convention. Erik H. Erikson, the Pulitzer Prize winner who established, perhaps more firmly than any of the others, the central concept of the social environment's influence on human development, was trained as a psychoanalyst in early modern Vienna, at the Ambulatorium. In Budapest the clinic's first director, Sándor Ferenczi, a lifelong intimate of Freud's, belonged to a circle of modernist Hungarian intellectuals, poets, and writers that included the left-wing philosopher Georg Lukács and the composer Béla Bartók.

Ferenczi, who died in 1933, believed that psychoanalysts who disregarded the "*real* conditions of the various levels of society" were forsaking the very people for whom everyday life is especially painful. In many ways postwar *début de siècle* Vienna found psychoanalytic theory and therapy less controversial than it is today. But almost since its inception and certainly since its arrival in America, anticlinical clichés have surrounded psychoanalysis from across the political spectrum.[5] Some critics suggest that individual psychological investigation precludes environmental advocacy and that psychoanalytic studies place the individual person at a remove from culture. Others have virtually made a career of invalidating psychoanalysis as nonscientific and purely ideological. Psychoanalysts themselves have alleged that clinical objectivity actually demands distance from politics, social policy, and social thought. As Wilhelm Reich, one of the field's most biting theoreticians, observed, "the conflict within psychoanalysis in regard to its social function was immense long before anyone involved noticed it."[6] But Ferenczi and Freud did recognize this conflict and, by 1910, had embarked on a far-reaching corrective strategy.

Among the radical changes wrought by World War 1, previously disparaged political attitudes were suddenly dominant within the psychoanalytic movement as elsewhere, while the first Austrian and German republics followed a craggy path into constitutional states. In 1918 Freud might simply have restated the 1913 principles that systematized his prewar approach to patient fees,[7] but he foresaw the history of psychoanalytic theory would ultimately rest on the history of its actual practice. The new democracies would require of working psychoanalysts, as of other professionals, greater public involvement and accountability. Accordingly, Freud argued for an alternative and nontraditional (even then) view of the collective social obligations of psychoanalysis. The Budapest speech on "the conscience of society" reflected Freud's personal awakening to the reality of a new social contract, a new cultural and political paradigm that drew in almost every reformer from Adolf Loos in architecture to Clemens Pirquet in medicine and Paul Lazarsfeld in social science.[8]

By the end of 1918 Germany and Austria's fundamental shifts in size and political outlook were underscored by the advent of "Red Vienna" and "Weimar Berlin" as modern models of urban reconstruction. In both cities the new governments' policies of aggressive social planning linked postwar economic recovery to a public works approach where highly original large-scale projects were instituted along with expansive cultural and aesthetic development. Freud believed that someday "the State will come to see these duties as urgent," and indeed the new governments promoted mental health and social services on a far broader scale than public health care had seen before. They drew on the new-sprung professions of utilitarian architecture, public health policy, and professional social work and emphasized the significance of high culture for the socialist cause. First-hand accounts of life in Red Vienna, its vast communities of public housing, its social welfare programs for families, its art and music, share an exhilarating quality of public commitment and civic pride. Interpretations of these accounts, however, are endlessly contradictory and ideologically driven, speaking of state intrusion and regulation to the conservative analyst, of social democracy's opportunism and the futility of gradualism in social change to the Marxist, and of fairness and affirmative action to progressives.

In 1919 Austrian women achieved universal suffrage, prompting government policies on health, housing, and family to change from patronizing individual charity to empowering social welfare entitlement—the privileges of citizenship. Public resources were invested in medical and dental clinics, family assistance programs, aid to children, and youth and mothers consultation centers. This array of programs was designed by Julius Tandler, the brilliant anatomist and university professor who transformed Vienna's welfare department into a system of professional assistance for families and children. Even visiting Americans were impressed. "One thing is clear," reported a delegation from the Commonwealth Fund. "It would be grossly inaccurate to think of Austria as a country in which health and social work is in a rudimentary stage."[9] The fund's representatives met with Otto Bauer, the sophisticated leader of the new Austrian Marxists and foreign secretary in 1918–1919. Editor of the socialist journal *Arbeiter-Zeitung*, Bauer spoke of the current social movement as a revolution in "the soul of man."[10] Urban culture, Vienna's Social Democrats believed, should encompass the worker's total life, from the privacy of individual and family life to public policy and the workplace. Among the psychoanalysts the left-leaning neurologist Martin Pappenheim, Eduard Histchmann's friend and a frequent guest of the Freud's, maintained that social change should reach "into the structure of family relationships, the social position of women and children, [and] sexual reform."[11]

In 1920 Adolf Loos, now remembered for his ruthlessly streamlined modernism, was appointed chief architect to the building department of the city of Vienna, then suffering from a chronic housing shortage. Anton von Webern, the brilliant avant-garde composer, was principal conductor of the Vienna Worker's Symphony and the Vienna Worker's Chorus (where he remained until 1934) and promoted some of the first performances of Arnold Schoenberg's modernist compositions. Schoenberg had trained himself as the organizer of the Social Democrats' workers' orchestra. Meanwhile in Germany, the Bauhaus director Walter Gropius's fame as the quintessential Weimar architect peaked with the production of urban construction. In its workshops for functional, exquisitely crafted furniture and daily utensils, the Bauhaus remade the idea of mass production. Its principles of streamlined design (many of which still seem modern today) were brought to bear on all the common material needs of everyday city life, from copper desk lamps to porcelain tea sets and from chrome-winged toasters to bentwood baby cradles. Art coexisted with economic reality, culture with politics, citizenship with the newly participatory structure of the state.[12]

Berlin in the 1920s was home to the Poliklinik, the psychoanalysts' flagship program for public therapy and to many the heart of the Berlin Psychoanalytic Society much as the Ambulatorium was to the Viennese. To the Hungarian analyst and teacher Sándor Radó, the Berlin analysts had forged a "wonderful society," a particularly spirited set of progressive practitioners so popular among the city's intellectuals that Karl Abraham nearly secured a professorship in psychoanalysis at the university.[13] International trainees in social work, psychiatry, child guidance, and psychology flocked to the Poliklinik not only from France and England but also from Egypt, Cuba, and the United States. "Please send me all available information concerning your Institute," wrote the Worcester State Hospital psychologist Norman Lyon in August 1929. "I hope sometime to teach Psychology and conduct a clinic in connection with the teaching."[14] From its modernist interiors designed by Ernst, Freud's architect son, to its educational projects, the clinic's efforts to meet the social obligations of psychoanalysis matched Weimar Berlin's social, political, and cultural outlook. Ernst had studied with Loos in his Vienna workshop and parlayed Loos's simple lines and unadorned surfaces into a community design for the clinic's waiting room. In their therapeutic practice the Weimar psychoanalysts debated nontraditional approaches to treatment and, on the social plane, they advocated for penal reform, sexual liberation, gender equality, and the decriminalization of homosexuality.[15] But even in Berlin, where Eitingon's wealth and Karl Abraham's efficiency as the society's director led to a simplification of Freud's formula for allocating pro bono services, pledges were made and patients seen at home. The public's demand for psychoanalytic treatment, which seemed to outpace any solution to the chronic inadequacies of time and space, was sensational.

Neither in Vienna nor Berlin was psychoanalysis truly disengaged from the overall network of available mental health services. Private health and mental health clinics, once restricted to the affluent or near affluent, now opened to all strata of society. But since at least 1916 governments had endorsed psychoanalysis as a form of psychotherapy to help shell-shocked soldiers returning from the front lines. And, while Alfred Adler had broken from Freud's ranks in 1911, members of Adler's highly popular Society for Individual Psychology staffed child guidance offices linked to Vienna's municipal educational system.[16] With its uncompromising emphasis on human sexuality, psychoanalysis was only one of many treatments available in modern psychology, but it was, even so, the most complex and controversial. At the Vienna Ambulatorium on Pelikangasse psychoanalysis was practiced daily by clinicians closely linked to Red Vienna's changing medical and sociopolitical agenda. And on Potsdamerstrasse in Berlin the Poliklinik offered the city's psychiatric patients a compassionate alternative to the Charité Hospital's institutional care, taking in those whom the medical and psychiatric establishments were ready to dismiss.

Although by 1938 the Nazis had so depleted psychoanalysis that one could walk through the academic centers of Berlin or Vienna without meeting an analyst, let alone a Jew, Otto Fenichel and his group of exiled colleagues argued their beliefs more fiercely than ever. The Berlin clinic was ended in 1933, Sex-Pol in 1934, the Vienna Ambulatorium in 1938. Even then Fenichel encouraged his former colleagues to preserve a critical, political attitude even though the Poliklinik had been aryanized (not technically closed) in 1933. In the *Rundbriefe,* an extraordinary series of circular letters written to and among his circle of activist analysts, Fenichel articulated the confrontation between those who faithfully held to the humanist Freud and a new kind of clinician aligned with ego psychology. Over the next ten years Fenichel would come to view the ego psychologist Heinz Hartmann's new theory of adaptation as neo-Freudian at best and, at worst, conformist and eerily pre-Freudian. Fenichel's group argued consistently, along with their colleagues in Ernst Simmel's Association for Socialist Physicians, that the importance of psychoanalysis lay precisely in its social, even Marxist, dimension. "We are all convinced," Fenichel wrote from Oslo in March of 1934, "that we recognize in Freud's Psychoanalysis the germ of the dialectical-materialist psychology of the future, and therefore we desperately need to protect and extend this knowledge."[17]

That the history of political activism in psychoanalysis has been consistently withheld from public view is puzzling. The careers of the second generation of psychoanalysts were exemplary. Freud's students were leaders in academia and medicine and even the military. Archival and oral history evidence, fragmented as it is, confirms that the early psychoanalytic movement was built around a progressive political core, closely allied to the cultural context of central Europe from 1918 to 1933, and that the free outpatient clinics were a practical implementation of that ideology. This narrative comes into focus once psychoanalysis is located in relation to the twentieth century's alternately reformist and conformist social movements of modernism, socialism, democracy, and fascism. Today Otto Fenichel's 119 *Rundbriefe* survive as eloquent documentation of the historical link between psychoanalysis and progressive politics, as classical in their epistolary form as Fenichel's benchmark psychoanalytic text, *The Psychoanalytic Theory of Neurosis*. As of this writing they are fragile sheets of old typing paper attached by rusting paperclips. But the *Rundbriefe* tell part of the story of the psychoanalytic movement's evolution from 1934 to 1945, of its active participants and their larger ideological struggles in Europe and America. Reconstructing other equally valid chronicles from personal memories, the few surviving documents, and widely dispersed archival fragments is a challenge. Nevertheless, the actual political affiliations of prominent members of the psychoanalytic movement are a matter of record. Among the declared Marxists were Erich Fromm, Otto Fenichel, Karl Landauer, Barbara Lantos, Georg Gerö, Frances Deri, Käthe Friedländer, Steff Bornstein, and Wilhelm and Annie Reich. Bruno Bettelheim, Grete Bibring, Helene Deutsch, Ernst Simmel, Willi Hoffer, Eduard Kronengold (Kronold), Siegfried Bernfeld, and Heinrich Meng identified themselves as Socialists. Among the known Communists were Anny Angel-Katan, Edith Jacobson, Edith Gyömröi, Edith Buxbaum, Marie Langer, Ludwig Jekels, and Wilhelm Reich. Eduard Hitschmann, Paul Federn, Karen Horney, Josef Freidjung, and Sigmund Freud were Social Democrats. Since then some of the analysts, like Erik Erikson and Karen Horney, have gained in stature while, for example, Helene Deutsch and Erich Fromm have faded from today's cultural landscape and others, like Wilhelm Reich and Sándor Ferenczi, have since reappeared with surprising strength. Like the *Rundbriefe,* which have disappeared from public view, the clinics have suffered a historical fate in stark contrast to the elaborate psychoanalytic training standards and private practice model now prevailing in psychoanalytic institutes and exclusive offices worldwide.

With their culture fragmented by terrorism, obliged to rebuild professional lives in a foreign language, and beset by screeching postwar nationalism, most central European psychoanalysts fled. But they still assumed that the goodwill and compassion generated by psychoanalysis would ultimately triumph if they tempered the stories of their radical pasts. Ernest Jones had been a voice of conservatism all along, yet his 1926 pronouncements of social conscience had set the British society's clinic on a course that, even today, continues to offer psychoanalysis free to London residents. The Centre Jean Favreau still thrives under the Société Psychanalytique de Paris, founded in 1920 and led for many years by Marie Bonaparte; its psychoanalysts provide free consultation and treatment to residents of the city of Paris.

Toward the end of World War 1, Ernst Simmel, who had served as an army doctor and director of a hospital for shell-shocked soldiers, wrote of the urgent need to participate in "the human economy . . . because of the waste of human life during the war years and for the preservation of all nations."[18] He believed that community was the lifeblood of survival. For Simmel, as for Freud, the free clinics embodied collectivity within psychoanalysis. The psychoanalysts joined in Europe's début de siècle struggle to build democracy without sentimentality and a better world. Helen Schur, a medical student at the University of Vienna in the 1920s and later wife of Freud's personal physician Max Schur, summarized this well. "I think they saw that this would be the liberation of people. To really make them free of neuroses, to be much more able to work, you know, like Freud said, to love well and to work."[19]

What follows is a history of that liberation.

1

1918–1922

SOCIETY AWAKES

"Treatment will be free"

1918

THE GERMAN psychoanalyst Max Eitingon wrote in 1925 that his colleagues could no longer honestly argue that "the factor of the patients paying or not paying has any important influence on the course of the analysis."[1] But Eitingon was merely announcing the fulfillment of Freud's forecast from the 1918 Budapest speech on the conscience of society. In that speech Sigmund Freud had explicitly disavowed his prewar position, "that the value of the treatment is not enhanced in the patient's eyes if a very low fee is asked,"[2] and had repudiated his earlier 1913 image of the psychoanalyst/ physician as medical entrepreneur.[3] Until the end of his life Freud supported free psychoanalytic clinics, stood up for the flexible fee, and defended the practice of lay analysis, all substantive deviations from a tradition of physicians' privilege and their patients' dependence. His consistent loathing of the United States as "the land of the dollar barbarians" echoed his contempt for a medical attitude he believed to be more American than European, more conservative than social democratic.[4] This broad revision in his view of doctors' fees from 1913 to 1918 resulted partly from the grievous material and psychological deprivations the Freud family endured during the war and partly from momentous shifts in the larger political landscape of the early twentieth century.

Freud's sense of civic responsibility was not new. As a child he had witnessed the 1868 installation of the aggressively liberal *Bürgerministerium* (bourgeois ministry) that promoted religious tolerance and progressive social legislation involving secular education, interdenominational marriages, a ban on discrimination against Jews, and a compassionate penal system.[5] He admired Hannibal and Masséna, a Jewish general in Napoleon's army, and was fascinated by the deployment of large-scale military strategies. The idea of becoming a politician seems to have occurred to Freud when, as an adolescent, he "developed a wish . . . to engage in social activities" and decided to study law.[6] Law school would train him in the skills of political leadership, and he would grow up to promote the Austrian liberal's agenda of social reform. But the economic crash of 1873 that shattered Vienna's private sector banks and industries, and the city's economic prosperity in general, struck the same year Freud entered the university. The young Freud was deeply affected by "the fate of being in the Opposition and of being put under the ban of the 'compact majority'" and reacted by developing what he later called, with irony, "a certain degree of independence of judgement."[7]

The experience of anti-Semitism first-hand at the university was, in Freud's life, a powerful motivation to uncover the roots of individual and social aggression. That Freud should focus on the social context of individual behavior was only natural. His model of the civic-minded liberal Jewish family, largely secular, highly accomplished and hard working, was engrained in cosmopolitan Vienna. "Our father was a truly liberal man," wrote Freud's sister, Anna Freud Bernays, about their paterfamilias Jacob,

> so much so that the democratic ideas absorbed by his children were far removed from the more conventional opinions of our relatives. . . . About the middle of the last century, the father was all-powerful in a European family and everyone obeyed him unquestioningly. With us, however, a much more modern spirit prevailed. My father, a self-taught scholar, was really brilliant. He would discuss with us children, especially Sigmund, all manner of questions and problems.[8]

Not surprisingly then, Emma Goldman, the early American feminist and anarchist leader, found much in common with the young neurologist and was enormously impressed when she heard Freud's 1896 lecture in Vienna. "His simplicity and earnestness and the brilliance of his mind combined to give one the feeling of being led out of a dark cellar into broad daylight. For the first time I grasped the full significance of sex repression and its effect on human thought and action. He helped me to understand myself, my own needs; and I also realized that only people of depraved minds could impugn the motives or find impure so great and fine a personality as Sigmund Freud."[9]

Other liberal activists like Sándor Ferenczi (figure 2), Freud's great Hungarian psychoanalytic partner, agreed. "In our analyses," he wrote from Budapest to Freud in 1910, "we investigate the real conditions in the various levels of society, cleansed of all hypocrisy and conventionalism, just as they are mirrored in the individual."[10] Sándor Ferenczi was an affable, round-faced intellectual and socialist physician who had passionately defended the rights of women and homosexuals as early as 1906. The charming son of a Hungarian Socialist publisher, Ferenczi pushed the limits of psychoanalytic theory further and faster than anyone else. In 1912 he established the Hungarian Psychoanalytic Society, home to major psychoanalysts including Melanie Klein, Sándor Radó, Franz Alexander, Therese Benedek, and Alice and Michael Bálint. In 1929 he revived the free clinic he had planned in Budapest at the university ten years earlier, during a brief professorship in psychoanalysis promoted by the revolutionary regime.[11] Freud's remarkable relationship with Ferenczi is conveyed in the course of over twelve hundred letters exchanged between 1908 and 1933, the year Ferenczi died of pernicious anemia. The epistolary dialogue between the two men is highly charged with personal feeling, records their far-ranging exchanges of psychoanalytic theory, and

2 Portrait of Sándor Ferenczi painted by Olga Székely-Kovács (Judith Dupont)

often alludes, in a sad sarcastic way, to the larger effects of social injustice on their patients. Ferenczi describes how the analyst must listen to the patients because only they truly understand how psychoanalysis fosters social welfare. When women, men, and children lead lives truer to their individual natures, society can loosen its bonds and allow for a less rigid system of social stratification. His analytical work with a typesetter, a print shop owner, and a countess had shown Ferenczi how each individual experienced society's repressiveness within their respective social strata, none more than the other but each equally deserving of therapeutic benefits. The high-strung typesetter was terrorized by the demands of the newspaper's foreman; the owner of a print shop felt crushed by guilt over the swindles he perfected to outwit the corrupt rules of the Association of Print Shop Owners; a young countess's sexual fantasies about her coachman revealed her sense of inner hollowness. And a servant disclosed the masochistic pleasure she obtained by deciding to accept lower wages from aristocrats instead of higher wages from a bourgeois family. "Next to the 'Iron Law of Wages,' the psychological determinants," Ferenczi summarized, "are sadly neglected in today's sociology."

What might seem to be Freud's postwar awakening to the harsher realities of life and to social inequality had actually been stirring for years, often in exchanges between the two same friends. "I have found in myself only one quality of the first rank, a kind of courage which is unshaken by convention," Freud wrote in 1915 to Ferenczi, and he postulated that their psychoanalytic discoveries stemmed from "relentless realistic criticism."[12] Indeed political reality called for scrutiny on many levels. In 1915 Freud was still loyal to Franz Joseph and to the Vienna where assimilated Jews thrived on high culture, intellectual pursuits, and a politics of social reform. But by then the war had started and the reactionary mayor Karl Lueger, a right-wing populist and anti-Semite, and the Christian Social Party he cofounded in 1885, had superseded the Viennese liberals and dominated municipal politics until World War 1. By 1917 Freud's family life and professional practice had been thoroughly disrupted. He wrote to Ferenczi of the "bitter cold, worries about provisions, stifled expectations. . . . Even the tempo in which one lives is hard to bear."[13] Sixty-two years old and frankly impatient with battles and the old idea of the absolutist state, Freud remarked that "the stifling tension, with which everyone is awaiting the imminent disintegration of the State of Austria, is perhaps unfavorable." But, he continued, "I can't suppress my satisfaction over this outcome."[14]

Even before war's end Freud's September 1918 address to the Fifth International Psychoanalytic Congress concentrated specifically on the future, not on the war or individual conflict. The speech appealed for postwar social renewal on a vast scale, a three-way demand for civic society, government responsibility, and social equality. To many of his psychoanalytic colleagues, diplomats and statesmen, friends and family members who listened to Freud read his essay on the future of psychoanalysis, that beautiful autumn day in Budapest augured a bold and new direction in the psychoanalytic movement. Anna Freud and her brother Ernst had accompanied their father to the congress, and the British psychoanalyst Ernest Jones (who could not attend) later claimed that Freud uncharacteristically read his paper[15] instead of producing a speech extemporaneously, and upset his family.[16] But in the cautiously festive atmosphere that predominated on September 28 and 29, Freud's speech before this sophisticated audience was far more seditious in meaning than in delivery. He would lead them along an unexplored path, he said, "one that will seem fantastic to many of you, but which I think deserves that we should be prepared for it in our minds."[17] He invoked a series of modernist beliefs in achievable progress, secular society, and the social responsibility of psychoanalysis. And he argued for the central role of government, the need to reduce inequality through universal access to services, the influence of environment on individual behavior, and dissatisfaction with the status quo.

"It is possible to foresee that the conscience of society will awake," Freud proclaimed,

> and remind it that the poor man should have just as much right to assistance for his mind as he now has to the life-saving help offered by surgery; and that the neuroses threaten public health no less than tuberculosis, and can be left as little as the latter to the impotent care of individual members of the community. Then institutions and out-patient clinics will be started, to which analytically-trained physicians will be appointed so that men who would otherwise give way to drink, women who have nearly succumbed under the burden of their privations, children for whom there is no choice but running wild or neurosis, may be made capable, by analysis, of resistance and efficient work. Such treatments will be free." Freud continued. "It may be a long time before the State comes to see these duties as urgent," he said, " . . . Probably these institutions will be started by private charity. Some time or other, however, it must come to this.[18]

Freud's argument concerned nothing less than the complex relationship between human beings and the larger governing social and economic forces.

Implicitly he was throwing in his lot with the emerging social democratic government.

Even in 1918 psychoanalysis was at imminent risk of premature irrelevance and isolation brought on by elitism. The same fervent independence that had driven the psychoanalytic movement, relatively marginal to Vienna's medical and academic communities and practiced by an eclectic group of free thinkers, now threatened its durability. Its economic survival depended on a new governmental configuration, one in which the state accepted responsibility for the mental health of its citizens. In a series of ideological positions intended to destigmatize neurosis, Freud was proposing that only the state could place mental health care on a par with physical health care. Individuals inevitably hold a measure of bias toward people with mental illness, and this limits our ability to provide trustworthy care. Redefining neurosis from a personal trouble to a larger social issue places responsibility for the care of mental illness on the entire civic community.[19]

Freud endorsed the idea that a traditional monarchy's power to set a country's laws should now be redistributed democratically to its citizenry. Like his friends and contemporaries the Austrian Socialist politician Otto Bauer and the Social Democrat Victor Adler, Freud believed that social progress could be achieved through a planned partnership of the state and its citizens. Citizens had the right to health and welfare and society should be committed to assist people in need within an urban environment deliberately responsive to the developmental needs of children and worker's families. In practical terms, he now demanded an interventionist government whose activist influence in the life of the citizens would forestall the increasingly obvious despair of overworked women, unemployed men, and parentless children. The political and social gains derived from the psychoanalysts' new alliances would, at the very least, confer legitimacy on a form of mental health treatment often practiced by nonphysicians or by physicians reluctant to join the establishment.

Freud concluded his Budapest speech with a demand for free mental health treatment for all. He developed the argument for founding free outpatient clinics in the smoothly systematic manner of a born statesman. The possibility of shifting psychoanalysis from a solely individualizing therapy to a larger, more environmental, approach to social problems hinged on four critical points: access, outreach, privilege, and social inequality. First, the psychoanalyst's "therapeutic activities are not far-reaching."[20] As if anticipating his critics, Freud noted how this scarcity of resources conferred on treatment the characteristic of a privilege, and this privilege limited the benefits psychoanalysis might achieve if its scope were broadened. Second, "there are only a handful" of clinicians who are qualified to practice analysis. The shortage of both providers and patients suggested that psychoanalysis might fall into the clutch of a dangerous elitism. This predicament must be overcome if analysts were to alert significantly more people to its curative potential. Third, "even by working very hard, each [analyst] can devote himself in a year to only a small number of patients."[21] This quandary is intrinsic to the intensive and time-consuming format of analytic work, but to Freud it also meant that analysts could not assume a position of social responsibility commensurate with their obligation. Individual analytic patients (called analysands in English, then as now) held to the same appointment at a daily hour five days each week until the treatment was completed. Their treatment usually lasted about six months to a year, perhaps less than we imagine today but, as Freud had commented wryly even in 1913, "a longer time than the patient expects."[22]

Freud's fourth point, that the actual "vast amount of neurotic misery" the analyst can eliminate is "almost negligible" at best compared to its reality in the world, reads like a simple disclaimer. But it is in this passage that the social consciousness of Freud's adolescence and university days reemerges. Human suffering need not be so widespread in society nor so deeply painful individually. Moreover, suffering does not stem from human nature alone, because it is, at least in part, imposed unfairly and largely according to economic status and position in society, a social inequality vividly depicted in Ferenczi's 1910 letter. Inequality, Freud summarized, is the fundamental problem, and he lamented how explicit socioeconomic factors confine psychoanalytic treatment to the "well-to-do-classes." Affluent people "who are accustomed to choos[ing] their own physicians" are already able to influence their treatment. But poor people, who have less choice in their medical care, are precisely those who have less access to psychoanalytic treatment and its benefits.[23] Psychoanalysis had become socially and economically stratified early in its development. At this crucial juncture in its short history, its lack of social awareness has rendered it virtually powerless. "At present we can do nothing for the wider social strata, those who suffer extremely from neuroses."[24]

Who could better reverse this course than this very audience? Freud's September 28 speech, born more of political anger than wartime dejection, had an astonishing effect on its listeners. The concept of the free mental health clinic may have predated the Budapest congress, but the number of organizational projects launched there by the assembled participants, especially Anton von Freund, Max Eitingon, Ernst Simmel, Eduard Hitschmann, and Sándor Ferenczi, was extraordinary. Eitingon and Simmel would open the

Berlin Poliklinik in 1920, Hitschmann would start a free clinic in Vienna in 1922, and Simmel would establish the Schloss Tegel free inpatient clinic. Ferenczi opened the free clinic in Budapest somewhat later, in 1929. Though Ernest Jones could not travel to Budapest to attend the congress because of war restrictions in 1918, he nevertheless started the London Clinic for Psychoanalysis in 1926. Melanie Klein, Hanns Sachs, Sándor Radó, and Karl Abraham were also in that audience and all became key players in the Berlin Poliklinik.

For the moment the grimness of the last few contentious months of 1918 gave way to political idealism, good company, and renewed confidence in Freud and psychoanalysis. "Under a walnut tree in the garden of one of those wonderful restaurants in Budapest . . . [we] chatted confidentially and privately around a big table,"[25] recalled Sándor Radó of their celebratory mood. As conference secretary and coleader of the Budapest society under Ferenczi, the young Radó and his colleague Geza Roheim, the future anthropologist, were pleasantly surprised to dine so informally with Freud and Anna Freud. Their conversations continued on the Danube steamer provided by the city for the analysts' transportation between their hotel and the meetings at the Hungarian Academy of Sciences. The visitors were hosted at the splendid new Gellértfürdö Hotel, still famous for its beautifully tiled thermal baths. Budapest's Mayor Bárczy and other city magistrates publicly welcomed psychoanalysis and graciously accommodated the congress with receptions and private banquets. Except for the avowed Viennese pacifist Siegfried Bernfeld and Freud, most of the analysts present in Budapest had enlisted as army psychiatrists and all attended the conference in uniform. High-level military and medical officials from Hungary, Austria, and Germany officially represented their governments' delegation to the convention and mingled with the families and guests of the forty-two participating analysts.

Freud's speech may have been seditious, but it must have been incredibly stimulating as well because so many of the analysts in the audience became powerful proponents of the free clinics. Among them the young Melanie Klein, who saw Freud in person for the first time at this congress, said she was overcome by "the wish to devote [her]self to psychoanalysis."[26] Klein would go on to become the originator of play therapy in child analysis, the framer of an extended dual drive theory, a truly principled follower of Freud. But at the 1918 congress she was still "Frau Dr. Arthur Klein" and mother of three, an analysand of Ferenczi's and member of the Budapest society since 1914. Anna Freud and Ernst, Freud's youngest son who had been fighting on the front lines for the last three years, would later become immersed in the free clinics. Anna, Freud's devoted youngest daughter and the only psychoanalyst of his six children, was a licensed teacher who developed experimental schools with new early childhood educational methodologies for Vienna's inner-city families. Whether or not in 1918 either Anna or Ernst were ever particularly disturbed by their father's speech, or merely surprised, both were nevertheless to join his social democratic platform shortly. Progressive politics, like psychoanalysis, struck them as a basic element of life.

The leader they had chosen to merge psychoanalysis and social reform was a wealthy Hungarian owner of breweries and an analytic trainee just appointed general secretary of the International Psychoanalytic Association (IPA). Anton von Freund (Antal Freund von Tószeghi) was a friend and patient of Freud and Ferenczi's. He was a young idealist with a doctorate in philosophy who believed that both his recent bout with cancer and his depression had been successfully treated with psychoanalysis. Toni, as von Freund was fondly nicknamed, donated two million crowns for the promotion of psychoanalysis by underwriting two significant projects, a publishing house and a major multi-faceted Institute in Budapest that would house a free outpatient clinic. "Materially we shall be strong, we shall be able to maintain and expand our journals and exert an influence," Freud wrote to Abraham after talking with von Freund about his plans. "And there will be an end to our hitherto prevailing penuriousness," Freud added.[27] The publishing enterprise, the Internationaler Psychoanalytischer Verlag (originally Bibliothek), started up the following year. Its first book-length project collected the 1918 colloquium's main papers into one volume, called "Psychoanalysis and the War Neuroses," with an introduction by Freud.[28]

The institute Toni Freund had forecast would help "the masses by psychoanalysis . . . which had hitherto only been at the service of the rich, in order to mitigate the neurotic sufferings of the poor."[29] He died before this vision could be realized, but Freud described it later as a project that would combine the teaching and practice of psychoanalysis under one roof, with a research center and an outpatient clinic added. A large group of analysts would be trained at the institute and then remunerated specifically "for the treatment of the poor" at the clinic. Von Freund and his friends anticipated that Ferenczi would be the director and Toni would maintain administrative and financial responsibility. Though a clinic would not actually appear in Budapest until 1929, such a scheme was in keeping with the municipal government's design for urban inpatient and ambulatory psychoanalytic treatment. The mayor of Budapest, Stefan Bárczy, promised to facilitate the allocation of von Freund's considerable financial legacy and, as Freud recalled, "preparations for the establishment of Centres of this kind were actually under way, when the revolution broke out and put an end to the war and the influence of the administrative offices which had hitherto to been all-powerful."[30] Indeed the huge political shifts sweeping Hungary, from liberal monarchist to radical left to dictatorial, undermined most of these promises. In seemingly boundless complex transactions over the next few years, the von Freund funds would shift between banks and what had been a considerable sum virtually evaporated. Apparently the public press in Budapest was less accepting of psychoanalysis than the municipal government and, once alerted to von Freund's bequest, sought out experts to testify against the clinic. "Psa is not a recognised science. No doubt [this testimony] is largely political (anti-semitic and anti-Bolshevik)," Ernest Jones observed to his Dutch colleague, Jan van Emden.[31] In other countries though, the free outpatient clinics, both the most crucial and the most polemical aspect of von Freund's project, were built along the lines laid out at that September 1918 conference.

In the midst of negotiations for the free clinics and, to some, for the future of psychoanalysis itself, Ferenczi, Ernst Simmel, and Karl Abraham made public their recent experiences with "war neurosis," the controversial psychiatric diagnosis of trauma among soldiers. All three physicians already had significant military and psychoanalytic experience (and all were destined to be a founder of a free clinic) before they came to the Budapest conference. Abraham, a self-confident man in his thirties with blond good looks and an adventurous spirit, recalled his first treatment of war neurosis. "When I founded a unit for neuroses and mental illness in 1916," Abraham remembered, "I completely disregarded all violent therapies[32] as well as hypnosis and other suggestive means. . . . By means of a kind of simplified psychoanalysis, I managed to . . . achieve comprehensive relaxation and improvement."[33] As chief psychiatrist of the twentieth army corps in Allenstein, West Prussia, Abraham had set up a ninety-patient observation unit with his Berlin colleague Hans Liebermann. Hungarian army officials were impressed by the results and decided to use psychoanalysis to treat the psychiatric symptoms seen among soldiers traumatized in the course of duty.

Figure 3 belongs somewhere within or after the next paragraph.

Ernst Simmel (figure 3), then the Prussian Royal Army's senior physician in charge of a specialized military hospital for war neurotics in Poznan (Posen), was among the first psychoanalysts to appreciate Abraham's work. Psychoanalysis could be conducted successfully under war conditions, he said, "but only rarely permits a more extensive individual analysis. I endeavoured to shorten the duration of the treatment . . . to two or three sessions."[34]

3 Freud and Ernst Simmel
at Schloss Tegel (Freud Museum,
London)

Simmel drew on his two years of intense field experience as superintendent of military psychiatry to develop the vivid interpretive diagnoses and treatments he described at the conference. In 1918 Freud arranged to have Simmel's observations published in a short but striking book, the first volume issued by the new *Verlag*.[35] "As a result of this publication," Freud said later, "th[is] Psycho-Analytical Congress was attended by official delegates of the German, Austrian and Hungarian Army Command, who promised that Centres should be set up for the purely psychological treatment of war neuroses."[36] By now only a few conservative psychiatrists still thought of neurotic soldiers as deviant or disloyal, and complaints of severe anxiety, phobias, and depressions accompanied by trembling, twitching, and cramps were viewed as genuine signs of illness.

Sándor Ferenczi's interest in war neurosis had military origins as well. The Hungarian government had acclaimed Ferenczi's work with psychologically injured soldiers early in the war. Initially a regiment physician on duty in the small Hungarian town of Papa, Ferenczi was transferred to Budapest and made director of the city's health services for soldiers with psychiatric disorders in 1915. The chief medical officer of the Budapest Military Command commissioned Ferenczi to design an entire hospital-based psychoanalytic ward in Budapest. Residential quarters would be adapted to treat men "brain crippled [by the war with] organic injuries and traumatic neuroses," modeled at least in part on the therapeutic institute in Vienna of Emil Fröschels, a colleague of the psychoanalyst Alfred Adler.[37] Thrilled that psychoanalysis had achieved scientific respectability, Ferenczi shared with Freud his dream of a "preliminary study [for] the planned civilian psychoanalytic institution," which would start with about thirty patients in 1918.[38] Istvan Hollós, a member of the Hungarian society then running the psychiatric hospital in Lipometzo, or Max Eitingon, now applying hypnosis with great success at an army base, or both together, would make excellent assistant directors, Freud suggested. Since 1915 Eitingon had supervised the psychiatric observation divisions of several military hospitals, one in Kassa (Kachau) in northern Hungary and the other in Miskolcz, a small industrial town in eastern Hungary. Together at the Budapest conference for the first time since the beginning of the war, Eitingon along with Ferenczi, Simmel, and Abraham began to set down policies for their civilian practice, derived from experience in military psychiatry. Of utmost concern was the threefold idea of barrier-free, non-punitive, and participatory access to psychoanalytic treatment. Sándor Ferenczi introduced the technical concept of "active therapy" during these discussions of war neurosis and initiated a clinical controversy that has lasted even until today. Throughout the history of psychoanalysis, and indeed much of modern mental health treatment, the debate between proponents of the therapist's direct verbal support of the patient, on the one hand, and the therapist's role as an interpretive facilitator of patient's quest for inner knowledge, on the other hand, has shifted from decade to decade. In all likelihood encouraged by Freud's interventionist speech on the role of the state, Ferenczi's own address proposed a psychoanalytic technique featuring time limits, tasks, and prohibitions.

For Freud, war neurosis was a clinical entity largely analogous to "traumatic neuroses which occur in peace-time too after frightening experiences or severe accident" except for "the conflict between the soldier's old peaceful ego and his new warlike one."[39] He was describing what we now call posttraumatic stress disorder or PTSD, a cluster of psychiatric symptoms (depression, hypochondria, anxiety, and hallucinatory flashbacks) experienced by men and women exposed to trauma. The diagnosis required drawing a necessary distinction between an involuntary psychological condition and somewhat more deliberate actions like malingering, lying, desertion, and lack of patriotism. For Simmel, who first articulated the concept of war neurosis, the designation had to be applied very carefully. "We gladly abstain from diagnoses out of desperation," he wrote, but warned that society could not afford to ignore "whatever in a person's experience is too powerful or horrible for his conscious mind to grasp and work through filters down to the unconscious level of his psyche."[40] The designation of "war neurosis," which encapsulated all the moral ambiguities of a psychiatric diagnosis, would resurface in 1920 when Freud was called by the Vienna war ministry to testify against the neurologist Julius Wagner-Jauregg.

"Political events absorb so much of one's interest at present," Karl Abraham wrote to Freud one month after the Budapest congress, "that one is automatically distracted from scientific work. All the same, some new plans are beginning to mature."[41] The month of November 1918 was as memorable for Austria as for psychoanalysis and indeed for the rest of the Western world. By November 10 Freud cheerfully advised Jones that "our science has survived the difficult times well, and fresh hopes for it have arisen in Budapest."[42] The following day, Armistice Day, Freud shifted from psychoanalysis to larger worldly concerns: the Hapsburgs, he wrote to Ferenczi on November 17 "left behind nothing but a pile of crap."[43] The map of Freud's political world was changing fast. From Schönbrun Palace to Madrid's Escorial, from the thirteenth to the twentieth centuries, the Hapsburg Empire's seven-hundred-year domination of Europe had spanned eleven countries and fourteen languages. Now it was over, leaving in its wake revolutions, newborn nations, and a few ambitious governments trying to relieve human suffering. In Germany, once the kaiser abdicated, the Social Democrat Philipp Scheidemann proclaimed a republic. Austria shrank both in physical size and in political power from the immensity of the Hapsburg Empire to a smaller, economically ravaged, but independent republic. At its height Vienna had been the capital of Austria, Hungary, Czechoslovakia, Yugoslavia, northern Italy, and parts of Poland. And while the new Austria was not currently faced with the pressure of managing a huge multiprovince administration, the government's need for effective leadership was urgent. Among these, the physician and Social Democrat Victor Adler had a particularly inventive political outlook that accommodated the atypical field of psychoanalysis. Scorned by Karl Lueger and the Christian Socials, Adler promoted a unique identity for the Viennese Social Democratic Workers' Party (also known as the Austrian Socialist, SDAP, or as the Austro-Marxist Party) grounded in the combined values of liberal intellectuals and workers' movements.

Victor Adler was a large affable-looking man with wavy brown hair, steel-rimmed eyeglasses, and a thick moustache. First as an *Armenarzt* (physician to the poor) and later as a government inspector touring factories in Germany, Switzerland, and England as well as his native Austria, Victor Adler's critical early observations of ordinary household life led him to join the politics of social reform. In 1886 he founded the first Social Democratic weekly, *Gleichheit* (Equality), and in 1889 the *Arbeiterzeitung* (Workers' Times), a journal that still exists today. His personality appealed even to those who resisted Austria's shift to a self-governing constitutional republic. Adler belonged to the Pernerstorfer Circle, a Viennese group that rejected nineteenth-century Austrian liberalism in favor of expanded suffrage, socialist economic structures, and cultural renewal based in art, politics, and ideas. Thus, he was at once a nationalist and a socially committed medical doctor whose personal attempts to meet the health concerns of poor people fueled a political vision of social reform.[44] Adler died suddenly the day the war ended, November 11. His friend Sigmund Freud, who yearned neither for the former monarchy nor traditional structure, wrote to Ferenczi that day. "We lost the best man, perhaps the only one who might have been up to the task," he said. "Nothing can likely be done with the Christian Socialists and the German Nationalists."[45] Viennese Jews had necessarily supported Franz Joseph because he offered protection against anti-Semitism.[46] Now the pro-Hapsburg Christian Socials were openly, and dangerously, opposed to Vienna's Jews. Freud and Adler had surely discussed these concerns along with their views on Viennese politics and culture and thought back on high school adventures with their fellow activist, Heinrich Braun.

An early figure in Freud's lifelong series of intense relationships with influential men, Braun seems to have inspired his friend's desire for a reformist's career when they met as adolescents at the Gymnasium in the early 1870s. Braun was "my most intimate companion in our schooldays," Freud recalled years later.[47] "Under the powerful influence of a school friendship with a boy rather my senior who grew up to be a well-known politician I developed a wish to study law like him."[48] Eventually Freud chose to study natural sciences and then medicine, but his adolescent convictions about social justice and the need for political leadership endured all his life. Like Victor Adler, Heinrich Braun became a prominent socialist politician and an expert on the theory of social economy. When Braun died in 1926, Freud sent a condolence note to his classmate's widow and made clear how deeply politics ran in the thoughts shared by all three friends. "At the Gymnasium we were inseparable friends. . . . He awakened a multitude of revolutionary trends in me. . . . Neither the goals nor the means for our ambitions were very clear to us. . . . But one thing was certain: that I would work with him and that I could never desert his party."[49] He never did. He shared with Braun, Adler, and yet another childhood friend, Eduard Silberstein, the background of the nineteenth-century tradition of liberal, scholarly, atheist doctors. As early as 1875 Freud asked Silberstein if the Austrian Social Democrats "are also revolutionary in philosophical and religious matters; I am of the opinion that one can more easily learn from this relationship than from any other whether or not the basic trait of their character is really radical."[50] The adolescent Freud wondered whether radicalism, philosophical or religious, in someone like himself was more central to a revolutionary position than even the progressivism of social democracy. This was to be Freud's journey: to craft a revolutionary position, to blend increasingly adventurous liberalism with science, to bend the depth and traditional graciousness of the humanities to serve the needs of the people. In the end the adolescent struggle was resolved through the discovery of psychoanalysis. Much later the adult Freud rented the apartment that had previously belonged to Victor Adler's family at 19 Berggasse, on a street of solid Viennese buildings down a steeply inclined hill near the University of Vienna. Victor Adler died the day before the Austrian republic was decreed, but his ideas had planted the seeds of the era known as *Rotes Wien*, or Red Vienna. Like the Weimar Republic, Austria's progressive First Republic would last less than twenty years.

In Red Vienna the birth of a social democratic state turned, even more than on Braun or Adler, on the influence of Dr. Julius Tandler, the University of Vienna anatomist whose role as administrator of the new republic's pathbreaking welfare system was hardly outweighed by his brilliant academic reputation. Now in his early fifties, Tandler had been a professor at the University of Vienna since 1910 and dean of the medical faculty during the war. He took over as undersecretary of state for public health on May 9, 1919. Over the next ten years Tandler fought for a vast extension of public health and welfare services and implemented a comprehensive political solution to the city's high rates of infant mortality, childhood illness, and, ultimately, family poverty. The Social Democrats "hoped to take away the shame of being born an illegitimate child," remembered the psychoanalyst Else Pappenheim. "Any baby born out of wedlock," she said, "was adopted by the city. It stayed with the mother who, if she was poor, was sent for six weeks to a home with the baby—but it was officially adopted."[51] Even a group of American physicians visiting Vienna were impressed. "Nowhere else have the theory and practice of legal guardianship for illegitimate and dependent children been pushed so far," they observed.[52] Actually pediatric medical care originated in Austria and the principle of guardianship, the state in essence substituting for paternal support of illegitimate children, had long been in effect. Within a few years of the war the extraordinary success of child services would dull most criticism. For Julius Tandler healthy children were simply the necessary foundation of a healthy state. Whether in the Vienna City Council or at the university, where his medical students included future prominent psychoanalysts like Erik Erikson, Wilhelm Reich, Otto Fenichel, and Grete and Eduard Bibring, Tandler's beliefs were as legendary as his irascible temper, his large white moustache, wide-brimmed hat, and bow tie.

Meanwhile Otto Bauer, the mathematician who had assumed the Social Democrats' chairmanship at Victor Adler's death, applied the party's platform of cautious progressivism to Vienna's economic recovery. Bauer's new government, which included the attorney and tax expert Robert Danneberg and Hugo Breitner, former director of the Austrian Ländesbank, sought to socialize housing without attacking private property, to build a viable government system based on parliamentary democracy, and to consolidate the country politically and economically. To articulate the complex partnership between urban architecture and social planning, Bauer hired Benedikt Kautsky, son of the theoretician of international socialism Karl Kautsky and editor of his father's correspondence with Engels and Victor Adler, as his private secretary. Robert Danneberg addressed questions of law and authored a range of new municipal ordinances. Finally, Hugo Breitner became councillor of finance responsible for fiscal and budgetary policy. Together they abolished the prewar taxation system and crafted an "inflation-proof" strategy to protect the city's revenue in an exceptionally volatile economic environment. They drew up a series of clever redistributive taxation measures that succeeded in balancing the municipal account books while allowing the government to continue functioning within the preexisting capitalist economy. Ten years later, in 1929, outsiders like the American representatives from the Commonwealth Fund who were completing their philanthropic mission in public health found that the strategy had been an impressive achievement on all economic fronts. "The Social Democratic city has run the gamut of experiments in taxation and has pioneered in municipal enterprises—housing for instance—in a fashion that arrests the attention of all Europe," William French and Geddes Smith reported.[53]

Between 1918, when World War I ended, and the mid-1930s when fascist incursions began in the streets of Vienna, the début de siècle was a gradual and at times painful breakaway from the alienating rule of monarchy. The October dissolution of the Austro-Hungarian monarchy had brought about the abrupt decline of a supranational empire of fifty-two million to a federal state of a mere six million, one-third of whom lived within the boundaries of Vienna. Concurrently the ascent of *Deutschösterreich*, the self-named rural Austria, led to conflicts with urban Vienna (both the greater area and the former imperial city) that would only end in 1933. Generally conservative and Catholic, agricultural landowners and laborers balked at the idea of sharing food, coal, and raw materials with the city, which to them represented decadence, taxes, and Jews. Red Vienna's brand of Austro-Marxism, with its belief in social democratic incrementalism in social and political change, sounded the alarm in traditionalist circles. But the support it received from the progressive avant-garde went far toward ensuring its survival. Once the term *Austro-Marxism* became synonymous with a unique alliance between the liberal arts and the health professions, it shed many of the negative images traditionally applied to movements of the left. Future humanitarian socioeconomic policy could be attained, the Social Democrats believed, through nonviolence and genuinely democratic elections. For the present however, construction of housing, symphony concerts for workers, school reform, ski trips, summer camps for urban children, and cash allotments made clear the party's commitment to improving the daily reality of human life. A genuine welfare system coexisted with public lectures, libraries, theaters, museums and galleries, sports arenas and mass festivals. The experiment's success turned on the confluence of several ideological streams that integrated a present-focused materialist, economic view with a reliance on traditional, liberal culture.

Vienna of the years between 1918 and 1934 reached an extraordinarily high level of intellectual production. Linked to Austria by their recent induction into war service, yet alienated from their nation by culture and religion, the modernist composer Arnold Schoenberg and his two celebrated pupils Anton von Webern and Alban Berg formulated the so-called Second, or Twentieth-Century, Viennese School of Music. These controversial composers broke with traditional forms of music and articulated the new twelve-tone system of serial composition. In February 1919 Schoenberg founded a forum for modern music, the Verein für musikalische Privataufführungen (Society for Private Music Performances), where composers presented chamber music, songs, and even operas that dismantled Vienna's musical heritage and featured the contemporary atonal medium. The Verein ran until 1921, with both Schoenberg's composition classes and some seats to the performances offered on a pay-as-you can basis. Modern music attracted a small audience. But the young Wilhelm Reich, still in medical school and befriended by Otto Fenichel, Grete Lehner Bibring, and other future psychoanalysts, most of whom played the piano, joined the Schoenberg Verein. In philosophy the Vienna Circle (including Rudolf Carnap, champion of logical positivism) gathered weekly at the University of Vienna between 1925 and 1936 to examine the relationship between mathematical and psychological worlds. And in medicine Guido Holzknecht, already a member of the Vienna psychoanalytic society, pioneered the use of radiology while Clemens Pirquet founded the theory of allergy. Still conscious of their past, institutions like the Bildungszentrale (the social democratic center for adult education) and municipal civic museums sponsored exhibits of Otto Neurath's pictorial statistics comparing everyday life after the war to the Vienna of long ago. The bridge between art and sociology was built on observations about families. Of all the cultural productions that linked psychoanalysis and Red Vienna, the new architecture for public housing was to demonstrate that communities constructed specifically to meet the needs of urban children and families met essential psychological needs as well.

"The living conditions in postwar Vienna were miserable," the psychoanalyst Richard Sterba remembered. "The official food rations were so small that one had to supplement them on the black market in order to survive. . . . At home and at the university there was no fuel for heating and the apartments and classrooms were bitter cold. . . . We [all] developed frostbite."[54] With the number of marriages and new families surging at war's end, Vienna's housing shortage became particularly acute for young people like Sterba. Returning former imperial civil servants and military personnel, newlyweds and even small families found themselves subletting rooms or renting "sleeping spaces" in existing apartments. The demand for housing grew stronger as workers were evicted from their sublets and left without alternative housing arrangements. Those tenement buildings where indigent families remained had neither gas nor electricity, and most residents shared water and toilets in the hallway. Inflation, unemployment, paucity of private capital invested in real estate, and drops in real wages added up to a major housing crisis. Rents had already been capped by the Mieterschutz (tenant protection, also known as rent control), a government decree of January 26, 1917, designed to shield soldiers and their dependent families from rent increases and evictions.

At its core Red Vienna, where Freud lived and worked, was "not so much a theory as a way of life . . . pervaded by a sense of hope that has no parallel in the twentieth century," recalled Marie Jahoda, one of the most influential modern social psychologists.[55] At the University of Vienna's Psychological

Institute, Karl Bühler, Charlotte Bühler, Paul Lazarsfeld, and Alfred Adler, combined the new "experimental method" with academic psychology and laboratory-based direct observation of infants. At the university's medical school Wilhelm Reich, Helene Deutsch, and Rudolf Ekstein had started to come together as a second generation of psychoanalysts with a specific, left-wing activist orientation. Reflecting on what Red Vienna meant to this incredible range of social psychologists, developmental psychologists, educators and psychoanalysts, architects and musicians whose calling emerged from an exceptional nexus of ideology and practice, Jahoda remained enthralled by its activist world view. *Revolutionism* was yet another designation for the spirit of Red Vienna. Helene Deutsch coined this term in her memoirs of her youth as an ambitious Polish-born medical student, as interested in political activism as in psychiatry and later psychoanalysis. As a young woman Helene Deutsch, whose striking classical features were set off by dark upswept hair, was the secret lover of the socialist leader Herman Lieberman and had, in his company, met the influential Marxist Rosa Luxemburg[56]. Deutsch was one of the few first women admitted to the University of Vienna's medical school, where she studied anatomy with Julius Tandler just before the war. She was also the only female war psychiatrist allowed to work in Wagner-Jauregg's clinic. As a physician she particularly admired the Kollwitz team, the socialist artist Käthe and her pediatrician husband (Berlin activists who later formed the Association for Socialist Physicians along with Albert Einstein and the psychoanalyst Ernst Simmel).

Wilhelm Reich was in Vienna too, a passionate young medical intern who stood out even among the two thousand other students. Like most psychoanalysts who lacked a political voice at the start of the war, Reich was radicalized by 1918. Reich, who would join the Ambulatorium as assistant director four years later in 1922, had just come out of military service and enrolled as a medical student. His own memoirs of Red Vienna speak of "everything in confusion: socialism, the Viennese intellectual bourgeoisie, psychoanalysis" to describe this era when all previous assumptions about the interests of government, individuals and society, were all called into question.[57] Soon after his first encounter with Otto Fenichel at the medical school, Reich read Fenichel's "Esoterik" and was enormously impressed because the essay's images truly captured the turbulence of Red Vienna.[58] As he recalled, the paper brought forward, for the first time, a written account of a woman's political and moral struggle over the right to use her body for reproduction, for sale, or for eroticism whether aimed at herself or others. Reich was challenged by just these same questions, and in fact his later network of free clinics offered free and confidential reproductive care for women. Meanwhile his friends Fenichel, Siegfried Bernfeld, and Bruno Bettelheim were involved with Vienna's complex *Wandervogel* groups and, like other young men returning from the front, applauded the movement's crucial transformation from its prewar pan-German nationalism to an "anti-war, pacifist and leftist" stance.[59] Actually, the young reformers represented only one aspect of the youth movement since it had recently split along ideological lines. Left-wing members affiliated with Socialism, Communism, and Zionism while others joined the Christian Nationalists and even more radical right-wing groups, precursors to Nazi organizations such as the Hitler Youth. Bettelheim's own left-leaning friends were specifically interested in radical educational reform. Inspired by the anarchist Gustav Landauer's ideal of spontaneous community then in vogue,[60] they met on Sundays in the Vienna woods. This was a vast and lush suburban park of inviting beer gardens and elaborate hiking trails, generally a playground where roaming groups of youths gathered for games, songs, and political discussions. Years later Bettelheim still enjoyed telling the story about the day Fenichel interrupted his group, wearing his military uniform. Fenichel was often inconsiderate, but this time he broke into their conversation and started to expound on the views of Sigmund Freud. Freud had just delivered a few of his famous university lectures and the dazzled Fenichel could hardly contain his exuberant fascination with dreams, dream interpretation, and sexuality. Bettelheim, for his part, was in less of a hurry but still curious. "While we had heard vaguely about these theories in our circle, which was eagerly taking up all new and radical ideas," Bettelheim recalled of his first introduction to psychoanalysis, "we knew nothing of substance about them."[61] Nevertheless, since the fascination seemed to infect Bettelheim's girlfriend as well, he dashed off to find the real Sigmund Freud. Before long Bettelheim had found his vocation—and recaptured his romantic relationship as well.

"It is good that the old should die, but the new is not yet here," Freud wrote to his great friend and colleague Max Eitingon in Berlin, just a few weeks just before the end of World War I. Freud's first glimpse of freedom from war was "frighteningly thrilling."[62] Even in October 1918 Freud had a real sense that remarkable changes at all levels of society were about to transform the world they had known. One month earlier, together with Eitingon and other members of the new IPA who had gathered in Budapest for their fifth international congress, Freud had plotted what he would meaningfully call "Lines of Advance" in the battle for psychoanalysis. They had approved far-reaching plans that would require local psychoanalytic societies to promote clinical research, standardized training programs, and free outpatient clinics. Their mood was confident and eager. The psychoanalyst Rudolf Ekstein remembered how "Anna Freud [and] August Aichorn were concerned not only with theoretical issues but also with practical issues of education. "In Red Vienna of course," he said, "there was Sigmund Freud."[63]

"The polyclinic will be opened in the winter and will grow into a Ψ institute"

1919

FOR YOUTH workers at community centers near the Prater, Vienna's area of seedy amusements and prostitution, the idea of establishing school-based treatment centers for children neglected by four years of war and starvation seemed like a deliverance. An advertisement for just this kind of center had appeared in the fall of 1919, not quite a year after Armistice, on a small bulletin board of the local Gymnasium, the high school on Zircusgasse. The poster also announced the imminent opening of an additional section of the *Volksheim,* a kind of university settlement house where workers took evening classes. The upcoming courses ranged from child psychology to educational reform. They were to be taught by Alfred Adler, founder of a new school of Individual Psychology, and by some of Sigmund Freud's adherents like Siegfried Bernfeld and Hermine Hug-Hellmuth. Adler and Freud were lecturing around Vienna and, beyond the intimacy of psychoanalytic circles, their now notorious differences were not so evident. In any case, given the depth of need among Vienna's children and schoolteachers, either analyst could count on finding an audience grateful for careful, caring, and methodical attention to child psychology.

Adler was an engaging speaker, impeccably outfitted in a tailored tweed suit, a white starched shirt, cigar, thoughtful demeanor, mustache, and wire-rimmed glasses. At eight o'clock in the evening, when Adler started to speak in the Volksheim, the small windowless classroom was already so crammed that even a larger room could barely accommodate the teachers, social workers, psychologists and school nurses already impressed by his new writings in educational psychology. The Gymnasium poster had announced that Adler would teach a semester-long course called Healing by Reeducation. His lecture would usually start with an enthralling case description, perhaps of Frank, a shy eight-year old boy from the slums who lied about the gravity of his mother's illness. Frank's teacher had seen his energetic mother hanging out the laundry, not dying at all. Why had the boy lied? Using Adler's analytic technique, she realized that Frank's tales were not "pathological lies" but, on the contrary, coping devices that emerged from his need to rectify painful feelings of family rejection and community neglect. Adler would start off his seminar with stories like these, volunteering some information and general principles and then asking participants for case examples. He could draw strikingly accurate analyses from small incidents of everyday life where children suddenly became important and the human need to belong to a communal society became meaningful.

The young psychologist Hilde Kramer found herself in that audience. She had volunteered to present the case of her difficult juvenile client, Ernest, and was struck by the clarity of Adler's explanation of the boy's psychological problem. Healing by reeducation was, she thought, a breakthrough technique, a pragmatic union of theory and therapy. For one, the concepts of "individualism" and "community" were not necessarily incompatible. Second, children were just as responsive as adults, if not more so, to the underlying meaning behind both these two terms and found them less contradictory. And third, little harm could come from reinforcing in children the dual message: that each child holds a particular value in the universe, and is, at the same time, obligated to use that value for the benefit of the community. Given Kramer's interest in the needs of postwar Vienna's children and families, starting some kind of independent therapeutic program along these lines seemed to be the obvious next step. Moreover Adler's increasing status in pedagogical and political circles meant that the kind of free clinical program that Kramer envisioned, with its social democratic features, would benefit a number of local families. The young psychologist's attempt to reach Adler with her ideas were encouraging, and, during the evening of one of his lectures at the Prater community center, Adler addressed her specific concerns. "Why not begin with a child guidance place (*Erziehungsberatungstelle*) for the good of the children and the parents?" he asked.[1] It was time to start the first child guidance center, the Child Guidance Clinic.

The new clinic's earliest patient was that same young Ernest, an anxious thin boy with searching eyes who exuded hostility and either sulked on a chair in a corner or abruptly ran off onto the neighboring roofs. Ernest was a firstborn, the spoiled nine-year old pet of hyperemotional parents who turned on his brother once this second (now the perfect son) boy was born. The child soured, assaulted his younger sibling, earned the position of family scapegoat, and became the family errand-running vassal. Ernest's mother then tried to have him placed in state custody, but the court refused to handle a "family problem" and remanded her to community services for assistance. Mother and child arrived at the clinic in desperation. Kramer hadn't yet told Adler, but eventually he heard of the child's arrival. "Try to help him," Adler encouraged Kramer. The therapeutic work she started then was called "Individual" psychology but in truth it drew in Ernest's entire social milieu including his family, his school, and his neighborhood. His mother calmed down once the intensity of her own despair was accepted and treated. Then her skewed attention to her son leveled off, and Ernest's anxious behavior subsided. When the parent's peer council at the school (a sort of psychological parent-teachers association) called an evening meeting to discuss whether Ernest's odd unruly behavior had become dangerous to the school's other ninety-nine children, his mother felt more supported than reproached. Adler reviewed the case. Only a child who is an entirely autonomous unit is dangerous, he commented, but Ernest's genuine ability to adapt himself cautiously to the community center and to the security and reliability of his classmates was a sign of health. Adler's reformulation of the child's pathology helped the Child Guidance Clinic staff promote his successful "reeducation" at school and at home.

This model for a child guidance clinic was to be replicated throughout Vienna over the next fifteen years. Most of the clinics were housed inside schools and doubled as laboratories for treating the children who suffered from lack of what Adler termed *Gemeinschaftgefuehl*, or community feeling. Adler instituted a citywide network of suicide prevention centers because, he believed, individual suicide was a form of community betrayal. The passion for community was second nature for Adler, who had started out his professional life as an *Armenarzt* but, unlike his namesake (the other famous reform-minded physician, Victor Adler), eventually chose a medical career over a political one. The Austrian "community physician" (*Gemeindearzt*) of the 1920s, a private doctor subsidized by the community, oversaw the management of communicable diseases, autopsies, and free treatment to the poor. This early work in public health gave Adler a practical template for his community-based programs and eventual psychological system. Increasingly popular with the Social Democrats, Adler attributed social inequality and human sense of inferiority to the pernicious overall lack of *Gemeinschaftge-fuehl*.

That May of 1919, in a landslide election that would be repeated in 1927, the Social Democratic Workers' Party (SDAP) triumphed over the Christian Socials in Austria's first secret, balloted election. Women voted for the first time under the umbrella of universal suffrage and brought to the election their concerns for family health and their acute awareness of the need for strong governmental action to stem the tide of tuberculosis, malnutrition, and poor housing conditions then decimating the city's children. Freud signed the electoral petition in favor of the Social Democrats.[2] The plebiscite ushered in a socialist government that lasted until its violent destruction by the Austro-Fascists in 1934. While the social democratic party had been an increasingly forceful presence on the Austrian political landscape since 1897, their representatives finally gained a majority in this election, winning 100 of the 165 municipal council seats. The new social democratic Rathaus, the city council of Vienna, used its firm majority to promote a highly innovative program of community policies and to redesign virtually every municipal resource.

Red Vienna's newly elected politicians and civil servants were at first uneasy about the presence of Paul Federn and other elected politician-psychoanalysts loyal to Sigmund Freud at the Rathaus meetings. Federn was an imposing man. Very tall, with a booming tremulous voice, brilliant dark eyes, and a long black beard, his appearance fell just short of menacing. But his social position was thoroughly standard for the psychoanalyst of 1919: a licensed physician, a representative for Vienna's First District, active in the Socialist Organization of Physicians of Vienna, and a board member of the Vienna Settlement Association. "Ideologically most analysts were liberals," recalled Federn's friend Richard Sterba. "Their sympathies, like those of most Viennese intellectuals, were with the Social Democrats."[3] With high moral principles and a passion for thoughtful relief work that, even many years later, caused his family to dub him a "one-man policlinic," Federn quickly became an asset to Vienna's new social democratic mayor Jakob Reumann.[4] Reumann was a kindly broad-shouldered former wood turner who had edited the *Arbeiterzeitung* since 1900. The mayoralty offered him a chance to demonstrate how effectively the new social democratic party could apply social welfare strategies to Vienna's postwar economic crisis. In addition to helping Vienna become a separate province, Reumann enforced broadscale public health and child welfare policies. His first priority was to rebuild a viable infrastructure for urban sanitation and food distribution, and he was hardly averse to receiving foreign assistance for the city's needs. Under such circumstances even capitalist countries seemed glad to offer assistance, and large American private charities like the Rockefeller Foundation and the Commonwealth Fund were generous (though inevitably ready with their own social agenda). Food and transportation for children were purchased by the European Children's Fund of the American Relief Administration, then headed by Herbert Hoover, who in turn believed that adults should be assisted—if at all—by the Friends organizations.[5] This stance, that adults with free will could more or less fend for themselves, shifted in 1922 when both American and Austrian funders decided to support unemployed families and underemployed academics. These private institutions saw little if any contradiction in their postwar goals of promoting international understanding and decreasing nationalism while disseminating the ideals of American democracy. In practice, however, Vienna's children, especially the war orphans, required direct emergency support from medical dispensaries, antitubercular programs, and newly trained nurses. When these child welfare funds arrived from Eli Bernays (Freud's American brother-in-law), the American Red Cross's postwar reconstruction project and the Commonwealth Fund the following year, Sigmund Freud joined Reumann, Paul Federn, and Julius Tandler on a committee to oversee their distribution.

The new Viennese government rallied around the right to housing and encouraged the development of an extraordinary collection of apartment buildings, the Vienna *Gemeindebauten* (figure 4), whose scale, scope, and combined social and architectural impact has not since been replicated. The Bauhaus-influenced buildings in Germany's central city of Weimar, designed

4 A communal housing block, one of the signature Wiener Gemeindebauten (Author)

earlier the same year (1919) by the renowned architect Walter Gropius, are generally better known today but are comparable in intent to the Wiener *Gemeindebauten*. Like Gropius's buildings, Vienna's *Gemeindebauten* celebrated modern mechanization with standardized and even prefabricated units designed to enhance human efficiency without sacrificing the equally human need for aesthetic gratification. The Viennese and the Weimar housing projects shared an underlying social democratic logic, that of the prewar theories and practices of Loos, Peter Behrens, and Bruno Taut. Art and craft together, functionalism joining aesthetics, reason and passion, Germany's Bauhaus studio school (in some ways like the Vienna Werkstätte) merged fine and applied arts to produce an exhilarating array of designs for furniture, lamps, rugs, pottery, jewelry, typefaces and book designs, dance and music. With the power of a heroic German myth, Gropius's theory and practice of communal "total architecture" envisioned the "new building of the future, which will be everything together, architecture and sculpture and painting, in a single shape, rising to heaven from the hands of millions of craftsmen as a crystal symbol of a new emerging faith."[6] The same could be said of the Wiener *Gemeindebauten*, the exceptional construction program that would rehouse thousands of families over the next fifteen years and was, as early as 1919, the centerpiece of Red Vienna. In Germany and Austria these expansive and beautifully designed buildings were fully congruent with the social welfare orientation of the psychoanalysts.

This housing campaign became a flashpoint in the political tensions between the city's ruling left-wing party and the nation's conservative, proclerical, and vehemently antisocialist majority. The Christian Socials—among them the conservative psychiatrist Julius von Wagner-Jauregg—also saw themselves as defenders of the average working-class family, still championing their enormously popular anti-Semitic platform originally promoted by Karl Lueger, Vienna's powerful mayor from 1897 to 1910. When Hitler was living in Vienna, from 1908 to 1913, he absorbed Lueger's vengeful hatred of socialists and Jews as well as the mayor's community-oriented rhetoric. Paradoxically, Lueger's administration also strengthened the city's public infrastructure and centralized the distribution of gas, electricity, drinking water, and the Stadtbahn, the sleek municipal railway with stations designed by Otto Wagner. And Austria had in place a national health department (a section of the ministry of public welfare) with remarkably modern sanitary laws, controlling water supplies and sewage, food inspection, communicable diseases, and building irregularities since 1870. Other large Central European cities saw comparable urban rebuilding plans developed after the 1918 revolutions brought in universal suffrage and parliamentary democracy. Nevertheless Vienna's innovative housing policies were unique and they categorically improved the lives of young Austrian workers and their families, at least one-third of whom lived in or near the capital. These were the soldiers just back from the front and their new families, or veterans and their dependents on the verge of eviction, for whom the total lack of construction of new dwellings meant homelessness and increasingly squalid urban conditions. Ultimately the extensive, imaginative housing reform was made possible by the city's new status as a province (*Bundesland*) in its own right, in charge of its own system of taxation. Independent from the rest of Austria, the governing Viennese Social Democrats believed that reform entailed the coupling of social and economic policies. They solidified their support among new clusters of voters including women and other previously disenfranchised groups, and consolidated their party by attending to both the housing crisis and the larger public health problems of tuberculosis and malnutrition.

The outbreak of tuberculosis (and ensuing infant mortality) was typical of postwar poor sanitation and food shortages, but in 1919 its carnivorous spread was a major threat to working-class children. Tandler lost no time in containing the damage. The charismatic anatomist now bridged his academic and emerging civic responsibilities with a particularly thoughtful system of aid to children. With the imaginative school superintendent Otto Glöckel and the pediatrician Clemens Pirquet, inventor of the skin test for tuberculosis, as partners, Tandler fought tuberculosis with a systematic program of social welfare and public health. Eventually this program would come to include school lunches, school medical and dental examinations, municipal bathing facilities, publicly sponsored vacations and summer camps, new day nurseries and after-school centers, and special clinics for childhood tuberculosis and orthopedics. With the unified health and mental health of the child in mind, pediatricians like Felix Tietze tried for a new kind of sociomedical specialization. Between 1920 and 1924 Tietze worked at Pirquet's clinic, the child health stations, a tuberculosis dispensary, conducted a survey on infant welfare, and advised the Commonwealth and Red Cross funders in Vienna.[7] As a result of this broad approach, by the early 1920s infant mortality had decreased by 50 percent and the general death rate by 25 percent. Nursery schools and kindergartens proliferated, increasing from 20 in 1913 to a 113, enrolling ten thousand children in 1931.[8] In newly secularized public schools hands-on learning and creativity superseded passive memorization. Many of the newer school programs were influenced by Maria Montessori's educational innovations and her faith in the child's innate creativity and joy of learning. Especially after 1924, Montessori child-centered methods saw a rapprochement between educator-psychoanalysts like August Aichorn and Siegfried Bernfeld (who provided free consultative services at the Ambulatorium) and other intellectuals dedicated to the welfare and education of the young. In this milieu Anna Freud's career as a *volksschul-Lehrer* (a "people's-school teacher") in an elementary school lead her to develop a series of public seminars on the theoretical and practical relationship between psychoanalysis and education. At the center of all this modernization, Julius Tandler steadfastly maintained that early childhood education and public health were conceptually inseparable, and he supported specialized programs like Clare Nathanssohn's nursery school for tubercular families. Clare Nathanssohn was a young political activist who would later marry the psychoanalyst Otto Fenichel and who had adapted Elsa Gingler's principles of yoga, body movement, and mind-body synergy to the needs of sick children. Since most of the tubercular children had been infected at home, the special school kept them outside in the fresh air, well exercised, and actively learning to care for their bodies.[9] Clare and her future husband subsequently joined the kindergarten movement, as did some of Vienna's most famous psychoanalysts.

When Fenichel met Clare Nathanssohn, she was an exciting young dancer who brought to their circle of friends the aura of heroic encounters as a youthful political prisoner seized for her left-wing affiliation during the fleeting Bavarian Soviet Republic (1918–May 1919). Clare was deeply affected by her activist experiences with Gustav Landauer in Munich, both by the city's lively culture of urban artists and workers collectives and by the community's violent repression by fascists, most notably Hitler, in 1919. She joined a collective (a twenty-person society that broke away from the Bauhaus movement) and decided to start a country nursery school near Darmstadt. Clare taught mind-body work to the small group then resettling the architect Peter Behrens's original 1901 artists colony. Behrens's community had been assembled according to the *Jugendstil* ideal of "total art," and even today the gorgeous allegorical mosaics on Love draw admirers to the scenic terraces and pergolas. The colony's beliefs in the curative forces of nature, music, and dance included Gustav Wyneken's ideals of school reform and led Clare to replicate her mentor's highly original school for troubled children.[10] When Tandler upheld Clare's efforts at the nursery school, her shift from a country schoolteacher for disturbed children to urban psychoanalyst was complete. Her teachings on mind-body therapeutic work eventually influenced Wilhelm Reich's later orgone therapy. "You can see how teachers got in contact with analysis," she recalled much later from her home in Boston. "It was a normal thing, of course. You could not ignore it."[11]

Erik Erikson, Anna Freud, August Aichorn, Siegfried Bernfeld, and Willi Hoffer were among the psychoanalysts who took early childhood education to heart. Politically they were Social Democrats. Like their sometime rival Alfred Adler, they attempted to tackle the effects of Vienna's crashing economy on the physical and psychological well-being of children. Eventually they expanded the original idea of carefully constructed nurturing environments for small children into a full-scale psychoanalytic research project on the interaction between society and early childhood development. Erikson in particular, a young German artist still using his birth name of Homburger when he reached Vienna, would explore the multiple influences of environmental reality on the development of the child's identity and individual personality. In 1919 however, even before Erikson reached her experimental nursery school, Anna Freud was working with an original young educator, Siegfried Bernfeld, a onetime leader of Austria's left-wing Youth Movement. Bernfeld was "tall and gaunt, with an ugliness that impressed one as beauty" remembered Helene Deutsch who, like Freud, found the young educator's intensity consistent with his idealism.[12] Bernfeld believed that social repression was an early impediment to children's development and that teachers generally reinforced the moral burden instead of lifting it. A passionate zionist and socialist organizer for the last ten years, Bernfeld wanted progressive education to start with kindergartens. He tried to persuade early childhood educators to actually use—not just showcase –a whole range of pedagogical techniques from hypnotism to Montessori's methods. Bernfeld was particularly fascinated by the possibilities of psychoanalysis. A year earlier he had been one of the youngest analysts present at the Budapest congress and now he was the newest member of the Vienna Psychoanalytic Society. Soon he would be introducing Anna Freud to Eva Rosenfeld and in 1924 they would found together another antiauthoritarian educational experiment, the small Heitzing school in Vienna. In addition to his psychoanalytic work and his original political writing, Bernfeld chartered the Kinderheim Baumgarten (Children's Home), a model kindergarten later directed by his friend Willi Hoffer.[13] The experimental Kinderheim also housed and fed underprivileged, displaced, or homeless children (including over 240 Jewish refugee children) with seed money drawn on municipal funding. Hoffer's own lectures on public education and his psychoanalytically based Vienna Course for Educators reached teachers from the city's nursery, elementary, and high schools.[14] The theoretical material in these lectures was informed by case illustrations from the authors' Kinderheim work with the child refugees, many under five years old, starving, handicapped, or traumatized.[15] The lectures were reprinted in the *Zeitschrift fur Psychoanalytische Pädagogik* and they still convey the earnest Austro-Marxist tone and the social service idealism of the first few generations of Viennese psychoanalysts.

Wilhelm Reich, the second-generation psychoanalyst perhaps most often associated with political radicalism, was just embarking on his lifelong quest for a successful fusion of social change and psychoanalysis. His Sex-Pol project started brilliantly but would ultimately come to haunt him. A farmer's son recently discharged from the army, in 1919 Reich was putting himself through medical school to become a psychiatrist. Muscular, thin, with darkly darting eyes and a square jaw, Reich seemed perpetually distraught in Tandler's classroom. Tandler was still teaching classical anatomy at the medical school then, though also running the city's new municipal welfare department. Both in the classroom and in the city legislature, Tandler inspired his audience to believe that bringing medical and social welfare expertise to the service of local government was the highest calling. For Reich, as for his friends Grete Lehner, Otto Fenichel, and Eduard Bibring, Tandler's message was a prophecy. Grete Lehner revered Tandler and thought he would do the same for politics as for anatomy. He could transform a grueling medical task into a "beautiful and deeply aesthetic experience," she said. "Hidden relationships were suddenly made clear."[16] His expertise in classical Greek sculpture offset the grim use of cadavers by turning them into lively illustrations, exercises, and specimens. One day, when Grete was sitting in the medical school's auditorium-style classroom between Eduard Bibring and Reich during Tandler's anatomy lecture (figure 5), Fenichel handed her a scribbled note to pass around to the other students. The message urged them all to join him in an exploratory new project. Fenichel, an intensely fastidious maker of groups, wanted to start a seminar to be convened by the students themselves where they could discuss topics not covered elsewhere in the medical curriculum. If idealistic students ran their own seminar, Grete thought, they could examine social relations and debate politics, religion, and sexuality with Tandlerian precision.

The four young activists set out to unearth modern psychological discoveries within and outside of the classroom. The University of Vienna's gray stone buildings consisted of eight connecting courtyards surrounding a large tree-lined square where students gathered without apparent constraint. Cafés serving apple cake under the arcades and, in the summer, beer gardens at each of the quadrant's corners were popular, though students especially liked

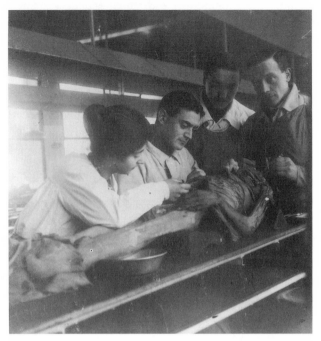

5 Grete Lehner, Samuel Singer, Wilhelm Reich, and Eduard Bibring, in 1919, dissecting a cadaver for Dr. Julius Tandler's class in anatomy at the University of Vienna Medical School (Archives of the Boston Psychoanalytic Society and Institute)

meeting under Gustav Klimt's frescoes of nudes hovering over the university entrance. Reich and his friends had recently heard the existentialist theologian Martin Buber address Jewish university students at an immense rally largely organized by Siegfried Bernfeld.[17] Buber was then translating the Hebrew Bible into German and developing his ideas for an inclusive modern spirituality. The crowd took quickly took to this humane new rhetoric and easily replaced, Reich said, an ideology of race-against-race with one of "people-with-people". Reich was as delighted by this conceptual shift as he was by Grete herself. He remembered her as "smooth and sleek, studious, a grave academician, at times naïve, and charming" who was, unfortunately for Reich, attracted to the more formal, frock-coated Eduard Bibring, a fellow war veteran then accelerating his studies. Nevertheless, when they found time to set their coursework aside, the three friends enjoyed tea parties, masked balls, and flirting in endless rounds of smoky bars near the university. Whether climbing the Rax mountains around Vienna or biking along the Danube, they loved to talk, to argue about sex and politics, and generally conspire to shake off the stagnancy of mankind. Student life was, like much of city life in 1919, financially strained but taken with Saturday tête-à-têtes at the Café Stadtthe-atre, heated discussions on newest developments in the Youth Movement over pastries in the mirrored cafés around the Ring, or cramming for exams over chocolate at the Volkscafé. Hölderlin's complex hymns (set to music) were performed in the Kammerspiele, the *Magic Flute* at the opera, and end-less theater, musical dramas, and philharmonic concerts added to their sense of Viennese cosmopolitanism. Such cultural experiences mattered deeply to these urban young doctors who would later join the Vienna Psychoanalytic Society, and even from Budapest their colleague Radó quite enviously noted how Viennese medical careers were motivated more by humanism than by scientific ambition. For the young educator turned psychoanalyst Rudolf Ek-stein, Red Vienna was a grand "*movement . . .* an ethics."

Otto Fenichel was a fairly short man, barrel chested even in his youth, with a soft wide face and a large smile. He wore climber's jackets and hiking boots and often carried a huge clumsy knapsack. By the spring term of 1919, Otto had persuaded his medical school friends Reich, Lehner, and Bibring to launch the new reading group they had furtively arranged in Tandler's anatomy class. Modern works on sex and psychology would be discussed, they agreed, and they would focus on alternative and nontraditional subjects ranging from scientific findings to sociopolitical texts. Their student-run seminar discussed genital physiology, masturbation, the clitoral-orgasm con-troversy, and homosexuality, all topics banned from the medical school cur-riculum. They also discussed psychoanalysis. Fenichel had just unearthed a copy of Freud's *Three Essays on the Theory of Sexuality* and found its argu-ments enthralling. He shared the book with his friends, and they scrutinized it chapter by chapter in their weekly meetings. The four were fascinated by the little text whose puzzles equaled anything they had seen in medicine. So they went to the source, Freud himself, for explanations.

Freud's office was just a short walk down Vienna's steep Berggasse hill near the university. Keeping to the Vienna medical tradition, Freud reserved one hour every afternoon for consultations. From his own experience as a trainee in Vienna, the Budapest-born psychoanalyst Franz Alexander remembered that, by then, the practice of calling upon 19 Berggasse was "not only natural but more or less expected" of early students and teachers of psychoanalysis.[18] In the days that followed their final class with Tandler, Reich, Lehner, Fenichel, and Bibring decided to visit Freud during this daily consulting hour. The four young Socialists, already comfortable with Red Vienna's so-cial welfare approach to health care, were also unusually well read in psycho-analysis. Freud must have been pleased by the young people's knowledge and by their inquiring attitude because he invited all four to attend weekly meet-ings of the Vienna Psychoanalytic Society. Luckily for Reich and his friends, Freud was by that time selecting "new members on the basis of personal and professional qualifications and of the lecture given by the prospective mem-ber." As the society's chairman, "Freud's personal opinion was always deci-sive," Helene Deutsch pointed out in her memoirs.[19] Then again, as Erik Erikson recalled from his own student days in Vienna, the psychoanalytic movement had amazing flexibility and if "the Freuds felt you had a certain sense of analysis, you could become an analysand of one of the most out-standing senior members without any further conditions." [20]

Medical school had brought Reich, Bibring, Fenichel, and Lehner together but Freud gave them a cause. Since 1902 Freud had gathered around him a like-minded cluster of protégés, friends, former patients, and current pupils, a group that would develop into the Vienna Psychoanalytic Society in 1908. "The closeness to Freud's work *in statu nascendi* gave us the feeling of participating in a major, future-shaping scientific and cultural process" recalled Richard Sterba, a psychoanalyst whose lyrical renderings of life in the Vienna society idealize Freud but also evoke a genuine pleasure in his presence.[21] The four medical students quickly gained favor with the society, all the while observing how Deutsch, Sterba, and Hermine von Hug-Hellmuth responded to Freud's comments or ideas. They were particularly attuned to sociopolitical content in those Wednesday evening roundtables and even more to the contentious dis-cussions at the Café Riedl (one of Freud's favorite Viennese cafés) where the psychoanalysts convened after the lectures.[22] By the next year Fenichel would be off to Berlin to work at the Poliklinik, and by 1922 all four partners in the sexology seminar would take on leadership roles at the Ambulatorium, but the Wednesday evenings at the Freud's remained with them forever.

Reich soon applied for full membership in the Vienna Psychoanalytic So-ciety. He had already turned over his paper "Concerning the Energy of Dri-ves" but felt sure that Freud would "shake his head and hand it back."[23] In his own narrative of personal development as a practicing analyst, Reich dated his first clinical session to September 15 of 1919. By Christmas he had two pa-tients, had started his personal analysis with Isidor Sadger, and was also en-rolled in Sadger's psychoanalytic seminar. Few members of the Wednesday circle seemed less politically involved than Sadger, and none more convinced of the absolute primacy of sexuality in human life. Himself haunted by homosexuality and fetishism, Sadger had the scabrous reputation of analyzing dinner parties guests down to the minutest intimate details. He exasperated even Freud with his ultra-orthodox adhesion to the theory of sexuality. Presumably Sadger analyzed Reich along these lines, and his influence on Reich's theories and the later founding of the Sex-Pol organization and clinics were more complex and important than Reich's own memoirs indicate.

Reich's personal development as a socially oriented psychoanalyst and his belief in the validity of Freud's theories matured simultaneously. Reich observed the city's people with a sociologist's outlook. He watched elderly ladies engaged in their morning chat about rising prices, asking of no one in particular when things would get better. At seven A.M. high school teachers discussed communism with a chimney sweep already covered with soot. Political groups attacked each other, whether Communist, Social Democrat, or Christian Social, all tainted by power-seeking and self-importance. By 1919 Reich saw himself moving further toward the left, looking forward to doing clinical work at the hospital, learning English, and giving his qualifying lecture at the Vienna Psychoanalytic Society of which he would become a member in 1920. Now convinced "that sexuality is the core around which all social life, as well as inner spiritual life of the individual, revolves," Reich successfully interpreted his patients' dreams.[24] Despite Sadger's analysis he was curiously ambivalent about the view then espoused by his friend and fellow medical student, Otto Fenichel, of pervasive sexuality in all things, because this seemed to the demanding Reich merely a perfunctory caricature of Freud's ideas. The friendship between Reich and Fenichel would continue for many years along this intense combative tone of political struggle and mutual interests. Then, however, Fenichel was largely occupied with the student seminar in sexology, his own merger of psychoanalysis and sexual education that he had initiated earlier that year at the university. Poet and physician, performer and writer, Otto Fenichel thought that even the most personal diaries "were always written with the thought that they would someday be read." So too with the narratives of psychoanalysis. Throughout 1919 and the early 1920s, this first known psychoanalytic seminar (Fenichel's discussions with Reich, Lehner, and Bibring) was to become enormously popular among the university's medical students ready to challenge the political and academic status quo. Tradition was being challenged everywhere.

Originally, when the first psychoanalysts formed the IPA at the Second International Psychoanalytic Congress held in Nuremberg in 1910, they had settled on a centralized membership organization with branches in London, Vienna, Budapest, and Berlin. By 1919, in large cities throughout Europe, the

United States, Japan, and India, similar groups had collected into local psychoanalytic societies to study, teach, and advance Freud's work. With organizations patterned after the flagship Vienna group, where leading members like Helene Deutsch accepted that Freud had to be defended and all his projects promoted, the local societies furthered the aims of psychoanalysis in public and in private. It was a battle, Deutsch said, "externally fought with and for Freud against the scientific and professional milieu from which one had sprung; internally it was fought over Freud himself, for his favor and recognition."[25] Outwardly the psychoanalysts struggled against the establishment while internally they vied for Freud's blessing, sometimes amicably and sometimes not, and for legitimacy both within and outside the IPA, their professional organization.

As a condition of its charter and its abiding membership in the IPA, a society's governance was held responsible for fulfilling two sets of resolutions conceived at the 1918 Budapest congress where Freud had delivered his address on the social obligations of psychoanalysis. The first official resolution was advanced by Herman Nunberg and concerned the pressing need to standardize psychoanalytic training. In particular Nunberg insisted that all psychoanalysts should themselves be analyzed. The practice of psychoanalysis was too new and already fraught with risk of corruption to be left to untrained clinicians, even psychiatrists, who lacked specific technical expertise. The basic tripartite training formula of theoretical coursework, supervised casework, and personal analysis was conceived in Budapest in 1918, implemented the same year, and ratified in 1920 under Max Eitingon's direction. The specifications developed in the mid-1920s by the International Training Commission (ITC), and articulated by Karen Horney as a member of the Poliklinik's education committee, were so widely accepted that they endure to this day.[26] But a second resolution formed at the congress focused on the development of walk-in clinics where "treatment shall be free" for prospective analysands of limited means.[27] Unlike the well-established outcome of the training resolution, the second is best-known today—if at all—for the role the clinics played in parlaying patients to psychoanalytic trainees in waiting. Nevertheless when the Berlin, Vienna, London, and Budapest societies organized their in-house psychoanalytic training programs, they also created external, community-based programs—the free outpatient clinics. And, in fact, the early twentieth-century psychoanalytic societies steadfastly sustained their outpatient centers with cash, skill, and in-kind donations. Taken together, the two resolutions implicitly expressed the psychoanalysts' efforts to reject conservative traditions and to supplant them with new mental health institutions under a far more progressive authority.

By 1919 plans for an official psychoanalytic free clinic were already afoot in Berlin. The Berlin clinic project had actually been drawn up at least ten years earlier in 1909 when Max Eitingon and Karl Abraham joined forces to promote psychoanalysis. By 1910 they had constituted the German Psychoanalytic Association (Deutsche Psychoanalytische Gesellschaft, or DPG) as a branch of the IPA, and within that the Berlin Psychoanalytic Society, as well as a training institute and even the first stages of their outpatient treatment facility. Berlin's creative energy appealed to talented urban newcomers like Eitingon and Abraham, both recently arrived from training in Zurich and both self-reliant Jews. "Things are moving! On the 27th the Berlin Psycho-Analytic Society will meet for the first time," Abraham had written to Freud in August 1908.[28] Their sketchy first Poliklinic for Psychoanalytic Treatment of Nervous Disorders appeared at the end of that year, a modest clinic that, ten years later in 1920, became the cornerstone of an already imposing branch society of the IPA.[29] Freud liked the winsome Abraham for his "unruffled spirits and tenacious confidence," but he had the greatest faith in Eitingon.[30]

Max Yefimovich Eitingon (figure 6) was a small round-faced man with short, dark hair parted carefully to the side, a neatly trimmed moustache, and

6 Max Eitingon (Library of the Boston Psychoanalytic Society and Institute)

a bemused air. In photographs, taken either as solo portraits or with medical or psychoanalytic friends, Eitingon's small frame and impeccably tailored suit put him at a slight remove from the group. Eitingon grew up in Germany, pursued a degree in philosophy at the university in Marburg, and then studied medicine. His family stood out, even among the rich fur merchants of Galicia, as powerful international traders with businesses spread throughout Russia, Poland, England, and Germany. In 1905, when he was twenty-four years old, Eitingon became a psychiatrist at the famous Burghölzli Clinic in Zurich. Two years later Carl Jung, who was still friendly with Freud and was Eitingon's dissertation director at Burghölzli, suggested he learn psychoanalysis. From 1907 forward Freud, who had cultivated passionate and generally disappointing relationships with men like Josef Breuer, Sándor Ferenczi, and even Jung, took to Eitingon with less ardor but great friendship. For the next fifteen years Max used his extraordinary wealth to provide indigent people with access to mental health treatment. By 1919 he had assumed many of the IPA's large debts first underwritten by von Freund. Even earlier, in 1910, Eitingon had financed the rudimentary independent psychoanalytic service that, after the 1918 Budapest congress, would serve as the blueprint for the Poliklinik. As an enterprise the Poliklinik was expensive from the beginning and after an initial outlay of about twenty thousand marks (roughly five thousand dollars) in the fall of 1919, the clinic saw its budget climb steadily along with the dramatic inflation of the German currency. Nevertheless, Eitingon announced, in an early December letter to Freud, that suitable premises had been found to house the clinic. Abraham, who was increasingly impressed by Eitingon's administrative capabilities, soon agreed that the Berlin society would rent the space if the price were within their means.

By November 1919 Abraham announced to Freud that "Berlin is clamouring for psychoanalysis" and regarded the Poliklinik as a fait accompli. "Eitingon will certainly be keeping you up to date with the business of our polyclinic. The plan is soon to become a reality."[31] On July 19 Eitingon's proposal to found a Poliklinik was passed unanimously by the Berlin society and on July 26 they were already discussing its implementation. On September 19 Simmel presented the Board with plans for publicizing the Poliklinik, and on September 26 Eitingon, Simmel, and Abraham were formally elected as the Clinic Committee.[32] The Berlin analysts grew ever more animated as they described to Freud the details of various preparations. "Things are *good* in our group. Enthusiasm is great and achievements much better than they were," Abraham wrote. "Your appeal in Budapest fell on fertile ground. The polyclinic will be opened in the winter, and will grow into a Ψ institute."[33] Abraham pointed to Ernst Simmel, one of the IPA's most serious new analysts and an avowed Socialist associated with the Ministry of Education through his political activities, as "an excellent force for the polyclinic."[34] Freud, for his part, was so pleased by all this activity that "on the occasion of the foundation of the Berlin polyclinic" he proposed "admit[ting] Eitingon to full membership in the committee."[35] Nothing now would stop Abraham, Simmel, and Eitingon from making Freud's social democratic reverie into a twentieth-century reality.

"The position of the polyclinic itself as the headquarters of the psychoanalytic movement"

1920

ON FEBRUARY 24, 1920, Freud dispatched his daughter Mathilde and her husband Robert Hollitscher, the Viennese businessman, to attend the opening ceremonies for the new Berlin Poliklinik für Psychoanalytische Behandlung Nervöser Krankheiten, the first psychoanalytic outpatient center specifically designated as a free clinic. The clinic's opening was "the most gratifying thing at this time" Freud wrote to Ferenczi, and Mathilde's presence alongside other prominent members of the psychoanalytic community added a measure of authority to the festivities.[1] The Poliklinik, as it came to be known, was the brainchild of Max Eitingon and Ernst Simmel. Their Hungarian friend and benefactor Anton von Freund had died just a month earlier on January 20, leaving the IPA some money but a much larger legacy of unfinished good works and his project for a free clinic in Budapest postponed. "In Berlin there is much better news [than] in Budapest," Ernest Jones commented to his Dutch colleague Jan van Emden. "They have money for the Policlinic."[2] And indeed Max Eitingon, moneyed and generous, took over where von Freund left off and financed the new clinic's start-up, now relocated to Berlin, from his private fortune. Eitingon would continue to underwrite the expenses of housing the ever growing Berlin Poliklinik, first at 29 Potsdamerstrasse until 1928 and then on Wichtmanstrasse until its involuntary end in 1933.

Part classical music, part poetry reading, and part ode to psychoanalytic inquiry, the Poliklinik's February 14 inaugural ceremony proved to be a splendid event. The daylong *Programme* of festivities showcased performances by members and friends of the Berlin Psychoanalytic Society, and included a Beethoven piano sonata, some Chopin, piano and voice pieces by Schubert and Schoenberg, and art songs by Hugo Wolf. Ernst Simmel read "Presentiment" and "Madness" from Rilke's *Book of Hours*. Abraham ended the day with paper on "The Rise of the Poliklinik from the Unconscious." The program's overall symbolist themes of human emotion, reality, and nature were reflected in the combination of traditional pieces from the mainstream of German culture with contemporary work suggesting modernity and subjectivity. For music Schubert and Chopin were mixed with Schoenberg, Vienna's avant-garde composer, identified musically with the Expressionists and politically with the Social Democrats. In poetry the psychoanalysts offset Rilke's romantic voice with the biting surrealism of Christian Morgenstern's satire. Rilke was still living in Europe then, enormously popular though still edgy, and, like Freud, an intimate of the Russian intellectual Lou Andreas-Salomé. By the time the day was over, the analysts could revel in a stylish celebration utterly consonant with the cultural overtones of Weimar.

In keeping with his modernist aspirations for the Poliklinik, Eitingon invited Freud's son Ernst Ludwig (figure 7), the architect and engineer who had trained in Vienna under Adolf Loos, to plan the clinic's physical layout and furnishings. Within a month Ernst had "won lasting recognition for himself in his designing of the polyclinic, which is admired by everyone," Abraham wrote to Freud in March.[3] Ernst had just arrived in Berlin at the invitation of his close friend Richard Neutra, his classmate in Loos's Vienna Bauschule architecture studio in 1912 and 1913.[4] From 1919 until his forced emigration to London in 1933, Ernst's years as a Berlin architect were filled with experimentation along the lines of the New Objectivity and the International Style of the 1920s. The commission to design the Poliklinik's interior space and to refurbish its musty quarters held particular appeal. "I love the conditions stipulated by an existing building of character, " Ernst said years later, "and very often old [ones] have great possibilities in their rooms."[5] This particular suite of rooms at 29 Potsdamerstrasse had been selected and rented as the clinic's site because of its ideal central location and easy proximity to the Berlin analysts' own private offices. On the fourth floor of a fairly modest residential building midway up a tree-lined street, the apartment's five interconnecting rooms were rearranged for treatment or consultation. Light-colored wood double doors soundproofed the consulting or therapy. An unadorned cane couch, a chair and a table, some

7 Ernst Freud,
the young architect, in 1926
(Freud Museum, London)

lamps, and simple portraits on the wall furnished the rooms. Ernst modified his father's luxuriantly adorned analytic couch, stripped it of ornamentation, and streamlined its shape to produce the model most frequently used today.

"The fascination of this task is to provide flats of convenience with the
minimum of alteration," Ernst explained in another context, a task made visible in his coherent restructuring of the Poliklinik's space.[6] For Ernst, as for
his friend Richard Neutra, modernism meant proportion, regard for the demands of the existing environment, and the use of natural light to integrate
the interior and the exterior of the home. Like Neutra, Ernst Freud's architecture was permeated with ecological and environmental sensitivity.
Throughout his career in Austria, Germany, and especially England after
1933, Ernst would design furniture for individual clients and revel in simple
functional lines, light woods, and natural fabrics. His architectural projects
ranged from factories to private houses but his particular talent was remod-
eling or "remoulding" houses and adapting them for modern living. Ernst remodeled furniture too. In 1938, when the celebrated ceramist Lucie Rie es-

caped the Nazis but retained her furniture designed by another modernist architect, Ernst Plischke, Ernst adapted it to her new home in London. His sophisticated built-in bookcases and cupboards, small walnut tables and armchairs made for sparse harmonious living. Ernst Freud's sense of the organic environment, a style he shared with Neutra, was already discernible in his 1920 designs for the Poliklinik. Dark heavy drapes shaded the consulting offices, while the windows of the larger meeting room, called the Lecture Hall, let in light through muslin curtains. The largest room was also used for conferences, lectures, and meetings. With a sizable blackboard mounted on the front wall and a speaker's podium, this room held approximately forty Thonet chairs. Ernst's use of commercially available furniture like these bentwood chairs reflected Loos's view that the architect's design should not influence the user's choice of everyday products.

Similarly simple, well-crafted furniture filled the clinic's small waiting room, consciously planned to promote a sense of community. Ernst had learned from his architect colleagues at the Bauhaus and in Red Vienna's Gemeindebauten to design public spaces with an eye to their therapeutic effect. Imbued with Alfred Loos's beliefs in unadorned forms and, wherever possible, built-in furniture, Ernst fitted the research library into one of the public meeting areas. In fact, Eitingon, foremost a Jewish intellectual who adhered to the curative powers of knowledge, specifically requested that Ernst arrange one room of the clinic as a reading room where all the psychoanalytic literature would be gathered and made available to client and clinician alike.[7] The Poliklinik's deliberately crowded milieu stood in stark contrast to the traditional medical office model with its separate doors and narrow access to the quasi-private practitioner. Clinic patients saw each other regularly and, confidentiality aside, could feel reassured knowing that a group of their peers had been admitted and were waiting for an analytic hour to open. Eitingon believed that this community atmosphere subtly motivated the patients toward self-sufficiency, in what would later be called forms of "milieu therapy." Once inside the analyst's room, however, privacy prevailed. Ernst effectively insulated the offices against sound with a series of new techniques (distinctive in his later architectural practice) including double-glazed windows and laminated doors with a plywood core for soundproofing. Altogether these measures were intended to dispel the more frightening aspects of beginning treatment. The prospective patient's first encounter with the Poliklinik was as scrupulously designed as the clinic's furniture and statistics.

The Poliklinik issued a formal announcement of its opening:

The Berlin Psychoanalytical Association
opened on 16th February 1920
a
Poliklinik for the psychoanalytical treatment of nervous diseases
at W. Potsdamer Str[asse] 29, under the medical supervision
of Dr. Abraham, Dr. Eitingon, Dr. Simmel
Consultations on weekdays 9–11:30, except Wednesdays.[8]

From its opening day the Poliklinik's unexpectedly large influx of adult and child patients was coordinated by Eitingon and Simmel. Their small staff of clinicians, all members of the Berlin society who had agreed to conduct free analyses, was barraged by requests from people with longstanding or chronic problems—both psychological and physiological—and by patients who had gone from one doctor or clinic to another. At least two and a half hours daily (except Wednesdays and Sundays) were allocated to these initial consultations, or intakes, which at first were conducted by the codirectors in tandem. The new patients "suffered especially strongly under their neuroses because of economic need," Simmel wrote, "or were especially given to material misery precisely as a result of their neurotic inhibition."[9] In the Poliklinik's first year 350 patients applied for free psychoanalytic treatment. Many of them walked in from the street, enticed by the name on the front door's classical brass plaque. But more and more were recommended by former patients, friends, or their personal physicians. Some patients read about the official opening of the clinic in local newspapers. The Berlin press had been fairly neutral, not nearly as flattering as the Vienna newspaper coverage of the Ambulatorium would be in 1922, but definitely more favorable than the Budapest clinic would see later in the decade. Berlin's *Die Neue Rundschau*, the Fischer Verlag's prestigious monthly magazine, published Karl Abraham's long article outlining the principles of psychoanalysis.[10] For the moment the city's academic and psychiatric communities were excited by the Poliklinik and willing to refer patients. While a *psychoanalytic* service was new to psychiatrists at the Charité, Berlin University's huge and magnificent teaching hospital, the idea of using a Poliklinik as an alternative to inpatient medical treatment went back at least a hundred years. The practice had started at the Charité in the late nineteenth century and had since become standard throughout Germany's medical system. In new fields like orthopedics or psychoanalysis intermediate-care polyclinics helped hospitals provide both academic training and general public health. Even before its formal opening the psychoanalytic polyclinic seemed so promising that medical faculty at the Charité considered nominating Abraham for a professorship in psychoanalysis. The position never did materialize but Abraham nevertheless informed Freud that "the polyclinic, which will definitely be opened in January, is arousing great interest on the part of the Ministry [of Education]" and that his collegial relations with the public health officials were bearing fruit.[11] The enthusiastic Konrad Haenisch, then heading Berlin's education ministry, had asked Abraham to draw up an account of their "first experiences at the polyclinic concerning the number of patients attending for treatment" and the size of the audience frequenting society lectures.[12] "The Clinic is well attended," Abraham said cheerily within a month of its opening. At least twenty analyses had been started and the flood of patients (of all ages, occupations, and social standing) continued to be so great that the Poliklinik never advertised again. "For the more distant future there is a project to start a special department for the treatment of neurotic children," Abraham added. "I should like to train a woman doctor particularly for this."[13] In June, barely three months after this note was sent to Freud, Hermine von Hug-Hellmuth launched the Berlin Poliklinik's child treatment program.

Hermine von Hug-Hellmuth was "a small woman with black hair, always neatly, one might say ascetically, dressed," recalled her companion from the Vienna society's roundtable meetings, Helene Deutsch.[14] Even before Melanie Klein and Anna Freud, Hug-Hellmuth had developed child therapies based on games and drawings and, as such, is know as the first practitioner of child analysis. Her views found their way into education, parenting, and child welfare facilities and her practice of treating children in their own homes was picked up by the emerging social work profession. Her beliefs in the impact of family and the larger environment on human development were consistent with Tandler's social welfare approach to children's mental health, and she managed the infusion of Freudian psychoanalysis into the city's growing network of family social services and schools. Fortunately Abraham had foreseen the need for a child analysis treatment and training section and invited Hug-Hellmuth to set it up. Yet her arrival in Berlin may not have been problem free. Although the diplomatic Eitingon (who spoke for the entire staff in his reports and letters to his colleagues) never stated so overtly, the controversy over Hug-Hellmuth's short and scabrous book, *A Young Girl's Diary*, surely loomed large. Published just the year before in 1919 as an authentic narrative of pubescent female sexuality, and perfectly synchronized with Freudian theory, the *Diary* proved to be largely fictional. The little book provoked such furor among the analysts that, as

Deutsch recalled, one of them "played detective and inquired in all the hospitals whether a man of a certain description had been admitted on the date when the diarist of the *Tagebuch* reports that her father fell ill."[15] The search proved futile and only further popularized the book. In 1923, the year she returned to Vienna, Hug-Hellmuth finally claimed the work as her personal editing of a genuine adolescent diary (perhaps her own). The adolescent's story, deceitful or not, contributed to the increasingly accepted twofold idea that adolescents and even younger children suffer from neurotic misery and that such afflictions can be treated with psychoanalysis as successfully as with adults.

We "cannot say that the factor of the patients paying or not paying has any important influence on the course of the analysis."[16] Arguably one of Max Eitingon's most paradoxical statements, the hypothesis that the fee itself has little or no significant effect on the course of psychoanalytic treatment was as insightful as it was controversial. He used quantitative data to confirm the feasibility of Freud's belief in public access to psychoanalysis, data that today disprove the conclusions of several class-based analyses of Freud's case studies.[17] He believed that fees for treatment should be discussed, despite some inevitable tension, between the patient and the administrator or clinician. Eitingon could personally handle an individual's pecuniary and clinical questions at once, but the larger social welfare concerns eventually raised by the issue of free treatment were strikingly complex. The Poliklinik functioned as a private charitable organization, generally independent of state supervision and of the regulatory oversight of Karl Moeli, director of the section for psychiatric affairs created within the medical division of Berlin's Ministry of Culture. Nevertheless the unusual fee scale generated disagreement both within the clinic and outside it and presumably created some anxiety for certain psychoanalysts accustomed to the private practice model. Melanie Klein, for one, was keenly aware of this. In her little personal diaries from the 1920s, Klein meticulously tabulated the clinical time she owed the Poliklinik down to the minute. Still, Eitingon was confident that being "entirely disinterested materially" in the patient would eventually strengthen the position and authority of the Poliklinik analyst. He confronted doubting analysts who feared—or said they feared, and one wonders about self-interest here—that forsaking the fee meant relinquishing opportunities to pressure a patient into tackling "complexes of vital importance." His threefold argument suggested that the strength of the "free treatment" rationale is implicit. First, Freud's Budapest speech specified that "these treatments shall be free," second, the Poliklinik had no formal guidelines for free treatment, and, third, the analysts' independence from the issue of fees would have favorable effects on their clinical work.

Free analyses were conducted side by side, at the same time and in the same location, as fee-paying analyses (figure 8). And the same, psychoanalysts treated all cases equally, regardless of the patient's ability to pay: fee-paying patients were not reserved for the senior analysts, nor was free treatment an obligation for the candidates alone. In effect, a sort of sliding scale of fees from zero upward eliminated the boundary between "free" and "paid" treatment. Senior analysts had little choice. Even Eitingon treated several patients gratis, though he was not known for his clinical acumen. Many of his colleagues, from Sándor Radó to Alix Strachey, agreed that Eitingon had excellent philosophical training and vast cultural sophistication but was too personally inhibited to command a successful clinical practice.[18] Nevertheless, the first three full-time salaried employees were Eitingon and Simmel as codirectors, with Anna Smeliansky as their assistant, each working up to fourteen hours every day. New staff members would be added as long as they met three distinct criteria that Abraham outlined to Freud. "Our conditions for working at the Clinic are," he wrote, "first, sufficient neurological and psychiatric training; second, sufficient knowledge of psycho-analytic literature; third, personal analysis of the candidate."[19] Hanns Sachs would arrive shortly in Berlin to conduct many of these didactic analyses. Volunteer society members covered for each other's illnesses and vacations, and they would "oversee the Poliklinik as Eitingon's

8 Treatment Room no. 2 at the Berlin Poliklinik (Library of the Boston Psychoanalytic Society and Institute)

representative during his trips," as Abraham was quick to reassure his international colleagues.[20]

"The position of the polyclinic itself as the headquarters of the psychoanalytic movement," Freud decided to write to Abraham, "would only be strengthened" by Theodor Reik's prospective move to Berlin.[21] Reik was a chronically impoverished literary man and the original model of the nonphysician analyst. His practice eventually created such furor that Freud was prompted to publish *The Question of Lay Analysis.* If Reik moved to Berlin, Freud thought, he could relieve Sachs of the burden of conducting all the candidates' training analyses, provide Abraham with a trusted replacement for the lecture series, and build up the stature of Poliklinik within the IPA and wider academic circles. Meanwhile his absence from Vienna would smooth out some of the home society's internal squabbling. But neither Abraham nor Eitingon welcomed Freud's idea of moving Reik to Berlin. They were quite happy with Sachs's abilities and, perhaps more important, unsure of Reik's political commitment. Besides the inspiring young analyst Otto Fenichel had just moved to Berlin from Vienna.

Following a summer full of equivocation about Reik, Otto Fenichel's arrival in Berlin signaled the start of lively new programming at the Institute. Fenichel organized and updated the clinic's record-keeping system (his forte) and launched a group that eventually became the celebrated Children's Seminars (*Kinderseminar*). The name of this meeting was attractive but misleading because it was not at all a pedagogical seminar on child analysis. In fact the Children's Seminars was a special self-sustained course for Berlin's younger candidates interested in the therapeutic and sociopolitical sides of psychoanalysis. Fenichel first proposed the idea to Eitingon, who agreed to support it, and then pulled together a discussion group much as he had several years before in medical school. Many years later the analyst Edith Jacobson remembered Otto Fenichel as "one of those who maintained their interest in sociological problems." Edith Jacobson herself would emerge, by the end of the 1920s, as one of the most radical of the left-wing psychoanalytic activists, second only perhaps to the more flamboyant Reich and certainly shrewder. Jacobson was profound and pretty, a smallish woman with intense deep eyes and shiny brown hair brushed back in a loose bun. She always remembered the Children's Seminars, without reservations, as that "special group [that] tackled the relations between sociology and psychoanalysis."[22] It would be from this circle that Fenichel would develop, by 1931, the inner circle of psychoanalysts specifically devoted to the expansion and circulation of Marxist Freudian thought. The immediate sphere around Fenichel has been described as political left, and correctly so, but claiming that they represented the "left opposition" in psychoanalysis is misleading because individual affiliations were merely a matter of degree.

Political ideologies aside, Eitingon insisted that the clinic's work could not be called unequivocally "therapy for the masses" for many reasons. First of all, Eitingon intended to remove financial obstacles to individual treatment, not to make psychoanalysis into a charitable cause. Second, the term *masses* could be conceptually misleading. As Fenichel later explained in his unflinching outline of dialectical-materialist psychology, psychoanalysts do not use the expression "mass psychology" to describe "a 'spirit of the masses.'" Attributing a universal unconscious to the individual psyche is so inaccurate, Fenichel wrote, that "C. G. Jung had to invent the idea of a 'collective unconscious' . . . which haunts bourgeois psychologies."[23] In contrast, psychoanalysis (even of many) explores how an individual's unconscious interacts with actual social or environmental conditions; it should in no way be confused with Jung's sentimental imagery. In practical terms the Poliklinik aimed to provide broadscale mental health treatment outside the medical establishment but still within the parameters of psychiatric practice.

Eitingon was fortunate that he understood the problem of marginalization in all its dimensions. He disavowed the idea that the Poliklinik worked on the "principle of free treatment," because he feared this concept would marginalize the clinic's function within an increasingly entrepreneurial state. And he feared that the preening specialists at the Charité would engineer a takeover of his facility. The Poliklinik positioned itself deliberately in contrast to Berlin's teaching institutions like the Charité where, as Simmel saw it, the "proletariat" and poorly insured people provided material for medical instruction while private "high fee-paying patients" were exempt from such abuse. Simmel tells the story of one of his first patients, a small disappointed woman who wandered away from the Poliklinik muttering "No ultraviolet lamps?" Shy and uncomfortable, she had answered Simmel's exploratory questions simply: "Yes, they say . . . I have a problem with my nerves." Apparently other clinics had dismissed her casually, as a mere annoyance, saying that she belonged to the group labeled "psychopaths" or "neurasthenics." With Simmel expounding on the "egalitarian character of psychoanalysis itself," access to treatment could hardly be predicated only on the patient's ability to pay.[24] Treatment decisions were based exclusively on patient diagnosis and need—not on the need of Institute candidates (or Charité medical students) for training material. Since the case's degree of urgency determined *how* the patient was to be treated, the diagnosis decided *if* the treatment would take place at the Poliklinik.

Patients were not stopped from paying for their treatment. They were simply not obliged to pay. Patients were expected to pay whatever they estimated they could afford. People who could not pay, like students, unemployed workers, or indigent men and women, were analyzed free of charge. Since an individual was admitted to treatment on the basis of diagnostic need alone, the mere ability to pay did not determine access to therapy. Patients' own reports on their financial status were believed: whether they said they could pay or not was not an important factor. The expectation that patients would "pay as much or as little as they can or *think they can*" (emphasis added) was more important as a practitioner's clinical issue than as an administrative one.[25] The initial consultation fee was about one dollar (in 1926 dollars), with subsequent visits decided on a sliding scale of twenty-five cents to one dollar. Fees were based on a case-by-case assessment of the patient's, or family's, income and on "responsibilities," the term used by the visiting American psychoanalyst Clarence Oberndorf to describe financial obligations such as rent and food. Obendorf's reports attempted to offer his skeptical New York colleagues a realistic account of how much the applicant could afford for treatment.[26]

In keeping with its status as a nonprofit private charity, general funds from the Berlin society, patient fees, and private donations maintained the Poliklinik (figure 9). Because all twelve members of the society treated at least one clinic applicant free of charge in their private office, the clinic could carry up to twelve nonpaying patients at a time. Alternatively, society members could donate the equivalent amount of their annual professional income to support the clinic. But even members who chose neither fee-free patients nor extra donations were bound to support the Poliklinik because a system of enrollment was built into the society's dues structure. In his letter of August 26 to Therese Benedek, a young Hungarian psychiatrist recently settled in Leipzig, Abraham described the requirements for admission to the psychoanalytic society and explained the fees. "The membership dues consist of 8.00 Mark annually for the Steering Committee of the International Association & 200.00 Mark for the local [Berlin] group. The magnitude of the latter dues is explained by the necessity to support the Poliklinik."[27] Actual patient fees, or receipts, covered approximately—and only—10 percent of the Poliklinik's operating budget. The Poliklinik's budget provided for salaries, rent, records, upkeep, and management of the facility. The permanent staff members collected small salaries, which, Eitingon commented, "bear no relation to their services or to the sacrifices they make." For example, the paid assistants each

Poliklinik der Berliner Psychoanalytischen Vereinigung

BERLIN W. 35, den   192

Potsdamer Str. 20
Fernsprecher: Kurfürst 9276

9 Letterhead from the Berlin Poliklinik's Stationery (Bundesarchiv, Koblenz, Germany)

received 75 marks, or $18.00, monthly paid out of the general funds of the Berlin Psychoanalytic Society. Such assets were most likely drawn on Eitingon's own bank account from which the IPA also received "a new Ψa fund to the amount of one million crowns ($5000)." As Freud was delighted to report, this "put an end to our most pungent fears."[28] Meanwhile the clinic's own expenses for eight months of 1920 came to 20,000 marks ($5000), with only 2,500 marks ($600) in receipts. October 1920 to October 1921 saw an allocation of 60,000 marks ($14,500) with 17,500 marks ($4,206) in receipts. Historically, mental health clinics with very open policies on access to treatment can be overwhelmed by patients; conversely only this openness of policy lets in patients according to their diagnostic need and specifically not according to their personal ability to pay. In consequence, Eitingon acknowledged, the Poliklinik's economic independence actually gave clinicians far greater access to patients than private practice.

Ernest Jones was then in London, enviously watching from afar as the Poliklinik grew in capacity and stature but reluctant to embark on such a project himself. To his friend Jan van Emden, Jones mentioned the Poliklinik's new funding and also noted the Berlin arrival of two inventive psychoanalysts, "Frau Klein of Budapest [will] analyse children . . . Sachs [is] analysing a number of doctors who wish to learn Psa and work at the Clinic."[29] Hanns Sachs, a member of the Vienna society since 1909 and coeditor with Otto Rank of the journal *Imago*, was to remain in Berlin as a master teacher and training analyst until he left for Boston in 1932. Jones would soon bring Melanie Klein over to London and eventually set up the British society's own clinic in 1926. But in 1920 Jones was still hard-pressed to put aside his objections to a clinic. "We have to think carefully before we throw the aegis of our prestige over an institution that can do psychoanalysis more harm than good in the eyes of the outer world," he wrote to his colleagues in Vienna and Berlin.[30] He found the recent spread of "wild analysis" alarming, despite the

Berliners' campaign to offer all new practitioners professional training, and he thought that "the relation between medical and lay workers [wa]s the exact opposite of what it should be." For Jones, nonmedical (or "lay") analysts had never really held the same level of clinical authority as physicians. Although Jones constantly invoked Freud's authority in psychoanalytic matters, he contested the belief that a medical education was fundamentally not beneficial (and might even hinder) effective psychoanalysis. He admired Brill's conservative exclusionary stance in New York. "I have not been so unsympathetic to the American point of view on lay analysis as most people in Europe," he later wrote to Eitingon. "I am even inclined to think that I should share it if I lived in America."[31] Despite his faith in Freud and his contempt for Americans, Jones took their side in the struggle to maintain medical dominance of the profession. No wonder then that the psychoanalyst Barbara Low's repeated offer to investigate the Berlin clinic on behalf of the British society was deferred for at least a year. Barbara Low was a friend and colleague of Alix and James Strachey and their Bloomsbury literary group. In the mid-1920s Alix and James would become Freud's master translators and would travel back and forth between London and Berlin for their analyses. Low was consequently comfortable with Berlin but her resolution, "that an enquiry into the organisation, financial and otherwise of the Berlin Psycho-Analytic Clinic be made as soon as possible with view to establishing a Freudian clinic in London," was tabled.[32] Four years later Low finally went to Berlin, and her report on the Poliklinik became the blueprint for the London Psychoanalytic Clinic. Jones, a physician, would become its director.

That July, although the Berlin Poliklinik opened with no apparent governmental hurdles, the project for a clinic in Vienna was much more cautiously received. Eduard Hitschmann, one of the unsung heroes of psychoanalysis and a forceful Social Democrat, insisted that psychoanalysts should have a free clinic and he battled Vienna's entrenched medical and psychiatric establishment in its pursuit. For two more years, until 1922, Hitschmann encountered governmental obstacles to opening the Ambulatorium. Few analysts were in a better position than Hitschmann to act on the Vienna society's interest in a free clinic. Respected by his peers as a "model of order and exactness in all his work and skill" and a great psychiatric diagnostician, Hitschmann seemed to relish confronting the starched medical bureaucracy all the same.[33] Competitive and energetic, and personally needled by the news of Max Eitingon's immediate success at the Berlin Poliklinik, Hitschmann was determined to organize a similar outpatient clinic. Most of the Vienna analysts were predisposed to start a free clinic. Their traditional medical ethos encouraged free services; they felt they should join with the new movement; and their self-interested motivations to gain legitimacy and build their practices were equally strong. "Every branch of medicine had a free clinic. So it wasn't so unusual for the socially-minded psychoanalysts to decide that we should have one too" said Martin Pappenheim's daughter Else, who emigrated under duress in 1938 while still a psychoanalytic trainee.[34]

In the end the Ambulatorium was shaped largely by Hitschmann's own abilities, but it was also determined by Paul Federn and Helene Deutsch's active socialist concern for the city's lower classes.[35] Yet, curiously, the beginning of the Vienna Ambulatorium was marked by distrust on all sides. Hitschmann's petitions for the establishment of a psychoanalytical outpatient clinic in the name of the Vienna Psychoanalytic Society were rejected both by the State Medical Department and the Municipal Council of the Medical Staff of the General Hospital. Unfortunately, even the new social democratic government drew a distinction between physical health and mental health and hesitated before granting psychological illness the same protections as tuberculosis and dental hygiene. Nevertheless, the galling resistance Hitschmann encountered over two years as he readied the Ambulatorium was directed far less at the free clinic as an institution than at psychoanalysis as a treatment method. Just as Freud had predicted in his Budapest speech, public support of their clinic would lag behind the psychoanalysts' own private charitable initiative. But Freud, who had raved about the opening of the Poliklinik in Berlin just eight months earlier, grudgingly wrote to Ferenczi that he "would basically be done a favor if [the clinic] never came into being. It is not suitable for Vienna."[36] He also suggested to Karl Abraham that the Vienna society's application for a psychoanalytic section at the general hospital went totally against his wishes. "Getting it would be quite unwelcome for me," Freud wrote, "because it would have to be in my name; I cannot devote any time to it, and there is no one in the Society to whom I could entrust its management."[37]

Freud's ostensible retreat from his 1918 Budapest manifesto followed a complex and interesting dynamic. The governing ideology of Viennese political culture was now unmistakably social democratic and Freud could afford to show a more reactive political side. On a personal level he felt burdened by old age (at sixty-four) and wary of increased workloads and managerial tasks intruding on his practice. He bemoaned an apparent dearth of independent leadership among the Viennese analysts. Vienna's psychoanalytic society lacked skilled administrators like Eitingon and even Jones, a situation perhaps created by Freud's preeminence but obvious nonetheless. On the political level, and in contrast to his earlier proactive demand for free psychoanalytic clinics, Freud was fearful of seeing psychoanalysis co-opted entirely by the left now that Vienna's leftward shift had been accomplished. He would hardly want the municipal government to legitimate their civic goals by exploiting his work. Freud needed to stay left of the right-wing party since the Christian Socials were openly anti-Semitic, but he also sought to stay clear of overt political commitment. It was a composite posture Freud would repeat periodically throughout his life as he sought to keep psychoanalysis above the political fray.

The Viennese psychoanalysts of the 1920s represented the entire political spectrum of the left, from Social Democrat to Communist. The fact that some moved far to the left does not mean that others were far to the right. "Most of the intellectuals, what here [in the United States] is a liberal was a socialist, a Social Democrat in Vienna" explained Grete Lehner Bibring.[38] Wilhelm Reich moved eventually to an even more radical left-wing position and openly took to the Communist Party. But other analysts like Paul Federn thought that Communists were hazardous to the nascent psychoanalytic movement, not because of their ideology but because they were subject to arrest or police supervision and could be relieved of their party affiliation if discovered in analysis. Social Democrats, on the contrary, were people like himself. With a mother who advocated for women's rights, a father whose practice as a family physician tended to the poor, and a sister who founded the first private social work agency in Vienna, the Vienna Settlement, Paul Federn epitomized the social democratic brand of progressivism. So it was important to distinguish between "Communist" as a political party affiliation and "Socialist" as a nominally Marxist political ideology aligned with the Social Democrats.[39] Sigmund Freud often repeated his opposition to Communism per se. But that was a different party; and the psychoanalysts remained, Freud and Grete Lehner Bibring included, "all social democrats because that was the liberal party for us."[40] The younger generation of Viennese analysts was deeply attached to the Austro-Marxists in city hall, while Freud and the older analysts with values grounded in a classical liberal tradition, simply identified with them.

Nonetheless, the twin beliefs that psychoanalysis had an implicit political mission and that Freudianism was progressive were widely understood by its practitioners, by the Social Democrats governing Vienna, and within at least the more avant-garde intellectual circles in Europe and America.[41] Emma Goldman, the American anarchist, had been "deeply impressed by the lucidity of his mind and the simplicity of his delivery" at Freud's 1909 Clark University lectures. Goldman recorded in her autobiography, *Living My Life*, how his speech echoed for her the themes of female sexuality and release from oppression she had first heard from him in 1896. Freud and psychoanalysis officially landed in America in September 1909 at Clark University's Twentieth Anniversary Conference held in Worcester, Massachusetts. Invited by the psychologist G. Stanley Hall to receive an honorary degree, the initially reluctant Freud was accompanied across the Atlantic by Carl Jung and Sándor Ferenczi. Freud improvised in German and delivered five lectures, each one developed around a specific psychoanalytic discovery. The final lecture explored how "civilization" demands repression and applies a particularly stringent moral code to the "cultured classes." America's ethic of puritan morality exemplified, for Freud, the repression inherent in civilization's moral codes. Challenging the somatic style then widespread in American psychiatry, Freud's ideas were ambiguously received. Nevertheless, the 1909 lectures represented a watershed in American behavioral and social sciences. For the neurologist James Jackson Putnam, the visit "was of deep significance," while the Harvard psychologist William James, the psychiatrist Adolph Meyer, and the anthropologist Franz Boas were more ambivalent.[42] The newspaper and magazine press alternately lionized and deplored him, setting the tone for a tense, unsettled relationship that lasts even until today. American resentment of Freud still lingers in many ways, but the feeling has always been mutual. Even in the mid-1920s Freud tried to avoid American questions about socialism and other controversial opinions, saying "politically, I am just nothing" to the Greenwich Village journalist Max Eastman, who had earlier published a book on Freud and Marx. At the same time, Freud advised Eastman that Lenin was carrying out "an intensely interesting experiment," rational enough for his serious scientific side, but anarchist enough to be accepted by some brilliant young analysts like Otto Fenichel and Wilhelm Reich.[43] Eastman was hardly dissuaded of Freud's progressivism.

Certainly by 1920 Freud was comfortable with current social democratic politics. As he told Ferenczi, he was delighted to receive an invitation to join Mayor Jakob Reumann's committee, headed by Red Vienna's guiding public health reformers Clemens Pirquet and Julius Tandler, to oversee an international child welfare fund.[44] Baron Clemens von Pirquet, who joined Freud and Tandler's child welfare project, was one of those extraordinarily inventive figures of début de siècle Vienna. A distinguished-looking pediatrician described as "exceedingly kind and polite though very nervous" by his laboratory's funders from the Rockefeller Foundation, Pirquet also introduced the concept of allergy into current medical language and pioneered modern nutrition with a system of measurements based on units of milk.[45] He was close to many of the psychoanalysts, among them Helene Deutsch, just finishing her term as a war psychiatrist and interested in childhood mental health. In some respects the project fit neatly with the Social Democrats' overriding interest in rebuilding Vienna around a core of child- and family-centered public welfare and their need to make constructive use of foreign moneys. In other respects, as Richard Pearce correctly observed, antagonism between Tandler and Pirquet, "the former representing the socialistic point of view and the latter the aristocratic," led to clashes over resources at the University of Vienna.[46] By the time Pirquet joined the American campaign of aid to Austrian children, the Commonwealth Fund had decided to help his famous Kinderklinik expand and repair its convalescent home for tubercular children. Several special grants helped replace worn-out technical equipment and surgical instruments used especially for operating on children. Subsequently Freud's wealthy and philanthropic brother-in-law Eli Bernays, now living in the United States, added a million crowns to the three-million-crown grant ($608,000) from a group of American physicians keen on building up Vienna's medical infrastructure including children's convalescent homes.[47] With images of the war's human wreckage still fresh, the Viennese decision to accept grants, even if preferential, from wealthy Americans was easy. The Americans, however, were responsible for administering these bequests morally and fairly. Notable among the foundations that chartered the course of modern child welfare and child development research, the Laura Spelman Rockefeller Memorial (LSRM) responded enthusiastically to the idea that cultivating good mental hygiene in childhood would produce healthy adults. According to most developmentalists including Freud, human character, personality, and even individual physiology are most vulnerable to environmental influences in childhood. A peaceful and productive postwar society would therefore be in want of attentive, progressive early education and social services dedicated to children's welfare. For the moment the LSRM was ready to invest directly in Julius Tandler's practical social services.

Freud was considerably more ambivalent toward other prominent Viennese doctors who were not affiliated with the Social Democrats. Among them the neurologist Julius von Wagner-Jauregg (figure 10) was then director of the city's principal public psychiatric clinic and, in 1920, as well-known a psychiatrist in Vienna as Freud. A thin man of dour appearance, Wagner-Jauregg's severe demeanor was underscored by a downturned mouth, a large waxed moustache, and a closely trimmed crewcut. Compassion was hardly his forte, but he was nevertheless an inspiring teacher and a formidable researcher who would be awarded the Nobel Prize for his 1927 discovery of

10 Dr. Julius Wagner von Jauregg
(Institute for the History of Medicine at
the University of Vienna)

malarial therapy for general paralysis. Nevertheless, in 1920 Wagner-Jauregg was charged by the city government's Commission of Inquiry on Dereliction of Military Duty with the lethal use of electrotherapy on shell-shocked soldiers. The commission, made up of prominent Social Democrats, invited Freud to testify as an expert witness at the October 14 and 16 hearings, where they investigated allegations of torture by military psychiatrists under Wagner-Jauregg's purview. Since 1918 the *Arbeiterzeitung* and other newspapers had published gruesome personal accounts of how the soldiers, suffering from war neurosis but accused of malingering and lack of will, were tortured in Wagner's clinic with "faradization" or electrical current to the point of death or suicide. Still a Hapsburg loyalist, Wagner-Jauregg joined patriotic duty to medical power and ordered isolation cells, straitjackets, and selective burning as therapy for soldiers he considered insufficiently energized for the war effort. But psychiatric brutality, even when passing as duty to the nation, simply outraged Freud. The psychiatrists had "acted like machine guns behind the front lines, forcing back the fleeing soldiers," Freud said on the stand.[48] Furthermore, he changed the tone of his written "Memorandum on the Electric Treatment of War Neurotics" from a clinical paper into a political statement.

He began the essay as a diplomatic colleague would, suggesting that Wagner-Jauregg was a man of principle who had acted against his better psychiatric judgement because of civic commitment to the interests of the state. While both men agreed on the symptomology underlying war neurosis, they disagreed on the treatment. But Freud ended with a withering critique of war and traditional military psychiatry. Conscription was not the patriotic duty of the state, he said, but the opposite, the "immediate cause of all war neurosis, [forming] rebellion against the ruthless suppression of [the soldier's] own personality by his superiors." Wagner-Jauregg's willingness to act in concert with the corporate state, by implicitly supporting governmental use of violence, dishonored the physician's humanitarian concern for the individual.[49] Freud had told Ferenczi that he would "naturally treat [Wagner-Jauregg] with the most distinct benevolence," adding that the events had "to do with war neurosis."[50] He had only wanted to show the court how their clinical and theoretical approaches differed without attacking his colleague personally. Just then the Viennese psychoanalytic society was formulating plans for its own free clinic, and Freud knew that the project would require at least nominal diplomacy toward his conservative rival. Wagner-Jauregg was eventually exonerated, but he continued to represent for Freud Vienna's old-time medical establishment and the dominance of a reactionary punitive stance in psychiatry.

All too soon, however, Freud found his courtesy to Vienna's institutional psychiatry and Wagner-Jauregg outmaneuvered. Hostile functionaries and a lethargic medical bureaucracy blocked Hitschmann's proposal for the Ambulatorium at each turn over the next two years. Since the license to open the clinic remained in the hands of the medical community's conservative opponents of psychoanalysis, Hitschmann enlisted the backing of his physician colleague Guido Holzknecht. Highly respected as a leading radiologist of the time, assistant in Hermann Nothnagel's clinic, and connected with the governing Society of Physicians of the Allgemeines Hospital, Holzknecht had also been since 1910 a member of the Viennese psychoanalytic society.[51] Holzknecht, Freud, and Hitschmann were friends and partners, jointly convinced that investigation of the unconscious mind and the interior body have equivalent aims. Holzknecht's genius in discovering tumors was the physiological counterpart to Freud's detection of the neuroses. Holzknecht and Freud also found themselves associated as reciprocal doctors and patients: Holzknecht, a former analysand, was the radiologist who treated Freud's cancer in 1924, and in 1929 Freud visited Holzknecht, who was dying of cancer from his own experiments, his right arm already amputated. Freud said, "You are to be admired for the way you bear your fate," and Holzknecht replied, "You know I have only you to thank for that."[52] Clearly, Hitschmann had found an influential spokesman and strategist.

Yet two full years of carefully planned tactical maneuvering would go by before the Allgemeines Hospital would officially designate an approved section for the Ambulatorium. Holzknecht's first personal intervention with the administration seemed to go well. On June 16 he optimistically noted his first auspicious visits to department heads and wrote to Hitschmann that "there would be room in the next months for an 'Ambulatorium for mental treatment' at Garrison Hospital No. 1. But how to commence? With whom to begin? I think eventually by association with one of the sections at the general hospital, though unfortunately it's impossible at mine. (Then again, nothing is really impossible!)"[53] Hitschmann followed his colleague's optimistic advice. Barely five months after the Berlin clinic opened, his petition dated July 1 was in the hands of the Senior Physician's Council of the Allgemeines Hospital, the local Public Health Authority of the State Medical Department, and the Society of Physicians headed by Wagner-Jauregg. The psychoanalytic Ambulatorium, Hitschmann promised, would not compete with the psychiatry department for patients nor decrease the use of medical therapy but instead would supplement other forms of treatment. Psychoanalysis could hardly be viewed as rivaling other departments of the hospital, "since psychotherapy, let alone psychoanalysis, is practiced at none." It had been inaccessible to the "wider masses until now" but was "ready for practical application on a broader scope. The Ambulatorium would restrict itself to underserved sick persons."[54]

An impressive red brick building housing the Military Hospital (Garrison Hospital No. 1) was selected for the Ambulatorium's location because of its convenient proximity to the General Hospital and because some of its treatment rooms had lain empty since the end of the war. These facilities could be put to use quite efficiently, calculated the psychoanalysts, since they would need at most a waiting room, another large area in which to examine prospective patients, and several small treatment rooms. Modest requests perhaps, but the hospital's branch of the Society of Physicians—the governing body of the Austrian medical profession—was in charge of allocating the facilities and saw no need to step up their unhurried decision-making process. Holzknecht, a member of that council (along with Wagner-Jauregg), relayed to Hitschmann, his friend and "most esteemed colleague," some confidential reports and instructions for future action: "Our proposal was not raised at the first meeting of the hospital's Physician's Council. I have done nothing about this, in order not to be identified as partisan from the outset.

I urge you to visit the director Dr. Glaser and, without pushing too hard, to inquire about the fate of the oft-submitted proposal, so that it does not vanish into the bureaucratic black hole."

Uninspired negotiations continued. For no clear reason, the hearing on Hitschmann's petition was switched from the hospital's local Physician's Council to the October meeting of the State Medical Board. As the doctors filtered out of that inconclusive session, Holzknecht stood around chatting sociably when suddenly the board's secretary alerted him that doctors Wagner-Jauregg and Jakob Pal were ready to listen to him. As "I read to them the introductory words of your proposal," Holzknecht reported on the events of October 23, Jakob Pal, a professor of internal medicine and also a board member, interrupted and nominated Wagner-Jauregg to examine the plans and deliver an expert opinion. The entire council agreed, unanimously. It was "the Austrian way," Holzknecht said dejectedly to Hitschmann. This time nothing could be done but to press Wagner.[55] And so the aristocratic Wagner von Jauregg, presumably still smarting from Freud's appearance at his trial, took the entire following year to examine the document, exercise his jurisdiction, and eventually come to an interim decision in July 1921.

In contrast to the sluggish progress of the psychoanalysts' petition for a free clinic, other branches of Vienna's new public health department moved forward rapidly. In November 1920 Julius Tandler was named councillor in charge of the Viennese Public Welfare Office, a post he maintained energetically until February 1934. Tandler saw a state- and community-based welfare program as the most expedient and viable remedy to Vienna's widespread postwar deterioration in almost every aspect of human life. In line with the cultural evolution of Red Vienna, a thorough reorganization of the health and welfare structure was called for and Tandler, working with Hugo Breitner, Otto Glöckel, Karl Seitz, and other Social Democrats, became its principal architect.

Tandler's theories proceeded from earlier models of social welfare benefits and entitlement like Bismarck's large-scale programs of domestic health, accident, and old-age insurance. In a curious ideological contradiction not unusual in nineteenth-century politics, Bismarck's progressive programs stemmed from a conservative motive, to create distance between German workers and the socialist movement—though it had the opposite effect. Like Bismarck but differently motivated, Tandler sought to bind workers to the state and vice versa. "In Germany," he wrote, "10–15% of all children born alive are provided for under the welfare system; in Austria the numbers are barely 4–5 in a thousand."[56] He wrote this admiringly, not because he believed that the state should override parental responsibility in taking care of so many children but because, by doing so, the state could prove its capacity to care for children whose lives had been placed at risk by larger social and environmental conditions. In Vienna a crippling environment had been created by the war. Tandler responded by centralizing all the city's welfare institutions into a single Public Welfare Office with professional and legal controls. His first concern, to curtail the patronizing policies of "Poor Care" charity by replacing them with modernized, planned, and far more respectful forms of direct assistance, led to further administrative reforms. Tandler's particular focus on the needs and rights of children corresponded, just then, to the emergence of new scientific studies of child development and new treatment techniques, as well as early childhood education and child analysis, all of which implied the necessity for social welfare services. The psychoanalysts agreed. The Ambulatorium, they believed, would shift free mental heath treatment from a stigma-laden paradigm of charity to that of social service.

Vienna's postwar social services offer a virtual map of the advances made by modern social work practice from the 1900s, when it was largely the province of upper-class benevolence on moral patrol, to the 1920s, when it grew into an educated profession. In Red Vienna some of the most powerful funders of social work and international social welfare, the Rockefeller Foundation and the Commonwealth Fund, collaborated with the city's health care leaders including Julius Tandler, Clemens Pirquet, and Guido Holzknecht. The Rockefeller Foundation's representatives watched Tandler's politics with some ambivalence but in general agreed with his goals. His sympathy for psychoanalysis was well-known, as was Holzknecht's, and they influenced every major social welfare campaign of those formative years. With international funders, city leaders, and local psychoanalysts united in support of progressive child welfare policies, the new profession of social work assumed its respected position within the welfare state.

Within each of Vienna's districts a woman appointed as a "welfare officer" visited the homes of children placed in care of families other than their biological parents, adopted children, and children born out of wedlock. She worked at the mother's advisory centers in residential areas and oversaw school medical inspections, looking out for family problems and signs of potential physical or sexual abuse. Supplied with extra cash, she could supplement a family's need in small ways, buying clothing or a pair of shoes for a child or new equipment for a father about to lose his job because he lacked masonry tools. Of course she documented her observations of the child's living conditions: the very nature of her work was defined by the successful coupling of practical assistance with the university's most current methodology, the direct observation of children's behavior. The core motive of a social worker was (and is) always subject to interpretation, and allowing her into the family home meant relinquishing jurisdiction over its members to the allegedly controlling state. But the opposite motive can also hold true, and a government can be more interested in assuring the safety and welfare of its children than upholding the false dignity of traditional family structures. As Tandler would reply to the Christian Socials' accusations that social workers took children away from families, "I can only say that we are doing our utmost to leave these children with their families in every possible case. But . . . the first thing we have to ask ourselves is whether the parents are really capable of bringing up their children."[57] In any society that sets great store by the idea of privacy, family home visits are experienced as intrusive and humiliating unless perhaps a medical emergency requires a physician at the patient's bedside. If patriarchal monarchist Austria asserted the supremacy of parental authority, then the welfare policies of Red Vienna affirmed the state's right to protect the child.

Given the Viennese preoccupation with child protection and Julius Tandler's own belief in the value of specific family-based assistance, the government standardized and strengthened the ties between the public child health centers and the supportive services provided in the home. New opportunities for teaching young mothers, not necessarily about sanitation, which was already quite good, but about nutrition and breast feeding or the treatment of fever and infection, led to the creation of a new occupation: the *Fürsorgerin*. Midway between a nurse and a social worker, but more influential than both combined, the title of *Fürsorgerin* had no actual counterpart in the United States. The Fürsorgerin's impressive stature came from a largely centralized health and social work system that placed responsibility for child care squarely with the government and therefore could normalize approaches to child welfare issues such as illegitimacy, orphanhood, and abuse and neglect of children. As a social worker, she (for it was largely a woman's profession) could count on the law to support her decisions, and, as a public health worker, her judgment was respected for the medical weight it carried. Trained *Fürsorgerinnen* were assigned, county by county, to assist physicians at the prenatal or child health stations as well as the families living in their geographic catchment areas. "Stations are found in all sorts of public and semi-public buildings—hospitals, town halls, store buildings, and municipal tenements which," the authors of the Commonwealth Fund's report declared of the Gemeindebauten dwellings, "are apt to be delightfully modern in style and decoration!"[58] Young children would not be deprived of care even if their overburdened mothers lacked the time for pediatricians. Instead mothers saw the Fürsorgerin in her rounds of home visits, reviewed the children's health, learned some safety tips, and procured some relief from the depressing load of everyday domestic life. Of the one hundred federally subsidized child health stations in Austria, the fifteen centers located in Vienna enrolled almost ten thousand and assisted another forty thousand children. In the year 1927 alone the Fürsorgerinnen affiliated with the health stations made over sixteen thousand home visits to enrolled infants and preschool children in Vienna.[59] True, the Fürsorgerinnen searched out parentless children or supervised the care of foster children as required by law, but mostly they referred children needing orthopedic or dental care to special clinics, or for tuberculosis to the health station, or for mental health care to the Ambulatorium.

The class clowns and the constant talkers, the cheaters and the liars, impudent or vain children, kids with poor grades, some depressed and some caught masturbating, by all accounts most of the children seen at the guidance clinic, were demoralized by family troubles. The entire municipal school system was now reorganized by the postwar Austrian Board of Education to regard children's social adjustment as important as their instructional needs. The choice was between Freudian or Adlerian pedagogy, but each group's allied educational institutions were imbued with psychoanalysis. Shaped by Willi Hoffer and Siegfried Bernfeld's kindergarten designs and by Alfred Adler's trademark Individual Psychology, the new Pedagogical Institute for the City of Vienna was simultaneously affiliated with the philosophy faculty of the university and with the Vienna Psychological Institute of Karl and Charlotte Büehler. The Büehlers, then Vienna's leading academic psychologists, were fine-tuning their methodology of laboratory-based, controlled experiments to understand child behavior. And when Adler spoke at the Pedagogical Institute, he enlisted a wide forum of educators, therapists, and school superintendents in the first program for teachers of child guidance clinics. He was personally engaged in setting up the first of what would eventually become an entire network of teacher and child guidance clinics. In a city district with sixty-seven grammar and high schools, 171 of the area's almost 20,000 children were voluntarily treated in 1920 (the first year of the program) on a case-by-case basis.[60] Most teachers had never considered problem students to be an organic part of the classroom, nor ever thought of them as depressed or isolated. Now Adler's method trained teachers to involve the entire classroom in building up the sense of *Gemeinschaftgefuehl*, or community feeling, among truant or rude children. Troubled children had bad problems, not innately bad character.

When Otto Glöckel, head of Vienna's reform-minded Department of Education in charge of school administrative policy, resolved to officially support Individual Psychology, Adler was finally afforded the chance to test his ideas in practice. The building at 20 Staudingergasse, one of the city's oldest classical structures, was remade into an experimental grade school based on Adler's principles of *Arbeitschule*, work and community. Spacious communal rooms were refashioned from once ornate chambers. Old wood benches, lockers, and even small metal inkwells were salvaged from the military and distributed to local children, most from poor families. Psychodrama, group talk, and individual therapy were used as educational tools in this extraordinary school setting where children themselves became coeducators, assistants, and hopefully cotherapists for their more disturbed classmates. There Oskar Spiel and Ferdinand Birnbaum incorporated depth psychology into the daily class agenda, providing modern progressive education for the next ten years to countless neglected, neurotic, learning disabled, or simply underprivileged children. Parents from the school's working-class neighborhood received the Adlerians' little illustrated journal *Elternhaus und Schüler* (Parental Home and Student) and free evening classes in child development. Glad to abide by the curriculum of the new Austrian elementary school, Spiel and Birnbaum tried to bridge the gap between individual psychology and psychoanalysis (a bridge Adler and Freud had failed to build) and strove for an intensely therapeutic atmosphere where every class was a community experience. Freudian psychoanalysis, emphasizing the inner self over against social determinism, also played its part in validating the individual child's right, as separate from the family, to be protected by the state.

Concurrent with this reorganization in conventional social values and gender roles, a sexual revolution seemed to flourish on virtually every level of society. Women were voting. Sexuality was openly discussed in popular newspapers and novels like Hugo Bettauer's *Wiener Romane*. Bettauer, a prolific Austrian writer whose novel, *The Joyless Street*, was made into a film by G. W. Pabst in 1925, would reappear throughout the early 1920s as a popularizer of psychoanalysis and a veritable champion of the Ambulatorium. Meanwhile the ambiguous idea of the procreative family, promoting at once maternalist and feminist images, imbued everyday life from urban transportation to municipal architecture. The student seminar on sexology started the year before in 1919 by Otto Fenichel and his friends Reich, Lehner, and Bibring was therefore hardly out of place, either within the university or outside of it. Now in its second year, the seminar planned to explore how traditional beliefs about sex could be retooled with the new psychoanalytic methodology and how to extrapolate a political agenda therefrom. For Fenichel, sexual freedom was as much a political issue as a psychological one. "Does man live from within or without?" was the anarchist title of an experimental symposium of June 22 in which he demanded outright that the participants give voice only to their feelings and resolutely expel all intellectual or scientific thoughts. Somewhere between a sermon and a harangue, Fenichel's highly charged two-and-a-half-hour speech explored a range of systematic yet humane solutions to social problems. Are science, philosophy, the youth movement, or politics best for mobilizing people to alleviate humanity's "great, glaring misery in all its colors?"[61] The company that night at his friend Hans Heller's elegant apartment included Reich's study partner and friend Desö Julius, a Hungarian student who had escaped to Vienna that summer after the fall of Béla Kun's government and who introduced Reich to the communist movement. Otto Fenichel's girlfriend Lisl was there along with his own sister and brother-in-law, Paul Stein, as well as Gisl Jäger from the Youth Movement, Gretl Rafael and Willy Schlamm, future publisher of *Die Rote Fahne* (The Red Flag) in Vienna. Annie Pink, who would become Reich's first wife and a prominent psychoanalyst, was there as well, still a member of the Youth Movement and a high school student. So too was Lore Kahn, a kindergarten teacher in training and Reich's pale sweetheart. Kahn died soon afterward of tuberculosis. When her grief-stricken mother falsely accused Reich of inducing Lore's death by causing her to have a disastrous abortion, Reich referred the mother to Paul Schilder, then professor of psychiatry at the University of Vienna.[62]

Different as they were, both Paul Schilder and Heinz Hartmann (the future champion of ego psychology) had worked at the university's psychiatric hospital but saw little if any contradiction between Freud's psychoanalytic and Wagner-Jauregg's organic biological views of mental illness. Wagner-Jauregg presided over the Psychiatric-Neurological Clinic, Vienna's center of clinical psychiatry, and most days were still filled with his research protocols based on electrotherapy and insulin shock treatments. Even Helene Deutsch, a military psychiatrist during the war, had worked on his experiments in round-the-clock shifts. Since women were precluded from official appointments, Deutsch lost her job when Schilder came back from the front, but she recognized in him "a very original and productive spirit" and seemed not to resent the institutional insult.[63] Deutsch used some of Schilder's experiments with humanistic hypnosis to draw out, for example, an elderly catatonic woman, intuiting that just behind her patient's blank façade a hidden consciousness was listening and inviting human contact. Evidently by the early 1930s most of the young analysts at the Ambulatorium were encouraged to study Schilder's model. Erik Erikson (then still using the name Erik Homburger), who had attended some of Tandler's classes, pursued further studies in psychiatry with Schilder. Paul Federn maintained friendly connections to the university clinic and later found that the application of psychologically based therapy to psychosis was invaluable. The clinic itself was not far from the Freud home on Berggasse, and Anna Freud attended afternoon training sessions while Deutsch was an assistant. In Anna's tightly controlled background as a grade school teacher, little had prepared her for the spontaneous outbursts and unmitigated pain of the psychiatric patients. But Anna learned quickly. She watched her friend Grete Lehner Bibring, also a pupil of Schilder's, apply his integrated model to her very first analytic patient, a prostitute with a compulsive neurosis. Grete had graduated from medical school at age twenty-four and started a psychiatric practice right away. Even after two years of experience at Wagner-Jauregg's clinic, Grete still looked back on Schilder's training as the best preparation for handling the florid psychiatric symptoms of, for example, a delusional, twenty-three-year-old polymorphously perverse clinic patient. Nonetheless, ten years were to pass before Schilder formally brought medical psychiatry to the Ambulatorium with the brilliant but short-lived Department for the Treatment of Borderline and Psychoses.

Meanwhile, on the main campus of the University of Vienna, the seminar in sexology grew ever more popular. After Fenichel had left Vienna for Berlin that fall, Reich assumed chairmanship and administrative responsibility for scheduling lectures and conferences. His outspoken interest in human sexuality was reflected in his choice of program speakers like Isidor Sadger (Reich's own analyst), then researching homosexuality and sexual perversions, and Eduard Hitschmann (figure 11), who was publishing studies on female frigidity. Reich's experience with authoritarian structure bred by four years in the military soon led him to divide the seminar into two branches, a biological group headed by Eduard Bibring and a psychological group, his own. The events were so popular, Reich reported, that thirty students and supporters turned out for a fairly plain lecture on "Drive and Libido Concepts from Forel to Jung".[64] As attendance grew, Reich encountered eager groups of radicalized university students, among them Fenichel

11 Eduard Hitschmann
(Institute for the History of Medicine
at the University of Vienna)

and Bernfeld's old friends and followers from the Youth Movement as well as young adherents to the Social Democratic Party. Soon what had started as a simple extracurricular activity at the medical school became a planned program of seminars for the study of sexology. Endocrinology, biology, physiology, and especially psychoanalysis were studied as new branches of the new discipline.

Among the occasional seminar participants who would eventually join Reich at the Sex-Pol clinics was Lia Laszky, a fellow anatomy student of Tandler's at the University of Vienna medical school. Lia was an elegant young bisexual woman with whom Reich was so obsessively infatuated and tormented he felt he might "wind up with Jauregg". Lia had a "soft face, a small nose and mouth, blond hair," Reich remembered, and, though poor, she thrived on Vienna's festive *vie de bohème*.[65] She lead Reich to Vienna's modernist music and opera and followed up their discussions about socialism with gifts like Gustav Landauer's book, *Aufruf* (The Call). Reich took to Landauer and Sterner's utopianist views immediately. Critics, then as now, have dismissed Reich as overidealistic and anarchist, yet his effect on psychoanalysis is almost unrealizable, and much of its impact lies in his clinical application of Landauer's ideas. Similarly, when Reich gave Lia books on psychoanalysis (like Hitschmann's) and personally intervened to secure her psychoanalytic education, she shifted her involvement away from the Wandervogel and sought to organize a left-leaning Youth Movement group for girls. More familiar names were to join Reich's subsequent efforts to organize Sex-Pol—Annie Pink Reich, Edith Jacobson—but, among his friends in the second generation of psychoanalysts, Otto Fenichel engaged most boldly with political activism.

Otto Fenichel was clearly a born orator and, when he returned to Vienna from another stay in Berlin that Christmas of 1920, he enthralled his friends for two full evenings on the subject of "On Founding a Commune in Berlin." Most of the members of the sexology seminar had heard about the Berlin Poliklinik though few except Fenichel had actually visited. But it was Fenichel who actually foresaw the many ways in which the Berlin Poliklinik would become, as Freud put it, an "institution or out-patient clinic . . . where treatment shall be free." He was fascinated by the Berlin model, the first and for the moment the only one of its kind, which formed a social nexus between the Poliklinik as a clinical service and the Institute as a regular psychoanalytic training program. The composite institution met Fenichel's expectations for collectivity, an interest that would dominate his personal and professional life.

In Vienna Freud and Rank announced in a circular letter to their colleagues that they would publish a year's end report on the activity of the Berlin clinic, either in brochure form or as a supplement to *Imago*, even before the real work of treating patients had started.[66] In Weimar Berlin and Red Vienna the idea that creativity could be blended with everyday practicality had particular intellectual and popular appeal.

"An Ambulatorium should exist for psychic treatment in the widest sense of the word"

1921

"IT IS PUZZLING," Freud wrote to Ernest Jones in March of 1921, "how little '*Gemeinsinn*' [community spirit] and tendency for organisation there is to be found among the better elements in American society, only robbers and pirates hunt in gangs."[1] His commentary, that "competition is much more pungent with them, not succeeding means civil death. . . . And success means money," is followed by Freud's even more distrustful query, whether "an American [can] live in opposition to the public opinion?" The questions reverberate with important themes, not only in the opposition between American and European psychoanalytic affinities within their respective cultures but also in Freud's understanding of culture as de facto community. Of course the term *community* was by now popularized in mental health circles by his former colleague Alfred Adler, but it played a fundamental role in Vienna's social welfare society as well.

News of the Viennese health authorities' rejection of the Ambulatorium petition was thus particularly galling when it reached the psychoanalysts in July. Hitschmann received the negative report a full year after he had recruited Guido Holzknecht to help shuttle the initial application through the myriad intricacies of the medical and administrative bureaucracy. Because the relationship between the conservative Physician's Council (Gesellschaft) at the Allgemeines Hospital and Wagner-Jauregg at the Vienna Psychiatric Clinic ran deep, their rejection of the psychoanalysts after a lengthy, cumbersome review was frustrating but hardly unexpected. Freud had despised the council, for him the worst symbol of orthodox rigidity, since the beginning of his medical career. Even when the Gesellschaft nominated him to an honorary membership in March of 1931, Freud thanked them unenthusiastically and described the event to Eitingon as "a cowardly gesture at the appearance of success, very disgusting and repulsive."[2] What was unanticipated, however, was the council's favorable opinion that "an Ambulatorium should exist for psychic treatment in the widest sense of the word."[3] Evidently Wagner-Jauregg was fairly conscious of his responsibility as a public health administrator. From his perspective the apparent problem was the applicability, or general reach, of psychoanalytic treatment, not the need for mental health treatment per se. But Hitschmann conjectured that the setback was based on two additional, more polemical premises. For one, a psychoanalytic clinic would cost too much if the minister of finance sponsored it as a state endeavor. And second, such a clinic would seem too limited therapeutically if it excluded all forms of psychiatric outpatient treatment except psychoanalysis—and was supported as such by the state. Hitschmann sensed that these ongoing problems with location and licensing foretold of future struggles with the broader issue of lay analysis and the very legitimacy of analytic practice. The path of persuasion seemed to have reached its limits: neither the analysts' enthusiasm for the project nor their public relations campaign seemed to move the local Health Authority closer to approving a license for the Ambulatorium. The Authority's resistance was discouraging, especially in Red Vienna, since every other branch of medicine already had its own free clinic, and citizens had access to heath care as a social right.[4]

"The sick adult, or the child who needs a defect corrected, is automatically given an opportunity to secure some medical care. Much time and energy which in the United States are used up by the nurse's efforts to arrange for free treatment . . . are in Austria left free for other activities," observed a delegation from the Commonwealth Fund. In their six-year effort to support children's health in Austria, officers of the powerful American charity commented repeatedly on the effectiveness of the Social Democrats' universal health care plan. In addition, private health insurance societies (*Krankenkassen*), founded in the 1880s to cover the poor, were expanded after the war to include most of the population. All government employees now belonged to this state-regulated contributory system, as did all wage-earning employees, domestics, and laborers. Thus, when Freud argued that "the poor man should have just as much right to assistance for his mind as he now has to the life-saving help offered by surgery; and that the neuroses threaten public health no less than tuberculosis," he was simply asking the state to include psychoanalysis in a universal public health system.

Nevertheless the government hindered the opening of the Ambulatorium for another full year, and refused to authorize a license for the clinic unless it guaranteed that only physicians would practice there. Even after office space had been secured and cooperation enlisted from key members of Vienna's Public Health Department and the Physician's Council, official objections showed no sign of relenting. Of course, Freud's controversial—at times hostile—relationship with the university and medical establishment may have impeded its first chances. But finally, late that summer, Dr. Tauber, an unusually imaginative officer in the public health service, offered Hitschmann a suite of vacant rooms in another section of the Military Hospital, Garrison Hospital No. 2. Unfortunately Tauber's original proposal proved unfeasible. The high cost of renovating the rooms and transforming military medical space into an arrangement suited to the needs of the Ambulatorium psychoanalytic patients was prohibitive. Another exasperating year would go by until Felix Deutsch, head of the hospital's cardiology department and also a psychoanalyst, rescued the project.

Would Dr. Tauber have assented more readily to Freud's clinic if Alfred Adler's own mental health clinics had not been running smoothly since 1918? Adler was by now celebrated for his work in child guidance. His first clinic was so favorably received by the Social Democrats that the Viennese authorities asked him to replicate them in each district. Eventually twenty-eight such centers were established. Somehow the theoretical underpinnings of individual psychology were less threatening to the medical establishment than Freudian psychoanalysis. Adler ran his own clinic as a training center for doctors, teachers, social workers, and psychology graduate students, all interested in participating in the workers' movements. Upon graduation these psychologists managed the clinics and generally worked in them without pay.[5] What more did Vienna need? Ultimately the stewards of Red Vienna did see the differences between Adler and Freud and found room not only for both of their therapeutic approaches but also for additional experimenters in psychotherapy and social welfare.

Wilhelm Reich's (figure 12) push to associate social welfare with psychoanalysis, both at the Ambulatorium and Sex-Pol, ultimately showed that such experiments were possible. A full generation younger than Adler, Reich had been active in student organizations and in the Social Democratic Party and was now working in psychoanalytic circles with his friends from the Youth Movement, Siegfried Bernfeld and Otto Fenichel. For the moment Reich was so highly regarded by Freud that, as a precocious pupil, he was allowed to start an analytic practice before graduating from medical school. Ecstatic,

12 Wilhelm Reich in his mid-twenties, at a Vienna café (Special Collections, A. A. Brill Library, New York Psychoanalytic Society and Institute)

and for very good reasons, he exclaimed "I am alive. [I] have two *paying* patients sent to me by Freud himself."[6] Reich felt no compunction about criticizing Adler, whose work he found sporadically interesting but largely dishonest and sanctimonious. "The socialist and psychologist of the individual, Alfred Adler, sits in the Café Central night after night, a luminary to his gaping disciples," Reich wrote when he had a chance to observe his rival. The students "listen as he ponders the problem of world socialism and rattles on about the struggles of feelings of community against the will to power, about socialist objectives, and meanwhile a dance of death is going on outside."[7] While Reich struggled to balance Adlerian objectivity with his own intense emotionalism, his friend Fenichel, who could slot everyone and everything into a particular category (Reich called this Fenichel's "pigeonhole" personality) disengaged politics from personality. "Yes, there an unconscious in a psychoanalytic sense," Fenichel said. But "in a philosophical sense, no!" Fenichel would later reactivate his spectacular planning skills in the mid- and late 1930s, when Marxism and classical psychoanalysis seemed hopelessly and absurdly contradictory to almost everyone else. Until then however, the two men remained friends, with Reich especially devoted once he found his name placed high on Fenichel's list of confidants. In 1921 they traveled together to the Wachau, a lovely region on the Danube, with Annie Pink and Berta Bornstein. Then they parted for the next few years, only to reunite with greater resolve in Berlin.

Meanwhile Max Eitingon was extraordinarily busy: he took on sole responsibility for every new patient screening at the Berlin Poliklinik because "discretion," he decreed, must be observed "even more than usual in this kind of work." Eitingon also assigned the senior analyst designated to carry out additional interviews, and at times allowed an assistant to follow up with detailed questioning. All applicants received physical and brief neurological examinations; patients with underlying or complex physical problems were sent to other clinics for tests like X rays or blood analyses. But it was always Eitingon who determined the patients' course of treatment and matched them with their analysts. He told his friends abroad how he was pleased to find the clinic doing so well after his absence, its performance and reputation growing together.[8] The size of the full-time staff grew quickly. Despite the sheer scale of their volunteerism, the clinic's expenditures more than doubled from 1921 to 1922, reaching 150,000 marks ($36,055) with only 25,500 marks ($6,000) in receipts. Eitingon estimated that their next budget would run to about 275,000 marks ($66,100).[9]. Hans Lampl was working there with Ada Schott, now specializing in child analysis. Karl Abraham, Hans Lieberman, Karen Horney, and Melanie Klein voluntarily took on nonpaying cases. Felix Boehm and Carl Müller-Braunschweig, two idiosyncratic analysts who would become, by 1933, Nazi collaborators and guide the ruinous aryanization of the Poliklinik, were still apparently serious analysts in the early 1920s.

Melanie Klein had arrived in Berlin from Budapest in 1921 at age thirty-eight and soon created a crucible for new ideas in child analysis. In appearance Melanie Klein never broke with her Hungarian roots. She wore marvelous whimsical hats and long dresses or long straight skirts and embroidered blouses. She had trained with two figureheads of psychoanalysis, the gentle Ferenczi and the mentoring Abraham. Her friend Alix Strachey, the British bohemian journalist and analytic candidate, wrote letters home and those from Berlin convey a real sense of the excitement Melanie generated at the Poliklinik. "*Die* Klein propounded her views & experiences on Kinderanalyse [child analysis], & at last the opposition showed its hoary head," Alix later wrote to her husband James Strachey. The evening of Klein's presentation, "the opposition consisted of Drs. Alexander and Radó. . . . [Then] everyone rallied to her & attacked the 2 swarthy Hungarians. . . . Two more women backed Melanie. One was Horney & the other [Josine] Müller."[10] Melanie Klein also had confidence that the more adventurous members of the Berlin society, especially Ernst Simmel, would stick by her. Her clinical practice widened as soon as she reached the city, and though her colleagues were generally uneasy about her methods of probing deeply into a child's unconscious, some like Felix Boehm and Karen Horney did allow her to conduct prophylactic analyses with their own children. Of course Horney was an experimenter herself. Klein's fellow Hungarian Franz Alexander (who fled political oppression along with Sándor Radó and came to Berlin in 1921) wrote that, like Melanie Klein, Horney was "always given to making her own formulations."[11] In later life Melanie Klein was bitter about her Berlin experience and complained that her only Poliklinik patients were either children or other analysts' deeply disturbed relatives or patients. Klein's account of the controversy surrounding her work was fairly accurate, but she was also very popular in the social life of the Poliklinik. Arguments aside, without the Poliklinik's atmosphere of tolerance and clinical experimentation, Klein might never have had the opportunity to observe children so closely.[12] The Poliklinik benefited too. With Klein on staff, fifty-two children under age ten obtained consultations that resulted in treatment. In contrast, only two patients over age fifty-six entered analysis in the same time frame, though almost fifty were interviewed. Child analysis as a method of treatment had begun in earnest while psychoanalysis of the elderly remained, as it would for many decades, remote. The child analyses Klein conducted in Berlin of "Egon" and the six year-old "Erna" were reported later in *The Psycho-Analysis of Children*. In the meantime, the children's treatment attendance and clinical progress were recorded virtually daily on clinic charts pre-printed on brown waxy paper.[13] These standardized forms, presumably laid out by the clinic's unofficial chart-maker Otto Fenichel, were folded in four like class attendance rosters. For the next three years Klein would use these documents to track her famous early child patients, "Kate," "Walter," "Heinrich," "Heinz," the three-year-old "Evchen," "Tanya," the six-year-old "Eva," and the ten-year-old "Ralph." Anyone treating analysands, adult or child, at the Poliklinik was required to use this practical format. The chart system easily allowed for treatment updates, quick notes and diagnoses, and ongoing comments about the patient's physical condition like a child's high fever or an adult's persistent cough. The charts also recorded payments and tracked the patient's life events like vacations and funerals. Best of all, once a chart was filled up, the statistics could be promptly turned over to Eitingon.

These numbers were tremendously important to Eitingon who, coincidentally, understood how the Poliklinik's presence in Berlin could either renew or destroy the delicate relationship between psychoanalysis and clinical psychiatry. The model of the polyclinic was not new to German psychiatry. Outpatient psychiatric services had emerged in the 1890s as urban psychiatrists sought to remedy their profession's poor public image. Academic medicine had already conceived of polyclinics as teaching facilities where students would combine supervised home visits to indigent families (*Hauspoliklin-iken*) with some regularly posted office hours, usually near a university hospital. At the Charité, socially aware psychiatrists had organized the first specifically psychiatric polyclinic and linked the external clinic to the hospital's neurological ward.[14] By 1909 the number of free or low-fee patients enrolled at the Charité had grown to six thousand annually, with twelve staff physicians attending to the clinic's hugely expanded mental hygiene and social responsibilities. Special care was offered to children, alcoholics, and people with sexually transmitted diseases. By the turn of the century, German psychiatrists succeeded in revitalizing their profession by combining innovative, state-of-the-art treatment on a one-to-one patient basis with communitywide mental health. This promise of a better kind of care for mental illness fit perfectly with Freud's 1918 Budapest image of the free clinic. Eitingon understood that the polyclinic model would diminish outside hindrances to psychoanalysis, attract both the middle and the lower classes, provide for the kind of intense clinical observation needed for basic scientific research, and leave room for questions of social welfare and mental health.

Ernest Jones (figure 13) saw no such thing. Until the Stracheys arrived back home from Berlin in 1922, Jones rebuffed the idea of building a clinic in London. That the larger political issues simply escaped him was, in itself, a sign of Jones's own position of privilege, as was his sense that he could persevere indifferent to the implications of social class on English psychoanalysis. In

13 Ernest Jones, checking his watch (Photo by Eduard Bibring, Archives of the Boston Psychoanalytic Society and Institute)

truth he was "keen on keeping out of politics," said the London psychoanalyst Pearl King. She described Jones as "a little man, decently dressed [who] kept people on time" in meetings.[15] At one of those well-run meetings of the British society, Barbara Low and Joan Riviere had engineered a particularly lively discussion of the Berlin clinic. Even Glover agreed to begin "something" more or less identical to the Poliklinik. That the question of a psychoanalytic clinic emerged at all was encouraging to Low and Rivière, but, according to the analysts' own records of the meeting, "no definite line was adopted as regards its formation."[16] For several years now the analysts had been without such basic assets as an official place to meet one another for case conferencing, let alone a clinic. But Jones, who was largely in authority and still ambivalent about the politically charged issue of free treatment, would not assent to a tentative plan.

Even during Europe's inflationary years of 1921–1923, Hugo Breitner and the Social Democrats' economic policies stabilized Vienna's municipal budget and maintained solvency without resorting to dependency on foreign loans. In redirecting the tax burden toward those landlords and large businesses that had remained wealthy after the war and had benefited from inflation, they generated enough revenue to finance housing and social welfare projects. Horses and dogs—the finer the pedigree, the higher the tax—were assessed selectively as were food and drink sold in luxury hotels and restaurants, beer, posters, entertainment, advertising, and auctions, with a moral charge inevitably creeping into such determinations. Tariffs on luxuries such as cars, servants, property, and fancy goods (basically anything but income) largely replaced indirect taxes from rent and consumer charges. But high culture was so meaningfully integrated into the Viennese life of workers and bourgeois alike that operas and concerts were taxed at a lower rate than movies and prize fights. Landlords and large employers, especially corporate entities like banks unaccustomed to taxes, were now paying them monthly and the funds were directed immediately toward public sector expenditures. Businessmen balked at the luxury taxes and claimed that such government interference would cause bankruptcies and increase unemployment. In fact, the opposite happened. The large-scale investment in public works employed blue- and white-collar workers by the thousands, and the newly enfranchised Viennese working-class in turn stimulated the municipal economy. Conservative and angry, the landlords and industrialists sided with the Christian Socials to dub the new policy *Steuersadismus* (tax sadism) since the strategy was, as in fact intended, shifting much of the fiscal burden from the working poor to the local moneyed elite.[9] In the new state's threefold housing policy, rents on preexisting apartments were frozen; then financing for individual houses was secured, and, following that, large-scale apartment complexes were built. Overriding any doubts, the commanding Danneberg articulated Red Vienna's ambitious egalitarian housing policy. "Until there is no shortage of housing," he proclaimed that winter, "it will remain inevitable the community must have the decisive word on the market of the lodgings and the rationing of the housing space."[10] On April 15, the National Assembly approved the Social Democrat's bill for a Federal Housing and Settlement Fund that allocated funds to build the *Siedlungsamt*, the settlement collective. Curiously, Danneberg found in Adolf Loos an architect with the necessarily resourceful mix of interests in classical housing, forthright ingenuity, and modernist ideology.

Loos, whose famous essay on "Ornamentation and Crime" condemned all forms of building decoration and especially the popular Jugendstil and the work of the Wiener Werkstätte, was appointed chief architect of Vienna's *Siedlungsamt* (or building collective) from May 1921 to June 1924. A small man with brooding deep-sunk eyes and a sharp chin, he was arguably the ideal architect to manage the ambiguous world of urban architecture. In many ways he was a true functionalist from whom Ernst Freud, then an apprentice in Loos's studio, learned the use of rational, refined space. When his stellar group of left-leaning architects, journalists, and intellectuals joined Red Vienna's housing project, building construction took on the spirit of a social movement. Loos predicted the streamlined forms characteristic of modernism; but he was also the kind of odd visionary who banned trees from gardens as "antisocial" because, he said, they occasioned disagreements among neighbors.[11] In a pattern that would blossom over the next fifteen years, Loos oversaw the construction of thirty inhabitable settlements where "the garden is primary, the house secondary."[12] The tradition of urban planting and self-sufficiency dates from that postwar period when food shortages and lack of housing led to the creation of workers' gardens, alternative shelter, and, indeed, squatters settlements. Actual building of the *Siedlungs* (settlements) started on the outskirts of the city when municipal support for construction became available on an individual or cooperative basis. Eventually some five thousand suburban cottages were built in workers' neighborhoods around Vienna, the kitchen in the dining room, the tiny bedroom only meant for sleeping, and an outhouse to guarantee that excrement would be recycled into the garden. That small green garden became the base around which the whole social organization and economy of this new family-centered housing revolved. Even today, approaching the city of Vienna by train or bus, the presence of the gardens and their vegetable patches, a few vines and some flowers climbing up the tool shed, is unmistakable.

"A Psychoanalytic Ambulatorium in Vienna"

1922

THE AMBULATORIUM opened with much fanfare on May 22, 1922, a few weeks after Freud's sixty-sixth birthday and more than two years after the Berliners had started the Poliklinik. After a full two years of strained negotiations with Vienna's entrenched medical patricians, Hitschmann welcomed fresh efforts by Paul Federn and by Helene Deutsch and her husband Felix Deutsch to restart the Ambulatorium project (figure 14). Finally this round of exertion paid off. The pivotal intervention came from Felix Deutsch, a physician specializing in heart disease at the Allgemeines Hospital and fairly powerful as director of the Clinic for Heart Diseases, the hospital's cardiology unit. For an insider like Deutsch the immense maze of the Allgemeines Krankenhaus finally yielded a suitable suite of rooms in an unlikely place, the ambulance entrance to the cardiology unit itself. The cardiology section, the Herzstation,[1] had survived as an independent unit of the hospital because of two of Vienna's stellar physicians, the pharmacologist Hans Horst Meyer and the cardiologist Rudolf Kauffmann. As early as 1915 they had recognized the critical need to designate a separate medical facility exclusively for heart patients. Now Meyer and Kauffman agreed with Felix Deutsch's plans and felt that the Ambulatorium's public health mission matched their own.

Undaunted by the hospital administration's stifling behavior, Meyer and Kauffman developed the Herzstation at the end of World War I after convening a board of directors similar to the psychoanalysts' own local society. They were particularly alarmed by the increase in chronic heart-

14 The Ambulatorium at 18 Pelikangasse, Vienna (Freud Museum, London)

related illnesses that, like the current upsurge of war neurosis, was discovered in young men who had been medically screened for military service. Among the Herzstation's medical examiners, young doctors like Tom Schwarz and Ernst Haudek supported Red Vienna's pro-family policies and understood that the vital postwar effort to rebuild the city's population required both practical and technical innovation. Fortunately the Herzstation quickly acquired new medical machinery, an X-ray machine and a therapeutic whirlpool. Pediatric services were added courtesy of the Commonwealth Fund. The affable Guido Holzknecht solicited funds from the Rockefeller Foundation (then also helping out Pirquet's child clinic and Dr. Löwenstein's tuberculosis institute) for a Potter-Bucky-Blende instrument and a respiratory chamber, helped manage the X-ray equipment, and trained the technicians.[2] Results of these X rays or *Orthodiagrammen* were carefully recorded and standardized charts made patient data available for medical review.

In many ways these medical charts were to be the Ambulatorium's lifeline. Meyer and Kaufmann believed that the Herzstation, conceived during the war, should last at least into the first year of peace. And since the whole hospital bureaucracy revolved around charts, statistics, and various forms of accounting, this huge archive of patient information essentially justified retaining the cardiac health unit to serve the civilian sector. The meticulously kept reports would lead to new protocols for the active care of sick people as well as retrospectively document war-related illnesses and anticipate military compensation claims. Administered by a close circle of friends and colleagues, as the Ambulatorium would be by the psychoanalytic society, the Herzstation society developed organizational bylaws and secured for Meyer and Kaufmann a mandate from the government of Lower Austria to add new therapeutic programs to their modest clinic.

Two small houses on the Pelikangasse, with gardens bordering directly on the military hospital, would accommodate the new EKG instruments and expanded treatment programs. The one-story smaller house, soon to share its premises with the psychoanalytic Ambulatorium, was remodeled so that the former entrance to a private home became a waiting room for trauma patients. The Viennese model of community-based cardiac clinic was applauded by civilians and veterans alike and replicated by public health departments in other Austrian cities. Its sports clinic was especially renown for quick, comprehensive medical exams of Austria's budding new athletes. In 1922 athletic training already featured gymnastics competitions, obstacle course running, and highly organized games so popular that, by 1931, worker sports events would culminate in the International Worker Olympics.[3] Unfortunately this popularity seemed to generate little capital, and Kaufmann's Herzstation society was obliged to seek funding again and again. So when Felix Deutsch approached Meyer with an idea for renting some space in the smaller building at 18 Pelikangasse, it seemed like an inspired solution to all parties' economic woes. The ambulance section of the Herzstation had rooms already equipped with soundproof doors, an arrangement compatible with the Ambulatorium's need for patient privacy and confidentiality. The four consulting rooms, which could be used only in the afternoon, were rented. A hall, or large conference room, was also made available and rented for evening meetings of the Ambulatorium staff. Helen Ross, the Chicago psychoanalyst who had trained in Vienna, remembered the meetings in that "big room on Pelikangasse, a long room with a long table and big heavy chairs."[4]

The struggle for a psychoanalytic Ambulatorium was not quite over. Concealed behind the Council of the Professional Association of Vienna Physicians, the conservative group of hospital psychiatrists mounted one further attempt to stifle the psychoanalysts. On February 11 the Physician's Council (the forceful Viennese physicians' financial association) repeated their "breach of trade" objections to the Ambulatorium. Bluntly stated, they demanded total regulatory control and occupational authority over nonmedical therapists. Psychoanalysis could be tolerated, perhaps, but only if practiced privately. The medical group barred the Ambulatorium from opening on the baldly self-serving grounds that it would damage the financial interests of Viennese physicians and that the clinic was superfluous. By now accustomed to these volleys, Federn, Deutsch, and Hitschmann set forth explanatory memoranda that led at length, on May 9, to a compromise from the council's executive committee. The council agreed to rescind their resolution if the psychoanalysts consented to abide by the stipulations that 1. the leadership of the Ambulatorium would uphold the principles of the physicians' financial association and 2. all aspects of psychoanalytic treatment, teaching, and learning would be conducted exclusively by doctors. In other words, all laymen (except patients) would be denied admittance to the facility. The analysts agreed, but Hitschmann was furious. "This clause," Hitschmann said, "makes it obvious how strong [was] the fear in Vienna lest the medical profession should suffer damage materially if laymen were permitted to become analysts."[5] Their "medical only" policy, he reiterated, was motivated by the raw greed of establishment physicians who objected to the Ambulatorium. Hardly a compromise at all, but after May 9 the clinic was indeed accepted into the hospital and permitted to function.

The Vienna Ambulatorium was inaugurated on May 22, 1922. Hitschmann and his colleagues proudly invited Freud to inspect the premises, publicly broadcast the opening of their clinic, and started their work at 18 Pelikangasse. Within a few days the cheering signs of widespread public and private attention became nothing less than exhilarating. Freud of course was pleased to accept personal congratulations from colleagues and friends and official applause from the IPA's branch societies. On May 24, Sándor Radó and Sándor Ferenczi, respectively secretary and president of the Hungarian Psychoanalytic Society in Budapest, greeted the news joyfully. They congratulated the Viennese and thanked them for the inspiration to set up a similar institution in Budapest, the very city where Freud first articulated the mission of psychoanalysis to society at large.[6] Radó and Ferenczi formally conveyed these compliments on behalf of the entire Hungarian Psychoanalytic Society's membership and flavored the remarks with tempered admiration. On May 30 Max Eitingon sent collegial congratulations from Berlin, penned on one of his elegant cream-colored note cards. He wished the Viennese great good luck on the clinic's opening and cheered them on toward the honest rewards of such work.[7] Finally Freud's wish "that individuals or societies may be found elsewhere to follow Eitingon's example, and bring similar institutions into existence" had come true.[8]

The self-assurance of these auspicious beginnings radiates from the group's official portrait (figure 15). Fourteen well-dressed men and women, the Ambulatorium's psychoanalytic staff, were formally photographed together at the back of one of the hospital's large carpeted rooms, far fancier than the sterile Herzstation. Wilhelm Reich is seated at the center of the front row with Grete Lehner Bibring, Richard Sterba, and Annie Reich Pink to his left. Hitschmann sits to Reich's right along with Ludwig Jekels, Anny Angel-Katan, and Eduard Kronengold. Behind them in the second row, Ernst Hoffmann, Ludwig Eidelberg, Eduard Bibring, Parker,[9] Stjepan Betlheim, and Edmund Bergler stand against a suite of heavy double doors, all the men wearing uniformly starched white collars and tweed winter suits. It is a portrait of the emerging second generation of psychoanalysts, of the young politically aware analysts favored by Freud to oversee the growth of the psychoanalytic movement with their publications, clinics, and training institutes.

Of course by 1922 the systematized curriculum for psychoanalytic training had only started to take hold. Franz Alexander, the first student to register at the Berlin Institute, likened this process to "medieval medicine when students gathered around famous teachers."[10] For him Freud was that model of

15 Staff of the Vienna Ambulatorium: seated (left to right), Eduard Kronengold, Anny Angel-Katan, Ludwig Jekels, Eduard Hitschmann (director), Wilhelm Reich (assistant director), Grete Lehner Bibring, Richard Sterba, Annie Reich; standing (left to right), Ernst Hoffmann, Ludwig Eidelberg, Eduard Bibring, Parker (?), Stjepan Betlheim, Edmund Bengler (Freud Museum, London)

the teacher, the self-appointed admissions officer, dismissing some candidates and taking genuine personal interest in selecting promising analysts like Wilhelm Reich, Grete Lehner Bibring, and the dozen others pictured as the staff of the Vienna Ambulatorium. Among Freud's cadre of young analysts were the left-leaning Annie Reich Pink, Anny Angel-Katan, and Edmund Bergler, who would join Reich's Sex-Pol by the end of the 1920s. Stjepan Betlheim, temporarily in Vienna to train with Paul Schilder at Wagner-Jauregg's clinic, became a pillar of Yugoslavian psychoanalysis and, in 1928, a founder of the Zagreb free clinic. Together with smart young doctors like Ludwig Eidelberg, a future director of the Vienna Worker's Neurological Clinic, the Ambulatorium staff forged a clinical approach to causality that struck a balance between the hospital's overt neurophysiology and the private practitioner's assertions of scientific neutrality.

Descriptive notices and small advertisements for the clinic soon appeared in the Vienna newspapers. Hardly a week after the opening went by before a long flattering article entitled "A Psychoanalytic Ambulatorium in Vienna" appeared in the *Ärztliche Reform-Zeitung* (Doctors' Reform Newspaper). Its unnamed author, no friend of the conservative dominance of medicine, sarcastically declared that "the claim that more poor people are not meeting the economic needs of doctors by trying out treatment in the Ambulatorium must be verified."[11] Partners in this charity happened to have inherited "a quite beautiful private practice," the article reported, and their income would be further enhanced now that individual "proof of impoverishment" was harder to obtain and a patient's social class or economic condition was less obvious. Not that the earnest efforts of the medical society—to protect doctors from improper use of the Ambulatorium—were very successful. Therefore, the witty journalist pressed on, doctors should be doubly concerned that the new outpatient program would be seriously abused. In the idea that poor people will take advantage of free care lay a classic set of contrasting ideological conjectures. The Social Democrats believed in universal access to health services, while the proponents of a conservative approach insisted that such total access to health care would just further corrupt an already lazy working class.

This ideological drama would unfold over the next fifteen years in the small two-story building that housed the Ambulatorium and doubled as the Herzstation's triage section for the Allgemeines Krankenhaus. Against the backdrop of the hospital's massive Beaux Arts structure, the Ambulatorium's modern clapboard siding and small windows looking out on the intersection with Lazaretgasse seemed like a gatekeeper's house on an opulent estate. Even the sidewalk narrowed in front of the clinic at 18 Pelikangasse, a short wide street leading from the main medical center, so that passersby had to hop onto the covered porch, actually the emergency entry for ailing cardiology patients, to avoid collision. Down the street and around the corner from Vienna's huge teaching hospitals and military garrisons, this incongruous wood-sided house measured not much more than sixty square feet on two floors. The German term *Klinik*, derived from the Greek word *kline*, which means "bed," denotes an acute care, inpatient hospital. The English language term *clinic* is, in German, "ambulatorium" and is derived from the Latin word *ambulare*, to walk around. And, indeed, inside the Ambulatorium's modest quarters psychoanalytic and cardiology patients mingled without distinction of illness or social class. Dozens of people a day streamed through the doors at 18 Pelikangasse, heart patients in the morning and analytic patients in the afternoon, the hallways barely accommodating the fluctuating groups of patients, doctors, administrators, equipment, students, and families. Psychological illnesses of every kind could be seen among the patients referred for psychoanalysis, from the lovelorn factory worker with uncontrollable blushing to the nymphomaniac patient who masturbated with a knife. On average the Ambulatorium registered between 200 and 250 applicants each year between 1922 and into the late 1930s. Inside the cramped medical offices with stretchers whirring by, Richard Sterba and his colleagues kept to those technical prescriptions for psychoanalytic treatment that—unlike his ideological reflection—Freud had not changed since 1913. "I adhere rigidly to the principle of leasing a definite hour," he wrote. "A certain hour of my available working day is appointed to each patient."[12] Office hours, held two evenings a week, were dedicated to outpatient consultations or intake sessions of up to two hours each. Since patients were seen every day of the week for an hour each, five analyses occupied five hours daily. Analysts rotated between their private offices, their hospital responsibilities, and their hours at the Ambulatorium.

Even in the last days of the Vienna Society, before the *Anschluss* in 1938, "every doctor had non-paying patients . . . and every training analyst treated two candidates free. . . . [All] analysts treated patients in the clinic."[13] The psychoanalyst Else Pappenheim felt this might be "surprising to Americans [today]," but the same anecdote has been repeated at different times, in different contexts, by Eduard Hitschmann, Grete Lehner Bibring, Richard Sterba, and even Freud. Every active member of the Vienna Psychoanalytic Society carried out an agreement, or initial pledge, to be "responsible for one or more free treatments" either at the clinic or in their private offices.[14] And candidates, who were still in training and not yet full-fledged psychoanalysts, could sign on with Hitschmann or, later, Wilhelm Reich, as assistant director of the clinic, and contract to cover in kind the costs of their training. The particular model of paying for psychoanalytic training by treating patients for free or contributing financially to the clinic's upkeep meant that candidates who had undergone a training analysis free of charge would have to work at the Ambulatorium two years without remuneration.[15] The advantages of this formula were at least threefold. For the clinic it assured that all staffing needs would be met. For candidates this plan sustained training analyses as a component of psychoanalytic education. And for current and prospective analysands these decisions implied that clinic patients deserve the same respect and sense of professionalism all too often confined to private practice, the same points on confidentiality and equitable treatment Ernst Simmel had made in Berlin.

Eventually all analysts treated gratis at least one-fifth of their practice, an unspoken custom shared by even the most accomplished doctors in Vienna.[16] In the privacy of their home offices or in the open and often less comfortable rooms at the clinics, analysts were known to volunteer up to a full day of their workweek. "Our pioneering analytic institutes of the past were poor," Anna Freud recalled years later, "and even to provide cases and treatment rooms for supervised analytic work stretched their resources to the utmost."[17] Helene Deutsch, Wilhelm Reich, and Richard Sterba were repeatedly summoned to undertake free analyses either at the Ambulatorium or in their offices. Lacking their Berlin colleague Max Eitingon's brilliant administrative skills but nevertheless desperate for a policy that would fairly and systematically apportion their patients, the Vienna society adopted the versatile Erlagschein voucher system. Within a medical community like the clinic an authorized signer could use the voucher to personally reimburse a colleague who had donated time to treat a patient. Senior analysts thus gained a reprieve from volunteer work, junior analysts were compensated for assuming extra clinical hours, and the Ambulatorium was assured of a stable economic footing, at least in the short run. Freud opted to participate in the Ambulatorium's voluntary self-funding (by way of the Erlagscheine), partly because he agreed with this approach and also because, by 1922, the city's professional classes were no more exempt from postwar economic hardship than the workers they treated.

But at times, the psychoanalysts decided, the formula would have to be stretched, and a monthly cash contribution to the Ambulatorium could absolve them from the responsibility of direct treatment. If Sterba's memory

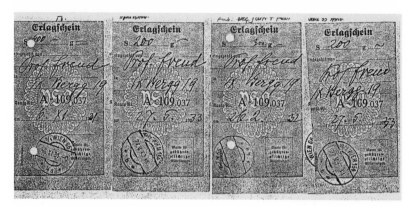

16 Sigmund Freud's Erlagscheine, or vouchers, endorsed to the Vienna Ambulatorium in 1931, 1932, and 1933 (Archives of the Boston Psychoanalytic Society and Institute)

served him correctly fifty years later, the monthly dues amounted to 100 Austrian shillings per person, then corresponding to roughly $25.00. "Each of us paid at this time [one] hundred shilling for not having a patient. . . . I have a pack of receipts of the hundred dollars which Freud paid every month as a subsidy for other analyses," Grete Bibring remembered.[18] The now famous Erlagscheine (figure 16), the vouchers Freud wrote out to the Ambulatorium, looked like beautiful old silks in her hands, perhaps the surviving artifacts of the vanished civilization of Red Vienna. But forty years later Bibring was not sentimental and repeated how senior analysts "were obliged, each of us, to take at least one patient, a clinic patient, unpaid clinic patient. [Whereas] those of us who felt they couldn't or didn't want to, or had no time or were too committed to take another clinic patient" paid a young analyst, even a young American analyst, to assume clinical responsibility for that patient. From the memoirs of Bibring and Sterba, and many others, it is clear that higher ranking analysts subscribed to an unwritten but very specific obligation to treat one or more patients at no charge and also to train one or more future analysts gratis. Thus until 1925, when Richard Sterba finally finished his psychoanalytic education, he not only received a free training analysis but was given three hundred or four hundred dollars a month as a stipend though he was actually indebted to the clinic by several thousand dollars. Sterba's experience was like that of most young members of the Vienna Psychoanalytic Society who, native and foreign alike, were compensated for their work at the Ambulatorium because they were, in essence, employees of the society.

And, yes, Freud too treated patients for free. Freud analyzed Marianne Kris, for example, at no cost intermittently from 1931 to 1938. "[Freud] treated me for free," Kris later informed the New York psychoanalyst Robert Grayson.[19] In the course of her analysis she questioned whether this gesture was more than professional courtesy, although she had barely the money herself. When Freud refused to let her pay for her analysis, she remembered that her father, Oscar Rie, was not paid for his services as the Freud's family pediatrician. But "it was very generous because it's very different," she explained. "When a pediatrician pay[s] a visit, he doesn't lose another visit he could make; while if one has somebody in analysis for that hour, you can't take anybody else." Freud frequently interrupted Kris's treatment because of illness or because he determined to use her hour for another patient or as a clinical experiment in fractionary analysis. Like Eva Rosenfeld in her own free analysis with Freud, Kris admitted that at times she felt "a little envious . . . [though] grateful enough. . . . That I didn't pay and that I had to interrupt . . . [did not] hinder the analysis although it might have made it somewhat more difficult—But I could express my feeling[s]." Freud's career is strewn with stories of free analyses: Marianne Kris, Eva Rosenfeld, the Wolfman, and Bruno Goetz are just a few.

Unlike Wagner-Jauregg's state-run psychiatric clinic or the municipal consultation centers, the Ambulatorium was privately operated by the Vienna Psychoanalytic Society in rented hospital quarters. Space and treatment rooms were limited even when analysts treated some clinic patients in their home-based offices. Their shared medical consulting rooms now had to meet a dual set of needs, the psychoanalysts' need for privacy and the Herzstation cardiologists' need for tranquil space. Grim conditions aside, the analysts relished the chance to demonstrate that the success of psychoanalysis did not depend on environment. These were stark surgical offices where the couch was a metal examination table and the analytic patients had to climb up a movable step ladder to reach the table top, then lie down on the thin springless mattress. Patients alone did not have to sustain the austere makeshift arrangements: their analyst sat angled behind the table on a simple bentwood chair without armrests. "After five sessions [we] felt the effects of so long a contact with the hard surface," Sterba recalled.[20]

Late one evening Grete Bibring was the last staff analyst about to leave the clinic when her colleague from the neurology department, the hospital's resident expert in epilepsy, sauntered into the Ambulatorium with a handsome nineteen-year-old law student. The young man's seizures were so severe, the neurologist said, that his ability to study was limited and, even worse, he felt incapable of socializing at the student law clubs because his fits were frequent and sudden. More out of collegiality than real interest in the new patient, Grete set about evaluating the student in the clinic's front office, the one opening onto a small courtyard garden shared by other medical departments. Sure enough, the interview quickly moved from present life circumstances to early childhood, and when they talked about his mother, the young lawyer lapsed into seizures. Toward the end of the very next session, and every night after that, he clambered off the examination table—the analytic couch—and, while shifting his conversation from the formal address *sie* to the more familiar *du*, seemed to throw himself at the terrified Grete and then fall into convulsions. As a physician, she could easily care for the physiology of the disease, but, as a psychoanalyst, she desperately hoped her young patient would articulate the latent content under the manifest expression of the epileptic fit so obviously imbued with oedipal symbolism. Eventually the barrier between the unconscious and insight disappeared and his epilepsy was cured. In her long adventurous life as a clinician thereafter very little scared Grete Bibring, but she always recognized the eerie swallowing sound of a patient about to convulse. And of course the question remained: if the symptoms could be cured by psychoanalysis, was the illness epilepsy or was it hysteria?

Equally challenging clinical debates recurred at the weekly Seminar on Therapeutic Technique and at evening meetings of the Vienna Psychoanalytic Society. The idea for the Technical Seminar, as it was to be called, first occurred when Freud suggested that his bright pupil Wilhelm Reich take a practical step toward systematizing clinical supervision at the Ambulatorium. The seminar's purpose differed from the scientific meetings of the society where theoretical presentations (supported by case material) were held around the conference table in Freud's office. In contrast, the Ambulatorium meetings were less theoretical, targeted to inexperienced analysts, and held around the conference table at the Herzstation. These seminars focused exclusively on individual analytic treatment cases, major clinical problems, and treatment failures. For example, Bibring chose to make her case for a psychosomatic basis of her young patient's epilepsy at a meeting of the Technical Seminar. There the less experienced candidates balked at her easy intermixing of psychology and medicine but were intrigued. Federn immediately quarreled with her and asserted that the cure in itself ruled out any diagnosis other than hysteria. Meanwhile, the gentle, gallant Ferenczi, visiting just for the evening, defended her. It was a splendid idea, he said, and Federn had no right to just wipe away the notion of psychosomatic epilepsy so thoughtlessly. Would epilepsy necessarily preclude a psychosomatic condition? So many patients on the clinic's waiting list suffered from medical conditions apart from their already oppressive neuroses. The first patient was analyzed, the second perhaps, but a third free patient could harden even the most altruistic clinician. Imagine analyzing someone for a year and a half (a veritable marathon in the 1920s), understanding his dreams and fantasies, his sisters and brothers, without ever learning his name or address! This anonymous patient became known as "the man with the cedilla under the 'c'."[21]

When the Ambulatorium opened as a treatment center, its founders simply intended to make psychoanalysis accessible to people who lacked the means to pay for private treatment. The Ambulatorium was maintained by limited private funds and functioned largely on a referral basis until 1926. Whether flexible or simply naive, the analysts never really expected psychoanalysis to become as lucrative as a traditional medical practice. For most Viennese patients in the postwar inflationary economy, devaluation of Austria's currency meant that paying 30 shilling fees was just too difficult. But by now many prospective patients and trainees came over from America, England, and Holland, and these visitors, these *Ausländer* (foreigners), arrived prepared to pay for their treatment and could do so in hard cash, dollars and pounds sterling. Freud took these eager foreigners into treatment or training analysis, and he was "terribly expensive and quite openly so," recalled Grete Bibring, because he lacked sentimentality and his conduct as a researcher (not as a doctor) justified the price.[22] He charged the *Entente* patients for missed sessions in order to repay friends for their wartime loans, to provide for his family, and even to support the widening circle of adherents like Lou Andreas-Salomé. But, like his Viennese colleagues, Sigmund Freud almost never took money from an Austrian candidate once inflation hit.

After 1922 Viennese citizens of even the middle classes were largely exempted from paying for the psychoanalytic treatment and training they sought, whether at the Ambulatorium or in Sigmund Freud's office. Generally the analysts had little compunction about redistributing the large sums they would charge the foreigners. In fact, Freud asked his friend Kata Levy to forgive this bias and hold confidential the fact that even he "can no longer make a living from Viennese, Hungarians, Germans. It is really no activity for a dignified old man. *C'est la guerre.*"[23] But the larger political issue Freud was navigating was really a form of local residency requirement. In Red Vienna, as in almost any social welfare system, tax levies passed through a municipal administration only to be apportioned back to the original local community in the form of public housing, parks, health clinics, schools, and libraries. Residency requirements distinguished between citizens and noncitizens by, for example, charging out-of-state residents a higher fee to attend a local public university. Thus the psychoanalysts of Red Vienna, Freud among them, comfortably charged the foreigners high fees while offering the same services free of charge to local residents, whether a poor medical student still living at home or a middle-class patient.

Within the city's politically charged environment, the Ambulatorium afforded Vienna's indigent families the same quality of mental health services traditionally reserved for private patients. The Ambulatorium's mission—to treat people regardless of their ability to pay—located psychoanalysis squarely in the social welfare ideology of Red Vienna. In 1922 New Year's Day celebrations were dedicated to Vienna's newly found independence and actual statehood, since the city had now separated voluntarily from Lower Austria by the *Trennungsgesetz* (statute of separation). The city—and now constituent state—of Vienna was independent for the moment of the wider Austrian political atmosphere of militaristic and religious conservatism. The right to legislate and to determine and impose taxes placed responsibility for solving urban problems directly on the city's government but also allowed for its particularly bold program of economic and social experimentation.

The social democratic program easily penetrated clinical psychiatry as well: Josef Berze, a specialist in brain research on schizophrenic disorders and, like Freud, a former intern in Theodor Meynert's psychiatric clinic, had given over the second half of his career to head the psychiatric hospital Am Steinhof. Dedicated to the residents of Vienna since its opening in 1907, the famous institution for the care and treatment of mental and neuropathological patients was integrated into the new welfare system after the Trennungsgesetz. Sloping down the Gallintzinberg hill in Vienna's Fourteenth District, the huge ornate asylum was laid out in sixty pavilions that housed twenty-two hundred "restive" and "semirestive" patients, teaching and research centers, the first hospital-based full program of occupational therapy, laboratories, and offices for administrators.[24] At times the institution's patient population doubled, as in 1914, when a military hospital and barracks opened on the grounds, or after 1918, when it served as a general medical facility and housing for war refugees. Even then the lushly planted valley cradled the graceful paths and stylized corridors of the institution's seventeen widely dispersed buildings. Otto Wagner had designed these buildings with open gardens, verandas, wrought iron balconies, and plantlike ramps leading to the modern reception rooms and large auditoriums for performances attended by patients and visitors alike. It is hardly surprising, then, that architectural innovation may have bred theoretical change in the mental health field. The relatively new field of psychology produced, in an unusual collaboration of what the existential psychologist Karl Jaspers called "asylum" and "university" psychiatry, a number of conceptual schools and a lively range of theories from materialism and physiology to psycholinguistics and psychoanalysis. Above all, the influence of Theodor Meynert was still felt: his pioneering emphasis on brain anatomy, his anatomical clinic in psychiatry, his teaching, and, most famous of all, his rejection of vague symptomatic descriptions and concurrent insistence that only findings grounded in empirical analysis could be called scientific. Meynert and his colleagues Hermann Nothnagel and Ernst Brücke may have staunchly supported Freud's personal petition for advancement to *Privatdozent* at the General Hospital in the late 1880s, but the next generation of Vienna's psychiatric establishment firmly supported Meynert's legacy of strict empiricism and followed Wagner-Jauregg's rejection of psychoanalysis. Periodically they still attempted to close the Ambulatorium.

On July 15 Josef Berze, now head psychiatrist at Am Steinhof and still Vienna's acerbic expert in the institutional treatment of schizophrenia, took it upon himself to report Hitschmann to the Viennese Public Health Office. He criticized the Ambulatorium's "one-sided therapeutic attitude," warned of encroachment on neurology and psychiatry, and demanded to know just how the clinic doctors applied their specialized knowledge.[25] Freud was awfully annoyed and, rising to the occasion, official to official, wielded his authority as chairman of the Vienna Psychoanalytic Society and led the opposing argument. On December 27 Freud appealed the Federal Department of Social Administration's decision to abide by Berze's Public Health Office written decertification and Wagner-Jauregg's verbal faultfinding. These experts criticized the Ambulatorium for not following Wagner-Jauregg's instructions and for establishing an independent self-supporting unit. Mostly though, Hitschmann's specialist qualification had not been proven to their satisfaction. So Freud reminded them of Hitschmann's eleven years of training in internal medicine at their own Allgemeines Krankenhaus, his further preparation at Krafft-Ebing's clinic, and his overall expertise in treating mental illness (or neuropsychiatric cases) on an inpatient as well as outpatient basis. The necessary records of these credentials were procured, and objections and threats from municipal authorities cowed by official psychiatry finally subsided. "In his capacity of physician, psycho-analyst and neurologist, Hitschmann was well fitted, and was appointed, to be the Director of the Psycho-Analytical Clinic in Vienna," noted a 1931 entry in the *International Journal of Psychoanalysis* on the occasion of Hitschmann's sixtieth birthday. "The attitude of the medical profession was for a long time hostile to the Institute," the record continued, "and the primary necessity for its reputation was reliability of diagnosis," which Hitschmann fulfilled admirably.[26]

Once sanctioned by the Federal Department of Social Administration, the Ambulatorium (figure 17) thrived for another sixteen years. The clinic grew to include a training institute directed by Helene Deutsch, a child guidance center, and a special department for the treatment of psychoses. Deutsch, whose "great virtue," her student Abram Kardiner remembered, "lay in her simplicity and her very sound common sense," had a gift for teaching psychoanalysis and thus easily articulated new plans for an educational program.[27] Though at first the official drafts outlined a separation between the Training Institute and the Ambulatorium, the two legally separate organizations became virtually interdependent. In fact, once the Vienna Training Institute was established three years later, the Ambulatorium became the candidates' major source of supervised cases. While ensuring the quality of the student analysts' work, Reich suggested during a planning meeting, the Ambulatorium would serve patients better by broadening its scope to include regular on-site training programs and informal conferences between students and their more experienced colleagues. Reich had just completed his postgraduate studies in neuropsychiatry at the University of Vienna clinic headed by Professor Wagner-Jauregg. What would work in hospital-based public psychiatry would be equally effective at the clinic, Hitschmann and Federn agreed, and so a new series of clinical and lecture courses first called Discussions on Technique were integrated into Reich's Technical Seminar at the Ambulatorium. Hermann Nunberg chaired the meetings for 1922, the first ten sessions of an exceptional project that would last until 1938 when everything else shut down too.

Meanwhile the ties between the Ambulatorium's Child Guidance Centre and Red Vienna's social welfare services for children were gaining strength. Freud had long been taken with Hermine Hug-Hellmuth's novel child-rearing ideas. "Strict upbringing by an intelligent mother enlightened by

AMBULATORIUM DER WIENER
PSYCHOANALYTISCHEN VEREINIGUNG

17 Stationery letterhead from the Vienna Ambulatorium (Archives of the Sigmund Freud Foundation, Vienna)

Hug-Hellmuth has done him a great deal of good," Freud had written to Abraham about his charming four-year old grandson Ernst Halberstadt.[28] In her lectures on early childhood education to Viennese women in private circles and at worker's educational societies, Hermine Hug-Hellmuth described psychoanalysis as a broad-minded approach to child psychology. She used stories from the Ambulatorium's child therapy program to help her audience picture her at work. Recently returned from a teaching assignment at the Berlin Poliklinik, Hug-Hellmuth believed that a strong attachment to the therapist is necessary for successful analysis with children. She was an active member of the Technical Seminar and taught her colleagues to scrutinize selected clinical features of children's early dreams and fantasies by using analytical methods now generally attributed to Melanie Klein. Hug-Hellmuth's attention to the needs of two social groups, that of the therapist and that of the patient, made for an auspicious beginning for the clinical facility she oversaw with great success until her sudden death in 1924.

The originality of mounting a separate child treatment program within a clinic devoted overall to the mental health of adults cannot be overestimated. Karl Abraham had conceived the idea and Hermine Hug-Hellmuth made it a clinical reality. Children were to be treated as individuals in their own right, not as miniature versions of adults. Esther Menaker, a trainee from New York, remembered evaluating a "pathetic little boy of seven who was referred by the Ambulatorium." She recalled that he was a bed-wetter, and that his mother, who was very poor, "was desperate about the laundry problems and the added work that his symptoms caused her. He was an only child, and his father was an unskilled worker."[29] Menaker's treatment style was more supportive (like Anna Freud) than interpretive (like Melanie Klein). Though her work with the young boy focused on his feelings, she could not ignore the family's severe social and economic conditions. Children like Menaker's young patient were sometimes accompanied to the Ambulatorium by their parents, but eventually many young people went to the center by themselves. As Hitschmann reported ten years later, schools and clubs, teachers, school doctors and personal pediatricians referred children "from all strata of the necessitous classes" to the clinic. The basis for this was twofold. In 1922 the state appreciated the need to protect the health and mental health of its young citizens. At the same time, children born after the war to Vienna's young, and often poor, families needed individual help to survive the stressful climate.

The problem of urban depopulation was answered by one of the new state's most controversial institutions, a marriage consultation clinic. Red

Vienna's municipal government and its social democratic council members here asserted their complex mix of maternalist pro-family policy, worker's health, and state subventions. Six centers for prenatal care and education had been opened, each one linked to a public child health station and staffed by a physician, a social worker, and a midwife.[30] To encourage procreation, the clinic offered marrying couples advice about sexual health, genetic strengths and defects, and healthy childbearing prospects—while ostensibly avoiding the more overt topics of sex counseling and birth control. Attacked as sacrilegious by the conservatives and as overly intrusive with eugenic intent by the liberals, the clinic lasted only a few years. Nevertheless its development signaled official recognition of sexuality as socially useful, especially in uplifting the moral standards of blue-collar families. "Sexuality was much more open because the Social Democratic Party insisted on it, on discussing sexual matters, on having clinics to give advice," remembered Else Pappenheim, then a student and herself an inquisitive adolescent.[31] In many ways Tandler's welfare policies were similarly paradoxical: at the heart of an apparently ultraliberal policy lay a struggle between the traditional maternalist stance and the radically new promotion of female sexual autonomy. In the case of the marriage consultation clinic, the state stood against mothers working outside the home, as though this contributed to the high infant mortality rate. The multiple social services eventually built into the Vienna Gemeindebauten reinforced this contradiction between the state's genuine assistance to families (in order to grow healthy children) and, simultaneously, the limitations this placed on women's lives (the demand to procreate). Even the two or three pages of "Menschen die einander suchen" (people who seek one another), the personal ads found at the end of each issue of Hugo Bettauer's highly popular journal *Er und Sie* (Him and Her), affirmed that the goal of human relationships was marriage and not promiscuity.[32] Nevertheless, Bettauer's corollary emphasis on the sexual origin of social problems conferred further legitimacy on both the marriage consultation clinic and the psychoanalytic movement. Sexual enlightenment was promoted as vigorously as the institutions of marriage and family because the argument that a healthy sex life made for healthy, happier workers was generally compatible with social democracy. Tandler launched a regional center for the treatment of alcoholism the same year and presumably with the same intent.

Troubled adolescents found an uncanny ally in August Aichorn. A former teacher in the city's public schools (and, according to Helen Ross, a former delinquent himself) and organizer of Red Vienna's municipal child care institutions, Aichorn developed special psychoanalytically based social services for disturbed or delinquent teenagers. He was then best known as a powerful player in city politics and Vienna's school reform movement and had only recently come to psychoanalysis. Aichorn had a kindly face with a long beard, soft wide shoulders, and long arms. He wore classic Austrian broad hats, wool coats, and pants with suspenders. When Aichorn became interested in psychoanalysis, he set about building a quasi-pedagogical therapeutic center for juvenile delinquents. This was the famous Jugenderziehungsanstalt Ober-Hollabrunn project, a residential institution supported by the current Social Democratic Party and set up first at the site of a former refugee camp and then at the St. Andrä residence. Aichorn was among the very first analysts who taught his counseling staff to work from the assumption that the delinquent posture of their young charges was conflict-driven antisocial behavior. Poor, angry, and hopelessly mortified in front of their teachers and more affluent peers, these children had been barred from local grammar schools for fighting, stealing, and running away from home (as often as not a way of surviving abuse). St. Andrä, with its the ample shaded courtyard, white-washed buildings, gardens, and barnyard lawns, was a spacious refuge for the city's distressed children and adolescents. Twenty grade-schoolers at a time would fill up the classrooms, small blond girls in braids and somber boys disarming their specialized teachers and tutors with that particular pleasing behavior bred of rejection and impermanence. Lana, a thirteen-year-old girl recently admitted to St. Andrä, had been caught stealing an apple from the street vendor's cart. In trouble with the law and truant even before this detention, Lana had balked at the reasoned didactic psychologist, an Adlerian based in her local school, who exhorted her to develop strength of character and responsibility to society. In contrast, her psychoanalytic therapist at St. Andrä believed that the unhappy child would draw internal strength from the powerful bond of the relationship between them. The therapist had been taught by Aichorn to accept that, in time, Lana and her therapist would heal the child's angry self fractured by insensitive parents and a punitive urban environment. Once her simmering impulse to lash out had been tamed by the reparative relationship, the child could rejoin the everyday life of friends, school, and neighborhood. For Lana as for the others, Adler insisted that misbehaving children failed to meet (for either internal or external reasons) the ideal social standard of "community feeling." Aichorn saw in this the inherent oppressiveness of demanding that all individuals conform to society. Instead, the crux of therapy, he held, should rest on the experience of a strong, positive emotional relationship (not unlike Donald Winnicott's later conceptualization of therapy as an emotionally corrective experience) that supersedes the child's unconscious impulse toward deviant behavior. Aichorn's clinical approach was less moralizing than Adler's individual psychology, and his own methods of reeducation addressed the appalling social and individual fears underlying the adolescent's angry behavior. The Hungarian psychoanalyst Franz Alexander worked with Aichorn, and his efforts to understand young criminals came largely from this rich theoretical milieu. After 1930, once Alexander emigrated to the Chicago Institute of Psychoanalysis, he focused on adolescent delinquency and consulted on Pioneer House, Fritz Reidl's project in Detroit. But in 1922 Alexander merely moved from Vienna to Berlin, taught alongside Abraham, and analyzed the steadily increasing numbers of patients at the Poliklinik.

That Berlin had become the actual center of the psychoanalytic movement was confirmed when the society hosted the Seventh International Psychoanalytic Congress in September, the last congress Freud attended. There the effect of his presentation, an outline of the new "structural" framework of the unconscious published the next year in *The Ego and the Id*, was simply astonishing. Rudolf Loewenstein would remain indelibly marked by Freud's speech as one of the peak experiences of his life, much like Melanie Klein's first encounter with Freud at the 1918 Budapest congress. Klein had already moved from Berlin to London, and Loewenstein would soon be off to Paris. Each would practice at their local society's clinics, but for now the conference guests were shown how the Poliklinik's professional community supported both clinical work and research. The treatment facility and the society had gained prestige, and psychoanalysis edged ever closer to acceptance by Berlin's mainstream practitioners. Psychoanalysis, it seemed, would reach much further into German cultural production among the avant-garde of Weimar intellectuals than it would into Austria. In Berlin Kleist's plays were revived for their psychoanalytic themes of the oedipal father and dreams, and later even the theologian Paul Tillich was impressed by the increasingly forceful influence of "the philosophy of the unconscious, initiated by Freud [growing] daily" in Berlin.[33] Felix J. Weill, a young political scientist whose doctoral dissertation on the "practical problems of implementing socialism" might have described the Poliklinik's own evolution, secured funding to set up a like-minded autonomous institute devoted to the analysis and social application of Marxist theory. This would open the following year as the prestigious Frankfurt School of the Institut für Sozialforschung (Institute for Social Research), whose faculty, with few exceptions, strengthened the association between psychoanalysis and left-wing critical theory. Meanwhile, at the conference, the analysts celebrated with parties and dinners. The grand finale banquet closed with Jones's humorous—he said so himself—speech about the Berlin clinic's anonymous patron, widely rumored to be Eitingon. Leaning on his gold-knobbed walking stick, Jones said, "In English we have two notable proverbs: 'Charity begins at home' and 'Murder will out.' If now we apply the mechanisms of condensation and displacement to these we reach the conclusions that 'Murder begins at home,' a fundamental tenet of psychoanalysis, and 'Charity will out,' which is illustrated by the difficulty of keeping secret the name of the generous donor of the Berlin Policlinic."[34]

By the time of the IPA's seventh congress the interest in coming to Berlin to teach, study, and work reflected the improved international relations that allowed for candid intellectual exchanges between eastern and western European psychoanalysts. Sándor Radó had recently moved westward, from Budapest to Berlin, to join the newly created institute. Fenichel traveled back and forth between Vienna and Berlin. Helene Deutsch, who would spend the next two years in Berlin's as Freud's special envoy, summarized the main events of the Berlin congress to the Vienna society's meeting of October 18 and described the state of the psychoanalytic movement including its theoretical advances. Not to be outdone by the implicit competition with Berlin, at the same meeting Hitschmann noted that the Ambulatorium's activities were progressing and announced that two lecture series would begin in early November. He would deliver An Introduction to Psycho-Analysis and Felix Deutsch would teach a special course called What Must the Practicing Physician Know About Psycho-Analysis? At times Hitschmann felt overwhelmed by his responsibilities as clinic director, but he also wanted to help his Viennese colleagues to promote their clinic much as the Berliners had done for the IPA visitors.[35]

By the end of the congress Poliklinik staff realized how their working conditions had been strained, in part because of the heavy traffic of patients, interns, and members, but also because of its constantly expanding pedagogical activities. "Our work," Eitingon complained "needs more and more space, but the housing shortage prevents [us] from extending our premises." Freud agreed, hoping "that individuals or societies may be found elsewhere to follow Eitingon's example, and bring similar institutions into existence."[36] Encouraging words indeed, but Freud was reminding the analysts of their need for vigilance and priorities in at least two areas. First, as even Jones had recognized (and as Eitingon and Simmel had done in Berlin), the psychoanalytic leadership throughout the IPA had to incorporate social services into mental health and not the other way around. Government-sponsored clinics could become bureaucratic weapons in the hands of traditional psychiatry's war on psychoanalysis. Second, psychoanalysis would succumb to its conservative detractors if only a few patients benefited. Amplifying on the point he had made in Budapest, Freud reiterated his indirect pitch for universal access. Free treatment, he suggested, should not be available only to people who are proven indigent but also—and equally—to those who are simply too poor to pay for treatment. Freud's words were based on the Poliklinik's obvious success but were also designed to soothe what Radó remembered as the "jealousy and envy of the Viennese increasing as the significance of Berlin" grew.[37] With the amusement of a father of rivalrous offspring, Freud bestowed uniform encouragement on all the free clinics, not just on the Ambulatorium's sibling dispensary in Berlin.

Can psychoanalysis truly reach all social classes? The record of the Poliklinik shows that the analysts tried. "And here for the first time analysis can present statistics to those who hanker after them, showing figures collected in a single place and in a relatively short time," Eitingon reported with a chuckle. In principle he placed quantitative analysis on a par with psychoanalysis. Laboratory trained and empiricist by nature, for the last few years Eitingon had struggled to decide which of the opposing designs—process-driven psychoanalytic narrative or outcomes-based statistical records—would best suit the clinic's reports. Drawing on the classical diagnostic categories advanced by the nineteenth-century psychiatrist Emil Kraepelin, Otto Fenichel and Eitingon attempted to establish a respectable clinical database of their own. No German-speaking psychiatrist would lack familiarity with Emil Kraepelin's textbook nosological system, already in its eighth edition by 1907. Karen Horney's medical dissertation had been directed by a pupil of the great clinical methodologist, and Helene Deutsch had studied the Kraepelinian approach in Munich. For them even the design of Kraepelin's original diagnostic cards (*Zählkarten*) from the Heidelberg University Clinic, printed in their bold roman typeface, demanded clear and objective assessments according to specific preformed lines of questioning. Tellingly, most of Kraepelin's data were based in observations of lower-class women, typical patients of the psychiatric clinic around 1900.[38] No wonder Fenichel and Eitingon, whose twofold aim was to treat people from this same lower social class but also to impart help without bias, sought less prescriptive forms of documentation.

In the end Eitingon and Fenichel produced two sets of charts. One was a clinical chart (figure 18) on which the psychoanalysts tracked their patients' progress; it was a simple design in outline form, with ample spaces for annotations and open-ended comments. But the other was a statistical chart whose copious preset diagnostic categories and checklists immerse the reader in a

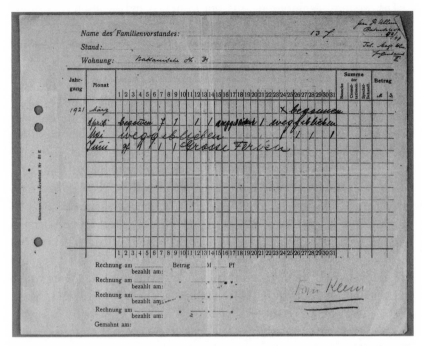

18 Melanie Klein's clinical case chart on "Kurt K.," a 1921 patient at the Berlin Poliklinik (Wellcome Library, London)

profusion of details that make the clinic come alive. In the context of the Weimar era, Fenichel's charts were planned in the style of the documentary authorship that deemphasized the author's own role in favor of the "new objectivity." Today the innovative techniques in journalistic photography and film developed by Weimar artists are well known. But in the early 1920s, when Otto Fenichel applied this documentary approach to psychoanalysis, he created an unusually striking report. Meanwhile, Max Eitingon, who oversaw the chart's content while Fenichel attended to form, disclaimed scientific responsibility for the statistics. The numbers "would be highly valuable [if they were] comprehensive, clear in every detail," Eitingon said, and if based on controlled comparisons designed to eliminate bias and interpretation. On questions like the length of time required for treatment, he commented that such detailed "statistics . . . would be the test of our courage to give the world" genuine evidence that psychoanalysis does—and should—take time. Overall these efforts did result in a calculated, eminently practical, striking representation of the clinic—and a skilled justification for the real value of statistics.

The two most significant reports, one from 1923 and one from 1930, showcase Eitingon's unerring eye for tracking patterns seen in the Poliklinik patients' social status, gender, and occupations. Under "occupations," he listed lawyers, waiters, a bandleader, a general's daughter, an architect, factory workers, captains, and a wide range of students and "bureaucrats." Artisans (25 male, 35 female), clerks (22 male, 41 female), civil servants (7 male, 3 female), teachers (16 male, 19 female), domestic servants and nurses (27, female only), tradespeople (23, male only), students (12 male including 5 medical, and 2 female with 1 medical), and professional (medical and academic, 56 male and 59 female) are listed under "Occupations." Married with no occupation (63, female only), widow (6, female only), and no occupation (2 male, 8 female) are other interesting categories. "Occupation" is the sole focus of one statistical table in the 1922 report, while five others cross-list occupation with age, gender, diagnosis, length of treatment, and treatment outcome. But the 1930 report attends to occupations far less. Here twenty-two occupations are counted by number of consultations only. Gender, age, and even length of treatment are not mentioned. "Bureaucrats" (office workers or civil servants) sought the most consultations (173) over ten years, and farmers the fewest (3). Still, that farmers should be counted is all the more interesting given Berlin's intensely urban cosmopolitanism. The categories of "no profession" (249) and "no profession given" (313), both of which could signify "unemployed," are listed with high counts. Artists, shopkeepers, and teachers are equal categories with 124 cases each.

Clinic applicants were counted by gender, age, occupation/profession, and diagnosis. Some men and women, who were seen only in for an intake consultation and whose cases did not warrant admission to treatment (or who were referred elsewhere) were counted separately. Displayed in several forms, from simple lists (or "classifications") to rather complex correlations, the data reveal the Poliklinik staff's careful (or Fenichel's obsessive) quantitative self-study. The numbers of consultations and treatments are listed by year, then by month. The lists are sorted into tables, which are then correlated to clinical and administrative factors: cases are counted by outcome (active, terminated, and interrupted or "fractionary"), by length of treatment, and by the year in which treatment was completed. In the 1923 report the statistical tables are scattered throughout the document and used to highlight specific issues. In contrast, the 1930 report (featuring Simmel, Fenichel, and Karen Horney's fairly polemical essays) summarizes statistics in a simple two-page centerfold. Still, it includes an elaborate table correlating diagnosis, length of treatment, and treatment outcome.

Another chronicle of life at the Poliklinik, the psychoanalysts' ongoing written and oral accounts of their cases, describes a continuous exchange of "brief communications" at the clinical gatherings of the Berlin society.[39] Simmel reported on the dreams of an epileptic female patient, Melanie Klein on a "Sunday neurosis" in a child, Franz Alexander on an obsessional neurosis in a homosexual. Of the three meetings the society held regularly (Radó said overzealously) each month before Abraham's death in 1925, one was designated for just such brief exchanges (*kleine Mitteilungen*). "The next meetings will take place on October 4th, 11th & 18th," Abraham wrote in his invitation to Therese Benedek. Benedek, an inquisitive young analyst who frequented the Berlin society while still commuting from Leipzig, found that the mix of kleine Mitteilungen and longer clinical papers dovetailed nicely with her own idea of case conferencing. She enjoyed the democratic nature of the practice-based "short communications, to which everybody brings whatever he happens to have," as she said, and was herself widely praised.[40] "This lady is of great value in her ability to attract young people as well as in her excellent practical work," Abraham informed Freud following one of her oral presentations.[41] The observation was not lost on Franz Alexander either: ten years later, with unprecedented terror sweeping Germany, Alexander brought Benedek and her husband to America. At the time though, Franz Alexander too found the meetings to be endlessly inspiring. Abraham "was a master at this type of presentation," he remembered. Where Abraham added only "a minimum of theoretical discussion, holding close to the facts and to their psychodynamic explanation," Simmel in contrast "liked to go into far-reaching theoretical abstractions."[42] In the nearly two years since the Poliklinik had opened, Simmel had developed an interesting range of political strategies. For one, he inserted deliberately technical expressions into the psychoanalytic language in order, he believed, to enhance the psychoanalysts' external credibility and to differentiate them from Berlin's less reliable providers of mental health care. Critics of psychoanalysis, then as now, have attempted to marginalize its practice as lacking scientific grounding and empirical verification. These reproaches stem, at least in part, from the significant number of new words, coined as scientific terms in Freud's German but selectively translated into composites of English, Latin, and Greek. The confusion was largely resolved with the 1926 publication of Jones's practical *Glossary*, which systematized definitions of psychoanalytic terms.

A list maker by nature, Otto Fenichel already had a better grasp of psychoanalytic phraseology than many of his colleagues. He indexed the diagnoses carefully, listing 36 clinical categories in the Poliklinik's 1923 report and

19 Intake and consultation room at the Poliklinik (Library of the Boston Psychoanalytic Society and Institute)

31 in 1930. Gender distribution was remarkably similar for both consultation and treatment (figure 19): within the ten-year (1920–1930) span of 1955 consultations, 969 were men and 986 were women; of a total of 721 analyses, 342 were men and 379 were women. These numbers refute once more the popular criticism of psychoanalysis as a treatment consumed only by bourgeois women and designed exclusively for them as well. The 1923 report contains an interesting cross-tabulation of gender and age: the category of thirty to forty year olds shows the widest gap in utilization (122 female:52 male) while the narrowest is among twenty to thirty year olds (65 female:72 male). Utilization is gender identical (6:6) among the ten to fifteen year olds. Hysteria is the most frequent diagnosis in both inventories. Women are diagnosed with hysteria far more frequently than men (95:10), leading to 271 consultations and 129 treatments over ten years. Obsessional neurosis is more equally distributed between women and men (25:37) and is the second most frequent diagnosis. Physiological diagnoses like epilepsy and bronchial asthma are interspersed with psychological categories including depression, mania, alcoholism, and paranoia. A small sample of war neurosis (3 males) and one female case of disablement-dole neurosis apparently intermixes psychological and physiological diagnosis. Altogether the statistical tables show an impressive attempt at social inclusiveness and a deliberate effort to treat people from generally isolated and economically unequal social ranks. The large

lower-class patient population resulted in no small part from Ernst Simmel's own social activism. This accounted for his work at the Association for Socialist Physicians with the pediatrician Karl Kollwitz (husband of the German Expressionist artist Käthe Kollwitz) and, to a lesser degree, his collaborations with one of Karl Abraham's favorite pupils, Karen Horney.

If Karen Horney is celebrated as the psychoanalyst who introduced cultural relativism into Freudian theory, her position as the only woman among the six founding members of the Poliklinik in 1920, and the first woman to teach there, has been underestimated until now. Horney's position as a teacher and thinker in experimentalist Berlin gave her the perfect context for beginning to formulate her pioneering ideas on the psychology of women, to question Freud's libido theory, and to explore the impact of culture on human development. She impressed Alexander with "her lucidity and stubborn refusal to accept current theoretical constructions as facts beyond discussion."[43] Horney was a slim woman with wispy blond hair tied back, strikingly large eyes, and the casual style of the well-schooled. She had arrived in Berlin in 1909, a medical student whose official studies culminated in 1915 with a highly academic clinical dissertation argued in the diagnostic style of Kraepelinian psychiatry. She also supported two other, and often contradictory, roles: that of upper-middle-class wife and mother and that of analysand, then psychoanalyst-in-training, with Karl Abraham. Like other Poliklinik analysts, she would cover patients' carfare if necessary so that treatment could continue.[44] In her theoretical work Horney endorsed and even embellished on Freud's social goals, though she remained less overtly political than many of her colleagues in Berlin and Vienna.

By 1922, in Vienna Wilhelm Reich's Sex-Hygiene Clinics for Workers and Employees, (Sexualberatungs-Klinik für Arbeiter und Angestelle) were emerging from community outreach efforts that he later subsumed under the rubric of "sex-political work." Several days a week Reich and his team of psychoanalysts and physicians would drive in a van out into Vienna's suburbs and rural areas, announcing their visits in advance. They would speak about sexual concerns to interested persons gathered at a local park. Reich himself would talk with the adolescents and men, the team's gynecologist with the women, and Lia Laszky (Reich's close friend from medical school) with the children. Upon request, the gynecologist also prescribed and fit women with contraceptive devices. The model pretty much replicated the prenatal and child health stations established by the Social Democrats and sustained by foreign aid from, for example, the Red Cross. Reich's overtly political group probably seemed more subversive. Though chased away or arrested by police for illegal activities, the group still distributed pamphlets with sexual information door to door. Reich would then give political talks in the evening. Calling for a "politics of everyday life," he focused on broad social issues without ignoring the more intimate problems people had brought to the team that day. There young people complained about lack of money, hampered freedom, frustrating work, and fear of unwanted pregnancies. Even when the police routinely disbanded the social hygiene meetings, where he criticized the "power of the state," Reich saw the officers as human beings hidden within the "custodian of law and order." From their repressive, often militaristic, function the police could be turned into "champions of the cause of social outcasts." Reich could show his listeners how to relinquish preconceived class barriers and allow the individual to emerge from class constraints. When he spoke about difficulties in marriage, family, and childhood or dilemmas that the unemployed, factory workers, youth, and women would have to solve by themselves, the audience's "awareness of the presence of 'protectors of class interests'[45] vanished completely." Reich was enormously charismatic and able to arouse empathy among his listeners by appealing to the fundamental humanity they held in common even with the police who guarded them. Thus, "it became strikingly obvious to all present that these officers and policemen were themselves employees, despite their uniforms. They had children, wives, marital problems, and housing and child-raising difficulties. Viewed in this way, from a practical, psychological perspective, class boundaries appeared entirely different from the way they were portrayed in purely economistic [political] party programs."[46] In his own writings Reich used the term *social work* to describe his community-based approach to mental health services, a unique blend of social action and direct services not unlike the contemporary social work paradigm.

Young women and adolescents drew Reich's particular concern. Girls had become pregnant unwittingly, simply through clumsiness or ignorance or, worse, by rape or incest. They were referred to the municipal birth control clinics, though not before an interview with a Sex-Pol associate who instructed them in sexuality and in the use of contraception. Many years later, when Edith Jacobson, a fellow traveler who had repudiated Reich, was asked just how this counseling could help with adolescents, she replied, "Surprisingly much."[47] Even in 1922 Reich saw that many of the pregnancies gratified the wishes of the mother or of the larger society to have a child. This had not been separated from the mothers' actual wish to raise a child or from their emotional and sexual needs. Thus, he came to champion abortion on demand, the "unquestionable right of every woman who was pregnant against her will to have an abortion." [48] Reich was advocating as much for the rights of the child as for the mother. Looking back at his 1937 writings, Reich observed in 1952 that "mothers did not count. Infant misery did not count. What counted was a sick moralism [of society]."[49] In other words, if society so strongly condoned the bearing of children, then society should shoulder some of the responsibility for its rearing as well. It was a mark of the oppression of women, and of children, that society demanded the production of children but was unwilling to assist them once the child was born. To relieve the subjugation of women, Reich believed, it was necessary to subvert the patriarchal structure of society. He put into practice what Engels had hypothesized.[50]

What were sex economic counseling strategies? Reich's case histories written between 1920 and the mid-1930s show him moving from cautious interpretation to a mannered, up front therapeutic stance. His own confidence in his dual therapeutic-political "ear" and his early training with Freud combined to permeate Reich's approach with a deep regard for human suffering and for the basic, urgent needs of the sexual self. Reich's words on the need to override his patient's patriarchal family and their efforts to preserve order and control, are particularly forward:

A woman of 35 who looked much younger than her age . . . had been married for 18 years, had a grown son and lived with her husband in an outwardly happy marriage. For the past three years, the husband had had a relationship with another woman. The wife tolerated this, understanding that after a marriage of such long duration there will be a desire for another sexual partner. For some months now, she had been suffering from her sexual abstinence but was too proud to induce her husband to have intercourse with her. To an increasing degree, she suffered from palpitations, insomnia, irritability and depression. She had made the acquaintance of another man, but moral scruples kept her from having intercourse with him, although she considered her scruples nonsensical. Her husband kept boasting about her fidelity, and she knew perfectly well that he would not have been willing to grant her that right which he took for himself as a matter of course.

A case likes this needs careful analysis. Continuation of abstinence meant the certainty of neurotic illness. To disturb the husband in his new relationship and to win him back was impossible for two reasons. First, he would not have let himself be disturbed and had openly admitted that he no longer desired her (and she him). There remained only the man she loved. The difficulty was that she was not economically independent and the husband, upon hearing of it, would immediately start divorce proceedings. I discussed all these possibilities with the woman and told her to think it over. After a few weeks I learned that she had decided to establish a sexual relationship with her friend and to keep it a secret from her husband. Her stasis-neurotic symptoms disappeared soon. Her decision had been made possible by my successful attempt to dispel her moral scruples.[51]

A large man who looked scruffy and elegant at the same time, Reich had a cantankerous style that managed to provoke everybody who spoke with him. But he obviously had amazing empathy as well, and his experience in the clinics alerted him to the special needs of adolescents. Neither his work at the Ambulatorium nor his private practice with disturbed adolescents had prepared him for the painful situation of the "normal, working Viennese teenager." After two years of Sex-Pol, he said, "the conflict between the scientist and the politician within me grew even more intense. . . . Gradually [I] learned to understand, to affirm, and to remove the deep-seated and completely justified mistrust that youth places in everything pertaining to authority and adults."[52] Through Sex-Pol Reich defined for himself how social work was personally and politically empowering. In clinical areas a worker's purpose was to advise current or potential clients about the personal costs of repressed sexuality, and in economic areas about the consequences of oppression. Reich pushed his advocacy role to the letter. He argued that the labor of the fourteen to twenty year olds (as factory workers, messengers, or servants) had already shaped them into adults, and he provided them with Sex-Pol social work, a blend of psychoanalytic counseling, Marxist advice, and contraceptives. The following unusually simple case had a pleasing outcome.

A girl of 16 and a boy of 17, both strong and well developed, come to the sex hygiene clinic, shy and apprehensive. After much encouragement, the boy asks whether it is really harmful to have sexual intercourse before the age of 20.
"Why do you think it is harmful?"
"That's what our group leader in the Red Falcons says and everybody else who talks about the sexual question."
"Do you talk about these things in your group?"
"Certainly. We all suffer horribly, but nobody dares to talk openly. Just recently, a bunch of boys and girls left and formed their own group, because they couldn't get along with the group leader. He is one of those who keeps saying that sexual intercourse is harmful."
"How long have you known each other?"
"Three years."

"Have you had sexual intercourse together?"

"No, but we love each other very much and we must break up because we always get so terribly excited. . . . We are almost going crazy. The worst thing is that because of our functions we always have to work together. She has had very frequent crying spells recently and I am beginning to fail in school."

"What do you two think would be the best solution?"

"We thought of breaking up, but that wouldn't work. The whole group we lead would disintegrate, and then the same thing would happen with another group."

"Do you do sports?"

"Yes, but it's no good at all. When we are together we only think of one thing. Please tell us if it's really harmful."

"No, it is not harmful, but it often creates great difficulties with parents and other people."

I explained to them the physiology of puberty and of sexual intercourse, the social obstacles, the danger of pregnancy, and contraception, and told them to think things over and come back. Two weeks later I saw them again, happy, grateful and able to work. They had overcome all inner and outer difficulties. I continued to see them occasionally over a period of two months.[53]

Reich recorded in detail the permutations of his own patients' sexual functioning, but he also scrutinized the transcribed clinical interviews and case charts of over two hundred patients treated at the Ambulatorium. If sexual disturbances exist in all neurosis (Freud's original thesis) and untreated neurosis results in a crisis, then patients who change for the better in therapy have healthier sex lives and also stronger coping skills. In Reich's mind the internal mind and the environmental context were inseparable. Turning away from an overly individualistic analysis of human suffering, Reich linked political oppression to neurosis and repressed sexuality or sexual guilt.

Wherever he went, Reich was as impressed with people's resilience as with their need for relief from oppression and for psychological autonomy, achievable through combined psychological and political assistance. Sex-Pol would eventually be turned over to the people it served, he believed, because workers would soon solve social problems on their own and assume leadership of society. The term Sex-Pol was an acronym for German Society of Proletarian Sexual Politics. "It was entirely within the realm of possibility," wrote Reich in 1937, "for the people themselves to organize children's clinics for the poor, or establish sex-counseling offices, or take various practical measures regarding problems."

Reich agreed with Julius Tandler, head of the Public Welfare Office, that sexuality and the construction of decent housing were essential and complementary components of the stability of workers and their families. The two men differed, however, in their ideological understanding of the issue. The government's inevitably more traditionalist bureaucratic position (even within a progressive administration) saw housing as a guarantee against moral decay and for the creation of families. Reich criticized this argument, stating that better housing would lend itself to freer, and therefore psychologically and physically healthier, sexual expression. Four people shared a single room in the standard housing design for Viennese workers: this lack of privacy, Reich claimed, did not lend itself to promiscuity.[54] On the contrary, it merely repressed working-class sexuality because its difficult conditions led to indifference to others and fear of disturbance. Reich was particularly concerned that crowded housing would restrain young people and, for example, dangerously expose those who were forced to seek shelter in dark doorways. He argued for sexual expressiveness for all, including the young and the unmarried, with a permissiveness that unsettled both the political left and the psychoanalysts.

2

1923–1932

THE MOST GRATIFYING YEARS

"This help should be available to the great multitude . . . "

1923

FOR YOUNGER ANALYSTS practicing at the Ambulatorium since its founding the previous year, the new Technical Seminar provided a sort of playing field where everything could be said, diagnoses criticized, and treatment theories argued with far less caution than the Vienna society's formal meetings required. At the beginning of 1923 Hermann Nunberg passed the seminar's chairmanship to Eduard Hitschmann. Every week thereafter for the next two years, Paul Federn, as the seminar's secretary and also deputy director of the Ambulatorium as of October 17, recorded the seminar's proceedings with a special compassion and intellectual flexibility. In the seminar minutes of the 1923 and 1924 meetings, Reich's zealous reasoning abilities emerge with a poetry all their own; Nunberg's theories unfold as conscientiously as those of an appellate lawyer; and Hug-Helmuth joyfully discovers that systematic child observation can be integrated into the psychoanalytic repertoire. In the early 1920s most Viennese analysts failed to explore the patient's psyche beyond Freud's psychosexual stages of human development or beyond whatever memories remained accessible to consciousness in adulthood. But Otto Fenichel, who traveled frequently between Berlin and Vienna, introduced the seminar participants to one of the Poliklinik's newest systems for separating psychoanalytic theory from technique. Theory should be separated from technique, he argued, because theory stresses research into the unconscious whereas technique is most significant for therapy. And because of the close examination of the therapist's own impulses required by analytic

training, particularly of the countertransference expected from new therapists, supervision at the Ambulatorium would have to be scheduled with uncompromising regularity.

One evening in October—for such meetings always happened in the evening after a full day's practice—Federn took the lead. A case in point had
cropped up during Rudolf Urbantschitsch's case presentation on the treatment of a twenty-one-year-old factory worker with unmanageable blushing
and violent bloody dreams. Urbantschitsch, the youngest and one of the few
Catholic adherents to the Vienna Psychoanalytic Society, "must [be] enjoy-
[ing] the transference feelings too much—a mistake into which beginners fall
all too easily," Federn cautioned.[1] Wealthy and aristocratic, Rudolf von Urbantschitsch was a gifted endocrinologist who had cultivated a long-standing
interest in psychoanalysis and, somewhat like the late Anton von Freund,
had outlined what Ferenczi described as a "great founding plan," a clinic and
research project to honor Freud.[2] At the age of twenty-eight this eccentric
physician was at once a monarchist and friend of the former archduke Ferdinand's daughter as well as an effective public speaker who promoted psychoanalytic thinking in schools, worker's halls, and medical societies. His intended consultation center had Freud as medical director, the archduke's
own Weilburg Castle in the nearby town of Baden as a site, and financing
from the *Bodenkreditanstalt* (National Credit Union). According to Ferenczi,
Freud and Anna knew that the Urbantschitsch scheme was illusory but were
nevertheless interested in enhancing the reputation of their flagship clinic as
a serious research center. But in deference partly to Hitschmann and partly
to Urbantschitsch's changeable character, the project was abandoned. Nevertheless Urbantschitsch continued to treat patients at the Ambulatorium.
At a later discussion of the rule of abstinence—the if, when, how, and
whether masturbation should be prohibited during analysis—he joined the
seminar participants in their struggle to standardize technique without sacrificing in-session spontaneity. Freud's own 1919 explication of the rule of
abstinence had actually been quite flexible. Of course, as analysts like Franz
Alexander later noted, Freud was invariably less rigid and orthodox in his
technique than most of his followers.[3] Hitschmann, for example, had started out clinging to Freud's "standard" but by 1923, as one can see from this
meeting, he was eager to set ideal and far more rigid schematic principles, in-
junctions, and prohibitions. He helped the group prepare exact patient
records, articulate statistical diagnostic profiles, and stay within a specific
format for writing up and presenting an analytic case study. From then on
each analyst seemed to fashion a personal therapeutic style. Federn's turned

on transference issues; Jokl wanted the analyst to listen for five months without intervening; and Reich stated categorically that no activity, masturbation or otherwise, should be prohibited even if it appeared excessive to the analyst. If anything, Reich said, the therapist should actively make it the central focus of the treatment. Reich was obviously working out the clinical theme for his paper on genitality that he presented three weeks later at a formal society meeting.

In his 1933 book, *Character Analysis*—perhaps his most accepted (if not significant) contribution to classical psychoanalysis—Reich developed a blueprint for thinking through a patient's characterological reactions to treatment. The event, such as masturbation, was in itself less important than the patient's unconscious psychological reaction to it and the analyst's as well. Even by 1933, when Reich seemed to have more enemies than friends, all agreed nevertheless that this serious technical work of the 1920s had ushered in a breakthrough expansion in ego psychology. Before launching into a new case study, Reich said, the analyst should decide whether to explore the patient's character neurosis (personality) or their symptom neurosis (handwashing). The difference is critical. In the mechanistic symptom perspective, a detailed study of a patient's excessive handwashing, for example, imparts a diagnosis of obsessive-compulsive disorder. But analyzing the character, not the symptoms, of that person might expose poor mental organization and a level of anxiety easily overwhelmed by the exterior world. Reich suggested that both character and symptom analysis could be combined if one understood that the symptom, the excessive handwashing, is actually the patient's unconscious attempt to gain a measure of control over their hostile environment. Reich called this "character armor." The symptom could be as easily rooted in environmental stressors like chronic poverty as in childhood trauma. Obviously Freud's vitalistic method appealed to Reich for several reasons. Psychoanalysts (more than psychiatrists) seemed to respect human beings' seemingly inborn ability to self-regulate, and psychoanalysis encouraged a physician to address human problems outside the sterile medical laboratory. When Reich first wrote up his concept of the individual "impulsive character," a study of the thieves and bullies at the Ambulatorium, he was anticipating his far broader 1933 study of human personality and psychological health. Similarly, Reich's energy and his eagerness to probe clinical material transformed an inauspicious academic exercise, the Technical Seminar, into a practical laboratory for the development of psychoanalytic theory in 1923 and 1924. The seminar was one of Vienna's most provocative and exciting centers for training new analysts.

"One evening in December 1923," Richard Sterba recalled from his days as a trainee,

> I went to the Ambulatorium to inquire about becoming an analyst. I was seen by an elderly physician whose name was Eduard Hitschmann. . . . I started my analysis in the early Spring of 1924. Since I did not have any money . . . I was not charged for my analysis. However, it was expected that in the future I would conduct the treatment of some patients from the ambulatorium gratuitously or for a minimal contribution to be paid to the ambulatorium.[4]

Sterba was far from the only candidate to experience such courtesy: Grete Lehner Bibring, Willi Hoffer, and Wilhelm Reich—in fact, almost everybody who worked in psychoanalysis at the Ambulatorium or elsewhere—were analyzed for free.[5] "In Vienna, for example, where almost all the training analyses are carried out gratis," Freud wrote to his friend Franz Alexander in Berlin, "I am afraid that renouncing any *preliminary* choice (of candidates) would threaten us with an excess of work."[6] Appraising a candidate's individual personality is inevitably subjective, the analysts agreed, but following formal or official requirements (which the administrative Eitingon presumably preferred) is merely a poor substitute for one-to-one interviews. Would a candidate understand the point of providing treatment at the free clinic, for example? To accept free services for oneself is meaningful too and indicates an open, nondefensive psychological posture. "Every training analyst in Vienna was obligated to train two students for free," Elsa Pappenheim explained. It was "not unusual for Vienna," she remarked years later, "but it does surprise Americans, I never paid for my analysis."[7] Her account easily confirmed both Grete Bibring's and Helene Deutsch's recollections that most analytic candidates indeed received a free training analysis.[8] That even non-Austrian analysts should be afforded this privilege in exchange for Ambulatorium service became a surprising sort of unwritten policy, another dimension of psychoanalytic social responsibility. True, Freud, Ferenczi, and many others relied on high American fees paid in dollars for economic survival after World War I. Even Red Vienna's new tax code structured a redistribution of funds from the more affluent property owners to the apartment renters, and the American psychoanalysts were obviously affluent.[9] But, in general, training all analysts presupposed negligible or nonexistent fees so that free analysis and free treatment were two sides of the same political coin.

The same held true for Berlin. In Freud's 1923 preface to the Poliklinik's first annual report, he wrote that "the clinics seem to be a social necessity particularly in our times, when the intellectual strata of the population, which are especially prone to neurosis, are sinking irresistibly into poverty." Faced with increasing numbers of unemployed teachers and young bourgeois men and women seeking treatment, the Poliklinik's seven full-time staff members toiled away at a daily combined twenty-five to twenty-eight hours of administrative tasks—exclusive of treatment. By 1923 the Berlin society members conceded that Eitingon's estimated budget of roughly 275,000 marks ($66,100), about double the previous year's, would be hard to meet given inflation and a weakening currency. What was necessary, proposed Felix Boehm in January, was to lay down a rule by which members would make a regular contribution toward a fund to support the clinic.[10] The very next month a six-member committee announced how the society could (and should) fund the Poliklinik as a center for psychoanalytic treatment and training. A psychoanalyst's monthly contribution would be fixed at 4 percent of the member's total income derived from analytic practice (i.e., the income of one day in the month) or less for analysts with temporarily reduced incomes or increased working expenses. The money would be collected at the second meeting every month and overseen by a three-member committee. Foreign members would pay half and do so quarterly.[11] Occasional donations came from friends and admirers. "Our polyclinic received from Fräulein van der Linden, who is here with Ophuijsen, a present of 100 guilders, now = 330,000 marks, which is useful even in present times," Abraham wrote to Freud.[12] The money would be used to increase the number of consulting rooms and to refashion the old facilities into classrooms for the institute. Meanwhile the Poliklinik's program of public lectures and introductory papers was flourishing and had the double advantage of publicizing for the clinic and fund-raising. The first courses were presented in the Poliklinik's elegant book-lined conference room. Sachs and Radó taught there and Melanie Klein organized a course on infantile sexuality specifically for kindergarten teachers. But by the end of 1923 classes could "no longer be held in the limited accommodation of the polyclinic" because the audience had doubled in size, from forty to eighty or ninety attendees. They moved to a "very nice lecture room in the Zentralinstitut für Erziehung und Unterricht,"[13] right across the street from the Poliklinik.[14]

Helene Deutsch (figure 20), now visiting Berlin as an analyst and advanced trainee, found that the city rekindled her social consciousness. She wrote to her husband, the psychoanalyst Felix Deutsch: "Somewhere in the world there is need and hunger, somewhere innocent blood flows, somewhere clouds of resentment and protest gather. . . . How it is fermenting and foaming down

20 Helene Deutsch
(Special Collections, A. A. Brill Library,
New York Psychoanalytic Society
and Institute)

there, how people suffer, how billows of the wave of social upheaval are tow-ering—that is history—the individual remains—where he wants to."[15] Of all the analysts in the circle that met at 19 Berggasse, Helene Deutsch was singled out by Freud and entrusted to go to Berlin to study Karl Abraham's clinical in-novations. The next year she would draw on her experience at the Poliklinik to assist Hitschmann with the Ambulatorium and start the formal education program in Vienna. As Freud explained to Abraham, she would "form a new Training Committee and organize the Ψα teaching following the Berlin pat-tern closely."[16] Deutsch did model the Vienna Institute after Berlin, and what in other hands might have competed with the clinic (the earlier organization) for attention remained in hers a progressive ally.

Ernst Simmel's understanding of politics was such that he always regarded women as equal to men, peers in the class struggle. Why then should a preg-nant woman be humiliated by medical educators simply because she is poor? In public medical institutions, he reported, she is forced "to expose her most difficult hour to hundreds of students and distant onlookers." He compared the vulnerability of a woman in childbirth to an analytic patient. The patient should be the sole focus of one doctor, in one room, for a full hour, regardless of her ability to pay. Moreover, the quality of free treatment would be identical to the quality of privately paid treatment. The idea that patient confidentiality and social class go hand in hand was hardly new: affluent patients buy a form of medical privacy from which patients are excluded. But the challenge at the Poliklinik was not so much making sure that poorer patients got private care but that individual care in itself could be justified ideologically. In other words, as Simmel would argue in *The Socialist Physician* of 1925, the paradigm of individual patient/individual physician is the stamp of bourgeois medicine. In contrast, the paradigm for socialist medicine is the group (medical teams/patient units) and is impossible to achieve without a structural reorganization of the whole health care system. Julius Tandler was attempting to do just this in Vienna. Both Tandler and Simmel shared a commitment to equality and both criticized bourgeois medicine, but Simmel was caught in a contradiction because he wanted bourgeois privileges for his patients. He hoped that the "fundamentally egalitarian nature of psychoanalysis" would transform this practice dilemma that, eventually, even radical psychoanalysts like R. D. Laing failed to resolve. Simmel did insist that the clinical staff could not choose their patients on the basis of "ethical or aesthetic considerations." Even Eitingon balked at the risk of overly personalized relationships with patients. He reprimanded Therese Benedek for saying hello and good-bye and for shaking hands with patients (a standard custom of Freud's), but demurred when she responded, "If I did not do that, I would not be myself and that would not be good for my patient."[17] Nevertheless, indigent patients were regarded with more respect and fairness at the Poliklinik than elsewhere, Simmel and Eitingon stressed, and they intended to make sure that this sense of social justice governed all their policies. They were appalled when fancier teaching institutions, and even the Charité, separated out "high fee-paying patients" but compelled the "proletariat and the ill insured [to] provide material for medical instruction."[18]

For Simmel, words like *proletariat* or exploitation or *egalitarianism* were charged with particular political meaning. Within a human society caught in a vast class struggle, Simmel thought, the "proletarian" class was oppressed by its lack of access to material resources closely held by the upper classes. Even more oppressive, limited access to nonmaterial resources like education and personal insight impeded the individual's natural Rousseau-like ability to be self-regulating. Depriving poor people of the use of psychoanalysis—the very instrument of liberation the rich used for personal enhancement—was yet another dimension of class oppression. Furthermore, callously placing human sickness on exhibit for the benefit (even if it is a teaching benefit) of training doctors gave the intrusive medical professionals an unfair power advantage over the patient: this Simmel called "exploitation." For poor people to overcome such oppression, Simmel believed, they must exercise their innate intelligence and develop insight. Psychoanalysis advanced insight (and conscious insight promoted personal responsibility) because it dislodged some of the individual's unconscious psychological obstacles. Just as Freud held "that the neuroses threaten public health no less than tuberculosis," so Simmel conjectured that public mental health services, psychoanalysis included, offset the damage wrought on individuals by social oppression. Convinced of the dual "egalitarian" nature of psychoanalysis, Freud and Simmel had enough faith in their theory to expose it to practice in their clinic. Later, Max Horkheimer, the influential Marxist philosopher who would lead the Frankfurt Institute for Social Research during its most fertile era, understood this well. "Freud's belief in Simmel as one of the few who understood him best and as a real brother in arms never changed," Horkheimer recalled.[19] Horkheimer oversaw the emergence of Critical Theory, the work for which the Frankfurt School is best known, and recruited talented sociologists, philosophers, psychoanalysts, and cultural critics to articulate the school's empirically based critique of modern society.

When Freud praised Eitingon for providing "the great multitude who are too poor themselves to repay an analyst for his laborious work" with equal access to treatment, he had already settled for himself the difference between paternalistic charity and the less stigmatizing forms of organized direct assistance.[20] Assistance was nothing less than a humane imperative in 1923, though the middle class of Vienna, the professors and scientists like himself, or the writers and artists and shopkeepers, were hardly a disaffected political group. And yet for many who were neither eligible for some of the targeted social assistance of the Social Democrats nor had recovered on their own from postwar deprivations, the prospect of destitution loomed large. It fell to several American philanthropies to assist the Viennese middle classes. The American Relief Administration (ARA), the Commonwealth Fund, and the Rockefeller Foundation, all of whom were already subsidizing programs for the city's children, mounted an emergency campaign in Austria. "We are at present feeding in Middle Class kitchens 13,540; in Middle Class Homes 3,334; professors 675 and students 3708, or a total of 21,257," Gardner Richardson reported from Vienna to Barry C. Smith, general director of the Commonwealth Fund. "No member of the middle class whose situation is proved to be destitute will be refused."[21] Nevertheless, of the 168,000 applications received for food, only 36,305 could be helped. Before more cash arrived from

New York, the ARA's clerks at 9 Elisabethstrasse had to turn down even urgent requests for medicines and medical equipment, payment of back rent, and railway tickets to reunite families or to send sick relatives to sanitariums. Smith and Edward Harkness dispatched a special emergency relief grant of $1,000 (roughly 73 million kronen, or crowns), an amount with significant purchasing power inside Austria yet little on the dollar exchange. The small checks were distributed by the association of Viennese Fürsorgerinnen and went for the purchase of shoes, bedding, or to redeem pawned family assets. A typical middle-class applicant, Mrs. F., lived in Vienna's ninth district at 18 Glasergasse. This educated fifty-five-year-old pensionless widow derived her only income of 200,000 kronen ($3.00) a month from subletting one room of her two-room apartment. She received two food packages in case her money had to be used for clothes or household goods. Then in June three additional allotments were earmarked for the middle class. The ARA's Middle Class Relief Department distributed $100 (approximately 7,000,000 kronnen) to fewer people and in larger amounts than had been given to the Fürsorgerinnen. Another $100 went toward middle class relief in Austrian provinces. And the Innsbruck University professor's mess received $200 to move into new quarters and to purchase kitchen utensils, dishes, and flatware.[22] This redirection of funds toward the middle classes, and seemingly away from the poor and working classes, was actually not so puzzling. The Social Democrats' deliberately redistributive economic policies were attending to the most vulnerable first. Their solution to the postwar fiscal crisis, which in the long term benefited all Viennese citizens, in the short term infuriated affluent families who felt they had the most to lose. When the American observers grumbled that "the salary of the university professor had exactly doubled between 1914 and 1920, whereas the salary of the working man had increased more than twenty times," they were, in fact, correct. What they saw as a source of distress, that the "only people in Vienna who were at all prosperous were the working class," the Social Democrats saw as validation of their economic strategy.[23]

By 1923 Vienna's municipal marriage counseling center was charting a record number of intakes. The institution of marriage, Julius Tandler said in his speech on "Marriage and Population Policy," gives children the benefits of "planned selection, and bringing up in legal and material security." Welfare, therefore, should guarantee the "optimal conditions in up-bringing" in order to insure that the family remain the basic unit of society.[24] Tandler's tone was that of a welfare advocate with a classic pro-family stance. He spoke about state-sponsored benefits as though they were unoriginal, everyday insurance. Of the three different approaches this assistance could take, he explained, the city could send families emergency cash payments or house them in government buildings or simply offer them an ongoing though minimal guaranteed income. But the important effect, regardless of the actual formula, was to safeguard children within their nuclear, biological family wherever possible. As a Social Democrat Tandler believed that government is equally responsible for maintaining children in families who are functioning well and for protecting those who are not. The image of a child, on its own, possessing the social right to a safe family environment was fairly revolutionary. Children's rights certainly predated the government of Red Vienna, and in the 1920s child-centered policies were debated on both sides of the Atlantic. Now the community of Vienna, as Tandler described it, claimed the explicit right to intervene in the life of a family if a child was judged at risk of significant harm. Christian Socials in the City Council responded vehemently, accusing Tandler of corrupting the sacredness of motherhood and turning children away from their families—and toward socialism. In a dispute evocative of virtually every known children's rights controversy, a battle of ideological assumptions ensued concerning the role of the family, the purpose of government, and the relationship between the two. Tandler, of course, thought that Red Vienna's postwar success proved, once and for all, that welfare simply helped children stay with their mothers and protected families against economic swings.

Of all the institutions undergirding the stability of Viennese working-class families, the Gemeindebauten, literally "community buildings," symbolized endurance, efficiency, and fellowship. The signature high-rise multiple housing units were supported by Karl Seitz, Vienna's new mayor, and built within the city. Within a new cultural paradigm that valued an urban populations' need for financial and visual relief, the Social Democratic Party transformed the city into a laboratory for new architecture. Adolf Loos had left the project in 1922, effectively ending the construction of suburban garden row houses. A return to individualized single-family housing was neither socially feasible nor fiscally advantageous. Incremental taxes had made housing speculation less attractive to private investors. Instead, the government responded to the worsening housing shortage with one of urban history's most extensive programs of municipal housing construction. A new building such as the Fuchsenfeldhof accommodated 212 apartments, a large cooperative store and several smaller shops, a child care facility, a central steam-powered laundry, and communal baths located within a large enclosed courtyard. Once again the team of Hugo Breitner, Robert Danneberg, and Julius Tandler was entrusted to oversee the banking, legal, and social-medical administration of the citywide building program. Breitner reintroduced the building tax in February, a tax imposed on major owners of land and business properties and on tenants of expensive apartments (only 0.5 percent of available housing) and raised almost half the necessary funds.[25] Over four thousand dwellings had been built since 1919. The City Council's February decision to build one thousand more that year was soon followed by work on the construction of another twenty-five thousand units, as functionalist and aesthetically progressive as the first group, to be completed at a rate of five thousand apartments each year for the next five years. Rent control held monthly payments to about 3.5 percent of the tenant's income, including utilities. From 1923 forward the building program was managed jointly by the city's departments of Public Works, Public Housing, and Public Health and Welfare, which also planned for the location of health care facilities like the VD immunization centers, kindergartens (figure 21), clinics, libraries, and other child and family services in each housing bloc.

"Air and sunlight for our children. . . . I looked up at Seitz like I was looking up at God, and he stood there and said those words. He made those council flats sound so good that all I could think about was, God, how I'd like to have one," recalled Frau Anna Müller, a Gemeindebauten tenant, a domestic

21 Community nursery,
Vienna (Author)

married to a metal worker and their young child. The mayor's election speech was not just propaganda.[26] The standardized apartments were generally small, most just over 400 square feet including a private lavatory, or 500 square feet with an extra bedroom. Unlike the typical dark and narrow prewar apartment, these small bright rooms had ample windows for direct daylight, adequate ventilation, electricity, gas and running water. Built-in kitchens, carefully researched and designed by Margarete Lihotzky, measured out to precisely 6'4" by 5'2.5" including sink and counter space, for maximum economy of steps and gesture. Lihotzky, an Austrian architect who collaborated with Adolf Loos from 1921 until 1925, designed the famous Frankfurt Kitchen, notable for its functionalism and aesthetic appeal. "Intensive studies," she wrote later of her partnership with Loos and the social scientist Otto Neurath, "in particular of the days of work, brought us to conclude that to every work task corresponded an installation of a certain type that would be the best, the simplest and the least tiring."[27] When Lihotzky and Joseph Frank teamed up with Wiener Werkstätte designers like Joseph Hoffman to develop affordable, aesthetically functional furniture, they aimed to be as practical and radically different from the traditional Viennese upholstery as the Gemeindebauten were from Schönbrunn Palace.[28] Low rents and protection against eviction reinforced family life and stabilized the city's population. A point system assessed eligibility for the housing so that young couples with children, especially workers who had been living in overcrowded tenements or with parents or in-laws, gained priority on the waiting list for new dwellings. Since the ample communal facilities relieved working women of the triple burden of job, household, and child care, feminists within the Social Democratic Party joined Otto Bauer in their ideological support of apartment housing. This rationalized time-and-motion Taylorization of housework can be criticized as a mere redomestication of the Austrian housewife, but social democratic planners like Lihotzky argued to the contrary, that coordination reduced the boredom of housework, left women more time for political work, and was therefore liberating. Other criticism of urban centralization by the governing labor elite suggests that planned housing weakened political motivation and contributed to placid embourgeoisement, when working classes, low-level white-collar workers, and laborers all live in the same apartment buildings and share abundant communal facilities. But rehousing at least 10 percent of a postwar population already depleted by disease and poverty and at risk of economic collapse overrode more than political indebtedness. With the Viennese working class's higher social standing came economic self-sufficiency, a new level of respectability, and, as Breitner and Tandler intended, a restimulated economy.

"The honor proceeds from the Social Democratic Party"

1924

BY 1924 fewer and fewer citizens of Red Vienna believed that psychoanalysis was either an arcane science or a dependent stepchild of psychiatric medicine. After the war the public's interest in psychoanalysis "actually moved faster than that conservative corporation, the medical profession," Paul Federn wrote, and medical patients demanded psychoanalytic information, referrals, and advice from their doctors in virtually all areas of specialization.[1] But the role of securing even greater popularity for psychoanalysis fell to Siegfried Bernfeld, who organized a special *Propaganda-Komitee* (publicity committee) for this purpose. "His fascinating personality, sharp sense and powers of oratory," Freud wrote of Bernfeld to Jones, made for a particularly imaginative leadership of a group from the Vienna society that required little to mount a creative public campaign around the city.[2] They sponsored lectures at municipal cultural centers like the Ärzte-Kurse, a continuing education program for doctors, the university's Internationale Hochschulkurse (international studies school), and the Academic Society for Medical Psychology. There were also courses at the American Medical Association of Vienna, the *Volksbildungshaus* "Urania" (a popular education project), the *Volks-shochschulen* (adult education courses), and a range of societies for women's and for workers' education. Felix Deutsch, Josef Karl, and Paul Schilder lectured at the university itself. Every few months August Aichorn, then chairman of education for the State Juvenile Department, discussed the application of psychoanalytic theory with directors of various child care institutions, schools, and clinics. These psychoanalytic events were reviewed more often in the press, and the public link between Freud's name and the governing Social Democrats grew stronger. The Viennese Social Democrats honored this bond and decided to reward Freud on his sixty-eighth birthday with a high-profile civic tribute of Citizenship of Vienna.[3]

The special distinction that city leaders offered Freud had to do with the Social Democratic Party—specifically the complementarity between psychoanalysis and the party's governing ideology. Freud was quite pleased. "This recognition is the work of the Social Democrats who now rule City Hall," he wrote to Abraham in early May of 1924.[4] "I have been informed that at midday on the sixth," he continued, "Professor Tandler, representing the burgomaster, and Dr. Friedjung, a pediatrician and a district councillor, who is one of our people, are to pay me a ceremonial visit." Freud was granted the status of *Bürger der Stadt Wien* (honorary citizen of the city of Vienna) on the occasion of his birthday. His friend Josef Friedjung, in his dual capacity as member of the Vienna Psychoanalytic Society and socialist district councillor specializing in child welfare, joined Julius Tandler, Karl Richter, and the mayor in the ceremony. Aside from a formal commendation on "the excellence of his contribution to medical science," the politicians praised Freud's humanitarian efforts and his ability to steer foreign benefactors toward Vienna's social causes, especially those of indigent children. For once the reward was the result of authentic idealism. "The honor proceeds from the Social Democratic Party," he wrote to his son Oliver, much as he had to Abraham, but added in this letter that "the Worker's Newspaper is celebrating me in a nice little article."[5] Actually the article in the *Arbeiter-Zeitung* was even more flattering. "A special obligation and gratitude falls to us Socialists," the Social Democratic newspaper wrote, "for the new roads which he opened for the education of the children and the masses."[6] True, Freud was morosely preoccupied with the idea that this sixty-eighth birthday would be his last, and the recent accolades struck a recurring note—perhaps, he wrote, the city government hastened the tribute knowing that this birthday would be the final one. Regardless, he enjoyed his relationship with Red Vienna's social welfare administration. More to the point, during the last six years Otto Bauer had overseen a remaking of the city and Freud was honored for his contribution to its new educational and psychological systems. By 1930, when the same medallion would be awarded to Alfred Adler, whose individual psychology was supported by Social Democratic Party officials like Carl Furtmueller, the role of psychoanalysis had expanded even further into the community.

Psychoanalysis had become so popular in Vienna that the Rathaus politicians turned over a city-owned building site at the lower end of the Berggasse, the street on which Freud lived, to house further psychoanalytic endeavors. The new building at Number 7, near both the medical school and urban transportation, would bring together the society, the Ambulatorium, and the Training Institute under one roof. But the building came without accompanying construction funds, and the plans for a centralized psychoanalytic establishment were set aside at least until 1936. In the meantime the thorny issue of lay analysis recurred again and again. Julius Wagner-Jauregg had reconvened the conservative Society of Physicians to examine the credentials of Theodor Reik, then practicing on the strength of his academic scholarship and psychoanalytic training with Freud. The challenge would draw Freud into the political fray the next year and prompted him to write *The Question of Lay Analysis* in 1927. But, more generally, as the programs of Red Vienna prospered over the next eight years, then leveling off, the psychoanalysts carried on the multiple clinical and educational functions of the Ambulatorium with surprising equanimity concerning the political situation.

Wilhelm Reich, now assistant director of the Ambulatorium, found his work with clinic patients to be mutually rewarding. The clinic allowed Reich to further his social interests by treating the emotional problems of poor and disenfranchised groups like laborers, farmers, students, and others with wages too low to afford private treatment. As an analyst he brought to the Ambulatorium a character well-versed in politics. "Material poverty and lack of opportunities," he believed, exacerbated the emotional suffering and neurotic symptoms of poor people.[7] Because sexual disturbances, the rearing of children, and family problems were inseparable from the larger context of social and economic oppression, Reich would eventually broaden the scope of psychoanalysis and add free sex counseling clinics to the outreach efforts already underway.[8] While at the Ambulatorium, though, Reich deliberately sought to treat difficult patients who had been diagnosed as "psychopaths," but were regarded as morally bad rather than "sick." Frequently antisocial, they showed tendencies to be destructive (of self and other) in the form of criminality, addictions, rageful outbursts, or suicide attempts. Psychoanalysis, Reich believed, would free them of rage and allow a more socially productive motivation, or energy, to emerge naturally.

Only twenty-two years old and barely graduated from medical school, the impassioned Wilhelm Reich assumed the position of first assistant chief to Eduard Hitschmann at the Ambulatorium in 1924. Over the next six years the two men, in many ways opposite in character, would work together as codirectors of the clinic. Reich seemed to be privileged with apparently limit-less visits to Freud, who bemusedly noted Reich's *Steckenpferd* (hobbyhorse), his obstinate conviction that neurosis, whether individual or social, is rooted in sexuality.[9] But he was genuinely well regarded by the analysts and espe-cially appreciated for his imaginative, charismatic chairmanship of the Tech-nical Seminar. Reich held these meetings weekly initially at the Ambulatori-um and, from 1925 until 1930 when he moved to Berlin, at the Vienna Psychoanalytic Society's Institute.[10] Reich's initial seminar papers, where he pursued his earliest theoretical sketches of a new therapy based on individual character structure, were surprising not only for their content but also for their structure. Psychoanalysis, he said, should be based on a careful exami-nation of selected unconscious character traits, later called ego defenses, that impede an individual's acceptance of their natural self in society. Else Pap-penheim, more a friend of Annie Reich than of Wilhelm, remembered the later popularity of "his book on character analysis that we all read. It was part of the curriculum. And," she commented, "he was very respected in Vienna at the time."[11] Reich called for a new approach to the analysis of individual character. In due course he devised the format of the in-depth individual case conference, a format that still endures as the standard method for systemati-cally summarizing and discussing therapeutic issues in clinical settings. Though a mere twenty-seven pages of handwritten minutes of the seminar's case reports have survived, the analysts' lively exchanges and imaginative cri-tiques make clear why these sessions were some of the most valuable activi-ties of the society.[12] The analysts met in the windowless conference room of the Ambulatorium and, in at least the discussions of January 9, February 6, March 5, May 7, and October 1, 1924, supported each other's efforts to treat all those who requested clinical treatment—without regard to fee. When Re-ich entered the conference room after a full day in the clinic, his relative youth vanished. He spread an electrifying energy all his own; his deep-set eyes, wavy hair, and high forehead of the rebellious German intellectual bare-ly tempered by the military mannerisms of a Prussian army official. Under his leadership the analysts developed not only path-breaking clinical proto-cols but also attended to the more mundane aspects of running a clinic. They formalized the staff, record-keeping, and statistical requirements of the clin-ic for both internal use and public scrutiny. As a branch society, the Viennese would send off these reports for publication and distribution by the IPA.

Reports from the IPA's branch societies' activities had shifted, as of 1920, from the *Zeitschrift* to the *International Journal of Psychoanalysis* (*IJP*). Local groups around the globe forwarded to the *IJP*'s editors the minutes of their scientific and administrative meetings. The most thorough reports came from Berlin where Eitingon and Fenichel's combined administrative talents produced an enviable array of detailed statistical tables. Not wishing to come in second best but skeptical of the dehumanizing effect of such accounting, Reich suggested an alternative model for the Ambulatorium 's statistical overview. The reports from Vienna, he said, would not merely depict past and present work. Rather they would be narrative portraits interspersed with numbers, diagnostic descriptions, and case notes on discharged patients. Reich and Jokl would organize follow-up studies and summon former patients, recontacting them as necessary. Careful wording of treatment plans (for example, designating an analysand "symptom free" instead of "cured") was a critical exercise in public relations, especially given the imperative for confidentiality and the Ambulatorium's relationship to public social services. Prospective patients must feel welcomed and former patients who had interrupted or ended analysis prematurely (or who had been intended for fractionary analysis) should feel comfortable enough to resume treatment.

Reich's beliefs were hardly unusual among psychoanalysts at the time. Nor was 18 Pelikangasse the only psychoanalytic outpatient clinic. What Hitschmann called "unauthorized competition" generally came from clinics formed by Freud's current rivals and former adherents like Alfred Adler and Wilhelm Stekel, a pacifist who had left Freud's circle even before the war. A case in point was the October 24 announcement published in a local Viennese newspaper, the *Wiener Sonn- und Montags-Zeitung* (the Vienna Sunday and Monday Times), just over the weather section. "The Society of Independent Analytical Physicians, under the leadership of Drs. Anton Mikreigler, Wilhelm Stekel and Fritz Wittels, opened an out-patient clinic to make possible the analytic treatment of the poor and needy. Come in regard to: sexual disturbances, nerves, epilepsy and spirit disorders. Open Tuesday-Friday, 6–7 in the afternoon, 8th District, Langegasse 72."[13] Faced with an apparent onslaught of new psychological practices in clinics around the city, some entrenched older members of the medical faculty at the Allgemeine Krankenhaus, over in Vienna's fifth district, sought to retaliate. This time, unlike their earlier efforts to block the Ambulatorium on professional grounds, they focused on the "problem" caused by large numbers of foreign students at the university. "The old professors have not been changed by the war and [are] still dictators, not open to the new psychology," Dr. Eversole wrote to Richard Pearce of the Rockefeller Foundation, "while great work and stimulation [are] being put [forth] by the younger faculty."[14] Apparently these "old professors" were overcharging foreigners, in part simply to cover the financial survival of their departments (Freud had done the same). But many did not understand the nature of medical progress and, by enforcing the rules of traditional practice, prevented new ideas from expanding into Austrian medicine. From the American Eversole's point of view, the foundation should give young Austrian doctors overseas study fellowships. From the perspective of Grete Lehner Bibring, Reich's friend from medical school just then finishing up her residency, the traditional psychiatry and neurology of Wagner-Jauregg's clinic was still pedagogically worthwhile. Jauregg's organic biological treatment approach was frequently useful as a supplement to psychoanalytic practice, Bibring found, but his academic conservatism was distressing. And Helene Deutsch (who had completed her wartime rotation there) warned that treating illiterate men and women this way resulted merely in their blind submission. Deutsch wanted to work with "the most hopeless patients, the ones who had locked up their entire emotional lives deep within them, unable either to give love or accept it." She recalled how "they would lie there in their beds, motionless and mute, as if dead, until after a period of 'observation' they were judged unpromising for further research, given the ominous diagnosis 'stupor,' and sent on to an institution for incurables." Her older, traditional—and all male—colleagues were convinced that she was wasting her time. But Deutsch persevered and "learned that one can penetrate the thickest wall of morbid narcissism if one is armed with a strong desire to help and a corresponding warmth."[15] The message was not lost on the Viennese press, and soon stories about human suffering and psychoanalytic help were appearing in the popular local journals.

Among the more daring of these periodicals, one of the most open to psychoanalysis was a Viennese news magazine called *Bettauer's Wochenschrift*. In mid-1923 the *Wochenschrift* published a series of enthusiastic articles on the benefits of psychoanalysis available at the clinic. The journal's "unsolicited publicity for psychoanalytic therapy," Richard Sterba recalled, "brought an influx of patients to the ambulatorium."[16] Sterba may have actually understated the magazine's impact since over 350 men and women applied in 1924 alone. Hugo Bettauer's novels, plays, and periodicals like *Er und Sie: Zeitschrift für Lebenskultur und Erotik* (He and She: A Magazine for Lifestyle and Eroticism), the *Wochenschrift* (Weekly), and *Bettauers Wochenschrift* (Almanac), all of which popularized psychoanalysis, sent more people seeking help at the Ambulatorium than therapists had time for. These widely distributed journals discussed sexuality candidly, called for unrestricted sexual emancipation, and openly advised psychoanalytic psychotherapy for people with sexual difficulties. References to Havelock Ellis, Magnus Hirschfeld,

Wilhelm Stekel, and of course Freud were written into *Er und Sie*'s leading articles. The reporters chose to comment on five central moral issues, the same issues Wilhelm Reich also picked: hypocrisy of the state, homosexual and abortion rights, a double standard for women, homelessness, and the distinction between natural and pornographic sexuality. In November 1924 the new question-and-answer column, "Probleme des Lebens" (Problems of Life) gave young people, women, and adolescents a chance to voice their familiar concerns. Soon words like *drive, impulse, sublimation, unconscious, complex,* and *instinct* appeared in the regular weekly column written by a *Nervenärzt* (psychiatrist), along with his direct recommendation to seek psychoanalytic help if the words matched their mood, and troubled readers flocked to the treatment center on Pelikangasse. These inexpensive twelve-to-sixteen page daily journals mixed currents of gossip, entertainment, and political satire with serious sex education columns, novellas, personal ads, and a clinical forum on both normal and "abnormal" behavior. "Lonesome: You are 29 years old, intelligent, educated, with a good job and you long for a companion who would share with you sorrow and joy. . . . This is no doubt a case which necessitates psychoanalytic treatment. Consult with the Psychoanalytic Ambulatorium, Vienna, Ninth District, 18 *Pelikangasse*, Office hours from 6 to 7pm."[17] The papers had seriously feminist side that condemned the oppression of women and rallied to their cause in tones firmly suggestive of Reich's work. "Daily one can observe the grotesque spectacle, the parents who permit their daughter to work eight hours a day in an office but prevent her from living her own life. She has to earn money, work under men and care for herself."[18] Readers who went to the Ambulatorium for psychoanalytic treatment, while perhaps neither sophisticated or psychologically informed, were fortified by Bettauer's advocacy, the postwar possibilities for a better personal and family life and, particularly among women and young people, a new sense of citizenship.

If the populist Hugo Bettauer lamented sexual hypocrisy and heralded psychoanalysis as liberation from social repression, the elitist writer Karl Kraus also lambasted bourgeois society's repressive sexual laws but famously mocked psychoanalysis as "the mental illness of which it considers itself the cure."[19] His celebrated satirical magazine *Die Fackel* (The Torch) published Kraus's own freewheeling criticism of the clichés and sensationalism of the general press yet, in a bald internal contradiction, advocated for gender equality, women's liberation, and generally much the same social agenda as Bettauer. Psychoanalysis represented a dividing line. At issue was less the theory of psychoanalysis than the feasibility of actually effecting individual and social change. Bettauer, who freely referred his blue-collar readers to the Ambulatorium, saw psychoanalysis as a genuine service that would relieve depressive overburdened human beings of their individual suffering and, consequently, improve their entire family and social system. Kraus by his own admission despised the idea of individual change but failed to understand the democratizing effect of personal transformation on the larger social and economic universe. Thus he accused Freud of blaming victims for their own oppressed predicament whereas Bettauer praised Freud for just the opposite, for relieving the individual of self-blame. Their disagreement epitomized the pro- and anti-Freudian argument that rages still today. But whatever intellectual confrontations inflamed Vienna's café society, in the 1920s the psychoanalysts believed in helping workers, students, maids and butlers, army officials and unemployed people cope with personal misery.

Some of the stories are incredibly sad. An anorexic sixteen-year old girl is in love. Her loss of appetite is total, and she is losing body weight so rapidly that her hair is drying up and falling out. Should the Ambulatorium arrange for individual analysis, or should she be treated along with her boyfriend? August Aichorn had been known to intervene actively in these situations with adolescents at his St. Andrä therapeutic group home. The severity of the young girl's condition seemed to be an emergency, so Hitschmann agreed to see the two young people together, in keeping with Reich's approach. But— one always must ask—is "couples counseling" really analysis? Another sixteen year old suffers from attacks of Wanderlust. Maybe he "longs to die in a far away, sunny landscape, the opposite of the narrow womb" or maybe he is running away from an abusive home. Are this adolescent's exhibitionistic tendencies really signs of schizophrenia? Yes, because he had a systematic delusional body image even as a four year old. He had probably been discharged too soon and would have benefited from longer-term therapy at the Ambulatorium since classical analysis was, after all, possible after puberty. In this way patients' cases were discussed for at least thirty minutes each, in clinical meetings held every other week at 8:30 at night in a basement room ostensibly stripped of its medical functionality but, in fact, still an emergency entrance for heart attacks.

Maybe he did resemble a white-haired German pastor with an abundant mustache, but Hitschmann could zero in on the comic and lighten up his most pretentious colleagues.[20] He stopped an exhaustive discussion on erythrophobia and schizophrenia with a joke: "The analyst must ask with his dying breath: What comes to your mind about this?"[21] Hitschmann's banter, recorded in clinical minutes and long remembered by Helene Deutsch and other analysts, brought welcome relief to the group of intense and austerely disciplined physicians. He and Reich were surely put off by Federn's cold use of the term *differential diagnosis,* a descriptive phrase borrowed from academic psychiatry to explore how a range of symptoms can cause one illness. But where Reich was combative, Hitschmann parodied the distant, scientific psychoanalyst more concerned with technique than relieving human misery.

Reich enjoyed these clinical debates immensely. Even in the 1920s some of Freud's colleagues were tempted to practice psychoanalysis along the lines of an idealized and rigidly "orthodox" protocol. In actuality most analysts, especially Freud, exercised nearly all variations of clinical flexibility. The dispute over what constitutes an appropriate length of treatment reappeared in every clinic and in almost every series of clinical notes. In Berlin brief therapy was eventually regarded as an official curative technique called "fractionary" analysis. In Vienna the clinicians asked whether they "should endeavor to achieve quick successes in order to shorten the duration of the treatment." Federn questioned the wisdom of discharging patients at their own request. But since after all nobody was ever symptom free, he agreed that interrupting the analysis could be a viable shortcut in treating the problem. Then again, lengthy treatment was just as debatable. To cite an instance, Reich accused Hoffer of retaining a thirteen-year-old patient in treatment too long because he felt like a beginner abruptly handed a difficult case. The boy was referred to the Ambulatorium for "educational problems," but in truth he ridiculed and insulted Jews and was a member of an anti-Semitic section of the Boy Scouts whose leader called psychoanalysis "Jewish filth." During the case conference Reich urged Hoffer to consult directly with Hitschmann, while Federn and Felix Deutsch dispassionately wondered if the youth was acting out an aggressive castration complex without knowing that the youth was circumcised. What emerges from this lengthy disputation on body image, sexual repression, and birth trauma among four men who are themselves Jews is an uncanny—perhaps naive—ability to detach from Vienna's dangerous anti-Semitism and concentrate instead on curing a young boy with school problems. The detachment presupposed, naturally, faultless trust between colleagues and in the outpatient system they were creating.

The Ambulatorium's reporting system required analysts, regardless of their status in the clinic hierarchy, to send Reich weekly written summaries. Oral reports, he thought, resulted in irrelevancies and disorganization. While the written reports were carefully collated by senior analysts, the oral reports, as the purview of less experienced trainees, were presented once every three months to the seminar and at least monthly to the supervisor. Anyhow, if distributing written reports placed patient confidentiality in question, the indiscrete character of the oral reports only added to the probability of turmoil. Accordingly a log was instituted to identify patients only by preassigned numbers. Interruptions of analysis, reduction or expansion in the number of sessions, and clinical difficulties were documented in writing. Signs of danger like suicidal or homicidal gestures, or ominous auditory or visual hallucinations, and major modifications in treatment were reported immediately. Such regulations were necessary because people with mental disturbances of every kind had found their way to the Ambulatorium. But with all of this ritualized supervision and accountability, what would happen to the spontaneous exchange of clinical ideas, the satisfying core of collegial exchanges? To safeguard the scientific nature of the seminar, a period for debating questions of technique was formally set aside for the end of every case presentation. Without these discussions, the Ambulatorium might have found itself too bureaucratic, just another one of Tandler's social welfare agencies.

Nobody knows now how many kinds of fringe and underground political people were treated at the Ambulatorium, but the analysts had to guard against lapses in confidentiality at all times. Even as danger closed in on the clinic in the early 1930s, analysts maintained this rule. Confidentiality meant that a patient's politics were protected from the couch to the conference room. Of course this level of trust was possible because analysand and analyst largely shared the same left-wing convictions. Most believed, Helene Deutsch later said, that social change was inevitable and "socialism was not a label [but] . . . a perfectly respectable thing to be."[22] Exit pass forgers, industrial spies from Russia, perhaps even incipient Nazis were in treatment, and so, for Grete Bibring or Richard Sterba, a patient's desire to join a political party posed no conflict with her ongoing psychoanalysis.[23] Sterba had exchanged his hospital job for a similar position as the Ambulatorium's resident psychiatrist. The new job entailed a loss of income but Wilhelm Reich broached the possibility of private patient fees to compensate for the pay cut. This proved to be difficult. As in-house psychiatrist, Sterba conducted five analyses of Ambulatorium patients each week. Still, he relished the opportunity and dispensed with luxuries in the thrill of adhering to his chosen vocation. Under the harsh lights of the Herzstation's examination rooms, Sterba was free to adopt a personality unique to mental health professionals—father and son, consoler and conscience, guardian of sexual secrets and protector of the intelligence of dreams.

Typically for Hitschmann, the stress placed on the Ambulatorium by his relationship with the state overshadowed his feeling of accomplishment. On the one hand, he was pleased that "our collaboration has always been most harmonious and the spirit of humanity and conscientiousness in dealing with our poor patients has at all times been eminently upheld." On the other, he chafed at the perception that the Ambulatorium was being held to different—and possibly more burdensome—sets of regulatory standards and civic demands than the Berlin Poliklinik. It was different from other municipal clinics in that it accepted only private funds while treatment referrals kept coming from government agencies.[24] The Viennese analysts had to cope with myriad referrals received from the municipal welfare authorities, the courts, Wagner-Jauregg's psychiatric clinic, health insurance societies, and the Matrimonial Advisory Center. "Here in Vienna," Hitschmann reported, "we were under the most rigid necessity of accepting only such patients as were *demonstrably without means*, so that for many years they contributed nothing whatever financially to our expenses."

Because the "salaries of the medical staff and fees of part-time physicians made very heavy demands . . . over and above the expenses of maintenance," as Hitschmann reported, fund-raising could no longer be left to spontaneous but inconsistent donations. In discussions of clinic administration at organizational meetings like the one held on May 7, 1924, Hitschmann, Helene Deutsch, Otto Isakower, and Dorian Feigenbaum agreed that the Ambulatorium's financial affairs had to be purposefully systematized. A 4 percent charge, they decided, would be levied on every member of the society to help defray the costs of the Ambulatorium, just as the Berliners had done for their own clinic.[25] This increased the Ambulatorium's cash on hand so that salaries could be paid, furniture rented, and publications issued. By 1924 the funding strategy, along with other occasional infusions of cash from enthusiastic analysts, had stabilized the Ambulatorium's fiscal situation and finally allowed for the financing of salaried positions. Members of the society who decided not to treat patients free of charge found themselves, according to the "one-fifth" rule, contributing to the salaries of a growing number of assistants and interns at the Ambulatorium. Reich even took to soliciting small monthly payments from nonindigent patients who could contribute to the clinic's administrative expenses. Many years later Wilhelm Reich recalled how his vigorous efforts to collect the 4 percent dues from his fellow analysts provoked Freud's expressions of pleasure in the early 1920s.

Obviously the Ambulatorium was no more immune to internal politics than to external ones. During the Eighth International Psychoanalytic Congress held in Salzburg that April, Siegfried Bernfeld asked Ferenczi to consider moving from Budapest to Vienna and take over the clinic since

Hitschmann was so disliked by his society peers. Hitschmann, he said, lacked personal initiative and the capacity to motivate younger analysts. Freud rallied to the invitation, lavishing Ferenczi with his "complete sympathy and highest interest" for the transfer and tempting him with elaborate incentives. "If I were omnipotent," wrote Freud, "I would move you without further ado." He offered to assign Ferenczi all his foreign patients, appoint him to replace Otto Rank as his successor, and even find him living quarters.[26] But both Freud and Bernfeld had to admit that the reach of Hitschmann's engagement with the Ambulatorium ran deep. Charges of inefficiency were barely credible since he was, at that moment, negotiating with the wife of a wealthy retired banker to invest in a new building for the clinic complete with an apartment for the resident director. Freud subsequently met with Frau Kraus that July and at several intervals throughout the year to iron out the details of the intended clinic, including its future director. But the building project never actually worked out. "The prospect of getting a house for an out-patient clinic," Freud wrote to Abraham, "has evaporated. The wealthy lady who wished to build it is now acting as if she were offended and is withdrawing."[27] Despite multiple incentives, the honor of being chosen and his personal devotion to the cause, Ferenczi finally decided to forego the Vienna offer because an even greater challenge—America—lay ahead.

For Sándor Ferenczi, the idea of founding a psychoanalytic outpatient clinic in America, "for which money is supposedly available . . . for two to three years," was irresistible.[28] In addition to a growing number of professional invitations for lecture series and consultations, this particular proposal came from Caroline Newton, a controversial figure on both sides of the Atlantic. Ferenczi neither accepted nor refused, first telling Freud about the offer as, in fact, Newton had requested.[29] In New York Newton was then at the epicenter of the escalating international dispute over the requirement for an accredited medical degree in order to participate legitimately in the psychoanalytic movement. The argument over lay analysis reflected in microcosm the differences between Americans and European psychoanalysts who, while less overtly murderous than the Montagues and Capulets, held equally intransigent views of each other. For Freud and the Europeans, psychoanalysis was above all a humanist endeavor best practiced by well-analyzed trainees regardless of their academic credentials. For Abraham Brill, as titular head of the American movement, psychoanalysis was a medical science to be guarded against intruders by physicians accredited by the American Medical Association. Thus when Caroline Newton, a social worker first analyzed by Freud in 1921 and more recently by Rank, attempted to open a practice in New York, the New York Psychoanalytic Association responded with outrage, and ejected her from their meetings for violating their privileged medical boundaries.[30] The resulting uproar prompted Brill to promote even more restrictive membership clauses and Newton, already a member of the Viennese society, to attempt a free clinic like the Ambulatorium in New York. Nothing could be more un-American than the combination of social work, lay analysis, European training, and provision to poor people of the kind of mental health treatment hitherto reserved for the affluent. The clinic project failed, but Ferenczi pursued his plans to visit America, only intensifying Freud's penchant for outrageous comments. "It is an extremely unfree society, which really knows only the hunt for the dollar," he wrote in 1921, calling the United States "Dollaria" and defying the Americans to start the kind of clinics seen in Weimar Berlin or Red Vienna.[31]

In Berlin, in fact, the Poliklinik's attention to the patient was different. Josephine Dellisch, a Poliklinik patient, was an unemployed schoolteacher who, like many, was ambivalent about her analysis. Did she truly lack the money to pay or was her financial distress a form of resistance against pursuing analysis? Her reasons were "mere pretexts—exhausted by the term—school moving to a crisis, no money to live in Berlin & no friends to help her—can't face taking a temporary post as governess, or giving lessons" wrote Alix Strachey to James, Freud's future English translator, in her letters from Berlin. Eitingon simply would not permit finances to come between her and treatment. He "twice said very impressively that the money 'was *there*,' only the question was how to press it into that lunatic's hand."[32] In other words, Eitingon believed that people like Dellisch had a right to treatment, regardless of their ability to pay. He, like Freud and other Social Democrats, had come to believe that payment and nonpayment alike were clinical issues and were more significant for the therapist than for the patient; eliminating the fee altogether could free analysands to explore and resolve impediments in their work and personal lives. Of course, in order to maintain this level of neutrality, the need to raise funds toward the Poliklinik's upkeep was unending. First the administrative committee checked to see how the Viennese balanced rental expenses, staff salaries, and patient subsidies. Next they decided to look for outside donations though society members' voluntary subscriptions and dues would continue in 1924, as in 1923.[33] New members saw this most starkly. Therese Benedek's renewed *Mitgliedskarte* (membership card; figure 22) in the 1924 Berlin Psychoanalytic Society identifies her dues quite specifically. In addition to the ten-mark fee collected for membership in the society, the secretary hand-entered a five-mark fee levied strictly for the Poliklinik. Predictably, the five marks scarcely compensated for the fees not paid by the clinic's patients.

Dellisch's financial and psychological predicament as an unemployed teacher was increasingly common in Germany of the mid-1920s. Like the distressed segments of Austria's middle class, Germany's impoverished university professors attracted the philanthropic attention of the Rockefeller Foundation. But after Raymond Fosdick of the Laura Spelman Rockefeller Memorial commissioned a confidential study of the country's "intellectual workers," the situation was found to be less dire in Austria. Approximately two hundred medical scientists were already receiving relief in the form of stipends, scientific literature, experimental animals, and laboratory supplies. Otherwise, "I find no critical situation demanding immediate action," Guy Stanton Ford reported from Berlin.[34] Berlin's affluence relative to Vienna's was noted by another Rockefeller deputee, H. O. Eversole, who reported that young men "had work in Germany but no sufficient material or clothing to go. It is an odd feeling on my part to assist young technicians to go to Germany," Eversole wrote to Richard Pearce in the New York office, "where they have work awaiting them, when we consider all of the propaganda

22 Theresa Benedek's membership card in the Berlin Psychoanalytic Society, with its additional fee for the Poliklinik (Thomas Benedek)

about alleged unemployment and hardship in Germany!"[35] Indeed the sheer number of libraries, academies, and special institutes was so large that at least one institution was likely to have the necessary books and periodicals. Salaries were low, but so were costs, and the standard of living of the "intellectual professions" seemed, for the moment at least, relatively stable.

For Berliners in early 1924, the practice of psychoanalysis was still avant-garde, a bit more culturally sophisticated and perhaps less clandestine than in Vienna. When "old friend Fenichel turned up," Alix Strachey wrote, he had already "migrated for a year or two from Vienna to get a little extra polish on his brain. A good idea."[36] And Helene Deutsch wrote to her husband Felix, that in Berlin "there is no mood of panic, no barricades, no starvation," despite the imminent elections and some of the harsher aspects of daily life like inflation and the landlord's perpetual threats of eviction in favor of Americans.[37] Alix, always the caustic but astute observer, in essence agreed with Helene about Berlin's atmosphere. "Most people seem apathetic" about the parade of trucks draped in German nationalist black-white-red flags and young patriots, she wrote to James from her favorite table at the Romanisches Café.[38] The Poliklinik analysts' festive social life unfolded in these cafés and in the concert halls, in weekend visits to the countryside, at the movies and cabaret shows, and in each other's apartments. Fenichel, Bornstein, and Wilhelm and Annie Reich liked to picnic in the woods by the Marditzer Lake and discuss what they were doing in psychoanalysis while Fenichel, who brought along his portable typewriter, remained ensconced in his manuscripts. Along with Radó and Alexander, they gathered at Melanie Klein's or the Abrahams for long soirees. The Eitingons held tea parties, hosted a literary salon, and had a hand in social gatherings of cultural émigrés from the Russian diaspora of the 1920s.[39] Alix, herself no stranger to refinement, was enthralled by Max and Mirra Eitingon's mid-Victorian house in the Grünewald. "I suspect the man of having taste," she wrote to James. "Or perhaps his wife. It was heavenly to lean back and look at rows & rows of bookshelves, & well-arranged furniture and thick carpets."[40] On a warm weekend in October Simmel led a travel party to Würzburg to see the Tiepolo trompe l'oeil frescoes in the Bishop's Palace and to drink Main wine at a choice local Ratskeller. Hans Lampl, Radó, Alexander, Jan van Emden, Josine Müller, and Hanns Sachs explored the lovely hill town of old houses and a rambling river. The same friends enjoyed Berlin's weekly succession of dances and balls, the Feuerreiter Dance, the Kunst Akademie Dance, and an occasional underground costumed ball—Simmel once dressed up as a Berlin nightwatchman—in the winter. Melanie Klein loved the balls and always wore wonderful hats. The famous golden decadence of Berlin in the 1920s, the sultry cabarets, the transvestite dance floors, the bars and amusement parks, surrounded the psychoanalysts and easily drew them in. "There is no city in the world so restless as Berlin," wrote the British diplomat and biographer Harold Nicolson. Married to Vita Sackville-West of London's Bloomsbury group, Nicolson was no stranger to either psychoanalysis or its encroachment on Berlin's avant-garde society. "At 3 A.M. the people of Berlin will light another cigar and embark afresh and refreshed upon discussions regarding Proust or Rilke, or the new penal code, or whether shyness comes from narcissism."[41]

Dedicated bon vivants, Sándor Radó and Franz Alexander joined these smoky arguments on occasion, but other Poliklinik analysts like Ernst Simmel seemed to relish discussing theory day or night. Simmel was especially attracted to left-wing political circles. At the institute he immediately joined up when Otto Fenichel called the first meeting of the Children's Seminar. Virtually identical in style and structure to the sexology seminar in Vienna, this was a semiformal study group that met every few weeks in private homes to explore topics outside the institutional curriculum. Fenichel soon pushed his case for a serious political focus and his friends, who would join him ten years later in a last-ditch effort to uphold Marxism in psychoanalysis, seemed to agree. Erich Fromm, Annie and Wilhelm Reich, Edith Jacobson, Francis Deri, Bertha Bornstein, Kate Friedländer, Alexander Mette, Barbara Lantos, and others gathered 168 times in groups of 5 to 25, from November 1924 until at least 1933.[42]

By 1924 Simmel had become increasingly interested in the interdisciplinary efforts of a highly original group of intellectuals, known since about 1930 as the Frankfurt School, who had opened their own academy in 1923 to explore social and psychological theory with uncompromising depth. The most philosophical members (Theodor W. Adorno, Max Horkheimer, and Herbert Marcuse) and the cultural critic Walter Benjamin would not affiliate with the researchers for at least five more years. But the psychoanalysts, led by Simmel, were already intrigued by the Frankfurt School's academic debates, which often paralleled their own theoretical approaches. Erich Fromm would join the school along with Karl Landauer, founder of the co-resident Frankfurt Psychoanalytic Institute in 1929. By then Landauer had already formed the Frankfurt Psychoanalytic Study Group with Fromm and his wife Frieda Fromm-Reichmann, Heinrich Meng, and Clara Happel. As the analysts diagnosed individual pathology, so the social scientists diagnosed the larger pathologies of Western society. Where the analysts probed interpretively into an individual's unconscious world, the Frankfurt School analyzed sociopolitical motivation and eventually emerged with Critical Theory, their own Marxist dialectical methodology. Most clearly articulated in the early 1930s by Max Horkheimer, Critical Theory analyzed facets of industrial culture and society, with a specific cultural emphasis on the reciprocity between political and economic factors. With their affiliated psychoanalysts critiquing Freud and their philosophers critiquing Marx, both from the left, the Frankfurt group did attempt a theoretical integration of the two perennially irreconcilable conceptions of the human world. This optimistic synthesis was one of the Frankfurt School's boldest attempts to break through traditional academic wariness and intellectual clichés. Eventually the Ministry of Education authorized the construction of a future home for the Institute for Social Research at 17 Victoria Allee in Frankfurt. It was a stark five-story stone building with small windows and few adornments, architecturally sedate but famous for housing Erich Fromm and the Frankfurt Psychoanalytic Institute. Until it was forcibly expelled by the Nazis, the Frankfurt School investigated the most nettlesome problems of the era, beyond the platitudes of party affiliation, and promoted a critically rigorous dialogue between psychoanalysis and Marxist theory.

Given the earlier opposition in Vienna to an official training program anything like that of the Berlin society's, let alone the Frankfurt School, Helene Deutsch was surprised to find a new regard for psychoanalytic courses when she returned after her year in Berlin. Deutsch was pleased and rallied her Viennese colleagues around the idea of attaching their training program to the Ambulatorium. "I turned out to be a good organizer," she recalled from her youthful community work with women.[43] At the same time, John Rickman convened members of the British society to review their own plans for a clinic and a training program in London. Whereas little came of the discussion there (London's clinic project was progressing, though slowly), in Vienna Deutsch aimed for an opening in the fall term of 1924. She envisioned a joint institute and clinic where the Technical Seminar would bridge the needs of students in the psychoanalytic training program and the senior analysts would teach more advanced courses. Deutsch prevailed and the Training Institute was started that October with only one major change from the Berlin system—in Vienna the clinic and the Institute were legally separate. Strategically, what appeared to be a concession to the local medical organizations and government authorities was actually a triumph: it allowed the analysts to train, for example, educators who had been excluded from the clinic by the government's insistence on medical-only personnel. The Institute was quickly swamped with applicants. Some came from Germany to escape the "rigid discipline" of Berlin, only to re-coil because they had underestimated the new program in Vienna.[44] Four candidates were selected for full training and soon joined the eight students who had completed their personal analyses and begun clinical work supervised by Hitschmann at the Ambulatorium.

"A warm sympathy for the fate of these unfortunates"

1925

"**I SUPPOSE** in the long run the success of a clinic would mean a general encouragement of Ψa," James Strachey wrote languidly from London to his wife Alix, still in Berlin, "and would eventually benefit us personally."[1] The British society had founded their Institute, organized a lecture series, set up a small psychoanalytic library, and hoped soon to open an outpatient clinic, John Rickman announced at the general meeting of the IPA in 1925.[2] Any London analyst interested in contributing to the outpatient effort was requested to contact the newly formed Clinic Committee. In January they tried to decide "who would give how much time to working there" and what would be a fair allocation of time. Rickman volunteered one or two hours a day, and Edward Glover and Douglas Bryan offered one hour each. In response, according to James Strachey, Jones voiced his habitual disdain. "Well," he huffed, "I'm sure it's extremely generous of all of you to offer so much of your time. As for myself, I shall be unable to give more than two hours a week."[3] Part of Jones's success was that, unless confronted by other analysts, he maintained a fairly neutral stance and allowed events like Melanie Klein's forthcoming arrival in London to unfold as though they happened without him. He had refrained from commenting when, at a meeting of the British society just a few weeks earlier, Strachey read an abstract (mailed over by Alix) of Melanie Klein's recent—and to date most controversial—paper on child analysis. Klein had made clear that psychoanalytic treatment "in the strictest sense of the word, was applicable even to very young children, though a special technique was necessary."[4] Presumably she meant interpretation of transference and attention to dreams and unconscious sexuality and aggression. At first glance, the reasoning seemed straightforward. When psychoanalytic treatment is applied to children, the theory, at least, is not much different from standard work with adults. But in practical terms the argument was tremendous: it suggested that psychoanalysts could effectively expand the use of their technique and reach out to more and more underserved populations without, for example, desexualizing their approach as Adler had done. Klein and her supporters' clinical stance would, by 1939, meet with fierce disagreement from Anna Freud who advocated for a more supportive, less intrusive approach to child analysis. Like her predecessor Hermine Hug-Hellmuth, Anna believed that classical analytic technique was inappropriate for children before puberty. But in 1925 most London analysts were energized by Melanie Klein's approach. As James Glover noted, making conscious the Repressed is never harmful, regardless of the patient's stage of development.[5] Of course these views on deep analysis of children needed to be validated by data collected first-hand, not by more theory, and fortunately the London clinic could make this possible. Meanwhile preparations for Klein's lectures in London were underway and even Karen Horney agreed to copresent a seminar paper with her contentious colleague. The group's theoretical wrangling felt merely academic since, unlike in Berlin, they weren't friends. Klein's companion and translator Alix Strachey knew this well and implored, six months later, "Why, oh why, is'nt there a Poliklinik in England?"[6]

Meanwhile, the five-year-old Poliklinik itself was facing a challenging year. Abraham fell ill; his death on Christmas day of 1925 would cast a brutal pall over the staff and patients. Max Eitingon had to take over completely. A powerful organizer and a teacher, he had joined Simmel in pursuit of the social obligations of psychoanalysis and intended to breach Berlin's class barriers and make psychoanalysis available to all who needed treatment. Paradoxically, he was enormously wealthy and just as generous: Karen Horney's daughters dubbed him "*der Rosenmax*" because he brought them roses whenever he visited.[7] But not all the psychoanalysts were sympathetic to his politics or convinced of his personal charm. Max had "considerable culture and encyclopedic interest," Sándor Radó said, but he was "totally inhibited and without a trace of originality or scientific imagination."[8] Yes, Eitingon had "paid every nickel that was spent" on Potsdamerstrasse, and later underwrote expenses for the clinic's larger and more sophisticated future facilities at 10 Wichmannstrasse. The famous inner-circle quarrels between psychoanalytic rivals emerged here, as the men vied for status as Freud's most devoted follower. Freud, it seems, always sided with Max whereas Radó, Jones, and even Ferenczi cast a dim view of their colleague. True, in the postwar inflationary economic climate, Freud sought out wealth in his endless quest to relieve the chronically impoverished psychoanalytic movement. But his attachment to Max was real, and the history of their *entente cordiale*, as he wrote later in 1931, was borne far more of genuine fondness and political beliefs than cynical rapacity. "In your quiet and irresistible way," Freud hailed Eitingon on his fiftieth birthday, "there was no task, however difficult and thankless, that you did not take upon yourself . . . and did not bring to a successful conclusion."[9]

The task of increasing the Poliklinik's clinical capacity had become urgent, and both Eitingon and Freud understood the need to staff it with socially conscious psychoanalysts. Luckily Siegfried Bernfeld, a prominent figure in Vienna's progressive education movement, agreed to move to Berlin. "Dr. Bernfeld should be taken into consideration, a first rate man, a brilliant teacher but who keeps his distance from the pathological," Freud had recommended as early as 1920.[10] The "pathological," of course, meant individual psychopathology, and Freud's figure of speech revealed a noteworthy awareness of possible left-wing opposition to individual clinical treatment. Berlin's local Communist Party in particular criticized psychoanalysis for its focus on the individuals' responsibility for personal success or failure at the expense, they thought, of the class struggle. In May the mainstream Berlin press resumed their attacks on psychoanalysis.[11] But Bernfeld, Freud suggested, was careful not to blame individuals in analysis for their own psychological condition, and instead focused on stressful social conditions that provoked the patient's anxiety. Part of the complicated political setting that persuaded Freud to send Bernfeld to Berlin was Ernst Simmel's increasingly popular Association for Socialist Physicians that included mental health in its agenda for public health activism. New publications like the *Der Sozialistische Aerzte* (The Socialist Doctor) made it all but impossible to ignore that psychoanalysts were recognized among medicine's left-wing activists. Now, if a critic accused the analysts of pandering to the rich, they could point to Simmel's inaugural issue. "Ever since the society of socialist doctors was founded twelve years ago," Simmel wrote, " we hoped to bring together all doctors who believe in the socialist idea. Today our organization has been consolidated."[12] In 1925 alone, in addition to the journal, the Socialist Physicians' Union sponsored public lectures on social hygiene laws, invited Alfred Adler to speak on individual psychology, and brought Julius Tandler from Vienna to speak on "Medicine and Socialism." Tandler, they hoped, would help them attain their primary goal, an overarching structural reorganization of urban medical care. The union's study groups explored legalizing the eight-hour work day (along with its health implications and cultural meaning), occupational health and safety, maternity leave for pregnant and nursing mothers, child labor laws, and socialized medicine. They fought for birth control and against the criminalization of abortion. Their actions took, in general, an optimistic view of the possibility of democratizing medicine and society. Albert Einstein, already an active member of the Socialist Physicians' Union, joined the artist Käthe Kollwitz to raise funds to aid the "Needy Wives and Children of Political Prisoners." As a key player in Freud's effort to boost the Poliklinik, Siegfried Bernfeld (figure 23) was a proven activist who agreed with Simmel's psychoanalytic direction, could work with Melanie Klein, and picked up where Hermine Hug-Hellmuth's work with children had left off. Psychoanalytically informed early childhood education, especially of underprivileged children, had driven much of Bernfeld's work, and he had just published *Sisyphus, or the Limits of Education*, an argument for radical reforms of traditional education predicated on an equally radical transformation of society. Bernfeld also understood that the clinic had to grow and that the training Institute was critical for this expansion. The affiliation between the clinic and the training program was, of necessity, close in Berlin and dis-

23 Siegfried Bernfeld (Special Collections, A. A. Brill Library, New York Psychoanalytic Society and Institute)

tant in Vienna. Clarence Oberndorf, visiting from New York, was truly awed by the complex organization, financing, and staffing policies of the Berlin Poliklinik and, in Vienna, the Ambulatorium.[13]

Independent of the Training Institute, the Ambulatorium had become a small but thriving autonomous treatment facility to which three important clinical centers—the educational guidance center, the department for the treatment of psychoses, and the Technical Seminar—were attached. Inevitably, the Ambulatorium became a forum for ongoing public debate concerning social services. Although the clinic asserted its financial independence from the government, municipal social welfare agencies freely referred needy clients to the psychoanalytic community. Red Vienna's health insurance societies, the law judges, and the juvenile courts, the mother-child counselors, the Matrimonial Advisory Center, and even the major Am Steinhof Hospital sent their troubled patients for treatment or evaluation. Other patients of every kind arrived from the countryside outside the city despite the highly charged political separation between social democratic Vienna, now really its own small self-governing state, and the far more conservative wider Austria. Not surprisingly, eventually even the ever diplomatic Hitschmann felt exploited by the Health Department's disingenuous maneuvers, on the one hand bestowing official legitimacy to the clinic with referrals, while on the other hand benefiting from their status as a free clinic and all the while failing to cover patient fees. The perennial dispute cropped up again on whether to continue separating mental and physical health or to join them. Barry Smith, whose Commonwealth Fund was then underwriting some of the city's largest child health programs, firmly believed they should be separated. "The medical work should include prenatal, infant, preschool and school work, and dental. . . . Too much attention is being paid to social work matters such as delinquency, dependency, illegitimacy . . . and relief rather than health," he complained.[14] Alan Gregg, Smith's counterpart at the Rockefeller Foundation, agreed that American grants should be limited to explicitly medical and scientific programs. Social services could be funded, but not under the same conditions. Gregg also recognized that Julius Tandler believed the opposite. As administrator of Red Vienna's child health programs, Tandler saw this differentiation as false and counterproductive. Tandler, however, was a skilled diplomat who kept the American dollars flowing into Vienna's children's services without sacrificing his signature fusion of health-care and social work.

The singular partnership between Tandler and the psychoanalysts remained solid, even in the face of Wagner-Jauregg's psychiatric establishment.

As chair of the powerful Society of Physicians, Wagner-Jauregg begrudged the analysts any possible infringement on their dominion and, perhaps cleverly, repeatedly stirred up the troublesome issue of lay analysis. This year was no exception, and Theodor Reik was the specific target. In March the lofty coalition of doctors issued another snarling ordinance, forbidding nonmedical practitioners from joining the clinic and threatening to close the Ambulatorium for failing to comply with their endless exacting instructions, statutes, and regulations. Once again Freud felt compelled to intercede and, in one of his long, elegantly sarcastic letters, asked Tandler to protect Reik. The magistrates' hostility toward psychoanalysis was undeniably influenced by the Society of Physicians, Freud noted, to the detriment of patients and researchers alike. Reik's credentials as an analyst were impeccable and the restrictions the doctors sought to impose on him were nothing short of malicious. "Should I refrain from referring a patient with foot pain to an orthopedist, or should I instead prescribe pain killers and electricity, just because I have made the medical diagnosis of flat feet?" The dispute escalated. Legal proceedings initiated against Reik expanded into a full-scale trial, with both Tandler and Freud testifying, to examine the application of psychoanalysis to education and child guidance. Finally, once both sides ran out of ammunition, the resilient little clinic carried on Hitschmann's "ideals for the public service" with state permission forever "subject to revocation."

As always, the Ambulatorium's waiting list of eligible patients was overextended. Wilhelm Reich, not half as impractical as his accusers would later portray him, went so far as to request small monthly contributions toward administrative expenses from patients "not entirely without means."[15] Evidently many people were turned away or simply not evaluated even for consultation. Urgent cases could wait for months before they could be treated, if at all. But at least once the efficient three-part reorganization of the clinic took effect, prospective clients could be triaged into age and diagnostically appropriate services. Unfortunately psychoanalytic diagnosis was never as precise as its practitioners (and opponents) would have wished; Helene Deutsch's amusing story reveals this disparity all too well. Her own office was on the Wollzeilgasse, about a half-hour's walk from the Ambulatorium on Pelikangasse. "How odd it is that what in my opinion is a harmless case of hysteria [on Pelikangasse]," Hitschmann quipped about their inconsistent diagnoses of Ambulatorium patients, "will often develop into a case of schizophrenia by the time it reaches the Wollzeilgasse!"[16]

At the busiest of the clinic's three departments, the Child Guidance Center, up to six analysts attended ten to twenty-five troubled child or adolescent patients each week after school and in the early evening. Between forty and seventy children yearly traveled daily by tram or bus for their analytic treatment, a one-hour appointment maintained on at least five consecutive days, for two to three months. This schedule suited both the children's daily timetable and the clinic's arrangement for sharing space with the Herzstation. But psychoanalysis was not always the treatment of choice for depressed children and sometimes the clinic's intake evaluator advised the family to take a less intensive approach. One day each week was reserved for other evaluations and consultations. An anxious child who excelled at sports activities but claimed to hate reading might be helped more by a change of after-school milieu than by psychotherapy. Changing schools altogether or enlightening the teacher might be an option for the phobic or obsessional child. And teenagers, who often went to the clinic in pairs for advice on sex or work options, formed a willing audience for evening consultations with Wilhelm Reich, then deeply involved in questions of adolescent sexuality. Teachers and parents were vital to the process; the Ambulatorium analysts largely subscribed to Anna Freud's belief that society's repression of childhood sexuality and "fear of immorality" interfered with the adult's compassion for the child. In her barely veiled criticism of Alfred Adler's desexualized character-building practitioners for whom "child analysis might [be] some special form of educational guidance," Anna Freud outlined how the anxiety of parents and teachers deprived the child of available help.[17] From there she advanced some further family-based guidelines for handling disturbed children, not yet as directive as family therapy but clearly involving parents in the assessment of their children's difficulties. In the friendly if chaotic atmosphere of the Child Guidance Center, Editha Sterba (who had recently taken over the center from Flora Kraus and the late Hermine Hug-Hellmuth) adopted Anna Freud's supportive approach. Anna Freud and Willi Hoffer were by then as familiar with the needs of Vienna's poor and working families as they were with Tandler's interventions. They had discussed child rearing with parents at the workers' education centers, and were known throughout Vienna's school and welfare districts. When social workers and district welfare workers (who had attended these discussions) visited local family homes, they found that families now viewed child analysis with fairly good will.

The year 1925 had started well at the Ambulatorium. The small staff was galvanized by the Training Institute's inauguration of its first class of fifteen students. Helene Deutsch was the director, Siegfried Bernfeld the assistant director temporarily, since he would soon move to Berlin, and Anna Freud the secretary.[18] The arduous four-term course of study was modeled after the

Berlin program and staffed by Federn, Hitschmann, Nunberg, and Reich. It was deliberately rigorous and difficult, requiring of the candidate a serious commitment of time if not money. When some shiftless applicants traveled there from Germany to worm out of the Berlin Institute's allegedly higher expectations, Hitschmann quickly denounced their opportunism and sent them home. A student's first year demanded personal analysis, clinical theory taught in lectures, seminars, case presentations and library research. Supervised clinical work, a second-year requirement, was best (though not necessarily) carried out with patients from the Ambulatorium functioning as the society's outpatient clinic.[19] Students were permitted to specialize in psychoanalytic work with adults at the regular clinic, with young people at the Child Guidance Center, or with more severely disturbed people at the special outpatient treatment center, which would not reach its peak in capability and services until 1929. To Freud, perhaps, it was not "a very big program," but to Edith Jackson, a visiting Boston pediatrician whose later letters show an impressive resolution to attend the seminar five nights a week, the pace was exhausting. Daily analysis, daily supervision with both Sterba and Walder, patient hours and language lessons, were grounds enough for napping through one of Anna Freud's lectures.[20] Reich and Bibring's Technical Seminar provided Ambulatorium analysts with an ongoing clinical forum or peer supervision. In midyear Reich's appointment as the clinic's first tenured doctor was honored by the whole society and came with a gift from Freud, a large portrait of himself, perhaps the only memento of Vienna Reich truly treasured, later displaying it in his study in Maine at least through the 1940s.

Freud's influence among Vienna's academic circles (except perhaps in the most conservative) was enhanced, then as today, by the seeming pressure to choose sides: somehow everyone was either praising or mocking psychoanalysis, proving it or refuting it, denying its scientific value or affirming its positivist grounding. Certain positivist academics even attempted to literally quantify Freud's *Group Psychology and the Analysis of the Ego* and translate it into the language of empirical reliability for Otto Neurath's seminar in social statistics.[21] At the same time, Marie Jahoda, then working with Neurath to develop the Social Democrats' Museum of Social and Economic Affairs, and Paul Lazarsfeld, the pioneering social scientist, found that these efforts were neither preposterous nor futile but rather joyous. Lazarsfeld, a childhood friend of Siegfried Bernfeld in the Youth Movement and now teaching math at the gymnasium, attended the Bühlers' influential lectures at the university and listened to Jean Piaget teach cognitive psychology at their Institute. Out of this emporium of theories in psychology came a new conceptual mix de-

scribed by contemporaries as the fourfold junction of quantitative and qual-
itative data and sociological and psychological data analysis. Traceable back
to its roots in Red Vienna, where opposites could coexist, this unique Austrian research methodology allowed for the systematic analysis of elaborate subjective experiences without forsaking their natural complexity.

The statistical data published by the Ambulatorium for that year was a case
in point.[22] Men outnumbered women as first-time applicants for psychoanalytic treatment, and more men than women continued as patients throughout the year. This gender pattern was not an oddity: more men than women
were in treatment, according to all the psychoanalytic clinics' reports
throughout Europe, and evidently in private practices as well. Of Sigmund
Freud's own forty-three recorded cases between 1907 and 1939, twenty-seven
were men and sixteen were female.[23] And as early as 1914 Karl Abraham wrote
to Freud on the subject of consumers of psychoanalysis. "My experience is
that at the moment there is only one kind of patient who seeks treatment,"
he commented, "unmarried men with inherited money."[24] For all of 1925 the
Ambulatorium's intake summaries show that over 300 prospective patients
were registered and that, of these, 182 (60 percent) of the applicants were
males and 122 (40 percent) were females.[25] These numbers cannot be con-
strued as mere isolated incidents of role reversal because the same gender
patterns were seen in each of the clinic's annual reports published before and
after that year. In all likelihood, Hitschmann's contemporaries Marie Jahoda
and Otto Neurath would have been delighted with these census-type descriptive numbers,which they called "social book-keeping," an "anti-
metaphysical" statistical style then widely used to illuminate issues of social
policy.[26] In the context of Red Vienna's policy of providing gender-neutral
social services, the fact that even before being accepted for treatment 60 percent of people desiring mental health services were men, and 40 percent were
women, was not at all unusual.

The significance of men using psychoanalytic treatment provided at the
Ambulatorium more frequently than women is brought into vivid relief by
three interesting statistical groupings where patients are categorized by occupation, diagnosis, and duration of treatment. First, in the classification of patients by occupation, seventy-seven are designated as "officials" meaning that
over 26 percent of the prospective analysands were salaried employees who
commanded a certain amount of respect and responsibility within their organizations. Second, while "housewife and persons with no occupation" take
up the next 22 percent, the category of "laborers" runs close behind at 20 percent. The term *laborer* is doubtless an even more pointedly male designation

than "*official.*" These numbers alone indicate that males constituted at least half the pool of clinic applicants. Once the sections of "independent professions (12 percent), university students (9 percent), teachers (3 percent), soldiers, servants, and school children" are added, the total number of males would expand further. Moreover, what gives the males the real advantage in this statistical picture is the third group of numbers, the psychoanalytic diagnoses noted on admission. "Impotence" was, at 12 percent, the most frequent primary psychological complaint registered in this year's consultations. Impotence weighs in three times as often as "frigidity." There are two times more diagnoses of "impotence" than of "hysteria," the clinical diagnosis perhaps most often associated with women. "Onanism" is diagnosed with the same frequency as "psychopathia" (delusional depression).

For contemporaries of the Ambulatorium psychoanalysts, then, the men's numerical advantage over women in three major areas—number, occupation, and diagnosis of applicants—did not imply male supremacy. It is difficult to appreciate that men attended treatment at the Ambulatorium without regard to the stigma of biased feminization and blame attached to psychoanalysis today. Several explanations may be offered, but the most plausible is the policy of universal access to care. For the last five years Red Vienna's health and welfare policies had ensured that, as Freud had said in 1918, "the poor man should have just as much right to assistance for his mind as he now has to the life-saving help offered by surgery." Red Vienna's urban planners had intended to ease the lives of proletarian women (with labor-saving domestic devices and community child care) and men (with onsite family supports including the marriage consultation centers). True, Tandler's maternalist policies and the network of child-centered clinics focused on ready access to mental health providers for mothers. But the clinics were built into the overall sociospatial structure of the Gemeindebauten and, therefore, the formerly private spaces of treatment rooms now became community areas. Since mental health services were included in the array of social services, men could approach treatment (for impotence, for instance) as a form of family support. Another factor was popularity. Psychoanalysis was widely discussed in fashionable newspapers read by men at their cafés. From pundits like Karl Kraus to enormously popular poets like Rilke, the prominence of psychoanalysis in the print media went far beyond the Social Democrats' local periodicals. Finally, a third consideration was the recent war and soldiers' experience with the psychoanalytic treatment of war neurosis. Impotence was one of the most prevalent effects of shell shock. "'Almost all' the neurological patients hospitalized in Budapest after World War I complained about 'their entirely damned up, or very strongly retarded libido and potency.'"[27] Impotence wholly undermined male identity, weakened men's traditional gender roles as husband and father, and deprived them of the biopsychological release of sex. In Red Vienna's culture of emerging democracy and openness, sexuality and psychoanalysis were building blocks for a better life.

The sweet funny stories from Helene Schur's days as a Viennese medical student bring alive the struggle of a "New Woman" whose personal choices for physical and psychological health were at once sanctioned by the state and condemned by tradition:

> You only had to go to a doctor [who] said that you were sick and needed an abortion. If you could say you had TB, then very prevalent in Austria, or any other *lungenspitzen catarh*, the doctor said you could have an abortion.
>
> A woman comes to me asking for an abortion. I said "Do you have a temperature?" She said "No." "Do you cough?" "No." "Do you sweat at night?" "No." So I went to the chief and asked "What should I do?" He said "Tell her to go home and talk with her friend and come back tomorrow." Next thing, she comes back and I say "Do you cough?" "Terribly." "Do you have a temperature?" "All the time." "Do you sweat at night?" "All the time." She got the abortion. That's how easy it was. There was *no* moral charge attached to it.

Perhaps less well known than her Weimarian counterpart (for whom abortion was still prohibited), the Viennese New Woman represented an educated and politically aware constituency and a significant focus of the government's renewal efforts. Housing, public parks, and an improved urban sanitation system: in almost every aspect of city life Red Vienna's standards of living were climbing. Relative economic stability had finally come to Vienna and to Austria at large, along with a friable but far-reaching democratization of the political system. Free and fairly destigmatized access to health and social services encouraged the creation and maintenance of families. In the dynamic organization of Julius Tandler's Public Welfare Office, social services represented the filter through which the government translated its family, hygiene, and educational policies into practice. Programs revolved largely around an idea of the "good family," an orderly patriarchal family with the breadwinning father and the caretaking mother of children. A sort of broad-shouldered female version of the heroic worker, serene in her capacity to lift and protect an armful of children, the good mother (Motherhood herself) was ubiquitously displayed in public sculptures. Popular weekly magazines, in contrast, featured the image of the slick New Woman, the voter citizen for whom the rational kitchen had been measured out, comrade to her husband, friend to her children. Since 1920 journals like Bettauer's *Wochenschrift* had helped women analyze for themselves the contradiction between monogamous reproductive partnership and the sexual freedom men were enjoying. Posters, pamphlets, and colorful leaflets handed out at the clinics featured photographs and stories by revisionist writers entreating women to alter traditional gender roles and promoting an image of the self-assured *garçonne* (boy-girl) with utilitarian loose-fitting clothes, sensible shoes, and bobbed hair.[28] Obviously the inconsistency between these two contradictory images of womanhood was inescapable, and the conflict was played out repeatedly in both the smaller and larger episodes of Viennese political culture. No more dramatic indicator of this contradiction can be found than in the experiences of young women who, in October, cheered the court when activist writer Hugo Bettauer was acquitted on charges of offending public morality—and, in September, mourned in front of 7 Langegasse, where he was assassinated by a former Nazi, Otto Rothstock.[29] As young mothers, and for that reason consumers of family services, these same women were caught in a kind of partisan tug-of-war along ideological lines, pitting "social worker as arrogant agent of social control" against "social worker as informed agent of an assisting government." Could the government genuinely balance its obligation to protect vulnerable citizens, like children, with the families' need for privacy and autonomy? The mothers generally thought so, but only the broadest access to social services (such that everybody from teachers to actors to children of unemployed waiters could socialize in the waiting room of a psychoanalytic clinic or a detoxification center) would prove it. This, of course, was the Ambulatorium's mission, but the entire history of Red Vienna was remarkable for its succession of similar community-based therapeutic ventures. For Helen Schur, then barely on the fringes of psychoanalysis, Red Vienna was a time when "you did something for people who didn't have money. Money didn't play such a great role. Nobody was really rich, but they cared more about others."

When Paul Lazarsfeld located the Institute for Social Psychology (Wirtschaftpsychologische Forschungstelle) within Karl and Charlotte Bühler's Psychological Institute, the University of Vienna at last recognized the potential for modern data collection in the social sciences.[30] Activist, curious, and friends with intellectual politicians like Otto Bauer and Käthe Leichter, Lazarsfeld and his associates sought to link their social policy findings to the needs of workers. The sponsor of an outpouring of research unequaled until the advent of Columbia University's Bureau of Applied Social Research in the

1940s, the Institute for Social Psychology produced studies of domestic servants, home workers, adolescent school dropouts, and, most significantly, for Red Vienna, the famous *Marienthal* study of unemployed adults. There were free clinics, community outreach programs, mother-child centers, marriage consultation centers, abortion counseling, and school-based child and adolescent services.

Alfred Adler's own child guidance clinic was one of the city's most successful practice-research endeavors. Late in 1925 the Viennese town council proposed the establishment of these child guidance clinics in each of Vienna's municipal districts. Adler's signature therapeutic model of individual [sychology would be practiced in local nursery schools, in grade schools, and in welfare work. The number of autonomous educational guidance offices grew to twenty-two, and there were as many as twenty-eight free psychotherapy centers around the city. Most of the psychologists who directed these clinics were already members or associates of Adler's Society for Individual Psychology and worked there without pay. Whether at the clinic he oversaw, at university lectures, or at evening classes held at the Viennese Volkshochschule (adult education center), this opportunity for training in the person-in-community methodology with Adler himself drew scores of doctors, teachers, social workers, and students worldwide. Viennese elementary school teachers brought their problem students, along with the child's parents, directly to the training sessions and interviewed them, presenting the cases for discussion and expert consultation before the participatory audience. Among Adler's most conscientious young interns, Lydia Sicher developed an outpatient clinic for adults and children. Like the new service her colleague Emil Mattauschek would assemble in 1930 at the Clinic of Psychiatry and Neurology at the Vienna General Hospital, Sicher's staff shared meeting facilities and treatment rooms with another outpatient therapeutic facility, the Mariahilfer clinic.

When *Wayward Youth*, August Aichorn's slim but seminal volume on the treatment of adolescent delinquency appeared with a foreword by Freud, the recurrent claim that Freud was oblivious to the political world lost another measure of credibility. Aichorn's lively little book relied on case examples of teenagers from the group residences he supervised, Ober-Hollabrunn from 1918 to 1920 and St. Andrä from 1920 to 1922. Thoroughly psychoanalytic as a model for treating disturbed adolescents (many of whom were also poor or without families), the theoretical treatise proposed the two-pronged approach of insight-oriented therapy and community responsibility to remedy the consequences of social disenfranchisement. Aichorn's "attitude to his charges had its source in a warm sympathy for the fate of these unfortunates," Freud wrote in his encouraging foreword, and he applauded the "great social value" of Aichorn's teaching and social work with children.[31] Much later, Anna Freud would reiterate her father's praise and note in particular that Aichorn's efforts confirmed how "all individual development, whether on social or dissocial lines, was the result of interaction between innate and environmental factors."[32] But 1925 was not the first time Freud declared his support of a project's underlying political mission, nor even of a class analysis of criminal behavior. Franz Alexander, whose own psychoanalytic theories of criminology were widely read by Chicago psychotherapists treating teen gang members, laughed at claims that Freud neglected sociological factors. The social democratic psychoanalysts simply did not believe that forensic psychology alone solved crime. From his student days in Freud's monthly seminar, Alexander remembered illustrating the unconscious motives of delinquency with the case of an obsessed car fan who repeatedly took long taxi rides, way beyond his means as a waiter, and inevitably landed in prison. To which Freud responded:

I do not see how this case can throw light upon the essential problem of criminality. If your patient had been the son of a millionaire, he might have become a record-breaker and as such a national hero. Only because of his social position and because he was a poor waiter, he could not give expression to his compulsion or hobby in a legal way.[33]

"Although absent from the opening of the Clinic, I am all with you"

1926

THROUGHOUT the early years of the free clinics, psychoanalysts in various countries followed a well-organized sequence, a "logical order," Ernest Jones would say, of first constituting a local society amongst themselves, next issuing a clinical journal, and finally organizing a training institute. After 1920 a fourth component was added, the outpatient clinic. The Berlin and Vienna societies had theirs and now so too would the British. "The chief news from London is good," Jones had told Freud just before Christmas of 1925, "an old patient of mine has given two thousand pounds to . . . start a clinic early in the New Year."[1] Jones had reason to be excited. This tremendous financial donation from Pryns Hopkins, an American industrialist named by the British society's as their own "Honorary Almoner," allowed the analysts to open their new clinic "for the purpose of rendering psycho-analytical treatment available for ambulatory patients of the poorer classes."[2] Freud was delighted. Not wasting any opportunity to bash the United States, he complimented Jones on his "good news. . . . I have always said that America is useful for nothing but giving money. Now it has at least fulfilled this function. . . . I am happy that it happened for London. . . . My best wishes for the thriving of your institute!"[3] Eitingon too sent a telegram with congratulations from the Berlin society.

The London Clinic of Psychoanalysis was officially inaugurated on Freud's seventieth birthday, May 6, 1926. At eight o'clock in the morning John Rickman welcomed the first patient to the newly leased premises at

24 The London Clinic for
Psychoanalysis on Gloucester Place
(Photo by Claudine Rausch)

36 Gloucester Place in the center of the city, London West 1 (figure 24). Other patients were delayed, however, until the following fall. At first the analysts occupied only a portion of the Gloucester Place townhouse and sublet the upper two floors. Building construction frustrated their attempts to develop a daily clinical schedule, and finally they admitted that necessary renovations would postpone their prospects for a fully functioning clinic until September. In spite of that Jones grew increasingly eager as opening day approached and dashed off note after note, barely containing his excitement in anticipation of Tuesday, September 24. Over their twenty years of fellowship Freud, who claimed to detest ceremonies, had come to realize how much Jones loved them and greeted his triumph with impeccable courtesy. "Although absent from the opening of the Clinic tomorrow, I am all with you and feel the importance of the day," Freud wrote to his friend.[4] The British society then formally delegated responsibility for the clinic to a board of managers. Ernest Jones greeted well-wishers as director of both the clinic and the Institute, while Edward Glover assumed the position of assistant director, and Drs. Douglas Bryan, Estelle Cole, David Eder, William Inman, John Rickman, Robert M. Rigall, and William Stoddart made up the remaining staff. Sylvia Payne and Marjorie Brierley, the only two women on the senior staff, interrupted their professional work to assume "domestic" responsibilities and oversee the care of the

building, supervise the maintenance and cleaning crew, and allocate the treatments rooms. And finally Warburton Brown, Marjorie Franklin, Lionel Penrose, and Adrian Stephen were appointed as clinical assistants allowed to conduct psychoanalysis under supervision. Jones was particularly pleased that he and Glover had arranged the control of analyses because the clinic would now be legitimately linked to the Institute.[5]

Later in November, in the last year of her quest for a permanent home for herself and her ideas, Melanie Klein arrived in London. Her relocation from Berlin could not have been better timed. The London clinic was just starting up and Klein was ideally prepared to contribute to its success. In some ways her decision to accept Jones's invitation to join the British society was tinged with regret, and she added a little goading as well. "Simmel is said to have made a positive pronouncement on my work and its prospects for the future," she wrote in her acceptance letter, "and to have expressed the hope that I will return with new stimuli from London to Berlin."[6] Instead she took to the London atmosphere well and stayed there, as always controversial, until the end of her life. After more than six years of strife surrounding her analysis of children in Berlin, Klein could now clarify her "ideas connected with education" and base them on "notes from the analysis of a child aged five years" with far less fear of her colleague's ill will.[7]. Melanie Klein was a diligent note keeper and attentive to the minutest details of her small patients' words and drawings. Her London work with "Alan," "Julia," "George," and "Richard" formed the core of *A Narrative of Child Analysis*. Like her democratic colleagues in Berlin and Vienna, Klein treated at least one patient at no charge daily or performed an equivalent service to the clinic. She kept notes of these appointments in tiny jewel-like pocket diaries, the identical size every year from 1923 until 1946, with maroon leather covers so worn they seem black, indistinguishable from each other except for the year stamped in gold. Many of her patients were children for whose play therapy she ordered painted wooden toys from a special supplier in Germany. The children's fees were noted, in Klein's own abbreviated German mixed at times with a touch of Hungarian, with particular reference to the accounts she maintained (until 1926) for the Poliklinik. "I am obligated to the Polik. for 26 marks, 6 k. for September," she scrawled on October 31, 1924.[8] She wrote in black ink with a classic fountain pen, but her penmanship was erratic and often sloppy. Some days she tracked her accounts in hours of service due to the clinic. "For the week [of May] 24–31," she noted on June 3, "I am responsible for 14 hours, 20" (figure 25). The same system of clinic duty applied now that Klein was in London. She also recognized that, as at her other clinics, candidates who could not afford to pay for their didactic analysis were seen as "clinic patients" by training faculty in lieu of the now customary outpatient responsibility. All told, the clinic staff treated about twenty-five patients daily. As at the other clinics, men and women of all ages and occupations lined up for the initial consultations. Arriving there on the advice of physicians or family, the prospective patients waited for intake interviews held alternately by Jones and Glover one day each week, Tuesdays at 5:30 P.M. An astounding one hundred such consultations were volunteered in the clinic's first nine months and, equally surprising, almost all the examinees became full analytic cases, with many staying on past the initial six months of treatment. The London clinic never broadcast its services to the public and never even advertised in local newspapers for its first ten years, but still the requests so far exceeded the staff's capacity that their waiting list reached back a full two years.

To avert a potentially overwhelming demand, the London analysts drew up a design for a waiting list before the first year was out. Treatment at the clinic was free of cost from the start and remains so even today. The waiting

 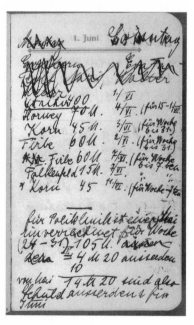

25 Melanie Klein's agenda from 1924 and a page of entries showing her earnings, patient hours, and Poliklinik dues (Wellcome Library, London)

list was divided into three rubrics: urgent cases, cases particularly well suited to students, and the perennial remaining cases. Since the entire enterprise revolved around the intake procedure, Jones and Glover were soon compelled to establish three more categories of patients not placed on the waiting list. An intake interviewer's purview is very broad, listening as impartially to the neurotic complainers as to the florid psychotics but mostly to generally well-balanced people overwhelmed by a wide variety of daily crises. Thus the first of the new categories, "on the spot advice," classified mostly parents and children with sudden school crises; arrests for petty crimes with an obvious psychological overlay like kleptomania, or perhaps domestic violence. The second category, "consultation with the patient's regular doctor;" was for complaints of ambulatory headache, asthma, epilepsy, narcolepsy, digestive disorders, and other occasional inquiries about somnambulism and tics. Finally the third group of patients, those whose presenting problems would be better helped at another medical facility, came with heart disease, drug addiction, and severe schizophrenia. The staff, who met quarterly, were satisfied with the therapeutic results and modestly estimated that some patients had been cured and several others "greatly benefited."[9]

In Vienna Grete Lehner Bibring and Eduard Kronold had teamed up with Reich and Hitschmann, the four together now constituting the professional staff of the analytic clinic in full force. Richard Sterba joined them officially after presenting his initiation paper "On Latent Negative Transference," which Reich found very impressive, to a Wednesday evening society meeting. This paper granted Sterba full membership in the society, but his admittance also gave the Ambulatorium an outstandingly loyal practitioner who would preserve the clinic's integrity until its unsolicited demise in 1938. Still, the team was more immediately concerned with the need to screen every prospective child, adolescent, and adult patient at intake and to engage them as soon as possible in psychoanalytic treatment. The highest numbers of children treated in the Ambulatorium's history were screened in 1926 and 1927. Even children under age ten (and elderly people ages sixty-one to seventy) were seen and counted, though they represented only a small fraction of the Ambulatorium's total patient population. As usual more males were treated than females, with about seven boys and five girls regularly accounted for. Little in their clinical experience had prepared the analysts to take on child cases, the "little patients from the ghetto," as the American Helen Ross said, and most of the analysts except for Hermine Hug-Helmuth and Anna Freud were novices.[10] One day Jenny Waelder-Hall, a pediatrician at the Kaiser Franz-Josef Hospital for five and a half years and already analyzing adults at the Herzstation, there took on her first child case, a young boy initially interviewed by Anna Freud. Fortunately the hospital was nearby, so while her medical responsibilities did not accommodate the clinic's odd afternoon hours, Waelder-Hall still opted to start her case the very next day. Anton, a shy nine-year-old school boy, experienced such profound night terrors that his school performance was affected badly and eventually al his family's routines were interrupted. Recurring images of violent beating scenes between his parents intruded into his sleep. He was haunted by the agonizing mental picture of a foiled attempt to rescue his mother at age three, thwarted when suddenly he fell—he was told later—badly injured, and the whole family landed at the police station.[11] Banned from games with his little playmates, Anton developed a lively fantasy life of invisible daytime friends and nighttime enemies. The delicate clinical dilemma posed by this case—how to relieve a child of exactly those unconscious fantasies that permitted his conscious daytime survival—impressed upon the child analysts the need for clinical oversight and guidance.

The concept of a seminar in psychoanalytic technique, by now Reich and Bibring's standard method for discussing adult patients, was easily transferred to child analysis. Since Anna Freud was the natural choice to lead the new weekly supervisory seminar, Monday evenings were assigned and Edith Buxbaum, Editha Sterba, August Aichorn, Grete Lehner Bibring, Marianne Rie Kris, Annie Reich, Anny Angel-Katan, Dorothy Burlingham, and Willi Hoffer joined the project, "On the Technique of Child Analysis." "So many people heard about our seminar and started to come that the meetings were full," Jenny Waelder-Hall recalled, "Kris, Waelder, everybody who was somebody and even nobody, came."[12] For Dorothy Burlingham, the seminar was one of her first official introductions to the life of Vienna's psychoanalysts. Anna Freud's future life companion Dorothy was the sad, rich daughter of Louis Comfort Tiffany and had recently brought her four children to Vienna. As her interest in psychoanalysis grew beyond the need for personal relief, she started to attend the seminar. Most meetings were still held at the Ambulatorium, she remembered, in the "smoke-filled lecture room of the *Herzstation* in the University District . . . a center for heart research during the day and psychoanalytic headquarters come evening."[13] But space at these "headquarters" had become so crowded by 1926 that the hospital administrators threatened, once again, to evict the clinic. In due time the Ambulatorium and the Institute were allowed to stay while the society meetings moved a few blocks away. Anna held her own seminars in a separate set of rooms on the Berggasse. The courtyard window of her waiting room was straight across from her father's, but Freud never joined the group because, as Jenny Waelder-Hall said, "he knew if he were present, none of us would function."[14] Challenged by the accelerating numbers of child patients referred by school teachers and beholden to the Ambulatorium's mission, the original seminar grew with wildfire speed and had to be reorganized into three separate, more manageable courses. The range of cases heard in the technical seminar on child analysis reflected the census of Vienna's working families, from Annie Reich's case of a runaway child prostitute to Dorothy Burlingham's attempt to involve an unschooled mother, a janitor, in the sex education of her eight-year-old daughter. Outside their common concern for the public good, very little had prepared the analysts for the class issues welling up in their work at the clinic. The eight-year-old girl was a perfect example of their naïveté. When Dorothy advised the mother to discuss sex with her daughter and explain "why it is useful and not dangerous," Waelder-Hall recalled from the case conference, the janitor let loose. Nasty pictures might be fine for the fancy analyst's children, she railed, but she cleaned a house full of bachelors, and who knows what her little girl would do! The small patient fled the Ambulatorium and just as fast the analysts realized that they had to acquire a whole range of new skills for working with families, school teachers, guidance counselors, and social workers. Small wonder that Adler's desexualized child counseling was meeting with such success among the Social Democrats. Adler's course on psychoanalytic pedagogy flourished precisely because it abated the prevailing discomfort (then as now) with the ideas of childhood sexuality, aggression, and fantasy among teachers of young children. Childhood aggression was viewed less critically by August Aichorn, also a member of the seminar, and his empathic responses to troubled children made him a vivid teacher. Aichorn led a seminar subsection on adolescence and delinquency, and ran it from his own little clinic in the basement at 18 Pelikangasse.

Because they were so poor, indigent and working-class adolescents were usually the last patients seen by municipal guidance counselors even though, as Aichorn and Reich knew well, their distress signaled more than just a troubled stop on the way to adulthood. Even capable parents became abstracted when their teenagers talked about the inevitable anguish of growing up, a personal torment that seemed to engulf all of family life in suffering. Aichorn and Adler, in contrast, were fascinated by adolescent depression and, now that their therapeutic approaches were better known, other therapists started building on their methods. As it happened, Professor Schroeder of Leipzig University's neurology institute decided to open an adolescent clinic in November. To start the new polyclinic and observation center for young criminal offenders, Schroeder first convinced hospital officials to set aside one large room, for visitors, and several smaller treatment rooms. His next addition was a Sunday afternoon lecture series, where local psychiatrists gave talks about their work at the adjoining observation center. Of course there were other facilities near Leipzig for girls and boys, but none provided treatment for trauma or complex oedipal situations. Schroeder's clinic was grounded in the methods Aichorn had published one year earlier, in *Wayward Youth*, and on Bernfeld's reports from the Kinderheim Baumgarten.[15] The Leipzig therapists identified with psychoanalysis and many were, in all likelihood, candidates in training at the Berlin Poliklinik. When Teresa Benedek, who moved easily between Berlin and Leipzig, took over direction of the local study group in October, she hoped that the sociologically oriented psychoanalyst Erich Fromm and Frieda Fromm-Reichmann, both of Heidelberg, would join either her group or the newly formed Frankfurt subsection of the Berlin society. Even the press was aware of activity within the psychoanalytic movement. At the top of the *Leipziger Volkszeitung*'s edition of October 13, 1926, an editor compiled a banner of flattering quotes about Freud on the occasion of his birthday. "There is a sociological aspect to psychoanalysis," the newspaper wrote, "which is sympathetic to social progress."[16] In the end Frankfurt's small society, with Clara Happel and Karl Landauer, emerged as historically more important than Leipzig, in no small part because it had affiliated with the distinguished Institute for Social Research.

On special occasions like his seventieth birthday that year, Freud helped out with the Ambulatorium's funding and turned over much of the 30,000 marks, about $4,200, collected by his colleagues toward a Psychoanalytic Jubilee Fund for the upkeep of the Vienna clinic (figure 26). Freud was pleased by this fund, raised largely by his pupils and his Hungarian colleague Sándor Ferenczi in lieu of gifts, and distributed its assets trusting he had been "faithful to the intentions of the donors."[17] Setting aside his cranky birthday mood, Freud thanked contributors like Marie Bonaparte whose imperial fortunes would survive even the economic crash of 1929. Freud teased her with his newest social democratic badge, the diploma certifying his honorary citizenship of Vienna (while subtly prodding her to fund a clinic in Paris). But Freud's impulse to support the Ambulatorium was not merely charitable. The redistributive economic policies of Red Vienna's financial decision makers, Robert Danneberg and Hugo Breitner, had taken hold, and surplus funds were invariably bestowed on institutions of social welfare. Vienna's independent status had served it well. "The absence of slums, the clean streets, the

PROF. DR FREUD

WIEN IX., BERGGASSE 19
20.Mai 1926.

Sehr geehrter Herr Kollega!

Zu meinem siebzigsten Geburtstag wurde
mir von dem stellvertretenden Leiter unserer
Internationalen Vereinigung ein namhafter
Geldbetrag als

"Psychoanalytischer Jubiläumsfond"

übergeben. Ich habe denselben zum grösseren
Teil dem Internationalen Psychoanalytischen
Verlag, zum kleineren dem Wiener Ambulatorium
zugewisen und hoffe, damit den Intentionen der
Spender gerecht geworden zu sein. Ich weiss,
dass Sie sich als Komitémitglied um das Zustande-
kommen dieser Sammlung besonders bemüht haben
und danke Ihnen herzlich dafür.

Ihr sehr ergebener

Freud

26 Sigmund Freud's Circular Letter apportioning funds to the Vienna Ambulatorium (Archives of the Sigmund Freud Foundation, Vienna)

well-tended parks . . . new workers' apartments and a number of very interesting schools for children and adults" impressed a visiting young American psychoanalytic candidate named Muriel Gardiner.[18]

Muriel Gardiner would become one of the most subtle and energetic antifascist fighters of the era. By the summer of 1934, with the fascists gunning people down on street corners, Gardiner would become an extraordinary clandestine rescuer and eventually, back in the United States, protector of the Social Democrat Otto Bauer until his death. But in the mid-1920s she was still attending medical school and psychoanalytic seminars. Her memoirs of life on both sides of psychoanalysis have the effect of introducing today's reader to the easy modes of exchange between Viennese psychoanalysts and even between analysts and patients. "Many features of analysis at that time would now be disapproved of in the United States," she wrote in her 1983 memoirs. Gardiner was born in 1901 to a wealthy Midwestern family. She was a Durant scholar at Wellesley, active in socialist politics on campus and founder of the Intercollegiate Liberal League with friends from Radcliffe and Harvard. In

1922 she moved to Europe, first for graduate work at Oxford and then to study psychoanalysis and medicine in Vienna. Her arrival coincided with Tandler's new social welfare system, and her interest in applying psychoanalytic understanding to education agreed with the mission of the Ambulatorium. At the time analysts "stated their opinions and tastes more openly and often discussed them freely with patients," she observed, adding that they were "less stringent in avoiding social contact."[19] For example, Bruno Bettelheim first met his future analyst Richard Sterba in public, social surroundings and settled practical matters like the daily appointment hour and the fee quite in the open.[20] For Bettelheim as for other analysands, pretreatment interviews with their prospective analysts were encouraged, even habitual, and were generally friendly experiences. Often the initial contact was an introduction by Anna Freud and Paul Federn to the atmosphere of camaraderie that was especially strong among the lay analysts. Erik Erikson, though generally ambivalent about his analysis with Anna Freud, remembered that she knitted, in session, a little blanket for his newborn son. Relaxing the social interactions between analyst and patient had political implications as well. Muriel Gardiner felt she could freely disclose her clandestine activities to her analyst Ruth Brunswick, not only because of the generally well-respected imperative of patient confidentiality but also because, she said, "I knew she shared my views."[21] And, most notably, Freud's own casework was striking for its blithe disregard of his own technical recommendations in the areas of anonymity (not revealing personal reactions), neutrality (not being directive), and confidentiality (not sharing patient information with a third party). He shook hands with his patients at the start and finish of each session and, in almost every arena, consistently deviated from his own instructions published in 1913. Each one of Freud's cases recorded between 1907 and 1939 reveals at a minimum his tendency to urge patients to take specific actions in their lives and also his pleasure in chatting, joking, and even gossiping with them. Much of this remains clinically controversial and, in terms of Freud's perhaps prurient curiosity and experimentation, has led to often justified accusations of impropriety. But his overt concern for his patients and his sociability emerge as well. Even earlier in his life, in 1905, when Freud's income barely covered his own family expenses, he helped out Bruno Goetz, a young Swiss poet with eye trouble and severe headaches. Freud read his poems with admiration, asked some questions and then said:

> "Now my student Goetz, I will not analyze you. You can become most happy with your complexes. As far as your eyesight is concerned, I shall write you a pre-

scription." He sat down at his desk and wrote. In the meantime, he asked me: "They told me you have hardly any money and live in poverty. Is that correct?"

I told him my father received a very small salary as a teacher, I had four younger brothers and sisters, and I survived by tutoring and selling newspaper articles.

"Yes," he said. "Severity against oneself sometimes might be good, but one should not go too far. When did you last have a steak?"

"I think about four weeks ago."

"That is what I thought," he said and rose from his desk. "Here is your prescription." And he added some more advice, but then he almost became somewhat shy. "I hope you don't mind, but I am an established doctor and you are a young student. Please accept this envelope and allow me to play your father this time. A small fee for the joy you have brought me with your poems and the story of your youth. Let us see each other again. *Auf Wiedersehn!*"

Imagine! When I arrived in my room and opened the envelope, I found 200 Kronen. I was so moved I broke out in tears.[22]

"In your private political opinions you might be a Bolshevist," wrote Ernest Jones to Freud that year, "but you would not help the spread of Ψ to announce it." [23] Jones, as always both deferential and impulsive, tinged their correspondence with a particularly emotional quality. Here, he bursts out with his own discovery of the political nature of Freud's thought. The spokesman for psychoanalysis divulges exactly that for which he castigates Freud. But he does not repudiate it. He understands Freud's fascination with change and is torn between loyalty to the man and loyalty to the psychoanalytic "cause."

The cause itself was far more politically focused than Jones understood it. By 1926 the IPA's plans for a network of training institutes and free clinics, laid out in Budapest in September 1918, had moved forward. The alliance between socialism and psychoanalysis was sealed in Berlin when Ernst Simmel was simultaneously awarded chairmanships of the Association for Socialist Physicians and the German Psychoanalytic Association (Deutsche Psychoanalytische Gesellschaft or DPG). Next, Siegfried Bernfeld and Otto Fenichel, still two of the movement's most politically dynamic members, officially joined the Poliklinik after leaving Vienna for Berlin. In July Bernfeld summarized their left-wing position in a comprehensive report delivered to the Socialist Physicians' Union. The address, called "On Socialism and Psychoanalysis," was attended by Barbara Lantos and Fenichel and most members of the Children's Seminars, and was published in a concurrent issue of *The*

Socialist Physician, the journal of the Socialist Physicians Union.[24] Bernfeld's essay made the case that psychoanalysis can have genuine meaning for the proletariat, but only if it is put to practical use in the class struggle. At a time when both socialism and psychoanalysis aimed to contribute to the nation's health, medicine continued to flourish in the private hands of the bourgeoisie. Once medical practice has been completely restructured and redirected toward the working classes, then psychoanalysis would follow. Perhaps psychoanalysis did not yet benefit the public in general as much as individuals, but it did explain some phenomena (like family conflict or group dynamics) that social science could not. Logically, the insights of psychoanalysis could be brought to bear on the class struggle, with the goal of individual psychological health. To members of the Association for Socialist Physicians like Heinrich Meng, Margarete Stegmann, Angel Garma, and the Viennese psychoanalyst-politician Josef Friedjung, Bernfeld's statement was the clearest expression to date of the argument that the two streams of psychoanalysis (the theory and the practice) have equally powerful influence. In other words, theory and practice together had a political impact that neither element alone could achieve. And as some younger DPG members and candidates, the group otherwise known as the Children's Seminars, saw it, Bernfeld had written their song. From 1924, when the Children's Seminars had first convened, until October 1933, when they were all forcibly disbanded, the group held 168 meetings in one another's homes.[25] Most of the meetings were devoted, naturally, to psychoanalysis and politics. But Bernfeld could explain the exact nature of a bridge between psychoanalysis and dialectical materialism that even Fenichel and Reich, who visited the Soviet Union on study tours for that purpose, were unable to build.

The enormous challenge of remaining the leader of a rapidly changing four-pronged organization—the IPA, the Berlin society, the Verlag, and the Poliklinik—fell to Max Eitingon with his masterful administrative skills. "It is very reassuring to me to know that the direction of the various organizations remains in Eitingon's hands," Ferenczi responded to Freud's equally reassuring note on the Poliklinik's post-Abraham fate.[26] On January 12 a memorial was held for Abraham, the founder and first president of the Berlin society. After dignified speeches by Eitingon, Sachs, and Radó, Abraham's portrait was placed on permanent display in the clinic's conference room.[27] Ferenczi cheered on his *Liebe Freunde* (dear friends), confident that together Eitingon and Simmel's talents would find the right solution to the administrative problems left by Abraham's death.[28] Eitingon quickly appointed a presidium of Simmel, Radó, and Horney until elections could be scheduled.

Loewenstein left for Paris and Alfred Gross, his replacement, moved on to Simmel's inpatient program, the Sanatorium Schloss Tegel, only to be replaced by Dr. Witt. By then the Poliklinik staff consisted of the directors plus seven paid assistants, ten senior candidates, and about fifteen members of the Psychoanalytic Society. Each one allocated four hours daily to clinic patients whom they treated either at the Poliklinik or in their private offices. Four additional unpaid assistants each volunteered the same four treatment hours weekly at the clinic. This number four seemed to be a standard of sorts since each patient regularly visited the clinic four hours each week.

Can individual treatment be shortened or speeded up? Is the analytic hour sixty minutes or forty-five, or can it vary? How many days each week are necessary for effective analysis? Just how many months should an analysis last to be complete? Are such decisions best made by the patient or by the clinician? Like the Freud-Ferenczi epistolary debates, these moral and practical controversies were argued often, though inconclusively, by the Poliklinik staff. Though Freud had foretold in 1918 that analysts would "have to mix some alloy with the pure gold of analysis" once free treatment became widespread, the Poliklinik staff found no suitable substitute for the analytic method and condemned as metaphorically "useless . . . the copper of direct suggestion." They refused to implement a priori time limits on treatment regardless of diagnosis. And while they experimented extensively with the concrete parameters of treatment, their sole definition of the course of analysis was "the process Freud created." To justify length of treatment, Eitingon referred to the Budapest speech and compared long-term therapy of the neuroses to the treatment of other chronic illnesses like tuberculosis: "the fuller and the deeper the success, the longer does the treatment take."[29] Active treatment was an innovation, an extension of psychoanalysis perhaps, but not a replacement. Though he mocked shorter-term treatment as one of those "hyper-ingenious, forcible interventions," which achieve little since they deviate from the path of the actual pathology, Eitingon nevertheless urged analysts to investigate fractionary, that is, time-limited or intermittent, regimens.[30] "He liked to experiment with interruptions," Franz Alexander recalled, "and the expression 'fractioned analysis' was frequently used."[31] A man of some contradiction and "a very charming character," from Alix Strachey's perspective, Eitingon viewed length of treatment as patient driven or, failing that, as a mutual decision between therapist and patient. He enjoyed developing advantageous *fraktionäre* schedules devised for patients like Josephine Dellisch, the impoverished Swiss schoolteacher who had befriended Anna Freud. "A month at Xmas, 3 weeks at Easter, etc., to suit her school-time—beginning in

December," Alix recorded.[32] The Poliklinik staff aimed for flexible solutions to practical clinical dilemmas, and the duration of the clinical hour and length of treatment were subjected to as much debate, or more, in the 1920s as today. Daily sessions were ideal, but since so many of the patients were working, analysis three times a week was more widespread. By 1926 the three-hour weekly treatment schedule was found generally adequate and retained as standard practice in Berlin. Ten years later, as founder of the new Chicago Institute for Psychoanalysis, which he modeled on his Berlin experience, Alexander still insisted on flexibility, that treatment be adjusted to the patient and not the other way around. Even if it meant curtailing the analytic experience, he said, "it is advantageous at times to change the intensity of the therapy by alternating the frequency of the interviews or by temporary interruption of the treatment."[33]

How long should an analytic session last? If treatment is an everyday part of life, an hour like any other work hour of the day, then maybe a thirty-minute session is just as natural a unit of time as the full sixty-—minute hour. Sixty minutes had been the standard length of a session until the 1920s when Karl Abraham and the Poliklinik staff took it up as yet another controversial debate. At first the analysts intended to "systematically and in every case reduce the length of the analytic sitting from one hour to half-an-hour," Eitingon wrote, because of their patients' crowded work and family schedules. Instead, each patient's session was set individually, with a total amount of minutes ranging from forty-five to sixty minutes. The deciding factor was the patient's responsiveness to "discipline"—perhaps another word for motivation. For one so accepting of mankind's Rousseau-like natural self-regulatory talent, Eitingon's statement that "despite their neuroses . . . [self-disciplined people] are not seldom to be found in Prussian Germany amongst civil servants and others" was sarcastic at best. Is the "discipline" a natural internal human motivation toward health? Or is it a response to external motivation, such as a fractionary schedule? Which would make greater sense clinically? As their friends from the Frankfurt School would say, the answer lay in the dialectic. An analytic interview, or session, could last from forty-five to the full sixty minutes since, in theory at least, only a balance of the practitioner's clinical assessment and the patient's discipline would lead to an appropriate scheme. Nevertheless according to Alexander, Eitingon's initial experiments with half-hour interviews proved "unsatisfactory" and what would become the standard fifty-minute analytic hour was instituted as the official norm. Patients were seen three to four times weekly, or more, with no time limits preestablished for ending the analysis. The Poliklinik was open from 8:00 A.M. to 8:00 P.M. daily. About three hundred analytic (full) hours were allocated weekly to clinic patients.

The possibility of modifying the length of the clinical hour also attracted the Viennese. In particular the staff of the Ambulatorium's later experimental Department for Borderline Cases and Psychosis found that the full sixty-minute analytic hour produced insupportable agitation in the patient. Reducing the session by a mere fourth, or fifteen minutes, seemed to contain the individual's anxiety and generally yield a more productive interview. But it would take at least another twenty years for the abridged time frame, the fifty-minute hour, to enter into the mainstream of psychoanalytic culture. After the Second World War the French psychoanalyst Sacha Nacht reintroduced the shorter forty-five minute hour and the three-time-weekly treatment schedule to willing practitioners at the clinic of the Société Psychanalytique de Paris.[34]

Since measuring the clinical hour had come under such scrutiny, naturally the duration of a complete course of treatment was examined too. How long should psychoanalysis last? How rigorously should analyst and patient hold to the daily schedule? Sándor Ferenczi had explored the clinical theory behind "fractionary analysis," the interval-based schedule now considered a precursor to today's "short-term" planned treatment and Eitingon had applied it.[35] At the same time, Ernst Simmel reintroduced experiments with effective, two- to three-session treatment he had started during the war. Later taken up in Vienna, fractionary analysis was not interminable but could be interrupted or divided into segments dictated by the patient's life. A pregnancy, a resistance to clinical change, military conscription were just some of the indications for legitimately interrupting the course of treatment. Unlike other therapeutic actions, a deliberate "fractionation" signaled either the end of treatment or simply a hiatus during which patients would practice (perhaps presaging Margaret Mahler's developmental theory) the options gained from new insights and then return—or not—as they chose. Analysts and their patients could set a mutually acceptable date for "termination," the planned end of treatment. Of course, the method of fractionary analysis was statistically satisfying as well because it allowed the analysts to document and count a type of "success rate": a completed analysis was a successful one, while the more ambiguous ones were merely fractionary—not failed.

Gratifying patients' father fantasies—and then inducing patients to renounce them? This sort of freethinking question could be asked and even acted upon by the Poliklinik's experimenters. The Poliklinik analyst's independence from financial interest in the patient offered both parties hitherto unknown clinical freedoms. In a manner reminiscent of Ferenczi's efforts at "mutual analysis," both analyst and patient could assess whether transferences changed according to the status of the patient and could use their freedom to experiment with these new forms of treatment. As Eitingon said, "in private practice [this] could never be undertaken, because it is only rarely that life allows so costly a performance."

"Of special value in the promotion of [psychoanalysis is] the establishment of Institutes and Outpatient Treatment Clinics"

1927

A TURNING POINT for Wilhelm Reich, as for Austria's political left, came on January 30, 1927, when a right-wing terrorist randomly shot into a crowd of Social Democrats in Schattendorf, a small town near the Hungarian border. What particularly enraged the workers and liberals was that the accused perpetrators were swiftly acquitted on July 14. Like Germany's paramilitary factions, Austria's conservative Christian Socials were affiliated with autonomous militaristic groups. Austrian reactionary forces had organized their own independent paramilitary factions, the protofascist *Heimwehr* (Homeland Guards), for just such occasions. The conservative Christian Social party had been defeated once again in Vienna and, though they held on to national leadership, they lost the city and its cosmopolitan culture—as important to Austrians as political power—to the Social Democrats. In fact Vienna remained allied to the Social Democrats until the end of the 1920s. But the end of the decade was marked by an intensifying struggle between the two profoundly different political parties, the urban, secular liberals of Red Vienna and Austria's ruling party whose rural Catholic constituency was still devoted to the monarchy. Even within the Vienna judiciary, though, conservative judges meted out lighter jail sentences to right-wing violence mongers, a policy that bred increasing tension between workers and party officials.

"Down with all politics!" commanded Reich, "let's get to the practical demands of life!" Protests erupted in Vienna the next day in response to the release of the *Heimwehr* soldiers. The spectacular demonstration moving swiftly down the street in front of his office interrupted Reich's morning analytic session and, together, he and his patient called it to an end. Workers had struck and occupied the inner city while the police readied their weapons. At daybreak police had launched an armed assault on the workers and Reich witnessed the massacre and the famous fire when the Palace of Justice burned down. "On that day" the image of the crowd and the police shooting at workers showed Reich "clearly that the socially suppressed individual is entirely different psychologically from the way rigid sociology of class antagonism describes him or would like him to be. . . . I saw, in short, that the real life of the working masses is lived on a completely different level from that on which the tumult of politicians and party politics rages."[1] The demonstrations were necessary and yet sadly futile. If rallies turned violent at every provocation, then the workers' movement would be nothing more than a collection of dissatisfied, disorganized poor people, incessantly shifting between causes. People had to be reached on a truly personal level to avoid reconstructing artificial class barriers between party organizers and demonstrators. Parallel to deep analysis that frees the individual from internal oppression and opens up the natural flow of energy, a fully deployed campaign from the left would deliver the common people from external oppression and release a natural social harmony. Like his colleagues of the period, Reich intended to do both at once, wielding psychoanalysis for the internal and social democracy for the external. Between its earliest planning stages in 1927 and its demise in 1934, Sex-Pol implemented psychological services and bridged Reich's theoretical link between human sexuality and organized political activities. He called this theory "sex-economy," meaning that human behavior and society would be naturally healthy and self regulating if people could be freed of cultural repression. As has been noted earlier, sex-economic practice, meaning counseling, outreach and reform, was referred to as social work. On that day in February, however, the conciliatory ways of social democracy had proved inadequate, and Reich joined the medical group of the Arbeiterhilfe, an affiliate of the Austrian Communist Party.

In 1917, a year before hearing Freud's speech on the advancement of free clinics, Ernst Simmel had already requested government approval for a psychoanalytic research institution including a sanatorium and a free clinic. Inpatient psychoanalytic treatment, he believed, should extend to people unable, for multiple reasons, to attend the outpatient clinic in the city. For Simmel, director of a World War I field hospital for war neuroses from 1916 to 1920, Freud's 1918 Budapest speech only confirmed the idea that inpatient care too belonged within the social obligations of psychoanalysis. His goal for a psychoanalytic sanatorium thus predated the Berlin Poliklinik. Actually all of Simmel's combined clinical and political ideas were bound up in the sanatorium project. For eight years now he had been raising funds to expand on the Poliklinik experience, and finally, in April 1927, sufficient financial backing came through to underwrite its inpatient counterpart. The German minister of health and education promised to send beds and to deploy state physicians there for training. It was an article of faith at the Poliklinik, and among members of the Socialist physicians circle, that the sanatorium would be as great a success as the clinic. While it never did attain prosperity, Ernst Simmel's Schloss Tegel Sanatorium survived for about five years as a nucleus of original clinical initiatives. The sanatorium also served Freud personally as an uncommonly peaceful retreat in a small renovated castle on the edge of Berlin.

In some respects the Schloss Tegel Sanatorium recalled the leafy suburban life of prewar Austria (figure 27). "It is half an hour by car from the city center, but beautiful and quiet, situated in a park a few minutes from Lake Tegel," Freud told Ernest Jones.[2] On April 1 Freud congratulated Simmel on Tegel's opening. "I wish you now what you need above all," he wrote, "a little luck."[3] The Tegel Sanatorium opened officially on April 11 for the residential treatment

27 Entrance to Schloss Tegel Park, Berlin (Author)

of profoundly troubled indigent people. The architect Ernst Freud, who welcomed the commission to design and refurbish the interior of the hundred-year-old health facility, lent the project his organizational skills as well. "He not only provided us with adequate housing," Simmel wrote to Freud, "but also helped me very much with advice in business matters. Whenever a danger threatened the development of the whole enterprise, he repeatedly gave us practical help."[4] Ernst converted the two-story building, previously used as a sanatorium as well, from its fifty large and small rooms accommodating seventy-four patients to a more functional streamlined setting for twenty-five to thirty patients. Faced with a dark old-fashioned Victorian edifice, Ernst decided that a large new double-arched entrance with plants and wicker chairs would open up the space and please patients and staff. Since his work was meant to promote a therapeutic environment, several large rooms were stripped of their ornamentation and converted into communal bathing and eating facilities reminiscent of the Viennese Gemeindebauten buildings overseen by his former mentor, Adolf Loos. Bauhaus-style white overhead lamps were hung from the ceiling to distribute light evenly over the patient and staff dining tables (the two groups shared communal meals). Hallways were cleared so that the rooms would open directly onto them, and a large area toward the back was fitted with an unusual round bathtub for hydrotherapy. The furniture was simple and bold, characteristic of Ernst's designs, with deep-seated upholstered armchairs, round tables, and the ubiquitous wood bookcases.

For venturesome psychoanalysts, the appeal of Tegel lay in its new variety of patients and their often turbulent behavior. As problems arose, the two chief physicians, Drs. Nussbrecher and Ludwig Jekels—both from Vienna—supervised the staff of analytically trained medical assistants and nurses. The clinical staff was stellar: Moishe Wulff, Edith Wiegert-Vowinckel, Irene Haenel-Guttman, Rudolf Bilz, Karl Maria Herald, Helmut Kaiser, Alfred Gross, Frances Deri, and Ludwig Fries, with Anna Freud's friend Eva Rosenfeld as facility manager. Many were staunch Social Democrats and several, in particular Frances Deri and Edith Wiegert, would later join Otto Fenichel on an ambitious project to infuse psychoanalytic practice with Marxist theory. Others, those politically closest to Simmel, were good-naturedly anticipating a time when they could start treating patients from a serious Marxist perspective, which they envisioned as a combination of personal insight-oriented analysis and community organizing. At its height Tegel supported a ratio of eight patients to one analyst. Only patients with intransigent organicity were sent back to the psychiatric units of Berlin's larger hospitals. Fortunately the owner of a small private psychiatric asylum located just a few minutes from Schloss Tegel agreed to house psychotic patients (at first only female) until the new sanatorium could accommodate them. They would be treated psychoanalytically by Simmel or his staff. The mentally ill population intended for Schloss Tegel were mostly referred by the Berlin clinicians and suffered from addictions and severe character problems or personality disorders. Otherwise they all too easily landed in prisons or asylums, victims of odd hunger cures or electroshock, death by suicide, or hopeless wandering from one physician to another.

The first patient was a small, acutely anxious woman who found illness, surgery, death, burial, and mourning so taboo she was ceaselessly compelled to perform ceremonial washing. At Freud's urging, her husband escorted her to the sanatorium because her obsessionalism went beyond the scope of ambulatory, unintensive outpatient treatment. Another sad woman was incapacitated by deformed elephantiasized legs: she had not stood straight for the last two years because, for her, all horizontal furniture was taboo and persecuted her (literally and metaphorically) to stay awake and wash herself, enduring night after night of torment. Not only did the patients suffer horrendously, but so did their families out of fear of phobic infection, grief, or sheer ruin from a spouse's kleptomania or a father's tragic gambling. Drawing on family therapy concepts later elaborated by Salvador Minuchin and Nathan Ackerman, Simmel realized that some family members felt constrained to heed the designated patient's every symptom at home, perhaps engaging with an anorexic daughter's endless preoccupation with food intake. In this case the suffering daughter was merely depicting the family system's collective neurosis. Therefore, Simmel posited, removing the symptomatic person from their brothers and sisters or parents, or their spouse, alarming as it may seem, allowed the patient some freedom to recover on their own. Didn't the new therapeutic community simply replicate the various symptoms of anxiety, depression, and obsessive ceremonials? Or impose on already fragile people "hypochondriacs philosophizing at table about the quality of their nasal mucous and persons in depression daily proclaiming in audible tones their wish to die?"[5] Critics would argue that such a protected environment was actually harmful to recovery because it promoted dependence and, therefore, inherently deprived patients of the opportunity to confront reality. "But one cannot take from a man what he himself voluntarily resigned: life in the real present," Simmel told the faultfinders. And since the patient's disturbed psychic existence is only a pseudo-reality, offering them a *new* reality is hardly a deprivation. The new reality is pleasantly neutral, with "physicians ready to help, kindly attendants, male and female, good food, artistic rooms and beautiful country surroundings."[6] For a while the freedom from financial worry is liberating for doctor and patient alike because, in a free clinic, neither can barter health for money. Treatment starts slowly, perhaps during walks in the park with the analyst, until the whole world of clinic, staff, and patients becomes a re-created phantom family, grist for the analytic mill, and ultimately a far-reaching authenticity.

Tegel could hardly afford to let a patient collapse completely, and the staff did take measures to prevent it. The physicians, nurses, and house personnel met early every morning to discuss cases around an oak table in the consulting room. The analysts reviewed what had transpired during patient sessions and Mrs. Bruenitzer, the housemother at the sanatorium, shared her observations of any new behaviors, noticed night or day. How to prevent a love affair, a suicide, a pseudo-cure, a rather amazing nonalcoholic intoxication in a recovering dipsomaniac? Faced with this last extraordinary patient's insatiable morbid cravings during detoxification, Simmel assented to double and treble portions of food and withheld scolding when the patient cut off tree branches and then smashed a coffee set. A special nurse was assigned to him alone and analytic sessions at the least sign of violence or anxiety resulting from withdrawal, day or night. Having thus recreated a total milieu of the mother-child intimacy of feeding, "the infantile phase spontaneously disappeared" and treatment progressed.[7] On the whole, however, Simmel demanded that patients conform to standards of civility accepted outside the facility, that they return to family or work in increments as treatment progressed, and that they become conscious contributors to their unusual Weimarian community.

The Schloss Tegel Sanatorium was eight years in the making, and it lasted barely five. Simmel's efforts to achieve an integrated healing community of patients and psychoanalysts never really abated. He developed some extraordinarily bold theories at Schloss Tegel, among them family therapy and the idea of complementary neurosis (codependency). He reintroduced therapeutic ideas like short-term psychoanalytic treatment from his earlier career directing a field hospital for shell-shocked soldiers. Simmel's technique combined, he said, "analytic-cathartic hypnosis with analytical discussion and interpretation of dreams . . . result[ing] in liberation from symptoms in two to three sessions."[8] But to bring his project to fruition would have required fund-raising proficiency as great as his clinical talent. Reminded of Hitschmann's two-year lobbying effort to secure government approval for the Ambulatorium, Freud, who ultimately intervened on Simmel's behalf as he had in the Vienna proceedings, remained encouraging. "I envy you the patience with which you are willing to go on in the struggle against those unreliable people, [the Ministry of Heath of the German government]. . . . The principle should always be not to make concessions to those who don't have anything to give but who have everything to gain from us."[9]

Meanwhile, in Vienna, Freud had new reasons to support innovative psychoanalytic projects. For one, his daughter Anna had embarked on a psychoanalytic undertaking of her own. A small new school, named the Heitzing School after its location in the leafy suburbs of Vienna, implemented an experiment in early childhood education designed by Anna Freud and her companion Dorothy Burlingham along with their close friend Eva Rosenfeld. Rosenfeld was a large-boned woman with brown hair piled high, long arms, and wide swinging gestures that could sweep a fallen child off the ground or a truckload of turnips into the car. Originally a Berlin relative of the Freuds', Eva had moved to Vienna fifteen years earlier to marry and was now in the painful position of surviving the loss of three of her four children. When her eldest daughter Mädi died a sudden accidental death in 1924, Eva began to consider designing a memorial that was more socially useful and more powerful than a typical shrine. Her life was full of psychoanalysis and teaching, and the Freuds were her great friends. With Mädi's death still painfully fresh, Eva drew on her own earlier teaching experience at Zellerhaus, a Berlin girls' orphanage, and set out to memorialize her child by building a progressive school. "The young women pupils for whom my house would provide a sort of research station" on their way to becoming the New Woman, said Eva, would live and learn "a model of household and gardening management." [10] But Eva also thought that the psychoanalytic component was essential to growth and development and brought Anna Freud, to whom she had been introduced by their mutual friend, the psychoanalyst Siegfried Bernfeld, into her foster home-based school. In 1925 Dorothy Burlingham joined the circle permanently.

When Erik Erikson, then a young German artist named Erik Homburger, arrived in Vienna that spring at the invitation of his friend Peter Blos to work at a new kindergarten, Anna Freud and the larger Freud circle took him in and "opened a life's work."[11] In the years he spent at Heitzing, until the school closed in 1932, Erikson and Blos and their colleagues were afforded months of trial and error to learn what actually educated children and what simply appealed to their sense of the game. Erik was willing to put children and adults on an equal plane (a reciprocity Anna Freud found too lenient) and to use a Dewey-like curriculum where education was based on classwide community projects. The children who thrived on the independence and self-sufficiency of the projects were those who, in Erikson's famous future work, already had a better sense of personal identity. It was relatively easy to have a progressive educational mission in a pleasant middle class district like Heitzing near a park, an ideal location for the small private school installed in the backyard of the Rosenfeld's large suburban home on Wattmanngasse. Technically, the Heitzing project was a communal private school for children and early adolescents. Some of the child residents were, however, foster children (*Haustörchter*) and actually wards of the state. The pupils ranged from Kyra Nijinsky, the dancer's daughter, and Vera von Freund-Toszeghi, granddaughter of the late Hungarian psychoanalytic patron Anton von Freund, to abandoned and disturbed street children, along with Ernst Simmel's son and Dorothy's four children. Burlingham built, furnished, and supplied the two-story four-room schoolhouse, designed by Erikson, while Rosenfeld contributed her management skills, as well as music and daily lunch for the next five years. The little school's curriculum was organized along selected psychoanalytic principles including dreams, symbols, and unconscious influences on human relationships. Erikson taught art, German, and humanities. Peter Blos, the school's director, taught geography and science and Joan Serson (who would marry Erik in 1930) taught dance. Marie Briehl, the future child analyst, and Dorothy Burlingham taught English. August Aichorn appeared in the afternoon for free discussions with the children, an ad hoc form of group therapy. The protected environment, with few rules and large special projects, could be seen as either chaotic or liberating for children, but, until its end, research produced by the school informed much of the emerging field of child analysis and significantly influenced early childhood teaching.

In her 1927 papers, "Four Lectures on Child Analysis," and in her seminars at the Vienna Society and at the local Kinderhaus for children under age six from working-class families, Anna Freud differentiated her supportive therapeutic approach from Melanie Klein's intense focus on the infantile unconscious. Almost two-thirds of the pupils at Heitzing were in analysis with Anna as patients and study subjects (as were children of fellow analysts as well), so her clinical authority was altogether pervasive. August Aichorn had a different, at times more questionable, influence at Heitzing. As a government official he held jurisdictional authority to intervene if a child was harmed by a family member. Anna was simply a private citizen, one who held enormous moral influence but little actual control and whose vision of the larger social world, at the time, was circumscribed. She could not disturb the well-reciprocated devotion to her father and she suffered, as well, from a timidity bred from staying exclusively within the individual analytic purview—a narrowness distinctly not shared by her father. Anna and Dorothy had taken to a simpler life, a country home with vegetable patches and seasonal flowers and an Austrian style of dress with long, wide patterned skirts and pleated white blouses. In 1927 this rusticity on a Viennese woman spoke perhaps of an Austrian allegiance, an unprompted conservatism that would reappear in some aspects of her later life. Nevertheless, at Heitzing and in her public life Anna openly admired Aichorn's therapeutic work with juvenile delinquents as well as Bernfeld's advocacy of school reforms and encouraged the leaders of Red Vienna in their advancement of special child guidance centers. She even fed her hungry child patients during their analytic sessions. Erik Erikson tells the story of Martha Freud, seeing the maid Paula Fichtl carry a plate of food into Anna's office, saying, "A costly affair, child analysis!"[12] Many of Anna's patients were private, but some were public foster children. Interestingly, the foster children were often the subjects of Erikson's research on child development. Erikson, who knew little about psychology before starting at Heitzing, found that the children from poor families "opened up data beyond those provided in the analysis of children whose parents could afford to pay for treatment." Many years after leaving Vienna he developed an ambitious metadiagram for identity and the life cycle, his famous eight stages of life that intimately interweave the psychological and social dimensions of human experience. In Erikson's schema people's successful resolution of epigenetic psychosocial "crises" revolves around their ability to conform to dominant Western culture by separating from the family, achieving autonomy, generating results, and gracefully aging out of society with a sense of personal accomplishment. Paradoxically, his research was conducted precisely on those individuals most alienated from the hegemonic culture.

On April 20 Sigmund Freud's name was published, along with Alfred Adler's, in the *Arbeiter-Zeitung*'s formal list of Red Vienna's thirty-eight most prominent citizens, praising them for their social and cultural achievements.[13] It was a crucial time in the ongoing expansion of the psychoanalytic movement as sibling Berlin and Vienna challenged each other regularly for dominance in clinical and theoretical innovation. "A feeling of community," Freud cautioned his quarrelling friends with the air of an exasperated father, would "enable you to unite . . . in your endeavors" around the work to be done at the Tenth International Psychoanalytic Congress, which he was not able to attend.[14] Berlin boasted of expanded facilities while Vienna gloried in Freud's presence. In Stuttgart the daily newspaper, the *Stuttgart Tagblatt,* published a long article about psychoanalysis as the theme for the town's "pedagogical week." The paper announced lectures by Bernfeld and Landauer and called on the city's educators, trainers, and doctors to "wipe out" neurosis.[15] Eventually, neither Berlin nor Vienna would sustain the movement in the face of Fascist and Nazi threats. But, for the moment, at least in Vienna, the earlier partnership between analysts and Tandler's social welfare institutions somewhat cushioned the field of child and adolescent psychoanalysis.

The renewed need for free clinics was not lost on the analysts and, as they would soon read in the most recent IPA statutes, "of special value in the promotion of [psychoanalysis is] the establishment of Institutes and Outpatient Treatment Centres, Clinics." [16] The surprise was not that the clinic reports became regular agenda items at every semi-annual IPA meeting after 1927, but that they had been judged less important before then. Hitschmann was quick to grace his first 1927 Ambulatorium report with the crucial passage from Freud's 1918 Budapest speech, that "the poor man should have [the] right to assistance for his mind." Hitschmann's foremost concern was how to publicize the Ambulatorium's urgent need for new quarters, while informing his readers of the clinic's improved legal status, without forfeiting the sense of ongoing struggle. Hitschmann and Federn had met with Tandler in January to discuss the clinic's pressing lack of space and to plead for government funding for new offices. At the same time, Josef Friedjung, a veteran member of the municipal council, had met with Mayor Seitz and sent compelling petitions to city officials. Over the last five years thousands of patients—mostly office workers, shopkeepers, and government officials—had found help and an indispensable sense of well-being at the Ambulatorium for the destitute, they wrote.[17] The Ambulatorium was by now one of Vienna's largest providers of mental health treatment (after Wagner-Jauregg's outpatient clinic) and was developing new services like the child clinic as fast as it could. Continuously monitored by the Public Health Department, the Vienna analysts had voluntarily paid the rent, lighting, and heat (and donated their time) completely on their own. Meanwhile the municipal doctors, health insurance companies, marriage counselors, alcoholism stations, and food pantries sent over an increasing number of patients. Hitschmann was still on the medical staff of the General Hospital and loyal to "the great clinical community in the heart of Vienna," as his colleague Josef Friedjung said.[18] Above all else, Hitschmann said, the analysts simply sought to promote the humanitarian purposes of psychoanalysis, but the five small rooms of the Herzstation in the hospital's shadow were severely inadequate for this mission. Nevertheless, Hitschmann's bid was unsuccessful and the city government, as in the years 1920 through 1922, refused to grant the analysts' requests. Instead the city was spending hundreds of thousands of dollars buying up as much real estate as it could and developing an extraordinary expanse of workers' housing, ultimately the stately signature of Red Vienna.

"Erbaut von der Gemeinde Wien in der Jahren 19": even today each set of buildings dating from the period of Red Vienna proudly preserves the words "Built by the Community of Vienna in the Years 19" on its facade. Grouped together and repeated on hundreds of buildings throughout the city, these bold large-scale signatures reveal a nexus of concerns from the sociopolitical discourse of the era. Effectively mottoes for the lasting impact of a fused relationship between citizen and state, the words refocus our attention on the interdependence of private life and public culture, an effect similarly conveyed by the free psychoanalytic clinics. At its core a fascinating dialectic between architecture and social science formed the basis on which social democratic city planners created for Viennese citizens an identifiable sense of place, addressed the social needs of families with children, and advanced the individual worker's potential in a democratic state. "Great tenements, as bold in architecture as they are in economics, proclaim their origin in staring red letters," reported an admiring release from the Commonwealth Fund.[19] The second great wave of municipal housing construction began that May and result in a total of sixty-three thousand affordable new dwellings for Vienna city workers. At its peak the project would employ over two hundred architects and engineers, many of whom had studied at the school of Otto Wagner. Influenced by new housing design in Germany and the West, the latest apartments were individually more spacious than the original Gemeindebauten and organized into immense structures with hundreds of dwellings spread over several city blocks. The distinctive *Mittelstandswohnungen* (middle class dwellings) each measured a comfortable 613 square feet and the kitchen was separate from the dining room. The residential sites were set back from the street, built around grand semi-enclosed parks, and accessed through a monumental common entryway. These were virtually self-contained villages, and daily life in these "superblock" dwellings of up to a thousand apartments whirred around an economy all its own. Large cooperative stores, dozens of product shops and workshops (*ateliers*), meeting halls, a bookstore, and large automated laundry and bathing facilities supported the communal lifestyle. At the open air baths men like the skilled metal worker Karl Potenski would meet up with their families. "I went straight from the factory to the bath where I met my wife and our child," he recalled. "The Kongressbad was open until 10 o'clock in the evening. Our child grew up on the sand of that bath. We played table tennis, we called it Ping Pong. It was our happiest time."[20] The huge internal courtyards (figure 28) buzzed with children charging toward the playing fields for after-school sports, mothers on benches, playgrounds, paths, public toilets, baby changing rooms, and milk bars. Social services and public amenities ranged from the tuberculosis clinic, perhaps several kindergartens and youth care facilities, wading pools for children and swimming pools for adults, to the worker's health insurance office and the pharmacy. From there the social workers, sometimes dreaded and sometimes welcomed, would fan out across the buildings to visit families in their homes. In 1927 many distributed the notorious infant layettes.

When Julius Tandler wrested from the Municipal Council the authority to distribute infant layettes to all newborns, regardless of family need, he was vehemently accused of pandering to the socialist propaganda machine. The baby clothes were attractively packaged in red gift cartons. *Motherhood*, a mother with child sculpture by Anton Hanak, was pictured on the front, and the parcels were further ornamented with characteristic Wiener Werkstätte borders and lettering. A listing of Vienna's thirty-four maternal-child consultation centers was printed on the inside.[21] The need-blind aspect of the distribution particularly enraged the opposition, which objected to any suggestion of civic entitlement, that childbearing women were entitled to this aid simply because they were citizens of Vienna and regardless of their economic status. If anything, the Christian Socials thought, the clothes parcels should go only to needy families. Tandler countered that the free layettes were educational, sanitary, and had a "beneficial effect on the young mother's inner state."[22] Psychoanalytic principles had touched social welfare and Tandler

28 Interior courtyard of a Viennese community dwelling (Author)

urged the municipal social workers (most likely trained by Aichorn), the district welfare officers, and the local health stations' Fürsorgerinnen to deliver the packages on their rounds to family homes.

At least thirteen thousand municipal layettes were disbursed that year alone by social workers making home visits. The social workers no doubt evaluated the physical and psychological milieu of the home as well and referred children or adolescents to the *Kinderüberahmsstelle* (Child Observation Center) if necessary. The mere mention of the home visitor could evoke the sense of a surprise attack, of the morality police prowling indigent neighborhoods to search out and remove children from parents whose only crime was poverty. In reality, her appearance was far more benign. Poor families could receive extra clothes and food vouchers, and the waiting list for housing could be shortened. Even more important, though, neglected children who slept in their clothes and shoes in "indescribable, filthy, really terrible" beds or a child "beaten black and blue" could be helped. So many families were helped that the number of reported incidents decreased by 8 percent in one year, from 3,324 in 1926 to 3,089 in 1927. Fortunately, numbers speak louder than rhetoric: children removed from homes because of "morals endangered" were only 2 percent of the total. But far more significant reasons for transferring children to nonfamily care included "relatives admitted to hospital" (30 percent), poverty/unemployment (14 percent), homelessness (16 percent), neglect (7 percent), and delinquency (8 percent).[23] Behind the social worker making this assessment stood the power of the state's new medical profession and the organized public health responsibility among doctors. School physicians and school dentists, tuberculosis specialists and guidance counselors fanned out across hundreds of child health stations and into community buildings and family homes. In effect, Tandler had finally succeeded in making government respond directly to the health and mental heath needs of dependent children.

In the United States of the mid-1920s the progress made by psychoanalysis was ambiguous: its popularity in official medical circles was also its undoing, Ferenczi thought, and led "to a tendency to be satisfied with a superficial acquaintance" with psychoanalysis.[24] Ferenczi reported at a meeting of the British society that the recent surge of interest concerned him because the conservative American values of individualism and self-sufficiency, and the general reluctance to be personally analyzed, were at odds with psychoanalysis as the Europeans knew it. He had delivered two series of lectures at Columbia University and at the New School for Social Research. The doctors' overwrought fear of encroachment by New York's lay practitioners caused Ferenczi to separate his courses in two, one for the medical audience and one for others. With no thanks from Freud, Ferenczi had pursued an incredibly arduous teaching and training schedule, placating the Americans with extra seminars, and lobbying all the while for new subsidies and funds. Freud's unsparing mockery of "Dollaria" and equally discouraging, distrustful view of the Hungarians seemed unduly harsh. A journalist had requested a speech about psychoanalysis for a documentary. "I would agree only if they gave me enough money to set up a polyclinic in Budapest," Ferenczi wrote wearily to Freud.[25] Yet in Ferenczi's absence from Budapest Imre Hermann had convened the Hungarian society with renewed vigor. Once Ferenczi returned in October he could inform Freud that he hoped "in not too long a time [to] find a house and home of an outpatient clinic" and that the Budapest society was engrossed in administrative plans to lay the clinic's foundation.[26]

Freud "knew exactly how things were in the world. But before he could go outside, he first had to know what was inside"

1928

IN 1928 Wilhelm Reich, intensely absorbed in activist politics but still working daily at the Ambulatorium, introduced a vision of social services freed of the boundaries of stigma and ideology. Reich decided to take psychoanalysis in a direction charted through social work, by the late 1920s a well-established profession in its own right, and, as noted earlier, used the term *social work* interchangeably with *sociological work*. "Following a conversation with Freud, " Reich recalled, "I explained my plans and asked him for his opinion. Sex-counseling centers were to be opened on a mass scale . . . [and] designed to serve the general public. Freud agreed wholeheartedly. He knew as little as I where it would lead."[1] And, indeed, under the umbrella name of Sex-Pol, Reich carried out his project of making social services directly available to consumers without waiting for them to become eligible or to make appointments for help according to a prearranged bureaucratic format. In Vienna and its suburbs Reich's free Sex-Pol clinics extended to the wider municipal community some unusually open medical and educational services and an abbreviated form of psychoanalysis. "Free counseling on sexual problems, the rearing of children, and general mental hygiene to those seeking advice" was available for the taking.[2] Reich's reliable outreach team, which included his old friend from medical school Lia Laszky, turned their energies toward three- or four-day traveling health fairs in a van fitted out with health care supplies. For mental health care they tried to carve out corners of privacy, also in the van. Adopting "free sexuality within an egalitarian society" as the motto for their organization, the Sex-Pol team performed a real service by offering valuable one-on-one health education.[3] On a larger scale their outreach efforts promoted awareness of the possibility of far-reaching sexual reforms that, Reich believed, must accompany social change. Sex-Pol counseling, Reich's extension of psychoanalysis and a component of his unique brand of "social work," was dialectical and bilateral: to understand fully that individuals lived symbiotically within and were a product of their overall environment, yet to address each person's unique experience of this environment.

About the same time that Reich opened his social work clinics, Freud remarked that analytically trained social workers would one day become a powerful force in the prevention and treatment of mental illness. With metaphors suggesting both a grand conquest and a tribute to Julius Tandler, Freud envisioned a social work association (funded by a rich American) strong enough to "mobilize a corps to give battle to the neuroses springing from our civilization." This "new sort of Salvation Army [would help where] . . . our civilization puts an almost intolerable pressure on us."[4] Reich saw himself literally rushing to the rescue and divulged his plans to Freud despite the increasing tension in their relationship. Apparently Freud more than encouraged Reich to move forward with this community work. "'Go ahead, just go ahead' [said Freud]. . . . I discussed details and he was enthusiastic."[5] Reich and Freud were ideologues, aiming to carve out a distinctly new form of clinical therapy with enhanced social goals. Their systematic blend of progressive politics and psychoanalytic drive theory had worked so far: it could now be seen at the Poliklinik and at the Ambulatorium. But the Sex-Pol clinics took this concept further and, for the next few years, in Vienna and Berlin, Reich built up its prevention work and emphasized an integrated person-in-environment treatment model, two of modern professional social work's banner practices.

At the end of the 1920s, Reich said, it was "new to attack the neuroses by prevention rather than treatment," and the corollary idea, that individuals were really inseparable from their larger social environments, was intriguing. To be genuinely effective, therefore, an analyst who tracks down evidence of a patient's early trauma (for example, deprivation) must also confront the societal pressures (deprivation's root, poverty) that created the individual problem. In this respect the Sex-Pol clinics "integrated the problems of the neuroses, sexual disturbances, and everyday conflicts to alleviate the misery" that, Reich claimed, derived from "social conditions rooted in the bourgeois social order." In other words, the analyst must be a social activist to be competent. But even social activism, as meaningful in the analyst's range of tasks as individual therapy, should rank second to the perennially ignored area of prevention. Analysts should actually tackle social problems even before they occur, Reich thought, and the Sex-Pol project, now occupying more and more of his time, was deeply involved in this attempt. Sex-Pol's preventive work extended from individual clinical therapy, to print literature widely circulated especially among workers, to popular lectures "to furnish information on sexual hygiene and the causes of and possible remedies for emotional difficulties." Reich aimed to vest individuals with the confidence to overcome repressive social constraints, both within themselves and in the world at large. He emphasized the importance of helping adolescents and young adults cope on their own terms with their emerging sexuality and of validating their experiences and feelings as normal. Reich advocated for public sanction of healthy adolescent sexuality, broad availability of contraceptives and abortion regardless of marital status or age, and women's rights to economic independence. This, he postulated, would prevent neuroses from emerging later in adulthood.

Reich repeatedly emphasized the extent to which Freud was aware of the impact of the environment on individuals. As Reich explained later in life, Freud "saw the whole social thing. . . . He knew exactly how things were in the world. But before he could go outside, he first had to know what was inside. He was very happy that somebody who knew the inside so well went out and tried to do something about it." To that end, Reich planned to expand Sex-Pol and open several more clinics over the next few years. He had already opened six, mostly in the outlying areas of Vienna. The centers included individual and couples counseling, sex education, birth control advice, and gynecological cabins stocked with diaphragms and literature on effective parenting. The waiting rooms were stocked with pamphlets and psychoanalytic classics. And of course, they had ample lectures halls where potential patients could listen to Reich expound on sexual guilt, social repression, and personal liberation.

As Reich spent more and more of his time at the Sex-Pol centers, Freud became concerned. How well was Reich managing the multiple demands of his private practice, the sex-counseling centers, chairing the Technical Seminar, and codirecting the Ambulatorium, all at the same time? Freud suspected, correctly, that Reich's enthusiasm for the Ambulatorium was waning. Now in its sixth year of autonomous operation, the Ambulatorium was so overwhelmed with referrals that psychoanalysts had started to turn away even urgent cases. The staff, comprised of one full-time physician as well as one full-time and two half-time junior physicians, found themselves treating forty to fifty people daily. Many were children. By now all grammar and high schools in Vienna were associated with a clinic, since eleven local child guidance clinics alone had opened under Alfred Adler's direction. Students and teachers alike benefited inasmuch as school age children had access to psychological services while their classroom teachers participated in either the free technical forums in individual psychology, or in the free psychoanalytic seminars based on Hoffer and Bernfeld's work. At the local health stations pregnant women and new mothers attended the highly popular lectures offered by Viennese specialists in prenatal care and early child development. More formal courses, enhanced by demonstrations and instruction in record keeping, were aimed at more specialized groups like nurses, welfare workers, and Fürsorgerinnen. Over 3,000 children enrolled in health stations were examined in 1928 alone, nearly four times each by graduates of these courses, while 6,515 children of all ages were visited at home at least twice each.[6] The Fürsorgerinnen assigned to local health stations regularly routed problematic children, with or without their parents, for assessment at a mental health clinic like the Ambulatorium. In theory the Fürsorgerinnen were supposed to provide the clinics with psychological assessments, but, in practice, most analysts seeing the children for intake had to start their examinations from scratch. Not all the Ambulatorium's analysts were pleased with these added patients. From time to time even the local newspapers mocked the seeming chaotic surfeit of mental health services, each school vying for subscribers yet bemoaning the overflow of patients. A notably sharp-edged dose of fun came from the Social Democrat's own newspaper, *Die Stunde*.

"Sigmund Freud, Alfred Adler, and Karl Marx—how do those names sound together? Aren't they mixing literary chocolate with economic garlic?

Last year, the Individual-psychologists under Alfred Adler's leadership tried to persuade us that their soul-searching could fit into Social-democratic theory like a new bed of grass in a large, somewhat overgrown lawn. Well," continued the editorial columnist who obviously loved to mix metaphors, "now the psychoanalyst Dr. Bernfeld proposes that Freudian theory is the genuine mediator between psychology and social progress. It is true that [Adler's] individual-psychologists, with their mummified concepts of Encouragement, Sense of Inferiority and the need for Validation, are a petty-bourgeois sect that can only prettify the bourgeois world with antique landscape etchings. . . . [In contrast] Sigmund Freud, one of today's few brilliant people, and his immediate followers [i.e. Bernfeld] have until now abstained from imprinting their theories as political engravings. . . . Are not Marxism and Psychoanalysis just as Marxist as

Individual-psychology, itself a branch cut off from Psychoanalysis? One soul-researcher accuses the other of not being revolutionary enough. Indeed, from Karl Marx to Sigmund Freud and Alfred Adler, this is simply the evolution from historical to hysterical materialism.[7]

It was an exquisite exercise in Marxism of the 1920s: who is the more revolutionary, Freud or Adler? Freud and Bernfeld had never said out loud that their *theory* was specifically Marxist, *Die Stunde* said, so it is actually more Marxist than the petty bourgeois Adlerians. Adlerians have all the trappings of social democracy, but their individual psychology (garlic) is actually riddled with bourgeois romanticism. Bernfeld is at risk of doing the same. In contrast, Freud the (chocolate) rationalist, who never vied for the Marxist title, has demonstrated a purer form of social democracy in praxis.

In an educator's variation on the "ratio of Marxism" question, the Viennese newspaper *Der Tag* reported on Bernfeld's hugely successful lectures sponsored by the Socialist Youth Teachers. The controversial group had led a vigorous campaign for school reform based exclusively on the most modern pedagogical-psychological theories and invited Bernfeld to discuss whether "Marxism corresponds better to Psychoanalysis or Individual-Psychology." Even Adler's influence on school reform, they felt, might be too old guard. Bernfeld willingly explored the relationship between Marxism and the psychologies of Freud and Adler, but his partiality to Freud was both obvious and well-liked by the Social Democrats. "Marxism is a science and can only harmonize with psychological education that proceeds scientifically," *Der Tag*'s reporter quoted. "Freud's psychoanalysis offers such a scientific approach. It originates—as do Marx and Engels—from love and hunger as the fundamental human drives. It investigates the influence of the environment on the basic drives of the individual."[8] The "spirited, sharply-biting" Bernfeld alluded to other theories like "mass psychology and racial memories," presumably a cautionary reference to links between Jung and the growing fascist presence, and the concepts of "community feeling" and "encouragement" that had led Adler to part ways with Freud. Just as they had requested, Bernfeld was able to present the Socialist Youth Teachers with a series of propositions inspired by Freud but grounded in Marxism. It was an easy answer to a complex question.

Anyone listening to Sándor Radó's speech at the opening of the new institute would have been struck by his claim that the Berlin psychoanalysts conducted "110 free treatment analyses everyday," not including the training analyses.[9] At their new quarters, Radó said, the Poliklinik's twelve training analysts and forty candidates carried on this stunningly large public practice. Obviously, the increased demand for psychoanalytic treatment had not been confined to Vienna. Moreover workspace at the Potsdamerstrasse facility had been strained for years. But once again Max Eitingon used his wealth to help the Poliklinik meet a crisis: he underwrote the clinic's move to the new and larger quarters at 10 Wichmannstrasse, the new location to which Radó so proudly referred in his Frankfurt speech. Otto Fenichel had already compiled enough statistical data to support this investment. Of the 721 analyses undertaken at the Poliklinik from February 1922 until January 1930 (the year this report would be issued), 363 treatments were successfully completed, 117 were still active, and 241 were deemed fractionary, in some way interrupted. Of the 363 completed (by cure or other closure) analyses, 70 patients were treated for six months, 108 for a full year, 74 for 1.5 years, 51 for 2 years, 29 for 2.5 years, 15 for 3 years, and 16 were analyzed for over 3 years. Fenichel was even able to indicate quite graphically how the Poliklinik's popularity increased over the years: of the 117 active analyses, or cases still current in 1930, 2 had started in 1922, 2 more in 1924, 4 in 1925, 9 in 1926, 17 in 1927, 40 in 1928, and now 43 in 1929.

The Poliklinik's expanded facilities took up six small suites arranged along the length of a balconied Berlin apartment building. With leafy views from their front bay windows, the suites ranged from spacious and well-lighted new rooms for consultations, lectures, and meetings to an upgraded intake/examining room for the attending psychoanalyst-physicians. The physicians' intake and consultation room was lined with classic glass-doored bookcases. Its rather spare space accommodated a square table with four matching wood chairs, plus an upholstered analytic couch (with pillow) and an armchair positioned behind it. Light came in through the large front window while incongruously ornate glass lamps brightened the patient entrances. Portraits of Freud, sometimes four per room, were arranged haphazardly along with bland photographs of other analysts. In the new conference room several dozen stately, high-backed wood chairs surrounded an immensely long seminar table at one end. This seminar section was separated from the larger conference area by two sets of large, lightly curtained French doors and enhanced by a mantled fireplace, open bookcases, woven area rugs, and the ubiquitous portrait of Freud overlooking the premises. In keeping with the airy simplicity of Ernst Freud's decorative sense, dense linen curtains sheltered a group of meeting rooms facing the street (figure 29). Just five years later the same curtains would take on an eerie significance when members "took great pains to draw the[m]" during a discussion of aryaniza-

29 Meeting room of the Berlin Society and Institute (Library of the Boston Psychoanalytic Society and Institute)

tion and, as Felix Boehm later reported, even to remove Simmel's name from the doorplate, lest it "do harm to our Institute."[10] Eventually the whole building was turned over to Hitler's government and renamed the German Institute for Psychological Research and Psychotherapy (Deutsche Institüt für Psychologische Forschung und Psychotherapie) or simply the Göring Institute, after its new director, Matthias Heinrich Göring. Even in 1928 Göring was already embroiled with the Allgemeine Arztliche Gesellschaft für Psychotherapie, a group of mental health practitioners led by Ernst Kretschmer until 1933—and by Carl Jung after 1933. But the Berlin institute was still doing well, in fact thriving, at its new location on Wichmanstrasse.

Erich Fromm was the keynote speaker at the inaugural series of lectures celebrating the 1928 opening of the Wichmanstrasse clinic. He was the first academic guest to be so honored. Visiting from Heidelberg, Fromm lectured on psychoanalysis of "persons of lower middle class" twice, once at the society's March meeting and again for Radó's training seminar. A slim man with neatly combed thick dark hair and a high authoritative forehead, Fromm struck a relaxed pose unusual for an academic. He had recently married the urbane psychoanalyst Frieda Reichmann. Within the last few years Frieda had startled the Heidelberg medical community with the creation of a private psychoanalytic sanatorium. Her clinic's external directors, an intellectual circle that met periodically at her home to discuss literature and theory, included Karl Landauer, Leo Lowenthal, and Max Horkheimer of the Frankfurt Institute. From the outset, the group anticipated that an outpatient clinic, similar to Berlin's, would be housed physically and intellectually within the emerging Institute for Social Research in Frankfurt. To Fromm and his colleagues, therefore, the idea of formulating psychoanalytic treatment specifically around the needs of Frankfurt's working people were not only plausible but practical and necessary. Coincidentally, Fromm's Berlin lectures represented an intrepid bid to address the seemingly incongruous duo of psychoanalysis and religion within the context of social justice. Many years later, far removed from his progressive Frankfurt colleagues, Fromm would attempt to develop a psychohistory in *Sigmund Freud's Mission* in which he essentially accused his mentor of failing to fuse these same three elements (religion, psychoanalysis, and society). "Freud's aim was to found a movement for the ethical liberation of man," he wrote, "a new secular and scientific religion for an elite which was to guide mankind."[11] Fromm maintained that Freud had committed a fatal error by remaining "blind to the social unconscious," whereas he—Fromm—understood that man and society are inseparable. Of course back at the Poliklinik in the 1920s, Fromm had launched a personal, and far more accurately Freudian, campaign to redraw social context around psychoanalysis. In this he was joined by Theodore Reik, who had left Vienna for Berlin in October, and by Ernst Simmel, who enjoyed the balance of sociological theory and psychoanalytic practice and reinforced this symmetry with case observations from the clinic. Unlike Fromm, Simmel made social medicine seem inevitable. In the buoyant mission statement of the Association for Socialist Physicians, Simmel declared that his group sought to "examine all questions of public health and benefits relevant to the laws and government of the State and the community. The Society also seeks to enlighten non-socialist doctors, to expand awareness of the socialist worker-movement and its goals, and to promote among Party-members themselves a better grasp of medicine and socialist society."[12]

The Poliklinik's move to Wichmannstrasse was hailed as a sign that the Berlin Psychoanalytic Institute had become, once again, the epicenter of psychoanalysis. Dr. L. Pierce Clark was one of many resourceful Americans, often from New England and Chicago, who wrote to investigate the "approximate cost for a course of training to become an analyst in the Berlin Psychoanalytic Institute."[13] Eitingon answered with his good English and characteristic mix of diplomacy and ruthlessness. The fee for a six to twelve month training analysis ranges "from $10 to $5 a lesson, depend[ing] on the candidate' s means. But," he added, "some very experienced colleagues are not prohibited—permit me to give myself as an instance—to ask more for one lesson in accordance with their standard of life."[14] The message from the Poliklinik was consistent: no one would be refused training or treatment for lack of ability to pay, but neither would the analysts sacrifice the opportunity to earn a living or support their clinic. These inquiries had become fairly standard by now, and, with the Poliklinik' s intentionally broad scope, by 1928 it reached a few of those surprisingly original characters attracted to psychoanalysis from afar. "I am just a little over forty years of age, in splendid health, a train dispatcher by profession, making a side hobby of writing magazine fiction and studying Social and Abnormal Psychology. I do not like to make a journey so far to study Psychoanalysis, but it seems as if no one in this country is interested vitally in anyone but the M.D.'s having a hand in curing people of their ills."[15] So wrote Mr. Claude B. Carter, from Columbus, Ohio, whose initial meeting with Dr. William Alanson White in Washington D.C. had resulted in his contact with Eitingon. And John Dollard of Yale University' s Institute of Human Relations thanked Eitingon for the Berlin training and wrote that "the 'Institute' is a bully institution and a fine example."[16] To established psychiatrists and psychologists in America, the Poliklinik generally represented a perhaps more liberal version of the psychoanalytic training also available in Vienna. But as the New York medical community steadily incorporated psychoanalysis into the elite reaches of its private practices, the division of labor among American mental health professionals became increasingly apparent.

Of the three principal groups providing psychotherapy and psychoanalysis, professional social workers (rather than psychiatrists and psychologists) have adhered most closely to the Poliklinik's approaches to urban mental health. In the stories of social workers like Margaret Powers, interesting historical linkages emerge between Europe's free psychoanalytic clinics and American social work as it is taught and practiced today. The young Margaret Powers was "a person of exceptional intelligence and balance," wrote Mary Jarrett in her 1928 letter recommending the social worker for training in Berlin.[17] Jarrett, the feisty founder of psychiatric social work and associate director of the Smith College School for Social Work, believed that supplying society with highly educated activists would reinvigorate the waning American commitment to public mental health. Interestingly, Max Eitingon and Mary Jarrett had started from the same ideological position. The 1918 "Training School for Psychiatric Social Work was a war emergency course. . . . Public attention to mental hygiene, stimulated by general interest in war neuroses . . . is beginning to create a widespread demand for psychiatric social workers," announced the 1919–1920 annual report of the Smith College School for Social Work. Jarrett even hired lecturers known for their connections to the Berlin and Vienna clinics. The prestigious faculty included Bernard Glueck, a New York psychoanalyst openly interested in treating people with psychiatric illness. "I have been very busy the past few months organizing a hospital for nervous and mental disorders," Glueck wrote to Eitingon in 1928, "where I hope to be able to use psycho-analytic methods in connection with patients that are not entirely suitable for office practice." Similarly, William Alanson White, who built St. Elizabeth's into a great psychiatric hospital in Washington, D.C. while advocating for far-reaching prevention of mental illness, was a Smith social work lecturer. On his official trips to Europe, White had been impressed by the widespread shift in perception of war neurosis, from the military and psychiatric establishments alike. In fact, even before the war he and Pearce Bailey had advanced "the recognition of mental disease as a possible form of injury resulting from the operations of war." But when White later visited Berlin's Charité, he returned to the U.S. firmly persuaded that all soldiers, from the newly drafted soldiers to veterans already suffering from "mental disabilities which were the result of military service," should be screened by mental health professionals.[18] Taken aback by this striking evidence of war's impact on human psychology, even Abraham Brill, founder of the New York Psychoanalytic Society, and Adolf Meyer of Johns Hopkins in Baltimore, agreed to join the rotating faculty of the Smith College School for Social Work. Margaret Powers was a student in their graduating class of 1918.

By the time she reached the Poliklinik in 1928, Powers already had acquired a broad background both in psychiatry and as a child welfare worker with the State Charities Aid Association, one of the Charity Organization Societies (COS). In the unpopular role of home investigator for families applying to adopt, she nevertheless focused on the concerns of the children who remained in foster care until their legal adoption. She disliked the moral tones of self-righteousness that alienated some of her social work colleagues from the poor, largely immigrant families on New York's Lower East Side, who were their clients. Neither was she under any illusion of virtue in poverty, and if children were beaten, starved, or prostituted by their parents, they had the right to alternative—and better—families. Powers went to Berlin because the Poliklinik's design was uniquely suited to the mental health needs of urban families in her native New York. A popular lecturer on psychiatric social work, she established the first professional social work department in the division of psychiatry at Cornell University Hospital. She also instituted clinical internships at Cornell for graduate-level students at the Smith College and New York (future Columbia University) schools of social work. Five hundred to six hundred patients, and often their families as well, were aided annually by her social work department. Even Stanley P. Davies, the usually noncommittal officer of the State Charities Aid Association, reveled in Margaret Powers's ability to set "the highest standards of casework [that] . . . served as a model for the development of similar departments elsewhere."[19] Powers naturally imported back to New York the Berliners' belief in individual psychotherapy, eligibility for treatment based on diagnosis instead of the ability to pay, and special techniques for working with children. Her deliberate infusion of the Weimarian ethos into private and public American clinics consequently changed professional social work education. Even the established urban mental health services at Ward's Island in New York and throughout the Northeast were influenced by the what Erik Erikson would call the "psychosocial paradigm." Today American social work is wont to follow in many ways the Berlin model of urban psychoanalysis, while American psychoanalysis remains generally allied to the more functionalist model of mental hygiene.

"The very group of patients who need our treatment are without resources"

1929

"THE CENTERS immediately became so overcrowded," Reich said of Sex-Pol, "that any doubt as to the significance of my work was promptly removed."[1] Once the Vienna newspapers announced that the new sexual hygiene clinics for workers and employees had opened, the work of the clinics took off. In January 1929 Reich decided to expand the Sex-Pol network of free community clinics, and add longer-term individual psychoanalysis to the brief contact of the outreach missions. The clinics gained ample encouragement from prospective patients who, for whatever reason, did not go to private therapists or other consultation centers in Vienna, nor to the Ambulatorium where Reich was still assistant director. From his office on the fourth floor of one of Vienna's ornate stuccoed buildings, equidistant between the Ambulatorium and the Allgemeine Krankenhaus, Reich coordinated the network's activities. By now six clinics had opened in different districts of Vienna, each clinic directed by a physician. Three obstetricians and a lawyer volunteered to be on call. Reich, who most enjoyed his position as scientific director but whose popularity as an analyst never abated, had to schedule a second daily consultation hour because at least ten people at a time would wait their turn to see him during his hour reserved for counseling. Thorough diagnostic consultations took about half an hour per person, however, and many prospective patients required considerable assistance.[2] The four psychoanalytic colleagues from the Vienna society who joined Reich—probably Annie Reich and Grete Lehner Bibring, with Siegfried Bernfeld and Otto

Fenichel on their trips back from Berlin—were similarly beleaguered. Their lack of time became particularly acute once the outreach lectures started, and Reich was impatient and demanding. He still thought of his psychoanalytic peers as collaborators in the struggle for human liberation, but was concerned that their commitment would waver under pressure. Nevertheless Reich reassured his Viennese colleagues that their ongoing activism and support was still effective.

Reich's professional image was considerably less well-established, however, among most of the Americans staying in Vienna for their psychoanalytic training. They were suspicious of Reich's membership in the Communist Party. One young foreign candidate warned O. Spurgeon English, a New Yorker then in analysis with Reich, that Communism was dangerously contaminating. "When I returned to the United States, as a result of exposure to [Reich]," he cautioned English, I "would not be able to obtain a position in any American university."[3] One evening, when English took his friend's advice and asked Reich to explain how his political activities affected psychoanalysis, Reich suggested he speak instead to Helene Deutsch as director of the Institute. Reich was nervous about leaving his reputation in one analyst's hands, especially since he and Deutsch had quarreled over practice issues at the technical seminar. Nevertheless Deutsch stated her "complete confidence" in Reich and told English that she had "never seen any evidence that his political views disturb his ability as an analyst."[4] Either Deutsch was being generous or she simply agreed with Reich's politics. By then some of Reich's more outrageous capers had caused even the generally sympathetic *Arbeiter-Zeitung* to denounce his "backfiring maneuvers."[5] The newspaper accused Reich of having tried—and failed—to install a Communist cell in Ottakring, a working-class neighborhood, and of misusing the name of the Social Democratic Party.

Not that Reich had abandoned his belief in the union of psychoanalysis and left-wing politics. He warned that the struggle for human liberation could only be maintained if "the discoveries and formulations of psychoanalysis are not watered down and that it does not gradually, without its apologists realizing what is happening, lose its meaning." His own Socialist Association for Sex Hygiene and Sexological Research would be challenged by just this crisis. Yet Reich still emphasized that "the proper study of psychoanalysis is the psychological life of man in society" in his essays written between 1929 and 1931. His class-based analyses placed workers' sexuality within a dominant bourgeois culture. Impoverishment of worker sexuality was a form of subjugation caused by enforced living conditions, especially

harmful to young people whose energy could not—and should not—be simply sublimated by sports events. After a two-month pilgrimage to Moscow (where his lectures failed to win over local audiences from the Communist Academy) in 1930, Reich was all the more convinced of the need for a universal sexual revolution. "The history of psychoanalysis in bourgeois society is connected with the attitude of the bourgeoisie to sexual repression, or, to put it another way," Reich stated, "to the removal of sexual repression."[6] Finally he asked with pointed candor if "the bourgeoisie [could] live side by side with psychoanalysis for any length of time without damage to itself?" If psychoanalysis and bourgeois society got together to make psychological care genuinely accessible to the community, the result might look like his own free clinics.

Reich urged his psychoanalytic partners toward ever more frank and intimate communication with the people they treated on an individual micro level. At the same time, he proposed that a "practical course in social economy" or academic sociology would benefit them on a macro level. Sound social reform would emerge from this form of psychoanalytically blended social work. Increasingly impatient with academic city planners and with "official sociology still compiling dead statistics," Reich viewed social work as a more direct and meaningful application of the social sciences than experimental research. Social science research on its own was too abstract and already a fairly useless exercise, with few publicly redeeming qualities except perhaps in its practical applications. Sociologists would learn much more about the frank realities of human life "not at their university offices but at the sickbed of society, on the streets, in the slums, among the unemployed and poverty-stricken," Reich wrote. Typical of his pronouncements on the deteriorating human condition, Reich demanded "practicality" even from an academic discipline and prescribed at least six years of pragmatic experience as "social workers" for sociologists, "just as physicians gain their [profession] through six years of hard work in laboratories and clinics." In this realm of social work Reich followed and then extended Freud's political thought. Like an analysis that frees the individual from inner oppression and releases the flow of natural energies, so—Reich believed—the political left would free the oppressed and release their innate, self-regulating social equanimity. By coincidence, Reich's extended his efforts to build up Sex-Pol just when his activist colleague Ernst Simmel was renewing his rounds of fund-raising for another controversial institution (supported by Freud), the Schloss Tegel inpatient facility.

"The very group of patients who need our treatment are without resources, precisely because of their psychoneurosis. I am constantly receiving letters

from morphine and cocaine addicts and alcoholics begging for treatment, which mostly I cannot give them, or only at personal sacrifice," Simmel pleaded to Minister of State Becker.[7] Clinically, the sanatorium had afforded indigent people a total therapeutic milieu whose "aim [was] to produce in our patients responsibility for themselves."[8] Becker was then the *Kultus Minister*, the Prussian minister of art, science, and education who professed to be responsive to Freud's work and honored by his annual presence in Berlin-Tegel. Would Becker and his important officials, however, agree to future funding of the sanatorium? Freud, who found the Tegel facility enormously beneficial to himself and more generally to psychoanalysis, resolved to explain the hospital's financial predicament to Becker in person. In a special meeting between himself, the minister, the Tegel staff, and Simmel, Freud brought back almost word for word, and certainly in concept and in tone, the final challenge from his Budapest speech. "It is difficult to support this work by private means alone," Simmel recalled him saying, "and its future depends upon whether you, for instance, Herr Minister, help us support such work."[9] Ultimately Freud held that, since the representatives of the state wielded considerable power regardless of the current regime, and that by definition they would remain unmoved by the plight of the common people, the analysts were responsible for providing their government with enlightened guiding principles. And as the hospital's financial crisis seemed only to become worse, Freud's response was to declare the urgency not only of preserving the institution but also of enhancing it with research and training programs. Simmel had actually planned to expand the Schloss Tegel facility, now a semiclosed institution, and develop a locked unit for people with severe psychoses. But, like most such establishments, the sanatorium was caught in a three-way confrontation between the psychoanalysts' experimental and humanitarian concerns on the one side, establishment psychiatry on another side, and the market imperatives of private land owners on a third. The von Heinz family, landlords of the nearby Schloss Humboldt, largely dispensed with charitable leanings and soon objected to the prospect of lower property values, for them a far more terrifying prospect than freely roaming psychiatric patients. "As most people would shrink from the idea of settling near an establishment for the mentally ill," the landlord wrote to Simmel, "the nature and purpose of which, after all, cannot be hidden, my land would lose its value in an undesirable way."[10] The government agreed. Despite Becker's individual declarations of support for Simmel's project, the German government fully concluded, along with the landlord, that such an institution would harm investment and real estate speculation. Meanwhile

Dr. Gustav von Bergmann, medicine director of the Berlin Charité, rendered a negative opinion in essence parallel to Julius Wagner-Jauregg's verdict on the Ambulatorium in Vienna. "It's not the misgivings of the medical faculty that are crucial," he said in casting his vote against the Tegel Sanatorium, "but the conviction that the psychoanalytic worldview is as one-sided as the purely somatic. . . . The principle of the psychoanalytic clinic as a program— as I see it—cannot be endorsed" even if psychoanalysis has merit when combined with medical therapies.[11] With or without the closed unit, state support was withheld.

A fresh, younger group of supporters rallied to Simmel's cause and started to rebuild the clinic's financial base with a series of fund-raising programs. Marie Bonaparte undertook a campaign to raise an endowment, similar to Eitingon's concurrent crusade to rescue the Verlag, in order to save the Tegel facility. She had stayed at the sanatorium and had, as Freud said "become intensely interested in the institution and decided for herself that it must not go on the rocks."[12] The French psychoanalyst René Laforgue suggested that IPA members should buy stock, even a very small amount, in the corporation. But by then the good faith of IPA benefactors like Pryns Hopkins was dangerously stretched. In March Hopkins had no sooner "given £1000 to the London Clinic [than] the Princess [Marie Bonaparte] asked for money to save Simmel's sanatorium."[13] Freud sent out his own plea letter worldwide and augmented his annual contribution, but the prospect of ongoing aid remained tenuous. Still, Anna, who had lived at Tegel for a few weeks while her father recovered from cancer surgery, remained optimistic about the sanatorium's future. Writing from Tegel, she conveyed to her friend Eva Rosenfeld how both peace and confusion descend simultaneously on the mind during analysis. In contrast, true country calm gives off enough peacefulness to help the mind rebound from city stress. "Tegel is . . . an island of safety in the midst of city traffic . . . ideal and more beautiful than ever," she wrote to Eva, who would move there late the next year. At Anna's urging, Eva would also start a period of fee-free analysis with Freud when he returned to Vienna. Meanwhile, prospects for Tegel's survival improved. "Dr. Simmel is in high spirits and full of hope," Anna reported.[14] And two weeks later she wrote to Eva about Laforgue's plan. "We are trying to found Tegel Incorporated, but are lacking a few rich people who could buy shares. I hope we bring it off."[15] The appeal was graceless and largely ineffectual, even among the London analysts who had valued the shares at £25 each.[16]

Anna Freud lost little time at Tegel. She taught one seminar at the Berlin Institute and another three-day course in child analysis at Tegel. She was generally pleased that some of the Berlin analysts, including Melitta Schmideberg (Melanie Klein's daughter), Jenö Harnik, and Carl Müller-Braunschweig, had met with her at Tegel—they had even rented a car for this October trip to the country—but Anna still felt like a stranger among them and far preferred her Vienna group. In the ongoing dispute between the Berliners and the Viennese over everything from human character to aesthetic pleasure to analytic technique, Anna caught on quickly to the Weimarian penchant for the "usable and useful" versus the Viennese inclination toward the "easy and pleasurable." Personally, though, she despised what she called the efficient Berliners' "ideals, their houses and antique furniture and conveniences" in favor of a more rural, simpler, and perhaps more communal life.[17]

The newest outpatient clinic was scheduled to open in Frankfurt, this one particularly exciting for its association with the candidly Marxist Institute for Social Research (Institut für Sozialforschung). Keeping up with the steady expansion of local analytic societies, Simmel's colleagues and long-time friends Karl Landauer and Heinrich Meng of the South-West German Psychoanalytic Society founded their psychoanalytic institute and its companion clinic in Frankfurt in February 1929.[18] In a bold and perspicacious move, Landauer decided to house the clinic on the premises of its intellectual partner, Max Horkheimer's Institute for Social Research. Now, as "guest institute" of the Institute for Social Research, the Frankfurt Psychoanalytic Society became, in a roundabout way, the first psychoanalytic group with enough status to be connected to a university. The University of Frankfurt, which the socialist theologian Paul Tillich (appointed as chair of philosophy the year before) called "the most modern and liberal of the universities" in the late 1920s, was a natural site for this association.[19] To celebrate the alliance of their clinic with the Frankfurt social scientists, Landauer invited all his IPA colleagues worldwide to participate in a series of inaugural lectures. They were delighted. Even Ernest Jones was so pleased that he announced Landauer's invitation to "the opening of a Psycho-Analytic Clinic in Frankfurt" to his colleagues of the British society and was tempted to show up from London.[20] The roster of illustrious speakers from Berlin attracted local media attention, and the psychoanalysts' ideas received generally positive reviews in the Frankfurt press. The *Frankfurter Zeitung* in particular devoted an entire issue of its supplement *Für Hochschule und Jugend* (For College and Youth) to the new series of lectures attended by physicians, students, and teachers at the Institute for Social Research. On February 16 Sándor Radó, Heinrich Meng, and Erich Fromm each delivered an inaugural address as a prelude to the Institute's forthcoming programs.

Erich Fromm, then head of social psychology department at the Institut für Sozialforschung and a lecturer at the psychoanalytic institute, lent an uncommon passion to his speech of the opening day ceremonies because he too, like his Frankfurt colleagues, had researched a fused external and internal understanding of mankind. "Dr Erich Fromm (Heidelberg) spoke of the possibility of applying psychoanalysis to sociology," reported the *Frankfurter Zeitung*, "for on the one hand sociology is concerned with human beings and not the mass mind, while on the other hand human beings exist, as analysis has always recognized, only as social creatures."[21] The reporters summarized his essay well. In Fromm's talk titled "The Application of Psychoanalysis to Sociology and Religious Studies," concurrently published in the analyst's pedagogical journal, he proposed that, from the beginning, psychoanalysis had understood that "there is no such thing as 'homo psychologicus'." The true challenge lay in grasping "the reciprocal conditioning of man and society" and that social relations are parallel to, not the opposite of, object relations.[22] Fromm's courses at the Institute would unavoidably present two apparently antithetical positions, but the difference between sociology and psychology was really just methodological, a question of form and not content. Like all the teaching analysts, Fromm outlined how his course material was based on data from the clinic. If the analysts could compare observations and plumb patients' case histories from the clinic, Karl Landauer warranted, the psychotherapists' chances of success would be determined by objective, empirical knowledge and not by so-called intuitive understanding. This approach existed already in Berlin, Radó had said in his opening remarks, where over one hundred "free treatment analyses are carried out everyday," not including the training analyses, by the Poliklinik's twelve lecturers. Now Frankfurt had the opportunity, as only the second psychoanalytic institution in Germany, to meet the population's need for treatment as well as the psychoanalysts' need for clinical data.

The Frankfurt analysts were caught in an interesting predicament. On the one hand they had too little room for a full-fledged treatment bureau until the next year and too few faculty to constitute a training facility. Conversely, their impressive affiliation with the Institut für Sozialforschung made them a collective center for psychoanalytic information, and the faculty was in great demand for public lecture tours, presentations in community education centers, and continuing professional education courses for lawyers, social workers, teachers, psychologists, and doctors. Bernfeld's Frankfurt speech on "Socialism and Upbringing" was the first in a series of four inaugural lectures. Conventional bourgeois education, Bernfeld explained, demands conformity and favors a sort of indoctrination into social norms. In contrast, socialists believe that education is a process of learning about one's self and others through personal struggle (hence psychoanalysis) and the development of group consciousness.[23] Anna Freud spoke about pedagogy as well, and Paul Federn and Hanns Sachs followed with two more open lectures on the meaning of analysis in sociology, medicine, and the mental sciences. Among themselves they bickered. Anna Freud complained to Eitingon that "Bernfeld draws the wrong conclusions from correct observation. Otherwise one might spare oneself the trouble of therapy."[24] And they also made amends. "What a warm heart you have, you dear man," Jones exclaimed in a burst of collegial reconciliation with Eitingon.[25] But publicly they stood as a united vanguard for psychoanalysis. The Frankfurt group centralized their educational advisory bureau just as their colleagues at the Ambulatorium had in Vienna, and added a research coalition of psychoanalysts and medical internists to teach their allied professions how to apply psychoanalytic technique. The constant intermingling of sociology with economic and psychoanalytic theory in discussions, lectures, research, and clinical treatment produced an exceptionally vibrant intellectual community. "There were personal, academically fruitful contacts between our lecturers and the theologian Paul Tillich," Heinrich Meng recalled as an example. In "one of his topics of discussion . . . [Tillich] established how strongly the young Marx emphasized humanism as the core of socialism."[26] At the Institute's peak many of its leaders focused their studies on the nature and roots of fascism and, in particular, on the rise of National Socialism. Unfortunately this intellectual pursuit was alarmingly prescient, and, with Nazi power increasing daily, their discussions were either futile or cause for exile. Four years later the inevitable choice would be exile.

In the weakening economic climate in Europe now also affected by the American Depression, Ernest Jones had little option but to appeal to the loyalty of the British society members in order to sustain the work of the London clinic. Late in October Jones proposed, as a cost-saving measure, to dissolve the formal barriers between the four components of the society. This was a logical decision since the same core group of members directed the Institute, edited the journal, chaired society meetings, and volunteered at the clinic. Besides, officers of the society held onto their titles and put them to use as enhanced connections to established academic and medical groups. Writing to Max Eitingon, Jones dismissed his friend's concern about the London clinic's viability by reminding him that Sylvia Payne, as the new "Business Secretary," consolidated all correspondence for the society, Institute, and clinic under her jurisdiction, while Edward Glover coordinated research and public programs.[27] For the nonmedical people these institutional contacts were particularly important tokens of legitimacy. However the present situation called for efficiency over prestige, and all members of the British society were unilaterally appointed as clinic assistants. All staff would treat one patient daily at the Gloucester Place facility or, as in the other societies, render an alternative but equivalent amount of service or money to the Institute.[28] Jones relished the plans afoot to fuse the society, the Institute, and the clinic into a single unit and, in virtually identical letters sent off to Freud and to Eitingon, described how he would "consolidate the new profession of psycho-analysis."[29] The most original element of the project—Jones called it "revolutionary"—placed lay analysts at the clinic in the same capacity as the regular staff. Thus as in Berlin and Vienna in different times, new clinical knowledge was discussed at the society but implemented only at the clinic.

While other analysts were formulating theories of child or adult development, Erik Erikson envisioned a longitudinal pathway through human life and established the markers for a steady transition from infancy to old age. Handsome and courteous, Erikson was an appealing young man. He had startling blue eyes, a square jaw, and the attentive demeanor of a born clinician. In the traditional style of the German intellectual, he kept a trim mustache and combed back his wavy blond hair. Erikson's now legendary psychosocial stages (as opposed to Freud's psychosexual stages) were conceived when working with adolescents at the Ambulatorium and were based on his experience there. His work with teenagers was supervised by August Aichorn, while Helene Deutsch and Eduard Bibring oversaw the treatment of his first adult patient. Erikson later said that he had decided to pursue a training analysis with Anna Freud once he became convinced, in his work with children at Heitzing, that psychoanalysis was compatible with art and had a strong visual component. Even today Erikson's eight stages are essentially a visual representation of human psychological development. The "stages" are charted diagonally rather than vertically to show that the sequence of stages, each of which chronicles how an individual appropriately resolves the struggle between their inner self and their outer, environmental or cultural demands, are "present at the beginning of life and remain ever present."[30] His model proposes that each stage has a healthy and an unhealthy resolution, notably the "Identity vs. Diffusion" of adolescence, and it assumes that this resolution lies in conforming to cultural norms such as independence from family, individualism, and personal achievement. Yet for all his emphasis on the "social" aspect of development and the construction of individual identity (the autobiographical undercurrent is conspicuous here), the strength of

Erikson's theory actually lies in the tools it gives the therapist for helping individuals explore their inner worlds.

Anna Freud was running three seminars at the Ambulatorium at the time, and had taught each of these courses at least weekly since 1926. Nearly every notable psychoanalyst from Vienna attended either her informal Kinderseminar[31] for younger analysts at the clinic, her weekly pedagogy seminar on merged psychoanalytic and educational techniques (largely drawn from her work at the Heitzing School) or her Technical Seminar on Child Analysis at the society's Training Institute. In her tireless pursuit of explanations of childhood psychological disorder, Anna invited experts on each stage of the life cycle to make presentations to the senior analysts who sat around a table while junior analysts sat behind them or stood. Aichorn, for example, taught adolescent psychology and juvenile delinquency. At another seminar Willi Hoffer presented a full case study of a child in analysis complete with behavior, dreams, and fantasies. Reich conducted a similar lively program analyzing case studies of adolescents and adults.

Heinz Hartmann, who was later to preach psychoanalytic orthodoxy under the guise of "ego psychology," had just returned to Vienna from several years at the far less conventional Berlin Poliklinik. Hartmann and his colleague Paul Schilder promoted a dual, or synthesized, psychoanalytic and biological approach to mental illness and wanted to test this formula in the treatment of psychiatric disorders. Despite the omnipresent lure of Wagner-Jauregg's powerful Psychiatric-Neurological Clinic where both had trained in the pathological-anatomical model of treatment, the two psychiatrists hammered out the plans for a new experimental department at the Ambulatorium. Specifically designed to treat adults with borderline and psychotic symptoms, the new section marked a milestone in improved relations between the psychoanalysts and the medical fixtures of native Viennese psychiatry. Some fifteen years earlier, during and just after the end of World War I, the psychiatric approach to adults with forbidding psychological diagnoses had shifted from accusations of malingering to a more sympathetic treatment of a disorder called war neurosis. Psychoanalysis had triumphed as the preferred form of treatment in all but the most conservative medical circles and had gained remarkable popularity even within military medicine. Presumably the same might happen now with other disorders. Unfortunately, no sooner had Schilder inaugurated the special clinic at the Ambulatorium in March, with plans for a systematic experiment in the psychotherapy of the psychoses, than he accepted a job offer from Adolf Meyer and left for the United States. Schilder's friend Eduard Bibring took over as the clinic's new director in September. Bibring too was a hospital-trained psychiatrist (figure 30), but, more important, he had been part of that lively group of Tandler's anatomy students who one afternoon in 1920 had visited Freud and emerged as his newest protégés. This same energy characterized Bibring's management of the new clinic, a confident initiative in keeping with Red Vienna but very much ahead of the times. Even visitors from America could see this. "The eleven-year-old republic of Austria," observed William French of the Commonwealth Fund," has built up a system of . . . care that is distinctive, flexible, and increasingly effective."[32]

If Bibring had not enhanced the Ambulatorium's newest therapeutic program, the Department for Borderline Cases and Psychoses, Hartmann and Schilder's psychoanalytic treatment model for people with schizophrenia, would not have attracted Ruth Brunswick, who joined in 1930. With Brunswick's expertise in treating severe depression and her unique compassion for people marginalized by mental illness, the clinic's work took an even more progressive direction. The standard in-depth evaluation of neurotic adults was eliminated in favor of a shorter, symptom-focused assessment questionnaire. Had the patient heard voices, or had visions, hallucinated? In order to forestall bias, a team of clinicians studied the patient's responses and then chose one of three possible treatment venues. First, patients who needed an extra questionnaire to confirm the presence of mental disease were re-

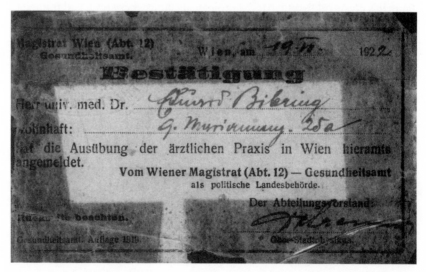

30 Eduard Bibring's license to practice medicine, issued in 1922 (Archives of the Boston Psychoanalytic Society and Institute)

manded to the regular adult section. A distinction had to be made between, for example, the organic hallucinations of the schizophrenic and the self-medicating alcoholic hallucinosis of the severely depressed. For patients to qualify for treatment in the psychiatric section, their psychotic or borderline symptoms could not be ruled out pending intensive scrutiny, and so they remained under observation and were eventually treated accordingly. Second, those who required an individualized treatment plan suited to their diagnostic category were offered less purely psychoanalytic forms of psychotherapy. Someone with a fragile hold on reality would tolerate with difficulty the anxiety stirred up by daily hour-long regimens of free association. And, technically, psychoanalysis could be modified: the full hour could be shortened to forty-five minutes, frequency reduced from five times to three times weekly, and perhaps the couch could be forfeited for a chair. Third, the analysts assumed the highly contestable position of allowing staff to offer classical psychoanalysis selectively to borderline cases or to people with incipient psychosis. Naturally aware of debates in this field, Eduard Hitschmann reported that nearly seventy cases of schizophrenia had been treated over ten years. Even the municipal hospital's psychiatric clinic, Wagner-Jauregg's own domain, referred patients. So too did the law courts: court officers were entitled to commute the sentence of offenders who agreed to manage their uncontrollable behavior with psychological treatment in lieu of incarceration. Social welfare centers, neighborhood physicians, and sanitoria where staff believed in a benign approach to mental illness sent referrals. Of course the Ambulatorium's own outpatient section sent over patients whose neurosis leaned toward psychosis. In retrospect, Bibring and his colleagues were naive in assuming that schizophrenia could be treated by analysis alone. But colleagues in Berlin were discussing this approach, and certainly in Budapest Sándor Ferenczi was experimenting with ingenious, if controversial, modifications in method that went way beyond individual style.

Under very different political circumstances, Sándor Ferenczi was also exploring options for instituting a clinic in Budapest. His colleagues in Vienna, Berlin, and London had successfully acted on the obligation to accommodate the needs of poor and underserved people for mental health services. Budapest's chronically inadequate public and private resources resulted in the actual loss of life, Ferenczi implied, in his overtly polemical introduction to a published case report. Ferenczi promoted the pamphlet, "From the Childhood of a Young Proletarian Girl," as a combined clinical summary and plea for understanding. In the gruesomely fascinating notes recording her first ten years of life, the nineteen-year-old daughter of an alcoholic underemployed father and despairing mother explored, with extraordinary precision, the relationship between social class and human misery. Ferenczi had been unable to stop the suicide of his precocious patient, but he did publish her *Diary* and let stand what Imre Hermann fondly called "subversive words for 1929."[33] "Rich children are lucky," the young diarist wrote. "They can learn many things, and [learning] is a form of entertainment for them . . . and they are given chocolate if they know something. Their memory is not burdened with all the horrible things they cannot get rid of. The teacher treats them with artificial respect. It was like this in our school. . . . I believe that many poor children learn poorly or only moderately for similar reasons and not because they are less talented."[34]

"Free or low-cost analyses . . . [were] at least a small beginning"

1930

BY 1930 Freud's bid for free treatment had taken shape much in the way he had envisioned over a decade earlier. Poor men and women in Vienna now had the same social right to mental health treatment as to surgery; mental illness was considered a public health threat much like tuberculosis; and decisions were made by committee, not by individuals, to start institutions where analytically trained physicians were appointed. Though outpatient clinics had been initiated by private charity, the state now recognized their value. Freud could not have been more pleased. The Berlin Poliklinik, he wrote, still "endeavors to make our therapy accessible to the great multitude who suffer under their neuroses no less than the wealthy but who are not in a position to meet the cost of their treatment."[1] Many factors converged then: the clinic's new location, its enlarged capacity and appeal to young academics, its political stance, and Berlin's reputation as an overall zestful urban epicenter. Yet the worldwide economic deterioration had struck, and the Nazi Party's sudden and powerful victory in the most recent elections was a shock. With the Nazis now Germany's second largest political party, Eitingon, Radó, and Simmel's concerns about the survival of psychoanalysis in a hostile environment intensified. They trained new analysts, analyzed patients five to six hours each day, taught new courses, and were generally driven to advance their own version of democracy. Even Freud's wife was drawn into the commotion: Martha, who enjoyed visiting Eitingon and his wife Mirra at their home on the Alteinsteinstrasse in Berlin-Dahlem, now called on the institute on Wichmannstrasse as well.

The demand for outpatient psychoanalysis was more variable than for inpatient psychiatry, but participation within predefined age groups and professions either increased or remained constant. Taking the clinic's demographic record as a whole, young adults had increased their usage fivefold in the ten-year span since 1920, so that by 1930 they were the most frequent consumers of clinical services. Eitingon screened almost all the applicants himself but, for many reasons, could not admit all of them to the Poliklinik. In fact, only half of the young adults between the ages of twenty-one and twenty-five who requested consultations actually received treatment (184 out of 372). The next demographic grouping, that of the twenty-six to thirty year olds, offered virtually the same picture: of their 358 consultations, 44 percent, or 160, resulted in a contract for analysis. Even among the so-called middle-aged men and women between the ages of thity-one and thirty-five years old, the pattern remained the same: the number of consultations (293) was just under double the number of ensuing analyses (128). Had the punctilious Fenichel analyzed Eitingon's data, he would have been pleased to discover that all cases seen during the 1920s were recorded in meticulous detail, from children under age five and to older adults ages sixty and above. A tremendous diversity of age, sex, occupation, and social standing formed the Poliklinik's overall patient base, but there seems to be little correlation between the patients' age and their diagnosis. Interestingly, despite the range of evidence to the contrary, clichéd assumptions that bourgeois women were the psychoanalysts' primary constituency because they were hysterical and could afford attention are still around today. False and catchy passages abound in the literature. "To be encouraged by a doctor to talk about oneself in the most prattling detail was a new and grand experience," Robert Graves once wrote, "especially for moneyed and lonely women who had had 'nervous breakdowns.'"[2] In truth, clinical institutions like the Poliklinik staked their historical reputations on contesting punitive measures taken against marginalized groups, women among them. The psychoanalysts believed that their theory allowed people to work productively and cooperatively, with fewer of the internalized restraints of a repressive society.

Seeking the same freedom from her starched New England breeding, the young Edith Banfield Jackson arrived in Vienna in January to be analyzed by Sigmund Freud. Edith Jackson was a rich, smart, and hardworking physician. She was a lean, long-limbed woman with a bob of chestnut hair and imperturbable green-blue eyes. Within a few years Jackson would become a financial mainstay of the psychoanalytic movement and, like von Freund, Eitingon, Marie Bonaparte, and Muriel Gardiner, fund ongoing psychoanalytic programs, socialize with the Freuds, and help analysts escape the Nazis. But in 1930 Jackson was new to Europe and kept to the pleasant routine of a recently arrived foreign analysand. She took daily German lessons in order to attend the Institute's seminars and work with children and dancing lessons for evenings at the Viennese balls. Every afternoon except Sunday she would leave the room she rented from Else Pappenheim's mother and walk to Freud's office on the Berggasse. Her analytic session, from five to six P.M., was held in English. "Working in the presence of Freud's mind is the most exciting experience I have ever had," she wrote to her sister Helen. "I find him a most lovable personality."[3] Analysis was difficult and made her moody, but Vienna's sophisticated array of evening activities easily cheered her up. All over the city the lectures, concerts, theater, and opera started at seven or seven-thirty in the evening. Jackson particularly enjoyed dances like the Artist's Ball where thousands of costumed men and women waltzed all night *en masque*. The more outrageous the costume, the more gleefully her analytic friends from the Kinderseminar gossiped about the dancer. The green cactus costume with a red cactus flower on the cap was her great favorite for the Concordia Ball. But the mushroom costume, the one she wore herself to the Concordia Ball (which she attended with another patient of Freud's) had a tight vest, an adorable white beret, and a round tulle skirt with the edges turned up. Meanwhile Jackson's new friends Anna Freud and Dorothy Burlingham drew Edith into the life of the Institute and the Ambulatorium and their own experiments in early childhood treatment. Ernst Simmel, now a specialist in psychotic disorders himself, invited Jackson to look in on his team at the Schloss Tegel. Jackson was particularly impressed by the originality of Simmel's work. At the *"Psychoanalytical* sanatorium,"[4] she wrote, "there are at present only 12 or 14 patients (capacity is 25). I don't know that we have any such institutions in America, but I hope we will have. For it is excellent for people who need analysis to have the benefits of such pleasant and healthful surroundings with a slight amount of supervision and regulation."[5] She met Ruth Mack Brunswick, another American analysand on the staff of the Ambulatorium, who was infusing the clinic's newest branch, the Department for Borderline Cases and Psychoses, with enthusiasm for the treatment of severe mental illness. Brunswick showed Edith her research on psychosis and her effort (shared by other analysts trained by Reich, Schilder, and Hartmann) to understand mental illness by interviewing psychotic or schizophrenic patients.

Wilhelm Reich is perhaps best known today as either an experimenter about whom people feel somewhat uncomfortable, for his orgone accumulators and rainmaking machines of the early 1950s, or as a patron of liberated sexuality mythologized by radical therapists of the 1960s. Others remember him for writing books like *Character Analysis* and for spearheading organizations like the Ambulatorium and Sex-Pol. Reich's history is often divided into the "good" psychoanalytic Reich and the "bad" Reich who lost his mind to politics and incipient schizophrenia sometime around 1930. In September 1930 Wilhelm Reich resigned from the Ambulatorium and moved from Vienna to Berlin[6] with his wife, the psychoanalyst Annie Reich. But he did not lose his mind. Between 1930 and 1934 Reich's involvement with psychoanalysis and activist politics continued unabated, his reputation intact. Berlin initially met his hopes for a more receptive environment than Vienna. Many of the younger analysts had also moved to Berlin—Otto Fenichel, Erich Fromm, Edith Jacobson, Siegfried Bernfeld, and Karen Horney—and agreed with Reich's immutable linkage of psychoanalysis and Marxism. They nicknamed him "the Character Smasher." Reich was personally dismayed by Freud's indifference (or worse) to him and deliberately avoided re-creating the factioned tensions of his last years in Vienna. He practiced and held seminars on character analysis in his home near Wichmanstrasse. Prohibited pro tem from working as a training analyst because of his resolutely character-analytic therapy, he nevertheless lectured at the Poliklinik and saw patients there. Soon Reich and Otto Fenichel, his old friend from Vienna's social circles, gathered around them an inner circle of younger colleagues self-described as dialectical-materialist analysts. "The existence of the psychic unconscious," wrote one of them, the analyst Alexander Mette, "is an incontrovertible point for the materialist science. Recognizing this won't modify its foundations anymore than, for example, the law of relativity."[7] Reich also joined the Children's Seminars (figure 31) that Fenichel had overseen since 1924. Its core participants, including Fromm, Jacobson, Kate Friedländer, George Gerö, and Edith Buxbaum, would form the heart of Fenichel's last organizing project in Europe, the *Rundbriefe* circle by 1934.

Emboldened, Reich began to reestablish his network of free sex-counseling clinics and move Sex-Pol from Vienna to Berlin. As in Vienna in the late 1920s, he assembled people for sex education discussions, contraceptive information, and short-term psychotherapy for individuals and couples. Annie Reich, Fenichel, Edith Jacobson, and Käthe Misch, still members of the Berlin Psychoanalytic Society, worked with him as advocates for sexual and political reform. He lectured to a student group on "The Fiasco of Bourgeois Morality," which Fenichel followed up with a conference interestingly titled "Dread of the Community." He then spoke to the Berlin Association for So-

31 Children's Seminar analysts on a picnic, "Self-Portrait." Standing (*from left to right*), Grete Bibring, Wilhelm Reich, Otto Fenichel, Eduard Bibring (*leaning into the camera*), unidentified woman; sitting (*from left to right*), unidentified woman, Frances Deri, Annie Reich (Special Collections, A. A. Brill Library, New York Psychoanalytic Society and Institute)

cialist Physicians, the group headed by Ernst Simmel, on the prevention of emotional problems. As he had in Vienna, Reich shifted among a range of political organizations but finally decided that expanding Sex-Pol would advance what he called "sex-political" themes the furthest. The sex hygiene centers had already registered seven hundred applicants over eighteen months, Reich reported in a speech to the World League for Sexual Reform.[8] He was one of the few psychoanalysts to join the German Communist Party and, perhaps inevitably, his mainstream reputation suffered when the Communists agreed to underwrite his sex-political organization. Since the turn of the century, the Communists had criticized psychoanalysis for being too individualistic and ignoring the economic root of human suffering. But they agreed with Reich that public health programs ignored mental illness or, even worse, prescribed routine advice. Seventy percent of the workers' problems were too severe for short-term counseling, Reich said, and even treating the

30 percent who might find their way to his clinics was inadequate. The Communists, who later repudiated Reich, as did the IPA, decided to subsidize the new Deutscher Reichsverband für Proletarische Sexualpolitik (German Association for Proletarian Sexual Politics). According to his second wife, Ilse Reich, the Reichsverband drew in more than twenty thousand members with a campaign very similar to Hugo Bettauer's popular crusade in Vienna: better mass housing, legalized abortion and homosexuality, free birth control and contraception, sex education, employer-based child care, and health insurance for mothers and children.[9]

In most matters Reich's political beliefs were those of the Viennese Social Democrats, taken further to the left but based in the idea of building feasible, specific social programs like housing and health care. The relationship between Reich and Freud was intense, ambivalent, and, by the 1930s, combative. Freud did have a political mission, the mission of the Social Democrats who implemented their idea of a centrally planned, redistributive state in Austria of the early 1920s. While Freud made it clear that "political unrest and economic misery certainly have the right to draw people's attention first and foremost to themselves," as he wrote to Ferenczi, personally he held off from overt involvement in a specific political movement.[10] Yet his disinclination to support outright "the Communist ideal" did not preclude him from having a political agenda since he "remain[ed] a liberal of the old school," as he wrote to his friend Arnold Zweig.[11] In fact, identification with a movement other than psychoanalysis would have blurred his agenda for human liberation. Reich understood this. For all the criticism he gave and got throughout his life, Reich spoke of Freud with admiration and excluded him from his general condemnation of psychoanalysts (who had, after all, ejected Reich from his own professional association). Former friends like Paul Federn and Otto Fenichel eventually proved disloyal. Ernest Jones blamed him for vicariously deceiving their leader and for shifting psychoanalysis away from private clinical practice to the wider political arena. "I am extremely sorry that so many members in Berlin and Vienna who had boycotted the only scientific Congress for Sex Research,"[12] Jones wrote to Eitingon, "should nevertheless be reading papers at the unscientific popular Congress for Sexual Reform."[13] But like so many of Freud's followers, from Melanie Klein and Ernest Jones onward, Reich saw himself as the lone champion of the true master and their interpersonal conflicts as merely human obstacles to the scientific progress of psychoanalysis. By 1930 Reich had switched to a more flamboyant rhetoric that would eventually alienate some of his closest friends, and Sex-Pol seemed to veer off on an increasingly left-radical path.

In truth his work hardly differed from Simmel's at Tegel or Eitingon's at the Poliklinik, but he did fail to persuade the analysts that he remained on their avant-garde.

Meanwhile, in Frankfurt, Erich Fromm and an elite group from the local psychoanalytic institute successfully opened a new clinic on a straightforward social democratic model. "Free or low-cost analyses . . . [are] at least a small beginning," Karl Landauer told Eitingon, of the plans he and Heinrich Meng had proposed.[14] The Frankfurt clinic, the last of the free outpatient treatment centers attributable to Freud's Budapest speech, would last only two years. Nevertheless, it was provided with modest but adequate assets for the moment, and the Frankfurt clinic was able to secure the level of serious academic authority that had eluded all the other clinics. Landauer's former analysand, the social philosopher Max Horkheimer, had just been appointed professor at the University in Frankfurt and simultaneously director of the Institute for Social Research. Landauer was thrilled. Horkheimer "has given his energetic support to psychoanalysis," he told Eitingon," and wants close collaboration between his institute and ours. We will, as far as I can see, move there and also have room for a treatment center." Freud too was pleased and sent Horkheimer letters of appreciation.[15] The clinic started small but promising and, except for its remarkable connection to its host, the Institut für Sozialforschung, it stayed quite modest. The customary ten to fifteen patient waiting list began even before the clinic opened. Eventually five patients at a time were seen by the part-time analysts. More homogeneous as a group than in Berlin or Vienna, the patients were almost exclusively intellectuals associated with the parent institute or its affiliates and chiefly young academics ages twenty to thirty. While the caseload was different—no farmers or laborers or even children were treated in Frankfurt—structurally the clinic was similar to those in other cities. Clinical sessions were scheduled to last forty-five minutes. Diagnoses were disproportionately male diagnoses: impotence, psychogenic sterility and hysteria and, typically for an academic milieu, "existential conflicts which have not been overcome, character disturbances, work inhibitions."[16] Interestingly, patients could transfer their analysis between the Berlin and Frankfurt clinics. Landauer, who saw the advantages of sharing resources between the two German clinics, sought practical advice from Eitingon. "I should like to ask you about the terms under which you appoint the assistants in the Berlin Institute. I mean most particularly the financial side," he wrote with the implicit understanding that Frankfurt's proficiency on the theoretical side was irreproachable. Erich Fromm, along with Landauer and Meng, consulted with community teachers whose primary and secondary schools had turned to them for advice on difficult pupils and adolescents with behavioral problems, in part to educate them on child development and in part to treat the teachers' own stress-induced neuroses. With Max Horkheimer heading the research institute and Meng, Fromm-Reichman, and especially Erich Fromm on the faculty, Landauer could take the integration of psychoanalysis and Marxism further than it had ever gone before.

Erich Fromm's career as a practicing psychoanalyst had started at the Berlin Poliklinik in 1926. A theoretically minded young man, Fromm was then as comfortable with philosophers like Horkheimer and Marcuse as with his left-leaning psychoanalytic colleagues from Berlin, Otto Fenichel and Wilhelm Reich. Once he arrived at the institute, however, Fromm's writings became increasingly critical of Freud. Like Reich, he valorized matriarchy over patriarchy (while equating Freud with patriarchism) and rejected the Oedipus configuration outright. In this he differed from Adorno and Horkheimer who, Fromm correctly believed, found Freud to be "more revolutionary" because he insisted on candor in regard to sexuality.[17] Later, once Fromm disengaged his work from the Frankfurt Institute's advances in critical theory, Horkheimer wrote to his old friend Lowenthal. "We are really indebted to Freud and his first collaborators. . . . Even where we do not agree with Freud's interpretations and use of [concepts], we find their objective intention is deeply right." What Horkheimer especially admired in Freud was his undiluted insistence that individual inner psychology exists per se and is, at the same time, rooted in the historical moment. For Freud the self is neither a simple product of the environment nor a mechanistic preformed personality but evolves in a constant process of redefining the relationship between inner and outer worlds. Proponents of critical theory gladly listened to this approach precisely because they thrived on examining the paradoxes and social contradictions of modern life. They accused so-called revisionists or neo-Freudians, like the post-Berlin Erich Fromm and Karen Horney, of diluting the bite of Freudian theory by desexualizing it and imposing a linear cultural template on the changeable nature of human development. Fenichel and Simmel agreed, accusing the neo-Freudians of conformity while asserting that orthodox Freudianism is all the more liberating for its emphasis on the unconscious and sexuality and for its tolerance of the irrational. Speaking at Simmel's memorial in 1946, Max Horkheimer said that Freud and Simmel were "relentless enemies of intellectual superstructures including the metaphysical hiding places of the mind. . . . They pursued, " he said dispassionately, "radical demythification."[18]

Once the Berlin society had publicly reaffirmed that "the obligation to treat free of charge one case at the Polyclinic still hold[s] good," Barbara Low reintroduced this still contentious discussion to the British society in London.[19] The British were unlikely to follow indiscriminately Eitingon's belief that members of the institute incur an actual obligation to work at the clinic or do other equivalent work. Both Jones in London and Hitschmann in Vienna had been duly following this principle, in fact, but, with resources thinning and without a strong political position, the British hesitated before making further commitments. The appropriate nature of the collaboration between the institute and the clinic, they decided, could only be arbitrated with empirical data. For the moment Jones had found a way to postpone the decision. Since data must be collected before it can be analyzed, a questionnaire would have to go to all members asking exactly how much time they were contributing to the clinic. The council would define the term *equivalent work* only after all the information had been gathered.[20] Perhaps the thornier issue of world politics loomed large in their decisions. Jones's good friend Franz Alexander, for example, was among the first analysts to leave Berlin for the United States.[21] Two years later, under Alexander's direction, the Chicago Institute for Psychoanalysis was born, the first and until 1948 the only American society to house an outpatient clinic.

By mid-November 1930 Budapest's new generation of city officials, whose predecessors had so eagerly vaunted their commitment to psychoanalysis, decided to delay the Hungarian society's request for a license to open the clinic. Like their London colleagues, the Hungarian analysts struggled to keep alive the prospects for an outpatient free clinic. Responsibility for the delay rested less with the judges themselves, Ferenczi's commented to his international colleagues, than with the university professors hired to evaluate the project.[22] These "experts" were already so hostile to psychoanalysis by the time they reviewed the plans that the application had to be temporarily withdrawn. But it was clear, just as it had been in Vienna from 1920 to 1922, that private (or private-public partnership) psychoanalytic initiatives would fare better than those seeking public approval. Margit Dubovitz had already launched a psychoanalytic clinic for children under the auspices of the Hungarian League for the Protection of Children.[23] The start-up of this clinic, partly subsidized by the government, was promising and made for much excitement in the psychoanalytic community. A psychoanalytic consultancy designed for children and parents from all social classes had been turned over by the National League to Ferenczi. Ferenczi enlisted Dubovitz, and together they charted out a system of social services to include safe homes for mothers and children, orphanages, organized holidays for handicapped and convalescing people, outpatient clinics, and a publication, the *Journal for the Protection of Children*.[24] By early May Dubovitz and her colleague Vera von Felszeghy had gathered substantive clinical material and were ready to lead a case discussion and report on the children's outpatient clinic to the Budapest society's monthly meeting.

"As a social-democratic town councilor, Dr. Friedjung has furthered our interests as psychoanalysts"

1931

MARTIN GROTJAHN was already a staff psychiatrist at the Berlin-Buch state mental hospital and, as he later wrote, no exception to the haughty reputation of university professors when he applied for admission to the Berlin Psychoanalytic Institute. Grotjahn's choice was politically significant. Despite its popularity in Berlin of the 1920s, the status of the psychoanalyst never really achieved that of the psychiatrist/physician, meaning that anyone inclined to pursue psychoanalytic training risked harming their academic career. Conversely, few organizations were more exciting to a socially minded psychiatrist, whose civic bent was increasingly confined to secretive meetings and coded plays, than the psychoanalyst's Poliklinik. Of course the analysts had their own exclusionary, and some critics would say elitist, practices. The grueling four-part admissions process consisted then, as today, of interviews designed to assess the candidates' personal motivation, capacity for empathy, and general equanimity—and to screen out individuals deemed unfit to treat others because of their particular neuroses. Grotjahn never forgot his admissions review. First came the interview with Max Eitingon, described by Grotjahn as a "shy, small man with a slight stammer," who afterward discreetly offered him financial support.[1] Next came the interview with the clinic's assistant director, Karen Horney. Horney's seven cats slept on the one comfortable couch in her office and her desk was piled so high with papers and manuscripts that Grotjahn felt both amused and a slightly wicked need to tidy up. Horney herself said very little. When Horney left, an elderly bald man with an enormous beard interviewed him, all the while staking out his own vehemently antipsychiatric position. Any student of theology or anthropology would bring a more open mind to the study of psychoanalysis than a psychiatrist, he said, but nevertheless he refrained from disqualifying Grotjahn entirely. The interviews culminated in a dramatic entrance by Wilhelm Reich, who asked a few questions without even sitting down and generally seemed to regard the interview as a silly formality. Grotjahn's candidacy was approved and his training analysis soon underway with Ernst Simmel.

At the center of Grotjahn's account of his training analysis lies a startling metaphor for that era—the cold use of cash. Ernst Simmel had a reputation as a technically meticulous analyst with radical politics but traditional scruples. His waiting room was noteworthy for its massive plain oak table designed by Ernst Freud and the glossy picture book of Charlie Chaplin. Now, however, Simmel insisted on being paid in cash. This kind of expedience was uncharacteristically cynical for him, but, then again, cash resources alone would make escaping the Nazis possible. His conduct was redeemed when, suddenly, in Grotjahn's fourth month of analysis, the peace of the daily session was shattered by a telephone call. A friend inside the Alexanderplatz precinct house had got wind of a Gestapo sweep and alerted Simmel that the secret police would shortly be sent his way with imminent arrest and a death threat. Grotjahn helped his analyst flee the Nazis by pushing him out a window into the backyard. In contrast, Felix Boehm, a non-Jew who remained at the Berlin Institute after its aryanization in 1933, also demanded cash, raised his fees, was constantly short of money, and often sent his maid to fetch his payment before it was due. In times of receding or less visible anti-Semitism, the analysts had carefully resisted the impact of such tensions on the Poliklinik. Now, with the Nazi presence in the treatment rooms, lecture halls, and seminars increasingly obvious, the analysts' sense of democracy and openness was fraying. Germany's economy had plummeted, violence roamed the streets, and the psychoanalysts were no safer (physically or financially) than anyone else. At a discussion of the Institute's deteriorating finances the Berliners resolved that, among other measures, candidates in training analysis should make a monthly contribution to the Institute equivalent to the analyst's fee for a single session. "The total fee of patients at the Poliklinik who become able to pay for analysis," the Berlin society decided, "shall be handed over to the Institute."[2] Nevertheless, when Barbara Low, in London, reported to the British society on her visit to Germany and the recent sociological and pedagogical activities of the Berlin society, she emphasized the public activities of the members.[3]

Faced with censoring rejection from within the IPA and with surveillance and penalty (or worse) from outside, Fenichel "called all left analysts in Berlin together in order to discuss," in a take on Lenin's famously pragmatic question, "what was to be done."[4] The IPA actively sought to moderate Wilhelm Reich, Otto Fenichel, and their Children's Seminars group's resolutely left-leaning approaches to therapy of internal and external worlds. Fenichel was removed as editor of the *Zeitschrift* and Reich's 1931 article on masochism was rejected without a disclaimer. But the IPA offensive only solidified their position. The group began to meet, regularly though informally, at Reich's house. For the first time since 1919, when Reich, Fenichel, Lehner, and Bibring had convened after Julius Tandler's class to discuss controversial topics outside Vienna's mainstream medical curriculum, the two leaders found themselves recreating the structure of a leftist caucus. Recently returned from a study trip to the Soviet Union, Fenichel helped the group integrate Reich's formulations into a Marxist-Freudian synthesis, plan rejoinders to the increasing political conservatism in the psychoanalytic journals, and explore the possibility of a new organization. In 1931 the friends could still devote their evening discussions to investigating the relationship between psychoanalysis, religion, and education in order to make clear the hazardous impact of what Fenichel dubiously called the "bourgeois-analytical viewpoints." After 1933, however, the group would assume a new appearance: it became a loosely organized network of psychoanalysts in exile, unified by their belief in psychoanalysis as dialectical materialism and bound together by Otto Fenichel's epistolary energy until 1945.

As the campaign against psychoanalysis (and other modernist venues) intensified in Germany and Austria, the Budapest city government seemed to rediscover its interest in the free clinic it had abandoned more than a decade earlier. On December 18, 1931, the municipality granted the analysts permission to open a polyclinic called the Allgemeines Ambulatorium für Nerven- und Gemütsskranke (General Ambulatorium for Nervous and Mental Patients).[5] Even after a full year of negotiations, the Ministry of Public Welfare still felt obliged to pacify the entrenched psychiatric establishment. "Since psychoanalysis is not an independent science but a part of general psychology and neuropathology," the local Budapest official said, "the [psychoanalytic] Association must express this in the title of the polyclinic." They agreed to call the clinic "simply a clinical agency for nervous and emotional illnesses in which, among other things, psychoanalysis is practiced," Ferenczi wrote to Freud.[6] In the end, the same government that had so vociferously impeded the clinic now inaugurated its opening with a laudatory address by the honorable Dr. Rostagni, town clerk. While the short opening program was perhaps more of a public relations gesture than a celebration, nevertheless Ferenczi recounted the history of the psychoanalytic movement in Hungary with joy. Bálint outlined the therapeutic work of the clinic and Hermann its training functions. The future held tremendous possibilities for child analysis, Margit Dubovitz said, despite the recent closing of a child protection society's psychoanalytic clinic. Alice Bálint, a former classmate of the celebrated infant developmentalist Margaret Mahler, would analyze children there. Istvan Hollós, a master administrator as well as clinician, shed a positive light on the relation between psychoanalysis and psychiatry. The Hungarian society collectively invited Dr. Ferenczi to assume the directorship of the clinic with Michael Bálint as deputy and Drs. Imre Hermann, Istvan Hollós, and Zsigmond Pfeifer providing consultations.[7]

In every respect 12 Mészáros Street (figure 32) was a central location for a free clinic in Budapest. Michael Bálint, Vilma Kovács, and her eldest daughter Alice (who later married Michael Bálint) happened upon the space in an imposing building at the intersection of Mészáros and Ag streets. The building, with its classical apartments and outer corridors on every floor, belonged to Vilma's husband, the architect Frederic Kovács. At the center of this typical Hungarian residential building was a squared courtyard where patients could easily find their way to the clinic's entrance on the ground floor. The concierge's children playing in the open yard rarely ventured to the clinic at the back left-hand corner of the courtyard, but occasionally the elderly lady herself would limp over, child in hand, and admit patients through the thick double doors during the daytime. The society had rented the five-room apartment out of its own funds and remodeled it into treatment rooms and a meeting area off the foyer. In the relatively large vestibule, one could see conference programs on flyers pinned to the right-hand wall, read an issue of *Gyógyászat* (Therapeutics), the journal edited on the premises, or simply select a chair from the two rows in the waiting room. The vestibule also functioned as a conference room, and a curtain could be pulled between the rows of chairs, one side for patients waiting to see their analysts, the other for perhaps an administrative meeting. Since the treatment rooms opened onto the waiting area, no effort was made to stop patients from meeting other friends and analysts, with the ultimate effect of developing the same sense of community as at the Berlin Poliklinik. Dr. Endre Almásy lived in a room off the clinic in exchange for a quasi full-time position as assistant.

In the hands of lay men and women like Edith Gyömröi, who would later

32 Doorway of the Budapest Clinic, Apt. no. 5 at 12 Mészáros Street (Judith Dupont)

join Fenichel's Berlin group of activists, the Budapest polyclinic expanded quickly. Patients paid very very little, maybe five pengö per session or nothing at all, and the analysts worked for free. Most analysts accepted referrals from their city's social service agencies, but the smaller, more private Budapest clinic accepted adult and child referrals only from physicians. The very first patients at Meszaros Street were, in fact, children. One tall pale girl, from a family so poor they ate nothing but potatoes morning, noon, and night, was brought to the clinic faint from crying for days. Her younger sister seemed fine, more concerned about her sibling's sadness than her own lack of food. "We tried to understand why the two children reacted to the same event so differently," said Judith Dupont, now a psychoanalyst in Paris.[8] Most analysts explore individual motivation and support the patient in varying degrees during this process. In Budapest you could see a new kind of psychotherapy evolve just by standing in the waiting room of the clinic, in part because of the intensity of Ferenczi's influence and in part because more children were treated there than adults. The psychoanalysts pressed for, and obtained, a new child protection agency, a worker's education program, and a social service center. Unfortunately, once society members finally secured government permission to open the clinic (an important achievement any time but especially significant when "the antirevolutionary and Catholic reaction [was] at the height of its power," as Ferenczi observed to his colleagues), angry words broke out with little warning.[9] The pressure of all this work caused squabbles to erupt among the staff and even outside the clinic. Local officials who had supported their efforts showed signs of dissent. Some of the more senior analysts ridiculed the industriousness of the junior, and mostly female, physicians and even withdrew their support for the clinic. Imre Hermann resigned as secretary. Within days of the opening, the analysts had turned on each other their anger at the Budapest professional community and the State Health Council, where, as Ferenczi told Freud, "every medical forum that was asked [for support] was rude and disdainful."[10] Friction also erupted between Ferenczi and Eitingon, with accusations of envy, pleas of poverty, and demands for sacrifice volleyed between Berlin and Budapest. But loyalty prevailed. This loyalty to the "cause" and to Freud was necessarily fragile and at times seemed to fragment. Nevertheless, in 1931 the Budapest analysts still held fast to the challenge their leader had proposed during the more festive aura of 1918.

Freud cultivated this loyalty unabashedly. He had decided to entertain a number of prominent Viennese Social Democrats and initially invited Josef Friedjung to celebrate his sixtieth birthday with a Sunday tea at the Freuds in October. No longer an active member of the City Council, Friedjung nevertheless maintained his threefold involvement in psychoanalysis, academic pediatrics, and child welfare. The child analytic work he undertook at the Ambulatorium, combined with his advocacy efforts among Vienna's lawmakers, endeared him to his colleagues. "Dr. Friedjung's interest in social questions," Hitschmann recorded in the *IJP*, and "his love of fellow-men caused him to enter politics and, as a social—democratic town councilor, he has exerted a beneficent influence in municipal affairs and furthered our interests as psychoanalysts."[11] Friedjung gladly returned the compliments and, unlike Freud, never hesitated to single out particular political qualities responsible for his colleagues' effectiveness as an advocate. Friedjung, Hitschmann, and Paul Federn had been friends from their schooldays and remained faithful to each other throughout their involvement with Vienna's experiments in social democracy. "Their alliance was not without importance in their city, all three having a reputation amongst medical circles there for sound training and early successes in practice," read Federn's *IJP* notice on Hitschmann's sixtieth birthday (July 28, 1931)."[12]

Indeed, since the early 1920s, and especially since their joint appointment on the City Council's child welfare funding committee, Freud and Julius Tandler remained in touch. They met periodically to discuss civic projects like the Bernays's child welfare program and, most likely, the Ambulatorium. "It is uncanny in such an old man, this vital strength, this sexual strength," Tandler wrote of Freud. Freud was "without a doubt a person who influences his time," Tandler said, and there was little controversy over his role in Vienna. "He is a person who is only accountable to his own law. . . . If he were not a Jew he might be Bismarck."[13] The greatest of these compliments was the allusion to Bismarck, the architect of social insurance and, for Tandler, the ideal social welfare administrator. Freud was impressed by the Social Democrat's ongoing campaign to fight rising unemployment with its controversial distribution of municipal layettes to jobless families. In his personal diary of November 29 he noted that his letter to Julius Tandler had been printed in that morning's *Neue Freie Presse*. The letter proposed a fundraising strategy that he had found effective in his various efforts to rescue declining psychoanalytic projects. People should be urged personally, he wrote, to pledge a regular sum to be collected on a weekly basis. Freud promised to contribute twenty schillings per day, except Sundays. "We hope many will be found who will possess the same high degree of awareness of their social obligations," the *Presse*'s editor commented, "as this internationally known Viennese scholar."[14] In fact this was Freud's characteristic course of action by 1931. "Being poor is no disgrace today," he wrote to Paul Federn as an explanation of his financial gift to the Ambulatorium.[15] Freud had accepted the Vienna society's gift of a handsome portrait bust by the sculptor Oscar Nemon and went on to acknowledge the members' "sacrifice at a time in which financial burdens worry us all." Then he said that, since he could not reimburse the society for its gift, he would like to see the three thousand Austrian schillings (about four hundred dollars on the official currency exchange, according to Ernst Federn) "used for the benefit of our Clinic and Training Institute."

Vienna's public health facilities such as nursing homes and tuberculosis clinics were brilliantly administered by Tandler, but their financial support was as likely to come from America as from the Rathaus. The Rockefeller and the Commonwealth Foundations were, just then, particularly keen on helping European medical institutions. But their generosity came with a social agenda. Maggie Wales, a handsome Bostonian woman, had been sent overseas by the Rockefellers to investigate exactly where the medical dollars went in various Austrian cities. Coincidentally, she was a friend of Edith Jackson and in February the two old acquaintances met for an evening of "opera and café."[16] Jackson was then attending Anna Freud's seminar at least four evenings a week from nine until midnight and thought Maggie might be interested. Actually psychoanalysis did not fit with Maggie's current agenda, but she was hardly opposed to the clinical world that enthralled her friend. By then Anna Freud was immersing her students in child development theory. Anna's seminars came alive with case examples drawn from her analytic practice, and from the Heitzing school project she intimately led with Dorothy Burlingham and their partner, Eva Rosenfeld. Eva, whose analysis with Freud gave her enough self-assurance to separate from her husband, had recently left Vienna to work with another member of the psychoanalytic circle, Ernst Simmel. In August she accepted the salaried position of house manager for his perennially failing sanatorium near Berlin and helped with its dissolution in 1932.

"Who are the seriously ill patients? The morphine addicts or the melancholics?" Anna demanded to know. "And what are the doctors like?" she asked Eva.[17] On the one hand Anna delved into Simmel's project with a seemingly prurient curiosity on the other hand she saw with discerning clinical acumen the myriad therapeutic conflicts that could impede solid patient care. One problem was the analyst's own risk of burnout. "I think that the most difficult thing about dealing with the kind of patients you have in Tegel must be the disillusionment associated with the question of how much pure and how much merely applied psychoanalysis they need and can stand," she wrote to Eva. The second problem, the risk of inaccurate assessment of the patients' capacity to tolerate the anxiety provoked by analysis, was even more grave. Gauging a prospective analysand's anxiety level was a critical factor in determining the success or failure of treatment, and only seasoned analysts like Ferenczi, Aichorn, and Simmel could rightly be trusted with this assessment. If less experienced clinicians were in charge, Anna worried, a symptom like agitation might be misread as energy, or dejection as simple depression instead of psychopathic withdrawal. Drawing an interesting link to child analysis, she suggested that the risk to psychotic people is compounded because, like children, they cannot recover on their own and additionally they lack the child's natural optimism. Unfortunately, because Tegel's minimal budget demanded low-priced personnel, most patients were treated by young inexperienced analysts, possibly interns, under Simmel's supervision. Could Simmel possibly have the time to teach, analyze, and administer the program simultaneously? "An enterprise that can only be kept going when people are fed into it to be devoured and annihilated by it," wrote Anna

Freud, drawing a dramatic analogy between the sanatorium and a child's fairy tale, "is not viable in this day and age. This is how dragons were served in the olden days."[18] Could Eva sustain Tegel on hard work alone?

Eva Rosenfeld's title of "Matron" was, as she said, "two-fold—to deal with the financial crises brought about by the crash of the Danat bank on the one hand, and to cope with the therapists, patients and nurses in the other. The latter might have been possible, although the work required immense physical resources: there were no lifts, nor any relief from the everlasting foot marches along the stupendous corridors—but the financial strain could not be borne."[19] As long as daily expenses were covered for the large number of patients, everyone was still hopeful. Financing the Schloss Tegel clinic had been worthwhile but difficult from the start. In its brief life Ernst Simmel had acted on his clinical vision, to apply psychoanalysis "for the relief of those patients whose extremity is greatest and who hitherto have been condemned to death in life."[20] And, true to Freud's Budapest speech, it was funded as a private charity by large Viennese and Berlin companies and by members of the Berlin society. Freud had supported the institution both morally and financially. Repeatedly, he urged his IPA colleagues to "preserve this instrument for our movement and make it available for future work."[21] Though Dorothy Burlingham, Raymond de Saussure, Marie Bonaparte, and others did join the fund-raising effort, ultimately the facility, which had declared bankruptcy in the fall of 1929, actually closed in 1931. The institution's buildings are gone today, though the actual Tegel castle and its red brick barns remain. And in recent years the lovely sloping park, where Anna Freud and her father each found a peace they could call their own, has been reopened for all to savor its ordinary walks.

"Male applicants for treatment [were] regularly more numerous than female"

1932

IN MARCH of 1932 the Ambulatorium celebrated its tenth anniversary by publishing its most extensive report to date on those who were "given the opportunity of undergoing an analysis, free of charge."[1] Some of Hitschmann's most trusted analysts had already met to discuss how the clinic's record should be promoted, and persuaded him follow the Berlin Poliklinik's example. An initial account would be published in the *IJP*, they decided, and followed up with a separately printed summary released as a brochure. The report was meant to detail how well the Ambulatorium had carried out Freud's 1918 mission statement, but it marked the clinic's role in sustaining Red Vienna as well. The Ambulatorium had become known, Hitschmann wrote, as an independent center where farmers, professionals, students, workers, and others who could not afford to pay for their therapy had been treated at no cost since 1922. The report also suggested that, as Helene Schur recalled as well, Vienna had become "a very progressive city [and] the health stations were excellent" in the early 1930s, despite the analysts' early encounters with a hostile medical establishment. "The hospitals were really very good," she said. "People had insurances when they worked; people who didn't have money were treated for nothing."[2] Even in the larger political arena the Social Democrats retained a safe 59 percent of the Austrian vote. For the first time, however, the National Socialists (the Nazi Party) participated in the municipal elections and gained just over 17 percent of the vote, with the remaining 20 percent going to the old-fashioned Christian Socials.[3]

Nevertheless, several psychoanalysts who were also social democratic representatives (like Friedjung and Federn) managed to remain in power despite the election of the conservative Engelbert Dolfuss as chancellor. Hitschmann and Sterba now favored supplementing their earlier 1925 account of the Ambulatorium's public health effectiveness, arguing that new data and some fresh interpretations would enhance the clinic's role in the city's social welfare system. That last report had been timely but dry and safe. This new publication would feature crisp statistical tables and categories, with patients counted variously by diagnosis, age, and sex and by occupation (or social class). Unfortunately, the document was unexpressive and dull and the statistical categories that promised to provide solid evidence of the Ambulatorium's impact on social welfare simply listed numbers. The tables counted applicants by pairs of years (from 1922/23 to 1930/1) and added them up into "grand total" sums. On average, the Ambulatorium registered between 200 and 250 applicants each year. Hitschmann paid little attention to the difference between "consultation/intake" and "treatment," and his few cross-tabulations make clear the effort involved in producing even this amount of information. In its own way, though, the information was accurate: the Ambulatorium's patient data provided evidence of an unexpected gender inequality in the use of psychoanalysis. Hitschmann had published the first (and perhaps only) longitudinal study confirming that males were more frequent consumers of psychoanalysis than females.

"Male applicants for treatment [were] regularly more numerous than female," Hitschmann said. He had sorted the applicants by age group and by gender and found that almost twice as many males had applied for treatment as females. Similarly, when he grouped clinic applicants by occupation and then gender, he found that males outnumbered females in almost all categories including school children and students. Over the last ten years 1,445 males had requested psychoanalysis, whereas only 800 applicants were female, less than half the number of males. The ratio of male and female applicants, constant for the Ambulatorium but still surprising to read today, was particularly striking within the twenty-one to thirty year old age group. In 1923 and 1924, when Bettauer's newspapers unabashedly promoted psychoanalysis as a remedy for the loneliness of youth, exactly half as many females (118) applied for treatment as males (236). The male majority was not without logic. In Red Vienna most social democrats, from Tandler to Reich to Hitschmann, commonly implied that the virile quality of psychoanalysis would free men to pursue occupations, self-fulfillment, and independence. Impotence, like other male illnesses, was related to the economy and carried little moral charge. "People do not die from deadly bacteria alone," Simmel contended, "but rather from the fact that anyone exhausted from brutal exploitation by industry becomes easy prey for whatever germs they happen to encounter."[4]

At the same time Simmel's friend Julius Tandler evoked the images of healthy working men (and nursing women) to boost an ardent pro-family message underlying his speech on the democratic relationship between the physician and the community. "Comrade" Tandler's speech on medicine and the economy was advertised (figure 33) not by one but by two of Berlin's socialist organizations, the German Social Democratic Physicians and the Free Society of Socialist Academics. The Ambulatorium itself was a hardworking place, a basement of a hospital cardiology clinic. Patients were "salaried employees, working class, professional, domestic service, teaching, without occupation, pensioners, and [university] students." In other words, they were often male and employed, precisely not the clichéd images of pale rich women with vapors. Impotence ranked as the clinic's most frequently recorded diagnosis, reiterating how psychoanalysis would give men—who already had more social freedom than women—even greater license to address sexual dysfunction, improve their sex lives, and, coincidentally, produce families and rebuild a vigorous state. The data could suggest that Freudian psychoanalysis was more acceptable to males simply because it was so openly

33 Advertisement for Julius Tandler's lecture in the *Socialist Physician*, spring 1932 (Library of the Center for the Humanities and Health Sciences, Institute for the History of Medicine, Berlin)

"about sex." Not that women were ignored. It was one of the accomplishments of psychoanalysis to assert that women did have sexual responses. That women of the "lower" classes also had sexual autonomy was an even more daring idea. Whatever larger gender ethos facilitated men's access to the Ambulatorium, the clinic's own disposition to treat women as equally sexual was avant-garde.

The two exceptions to the male plurality in Hitschmann's tallies can be found in the occupational categories of "domestic service" and "no occupation." Here women (296) appear over four times more than men (66). Women's enrollment in Tandler's maternal/child consultation centers or other family assistance programs probably accounts for the increase. The community lectures in child development, the support of the municipal social workers, and the local newspaper articles were among most visible forms of promotion for psychoanalysis, and many were targeted to women. Consequently, poor women or those with "no occupation" sought assistance not for hysteria but for relief from the same problems plaguing the men—depression, lack of occupational satisfaction, and sexual dysfunction. By the early 1930s an interesting and unexpected profile of the Ambulatorium's patients had emerged. For one, the male and female clients had largely the same psychological complaints (and, presumably, the same sense of sexual dysfunction). And, second, the clinic population was eclipsed by young adults regardless of gender or social class. In the ten years covered by the report, the twenty-one to thirty year olds were the only group that reached over one thousand (1,083 specifically). They were by far the largest single classification of consumers and the only group that came close, though a full 50 percent smaller, were the thirty-one to forty year olds (537). At either end of the age curve after that, children under age ten and elderly people ages sixty-one to seventy were seen and counted, but represented only a small fraction of the total patient population. In 1926 and 1927, peak years for children and seniors, Hitschmann counted seven male and five female children and five seniors. In contrast, no seniors and only a few children were counted in either 1922/23 and in 1928/29. It is possible that the child patients, who were treated at the separate Child Guidance Center, were undercounted in this report.

Vienna's Child Guidance Center was thriving, now that August Aichorn had taken over, on a consulting basis, after retiring from public service.[5] The Heitzing School had closed and, along with it, Aichorn's periodic teaching there, which he replaced by a solo practice of free short-term therapy, referrals, and advice to children and their families. Aichorn remained an ambiguous figure in the analytic community. Well-liked by both Sigmund and Anna Freud, he came from a conservative Catholic family allied to the Christian

Social Party and would (and could) remain in Vienna through the war and beyond. Aichorn's gift was his deep unyielding empathy for troubled children.
He treated them with compassion and respect, and he was the most likely psychoanalyst to pull together the various schools of child psychotherapy. Upon
his occasional absences his colleagues Editha Sterba and Willi Hoffer continued the Child Guidance Center's work of evaluating and treating young school
children referred by the welfare services. For most analysts dividing up the
work day posed no problem, and many taught in the morning, analyzed patients in the afternoon, and in the evening attended seminars and clinical presentations at the Vereinigung. But best of all, the society really felt like a refuge.
"The Berggasse is the center of everything," Anna Freud observed, "and we re-
volve around it sometimes in smaller and sometimes in larger circles."[6]

The Berggasse salon drew Siegfried Bernfeld for a brief visit to Vienna from
Berlin in January. Bernfeld's shock of dark hair and angular features enhanced an already powerful presence and his audiences were quite taken with
his lectures on child neglect, adolescence, aggression, and sexuality. At one of
the Vienna society's winter seminar meetings, Edith Jackson, whose future in
American child psychiatry would use Bernfeld's theories to alter conventional medical care, found him "a marvelous speaker, clear, fluent, precise and
picturesque with humour that bubbles up through the easy flow."[7] Neglect is
not a simple concept, he insisted.[8] A neglectful family's sociological milieu,
or environment, is so profoundly influential that two children who might
start out with identical psychological dispositions are each affected very differently. At the end of the seminar two male teachers asked Bernfeld exactly
how to respond when adolescent boys request advice on sex. Should they
have intercourse or not? Do masturbation, abstinence, or early intercourse
cause any permanent harm? In the developmental course of puberty, is there
a normal sequence for erotic thoughts, masturbation, homosexual activity,
and heterosexual activity? Bernfeld would not be lured into such banalities.
The truth, he insisted, is that these generalizations are impossible because all
human development is a joint product of the individual's family history plus
their socioeconomic status.

Bernfeld may have overemphasized the theme of individual aggression (or
misread his audience) in his lectures on adolescence. Many Viennese analysts
found it quite galling and dismissed it as the present thinking of the "Berlin
School," preferring Anna Freud's current perspective. Between the late 1920s
and 1936, when she would publish her classic book on *The Ego and the Mechanisms of Defense*, Anna Freud reframed the role of the ego and granted it
eminence in human psychological growth. She also insisted on respecting the

psychological particulars of each developmental stage. In other words, a clinical technique that might help a six year old resolve his oedipal system would be inappropriate for an adolescent attempting to form an individual identity. Though Anna felt that Bernfeld's tally of therapeutic successes was exaggerated, she generally agreed that his approach was interesting and clinically valid. "Fractionated analysis," the unconventional treatment strategy adopted in Berlin, could be particularly effective with psychologically wounded adolescents.[9] Nevertheless, during a case presentation at her own seminar one evening, Anna argued that Bernfeld's treatment of aggressive adolescents like "Danny" was hindered because the analyst had disregarded the patient's age-specific stage of development. A fifteen-year-old German boy, Danny coarsely berated his mother and blamed her for his gonorrhea (she "locked me up") but also shielded her ("my fault for masturbating"), did well at school, and rejected psychoanalysis. What to do? Within a few minutes the seminar listeners had advanced a "fractionary" plan of gradually decreasing the analytic hours, systematically refraining from deep analysis, asking the patient for feedback, and inviting him to return should he feel depressed (an internal condition) or humiliated (an external condition).

Unlike Reich, Bernfeld rejected the idea of an overarching sexual narrative. No sexual action is universally harmful or helpful because each individual is a personal amalgam of early childhood history, individual personality, and social environment. Reich and Bernfeld also differed on their views of family life. Whereas Reich thought of the family as an insidious microcosm of patriarchy and bourgeois capitalism, Bernfeld was generally more forgiving. Several years earlier, Reich suggested to Freud that Sex-Pol would be "treating the family problem rigorously" in an immense campaign against moral hypocrisy. To this appealing but unlikely proposal, Freud replied, 'You'll be poking into a hornet's nest.'" By 1932 Freud distinctly favored Bernfeld over Reich and was "always glad to see him. He [was] a brainy man," Freud mused.[10] "If there were a couple of dozen like him in analysis" he would worry less, and he hoped that Bernfeld, now in Berlin, would transfer back to Vienna for political reasons. Freud bluntly quipped that Hitler has made many promises, and the one he could probably keep is the suppression of the Jews. But, if Bernfeld realized the significance of Freud's challenge at the time, he didn't let on. He returned to Berlin and to his sympathetic group at the Socialist Physicians' Union, which was, sadly, busier quarreling with other left-wing groups than planning a campaign against Hitler.

Soon after Bernfeld's return to Berlin, the Socialist Physicians' Union convened a meeting entitled "National Socialism: Enemy of Public Health." Here

Ernst Simmel offered the broad outlines of a Marxist solution to Germany's worsening economic problems in combination with a psychoanalytic explication of Hitler's Nazi activity.[11] Overtly, Simmel seemed more interested in resolving the public health crisis than in alarming his audience, but he built his argument so strategically that, by the end, fascism and the quest for corporate medicine had become one. Formerly idealistic physicians, he thought, felt unable to spend enough time with their public patients, whose sheer numbers made for an assembly line practice, exactly the situation he had deliberately sought to avoid at the Poliklinik. This exploitation of the doctors represented, to him, the simultaneous rise of capitalism and of fascism. Simmel explained that the ruthlessness required for this kind of competition was so merciless that it undermined mutual human trust and ultimately led to war. A fascist government does the same thing: it replaces spontaneous individual human creativity with a totalitarian purview. In capitalism the corporation's suppressed aggressive drives are released and, if unchecked, triumphantly acquire the rival's private property and wealth or profits. In fascism the government unleashes its aggressive drives to gain property and power through war. In the end, both capitalism and fascism have war as a natural continuation of their goals. Hitler, he warned, was advancing on both fronts. Simmel's argument was sophisticated and thoughtful for Berlin in 1932. Reading these passages from *The Socialist Physician* today, Simmel's warning may seem obscured by the language of Marxism. Unfortunately, the rhetoric also hid the real value of his political insights exactly when Hitler's weapons started to fire. The Nazis had become Germany's largest elected political party, and Hitler had already put to use the vicious *Sturmabteilung* (SA, or brownshirted Stormtroopers) and the *Stahlhelm* (SS, or Steel Helmets) militia to support his case for seizing power.

Over the next few months Schloss Tegel, Ernst Simmel's brilliant inpatient clinic that had always been more of a concept than a working reality, deteriorated so severely that staff realized it would not survive. "The experiment broke down," Eva Rosenfeld remembered, "when parents and relatives of the patients wrote and declared themselves insolvent."[12] Families refused to take back their burdensome, mentally ill members who had finally, they thought, found appropriate caretakers. Some patients were discharged to institutions further away from the city,others to their own homes where they could live independently as cleaners and cooks. Those tasks accomplished, Eva stayed on to manage the termination and find jobs for the staff. Like her friend Anna Freud, Eva had never really thought this would happen. "Ever since I have known Tegel, the specter of dissolution has hovered over it. It was so beautiful and perfect in its principles and objectives," Anna eulogized, "like a sort of dream; its insufficiencies and defects and the tight money situation didn't seem to fit in but to be added on as if by accident. I always had the feeling that they might disappear and then Tegel would be what it can be."[13] But in the end the money simply ran out and not even Rosenfeld could be paid. Five years after Simmel officially closed down Tegel, Eva Rosenfeld found her life and livelihood at stake once again. "Having had vast experience in this type of work," she wrote to Glover in London, "I would like to offer my services as supervisor and matron in hospitals (also organizing and training staff for mental hospitals). For more than ten years I was a supervisor in homes for drunkards and criminals and in Dr. Simmel's Psychoanalytic Clinic, and I am sure I would always be able to do practical therapeutic and research work as a nurse." [14] Ultimately she returned to private practice in London and maintained an intermittent, if intense, relationship with Anna. What served Eva best for the next forty years was the superb analytic couch Ernst Freud had designed for her as a gift in Berlin of 1932.

Freud and Reich were wary of each other. In his diary entry dated Friday, January 1, 1932, Freud wrote, "Step against Reich."[15] He was responding to the controversy provoked by Reich's proposed use of Marxist vocabulary in a 1931 psychoanalytic paper. Freud's move was shaped by a range of possible factors. Either he was increasingly influenced by Jones and the more conservative members of the IPA or simply more wary of reactionary infringement than he had let on until now. Kurt von Schuschnigg had just been made minister of justice, a step aimed at helping Austria's Chancellor Engelbert Dollfuss repress the Social Democrats. The Nazi Party's popularity was growing as fast in Austria as in Germany. Or perhaps Freud took this opportunity to act on Paul Federn's suspicion of incipient schizophrenia in Reich. Whatever the explanation, Freud did indicate that overt left-wing political action could compromise the scientific credibility of psychoanalysis, already under attack from the medical, psychiatric, and academic establishments. Conversely, according to Helene Deutsch at least, Reich's "political radicalism" was specifically not the cause of their estrangement; the problem, she thought, was Reich's overbearing personality. In his theoretical work Freud broke with history; in practice he protected his discoveries. Freud and Reich were ideologically compatible on a metapolitical level—but certainly not without tension on the micro level.

Freud was not much happier with Franz Alexander, one of the earliest analysts to leave Germany for the United States. The first American outpatient psychoanalytic clinic was founded that fall in Chicago under Alexander's direction. The clinic's "basic purpose [was] the purpose of psychoanalysis everywhere," he stated, "to make available the healing services of a group of specialists to those in need."[16] Alexander was a broad-shouldered and square-jawed man intent on disseminating psychoanalysis in America. Born in Hungary and trained as a physician, Alexander had worked first with Ferenczi and then, after a dozen productive years in Berlin, refused to yield anything to the Nazis. He agreed with his psychiatric mentor Emil Kraepelin (still alive and politically engaged in Germany) that sanatoriums should be established to treat "social diseases" like alcoholism, syphilis, and crime itself. Now in his mid-forties, Alexander adhered to the medical character of psychoanalysis and, he believed, its natural pairing with psychosomatic medicine. Although analysts could easily imagine which psychological symptom matched which physiological ailment, few had researched the actual forms a mental illness converted into. Franz Alexander called this "specificity" and hypothesized that specific linkages existed between damaged internal organs of the body and their corollary psychiatric disorders of the mind (liver and depression, spleen and anxiety). At first his controversial research attracted serious funding from prominent Chicago investors like Alfred K. Stern. To most analysts' surprise, even the Rockefeller Foundation responded to Alexander's proposal to fund empirical research on mind-body conjunction. Alexander could reconcile seemingly contradictory ideas, accepting at once the relational qualities of psychoanalysis and the biological nature of mental illness while persuading rich Americans of the scientific value of this inquiry. His colleagues were far more skeptical of the results. "The research does not amount to a row of peas," the customarily uncritical Brill wrote to Ernest Jones.[8] And when Alexander decided to help Karen Horney's emigration by designating her as the new institute's associate director, Brill fretted over the expense. Jones and Brill couldn't believe that Alexander and Horney were charging fees for analysis when, specifically, "the Institute is not supposed to take any cases that can afford to pay regular fees."[9] Ironically, while this reproach came from the IPA's two most candid opponents of free clinics, Alexander and Horney asserted their allegiance to the Berlin model. Their clinic was "the backbone of the Institute," Alexander said, and they charged patients only "what they could afford. Some were treated for nothing." On average, the 125 patients seen each year until the mid-1950s paid roughly $3 per hour. The Chicago Institute for Psychoanalysis's scientific meetings made ready use of the Poliklinik's experimental techniques, and active therapy, conscious use of informality, and, most notably, treatment flexibility were practiced in the very first year. Like Richard Sterba reminiscing about the Vienna society, the American analyst Ralph

Crowley remembered how "psychoanalysis was forward looking: it was a rebellion against old ways and old ideas. . . . The field was full of excitement and controversy. . . . Psychoanalysts were interesting people, devoted, not to achieving personal and financial security, but to experiment and exploration, and to the personal growth of themselves."[10] Unlike Sterba, however, there is little sense of a wider political endeavor. Perhaps this explains why none of the American psychoanalytic institutes, except for Chicago and Topeka, advanced free outpatient clinics. Until at least the mid-1950s the psychoanalytic societies in Boston, Detroit, Philadelphia, New York, Washington, Los Angeles, and San Francisco adopted training programs but, as Alexander commented in 1951, "they have restricted themselves primarily to theoretical instruction and clinical work with private patients."[11]

Two of the other European clinics, London's and Budapest's, were planned with the same mix of voluntarism and financial support as the Ambulatorium. In London Pryns Hopkins's Christmas donation included a hint that he would continue to support the clinic if he could. The clinic analysts, who did not contribute financially, agreed their work was both voluntary and separate from their teaching or administrative duties to the institute. These two decisions came from the board of the British society in its well-intentioned oversight of the clinic's plans. In June, for example, the board agreed that one colleague's role as translation editor for the *IJP* could exempt her from taking on clinic cases.[12] In Budapest, meanwhile, the clinic was thriving. "We are positively overrun," Ferenczi wrote to Freud, "and are striving to master the difficulties that are arising in this manner."[13] The difficulties were in large part financial, and, when Freud sent around a special petition to local society presidents appealing for support for the Verlag (the psychoanalytic publishing house), Ferenczi reluctantly reminded him that, at least in Budapest, any extra resources were directed to the clinic. Vilma Kovács, like himself, had already contributed fourteen hundred Hungarian pengö each year toward its maintenance.[14] The other analysts earned barely what they needed to survive: they donated time but could hardly be expected to contribute cash.

3

1933–1938

TERMINATION

"The Berlin Psychoanalytic . . .
Policlinic . . . came to an end"

1933

AT FIRST the Berlin psychoanalysts contended with the political events of February 1933 in a mood for bargaining and Freud's encounters with the new fascist world were uncharacteristically compromising. Hitler had been named chancellor of the Reich on January 30. Hermann Göring, the politically powerful cousin of Matthias Göring and future scourge of the Poliklinik, was appointed Prussian minister of the interior and immediately expanded the ranks of the SA and SS, the Nazi police forces, while issuing decrees on who was—and was no longer—acceptable to the state. On February 28 opposition to the regime became a punishable crime and the next month, on March 23, the Reichstag voted for the "Enabling Act" (*Ermächtigungsgesetz*, or Law for Removing Want), setting the stage for Hitler's rule by decree for the next four years. Many affected by this first wave of Nazi harassment discovered their fate only by learning they had been fired. Non-Aryan state employees were dismissed and, since the Nazis now insisted on homogeneous control over every political, cultural, and social institution, virtually all artists, scientists, actors, teachers, and musicians were threatened with suspension.

Freud's unclear but, for the moment, conciliatory stance on the disposition of the Institute—a stance that Ernest Jones would later misinterpret—lasted through mid-March. When Freud finally outlined three possible actions the Berlin society could take, he did so at the urging of Max Eitingon, who understood, earlier and more accurately than anyone except perhaps Wilhelm Reich, the impact of Hitler's recent coup. Eitingon could dissolve the Institute and leave, Freud advised, or he could preserve it temporarily by handing over control to "Christians of purely German origin" like Felix Boehm and Claus Müller-Braunschweig.[1] Should the Institute survive simply because someone like Schultz-Hencke had replaced the non-Aryan Eitingon, its misuse would lead to disqualification and expulsion from the IPA. Psychoanalysis would survive in Germany, Freud concluded, as long as Eitingon stayed. But, by Easter, with the catastrophic dimensions of Hitler's agenda coming into full view, Eitingon chose the latter course. The change in leadership was not without controversy, however, and the extent to which Boehm and Müller-Braunschweig cooperated with Nazis to maintain a corrupt façade on German psychoanalysis seems to have been far-reaching. Even Ernest Jones and Anna Freud, the two self-proclaimed "pillars of Eastern and Western Europe," showed troubling conflicts of interest.[2] "I prefer Psycho-Analysis to be practiced by Gentiles in Germany than not at all," Jones (as president of the IPA) wrote to Anna Freud two years later. Freud may have suspected Jones's predilection all along.

On April 8 the newspaper *Gross-Berliner Ärzteblatt* complied with Hitler's order and published the regime's decree for all medical organizations to "change" (i.e., aryanize) their governing boards under the direction of the German Medical Council. It was a watershed event for the Berlin society, as for most groups in Germany, and determining how to comply was far from easy. According to Felix Boehm, who was present at the first meeting (but whose ambiguous position should be remembered), the psychoanalysts debated whether or not a vote altering the racial composition of their board would, or should, permit psychoanalysis to survive in Germany. This "Extraordinary General Meeting" took place on May 6. The psychoanalysts drew together the thick dark curtains that shielded the Poliklinik's meeting room from the swastika-draped Wichmanstrasse. The training Institute could come through more or less unharmed, they reasoned, because of its status as a research center. But the Poliklinik was at greater risk since it mainly provided therapeutic, if not outright medical, services to people with mental illness. "They will ban [psychoanalysis] anyway," Freud had forecast by this time, but he too questioned the pressure to acquiesce to the German Medical Council.[3] Preserving the status quo would serve, at best, as a "handle" to delay the government's obstruction. In the end they voted against the aryanization. For some members, including a few like Frances Deri who had already left Germany, refusing to modify the board was the more dangerous action. Others changed their votes in highly charged last-minute decisions. Ernst Simmel, Clara Happel, Eitingon, Landauer, and Meng were among the fifteen "no" votes. Felix Boehm and Carl Müller-Braunschweig, and Edith Jacobson voted "yes" with four others. Teresa Benedek, Fenichel, and three more abstained. Fenichel's hostility to the new German leadership did not stop him from thinking dialectically: while his reasoning mind told him to approve the measure, his heart opposed it. "If I were sure that the vote would be in favor of change, I should vote against it, as my feelings tell me to."[4] Nonetheless, several years later as the analysts were struggling in exile, Fenichel conceded that they had miscalculated the level of danger in presuming that psychoanalysis could survive with any integrity in fascist Germany. "I must confess that at the time I and Edith Jacobson, in opposition to Reich, represented the contrary position," he wrote.[5] Whether or not he knew that Jacobson had secretly joined Neu Beginnen (New Beginning), an early stronghold of social democratic resistance, her membership in the anti-Nazi group did little to reduce the political imprudence of the psychoanalysts. Quarrels between old friends had blinded them from choosing the better course, to simply dissolve the DPG as Freud (and apparently Wilhelm Reich) had proposed.

Felix Boehm had served as secretary and lecturer at the Berlin Institute and as an analyst at the Poliklinik under Eitingon. He was a fairly short, pale man, with combed-over, thinning brown hair and deep-set eyes. A psychiatrist and self-appointed expert on the "problem" of homosexuality, Boehm eventually advised the Wehrmacht on its "dangers" and recommended surveillance and "retraining" of homosexuals, especially those in the Luftwaffe. By the time the Nazis took him at his word with a program of imprisonment, sterilization, and eventual extermination of homosexuals, the "gross, arrogant and misogynist" Boehm professed his opposition to their policy.[6] Nevertheless, according to John Rickman, Boehm wartime's military duties entailed deciding if deserting soldiers were malingerers or not, with alarming consequences. "If they were malingerers," Rickman reported, "they were—[Boehm] drew his finger across his throat and made a noise like "esh" and chucked his thumb over his shoulder and then shrugged."[7] Even in 1933, as the new president of the DPG, he could pick sides, and, unfortunately, his affinity for the current political regime proved resolute. Boehm repeatedly and specifically chose not to check back with Eitingon, or even Simmel or Fenichel, on handling the Poliklinik's worst crisis since Abraham's death in 1925. Instead he proceeded to work directly with Nazi Party members within the German Medical Council. Thus, the first sign of an unseemly collaboration between the Nazi rulers and the new institute director had come even before the Extraordinary Meeting. Poliklinik analysts returned to work one day to find that Boehm and Müller-Braunschweig had effectively convinced the Medical Council not to harm the Berlin Institute because it would be so helpful for the Nazi state. The treatment-based Poliklinik, however, had to be refashioned as a non-Freudian psychiatric center. Boehm and Müller-Braunschweig accepted the orders, but others were considerably less sanguine. Even Ernest Jones was skeptical of the outcome. "Two Gentiles, Boehm and Müller-Braunschweig, have now got in touch with the Nazi authorities," he wrote to Brill, "and secured a promise not to interfere with the Institute or the practice of psycho-analysis in Germany. How much this is worth, or what conditions it has been obtained on, I do not know."[8] Within the next two years Boehm would join Werner Kemper, Harald Schultz-Hencke, and Carl Müller-Braunschweig, as directors of the racialized Deutsche Institut für Psychologische Forschung (German Institute for Psychological Research), otherwise known as the Göring Institute, in honor of its founder, Matthias Heinrich Göring, and his famous cousin, the Reichsmarschall Hermann Göring. The Göring Institute was to embody the nazification of psychoanalysis. In a sense Boehm, in crossing between the psychoanalytic and political sectors, put himself in a position similar to many of the original psychoanalytic activists. This time, however, the "cause" was fascism and the "movement" was exclusion of all non-Aryans, with a heated emphasis on Jews, homosexuals, and Communists.

Meanwhile, the regime started to round up Jewish doctors in their campaign against psychoanalysis, and Felix Boehm's practice of appealing to the good will of Nazi party insiders became more shrill. Charité (figure 34) faculty had accused Fenichel of forming a Communist cell within the society. Rather than focus on Fenichel's defense, the Children's Seminar group chose to disband after his last lecture, "Psychoanalysis, Socialism, and the Tasks for the Future."[9] Freud and Adler's works were burned in a huge public display of anti-intellectual venom. The Schloss Tegel buildings were seized by the Mark Brandenburg group of the Nazi SA. Simmel was detained as the former director of the Socialist Physicians' Union, and Jones, unusually upset, wrote to Brill. "Simmel . . . was arrested a fortnight ago but luckily got out of prison after a few days."[10] Brill and Jones discussed raising funds to send him to New York, but Simmel fled for safety to Switzerland. In the middle of this, Eitingon packed up his private consultation rooms and sent his furniture over to the Poliklinik where he now practiced, if at all, solely out of his director's office. On September 7 he held his last analytic sessions and on September 8 left to prepare his move to Palestine. Eitingon did renew the two-year lease on the Wichmanstrasse quarters but sent Boehm and Müller-Braunschweig to

34 An outpatient department at the Charité, Berlin (Author)

negotiate with the landlord. Somehow Jones found out and, once again, misinterpreted his colleague's action. "There is a rumour that the Berlin clinic is closed," he wrote from London. "In a short note from you five weeks ago you promised to send more news in a day or two, but I have heard nothing since."[11] Jones's concern about his friend betrayed his cautious diplomacy on three fronts. For one, he underestimated the danger of Hitler's recent and imperious nomination as chancellor. Second, he was personally and inappropriately offended that Eitingon had been too busy planning his escape to answer someone who was neither a Jew nor, after all, in life-threatening danger. Third, Jones really did know what was happening. Six months earlier van Ophuisjen had circulated polite but dire warnings about the Boehm and Müller-Braunschweig team. "The German Society is not in a position to fulfill all the written and unwritten conditions imposed by membership in the IPA," he wrote. "But this is an emergency."[12] The warning, such as it was, was ignored. Instead Jones focused on the deisgnated scoundrel Wilhelm Reich who, openly Communist and psychoanalyst at once, set everybody on edge without even being present. The psychoanalysts had determined to expel Reich from the Berlin society without informing him of their decision. The decision to put the blame on Reich, in effect to scapegoat their most outspoken member, helped to pacify the governmental German Medical Council and, for the moment, placate many of the psychoanalysts as well. Boehm effectively used Reich's expulsion to prove the society's rejection of Communism and secured an official promise that no action would be taken against them except, perhaps, by the governmental agency known as the Kampfbund für Deutsche Kultur (Combat League for German Culture).

The Kampfbund, or KDK, however, was not so easily convinced that the Poliklinik had abandoned its political convictions. Established by the Nazi party in 1929, the KDK had the specific mission of repudiating all evidence of modernism while, at the same time, fostering "native . . . characteristic . . . total cultural Germanness." [13] Modernist painting, architecture, music, and poetry were labeled *"Nigger-kultur"* and *"kultur bolshewismus,"* and psychoanalysis was called "Jewish-Marxist filth."[14] Both individuals like Freud's ally Thomas Mann and Simmel's friend Käthe Kollwitz, along with Bertold Brecht and Paul Klee and modernist institutions like the Bauhaus (including presumably Ernst Freud), now headed by Mies van der Rohe, were officially scorned as unsuitable to the KDK's racialized theories of culture. Apparently, to the KDK, the Poliklinik's intellectual prestige was more threatening than its medical reputation, and, when Nazi officers appeared at the Poliklinik to ask Boehm (to whom Eitingon had officially transferred responsibility for the clinic) how many members were Jews, they were actually routing out modernist intellectuals. For the Nazis, modernist art, music, architecture, and psychoanalysis were all one. Boehm chose to disclose every detail because, he said, a police officer in uniform had personally gone to the Poliklinik to ask exactly who was treating cases there, how many had a German license to practice, and how many possessed German nationality. But the KDK's arrival was not at all the opportunity to preserve the clinic's independence Boehm believed it was. Evidently the Nazis simply enjoyed meddling with the internal concerns of progressive organizations, an enervating routine they perfected with Mies van der Rohe and the Bauhaus. Meanwhile, in his memo of September 29, Müller-Braunschweig announced that he would "explain [psychoanalysis] in a suitable way to the authorities in the new government."[15] He and Boehm suggested that, really, the government should differentiate between two distinct types of psychoanalysis. One type, advocated by Wilhelm Reich, focused on sexuality and politics and had permanently alienated many of his associates except for Simmel (arrested not long ago) and his old friend, Otto Fenichel (recently accused). But another type could present valuable opportunities for the new National Socialist state. Psychoanalysis could develop worthy human character and citizenship, Boehm said, and quite a few of the remaining German analysts endorsed this formula. Boehm's strategy, of disavowing the sexual predicates of psychoanalysis and instead reinforcing its potential for conscious character building, worked. In addition, "it goes without saying that there are no foreign Jews working with them," Müller-Braunschweig and Boehm reassured the district medical office in Berlin.[16] The chief of police now objected less to the existence of the Poliklinik than to the Institute's ongoing training programs, especially of laymen, without a special license. Official psychoanalysis would be streamlined, simplified, and racialized. "There will hardly be any difficulties between the Jungian group, the school of applied characterology and that of autogenic training. The actual problem child is and remains psychoanalysis," the psychiatrist Fritz Künkel wrote to Göring.[17] But he knew how to make that change. "Above all the rules must be framed in such a way that the psychoanalysts give up their splendid isolation. I should like to characterise this point of view as 'softening up the crust of the old school.'"

Now that the chief of police and the KDK had been pacified, Boehm approached the Ministry of the Interior headed by Hermann Göring. For psychoanalysis in particular, the Ministry of the Interior proved to be one of the most difficult Nazi agencies to influence. The Ministry of the Interior was one of the Nazi Party's mythically monstrous agencies that made mental health treatment into a paranoid's worst nightmare—judgmental, deceitful, inhumane, and ultimately a feeder for the Nazi extermination program. Boehm believed that IPA analysts were ungrateful to him for preventing the Ministry of the Interior from closing their doors. In fact, they knew he had opened them for the worse. While the post-1933 Institute provided educational courses whose titles could be easily changed, the Poliklinik, as a treatment center, would be transformed into a horrible triage center where psychoanalysts condemned their patients to death. By 1938 the Poliklinik, now a virtual psychiatric guillotine, would be bloated with Nazi money and personally endorsed by Hitler. Whether or not the IPA could have predicted this is unclear. How much did Jones really know when he decided, at an IPA business meeting of August 29, 1934, to exclude activities of the clinics from the reports of the branch societies? Two years later Anna Freud and Eduard Bibring would reverse this decision and ask the branch society directors to report precisely on the activities of their clinics.

In 1933, however, Felix Boehm could still persuade most people, from interior ministry functionaries to Ernest Jones, to abide by his decisions. When Boehm and Müller-Braunschweig shared their proposal for integrating the Berlin society into the new government by splitting psychoanalysis into two types, Ernest Jones seemed delighted. "Boehm saved psychoanalysis," he wrote to Anna Freud.[18] The Dutch psychoanalyst van Ophuijsen was more skeptical and wondered if such extreme measures were necessary. To him, both Boehm and Müller-Braunschweig were confirmed Nazis. But Anna went along with Jones. "I hope you will overcome all your difficulties in the near future," she wrote to Boehm after hearing from Jones in October.[19] Paradoxically, Jones did mount a large effort to rescue analytic refugees, secure emergency funds, and disperse them around the world. As early as April he started a series of presentations to the British society that revealed the deep contradictions in his character and beliefs. First he proposed a "vote of sympathy" and discussed practical assistance for their colleagues, including "the possibility of German analysts finding work in England."[20] By June he announced that Maas, Cohn, Fuchs, and Jacobson would be welcome to settle there.[21] Maas had pledged to establish "a sanatorium run by German psychiatrists who had an English and American clientele," and, as Jones told Anna, he found possible "connections to the Clinic promising."[22] But privately Jones complained to Brill that, since none of the analysts had "enough money to go to America" and he had no idea how they would earn a living in England, this "distressing time with the German refugees" threatened to overwhelm the resources of the British society.[23] Jones insisted that his steadfast support of Boehm and Müller-Braunschweig's compromise with Göring should not be understood as an abandonment of his fellow analysts.

By the end of 1933 Berlin's latest form of psychoanalysis was well on its way toward unity with Germany's new official medical association. In what reads like an obituary titled "The Psycho-Analytical Movement," Jones (as *IJP* editor) described how, "with the changed political situation in Germany, the German Psycho-Analytical Society and the Berlin Psycho-Analytical Institute (Policlinic and Training Institute) came to an end. Most of the members left Germany."[24] By the time Jones published his dreadful news, only nine Jewish analysts were left in Berlin. What made this news such a travesty of truth, however, was that the Berlin Institute did not technically close in 1933. Instead it was aryanized, the teaching and training staff purged of Jews, the clinic's operations and principles absorbed into Nazi ideology. With most of the Jewish analysts gone into exile, Matthias Göring launched the racially streamlined German Medical Society for Psychotherapy, made himself president, and promoted Carl Jung to vice president.

On May 1, 1933, Matthias Heinrich Göring joined the National Socialist Party.[25] He belonged to five other Nazi organizations as well, three of which were extreme right-wing arms of the Nazi movement. He joined the SA and the SS, Hitler's terror police designated to search out and kill the opposition, as well as the Dozentenbund, or Lecturer's Alliance, a Nazi organization charged with uprooting independent-minded professionals and university academics.[26] As Göring had been a specialist in nervous and affective diseases since 1922, he also affiliated with the Ärztebund (NSD, or National Socialist German Doctors Alliance), and the National-Sozialistische Volkswohlfahrt (NSV, or National Socialist Peoples' Welfare Organization), which aided families, mothers, and children. With his soft, broad shoulders, high forehead, and an ample gray beard, he hardly looked the part of a militant Nazi loyalist. Yet, before long, he required all members of the Institute to read *Mein Kampf* and attended every social and professional function. Often accompanied by his wife Erna, he monitored all discussions, whether held at the Institute or in private homes, and eventually secured adherence to National Socialism from those who remained in Berlin. He insisted on abolishing all Freudian terms like *Oedipus* and *childhood sexuality* from the teaching and practice of psychoanalysis and contended that such concepts endangered the very existence of the Institute. "Now that Freud's book have been burned, the word 'psychoanalysis' must be removed," Göring wrote.[27] "So must the words 'individual psychology' which could perhaps be replaced by 'applied characterology.'" Carl Jung, Göring believed, was the best person to rewrite this language and, ultimately, to develop the *Neue Deutsche Seelenheilkunde* (New German Psychotherapy, or, literally, soul-health science).

With Carl Jung in place, Göring set out to revamp psychoanalysis in Germany. He thought he understood the relationship between Jewishness and Freudianism, and he and Jung began to replace this with the new German psychotherapy, presumably distinct from a "Jewish" psychotherapy. As Göring's liaison to mainstream psychoanalysis from 1933 until 1936, Jung would travel frequently from Zurich to Berlin to give lectures and seminars. The two men coedited the *Zentralblatt für Psychotherapie*, the Institute's official journal, which supported their belief in Nazi racial goals. Shortly after the March 1933 Enabling Act ratified Hitler's dictatorship and closed down the Reichstag, Jung agreed to an interview on German radio. Already all Jews had been compelled to abandon tenured positions in universities and were forced from the official civil service; Jewish businesses and professionals were officially boycotted; SA attacks on individual Jews were virtually sanctioned by the police. All non-Aryan (and all Communist) doctors, psychoanalysts among them, were precluded from participating in public or private health insurance programs and were thus, for all purposes, deprived of income. Since psychoanalysis was not de facto banned, those who remained in Berlin could still technically practice under the auspices of Göring and Jung's new association, the Deutsche Allgemeine Ärztliche Gesellschaft für Psychotherapie (German General Medical Society for Psychotherapy). The new association might have persuaded some analysts to stay, but they found its obligatory new German psychotherapy, where all mental illness was a question of race and all mental health one of racial hygiene, abhorrent.

And so the exodus began. Annie Reich, now separated from Wilhelm, went to Prague with her two children. Kate Friedländer and Barbara Lantos moved to Paris. Fenichel went briefly to Sweden and then to Prague. Theodor Reik, René Spitz, Berta Bornstein, Hans Lampl, and Jean Lampl-de Groot returned, temporarily, to the slightly safer city of Vienna. Helene and Felix Deutsch were already in America, as was Franz Alexander. After the Danish government refused him permission to open a psychoanalytic clinic in Copenhagen, Reich again moved, along with Sex-Pol and his resilient publishing company, to Oslo. Still determined to promote dialectical-materialist psychology, the heart of his joint work with Otto Fenichel in Berlin, Reich continued to practice and to promote sex economy, the closely bound aggregation of sex, psychoanalysis, and politics. At this point Reich's mind may have genuinely deteriorated, and he probably knew it. "If I were not so certain of what I am working on, it would appear to me as a schizophrenic fantasy," he admitted to Fenichel and Edith Gyömröi.[28] Reich's behavior had always been erratic and, to many, offensive, but he was also powerful and brilliant and sexy. He was, in many ways, an anxious man who had managed his depressions and obsessions quite well over the last fifteen years. Whether one attributes his downward progression to stress caused by forced immigration or to a characterological kind of paranoid personality, it is important to separate his politics from his psychology. Reich lived in a world in which undisguised support for one's community of friends (especially Freud) included permission to critique one another's beliefs. In one sense he thrived on this. But his ruthless demand for political purity combined with fairly idiosyncratic research in sex economy designated Reich, in the course of the next few years, as the problem child. He was targeted by psychoanalysts at all points along the political spectrum: to the Marxists his focus on sexuality was too controversial, to Freud he was too Marxist, and to the conservatives he was too Freudian.

That relentless conservative threat was now bearing down on Vienna as well. Though it lacked the explicit terrifying power of the German Nazis, the electoral triumph of the Christian party was cause for concern. Chancellor Dolfuss suspended the parliamentary constitution, banned the SDAP, and, while he officially disallowed the Austrian Nazi Party as well, he formed his own coalition with the paramilitary Heimwehr. "The political situation is of the greatest interest here," Edith Jackson observed with characteristic New England reticence in letters to her Bostonian sister, "only it is almost impossible to know what it is. No one knows from day to day what new direction it will take."[29] Nevertheless, as the year advanced, Jackson's Jewish friends became visibly more affected by the Nazi's growing strength. They knew that all of Alfred Adler's school-based child guidance clinics had been closed. Some of the analysts were already leaving for Prague, London, and the United States. When Erik Erikson left for Boston with his family, Edith Jackson (with whom he had worked at Anna Freud's nursery) set up a contact with her sister. The analysts endured the pressure of Germany's Election Day, now called Republic Day, in Vienna. "The streets are as quiet as can be," Jackson wrote on November 12. "All celebrations have been prohibited. There are policemen on corners everywhere to ensure the maintenance of the prohibition. There seems to be no attempt to overstep it. There is no threat, no alarm— just a Sunday quiet. . . . One still doesn't know what may burst forth at any moment. But the fear of something desperate happening has already lasted so long that it isn't acutely felt anymore."[30]

Just this kind of numbness seemed to prevail over the Ambulatorium in 1933. Hitschmann's mid-October report on the state of the clinic did little for the society's mood; nor did Edward Bibring's treasurer's report, which he presented as the clinic's new vice chairman. At the same time, Hans Lampl, widely regarded as a particularly thoughtful colleague, carefully prepared his remarks on his recent experiences in Berlin. Contrasting the Ambulatorium's position to the Poliklinik's and pointing to the conditions under which the German clinic would more or less survive, he seemed to spare Freud, Anna Freud, and his society friends the increasingly tyrannical reality of Nazi life. Lampl's account deliberately fell short of alarming the Ambulatorium's governing council, perhaps to protect Freud. The board did agree to curtail some of the society's public lectures and consulting functions. But Hitschmann, who had rescued the Ambulatorium time and again, insisted on keeping the clinic open and active. Exploring everything from fixed fees to paying lectures, the psychoanalysts invoked the spirit of Budapest 1918 and decided instead to voluntarily decrease their personal salaries. At the same time, those who made financial contributions in lieu of work at the clinic would increase the sum of their Erlagscheine.[31] General dues would remain fixed at an affordable ten shillings while the substitutive contribution would be raised to twenty shillings a month. Some analysts worried about the widening fascist presence in Vienna while others fretted over the clinic's everyday finances, but everyone agreed that they were facing an unprecedented kind of emergency.

To alleviate their own distressed financial position, the London society was ready to rent out the maisonette adjoining the building. Instead, the board decided to convert it into treatment rooms.[32] Melanie Klein's work with children was so influential by now and she had attracted so many new patients that the expanding Children's Department required more treatment rooms, more experienced analysts, and even more analysts in training. She became the famous theoretician while Marjorie Brierley supervised the caretaker and the clinic's general upkeep. The staff suffered, but the society thrived, while Ernest Jones extended his vacillating reach farther into the grim territory of the IPA in Austria and Germany.

Even in the middle of the universal disaster Hitler had engineered, Otto Fenichel's activist group of psychoanalysts effected a small miracle. They, and quite possibly psychoanalysis itself, survived in exile precisely because the political raison d'être they had developed in the 1920s prepared them for the hostile demands of a capricious and dangerous government. Some, like Reich and Gyömröi, had sided with the Communists, while others, especially Fenichel and Simmel, stayed with the rivalrous Social Democrats. As unapologetic Marxists in an increasingly capitalist world, they were frightened but not intimidated by the Nazi's arcane authoritarian practices. Now, with anti-Semitism spreading as the official state position, Matthias Göring's cousin, the famous Hermann Göring, built the first concentration camp to eliminate offenders. Göring's racial pandering was so vicious that almost all members of Berlin's "wonderful society," as Radó called it, realized they had to leave their country in a hurry. Still, they carried their identity as social reformers with them. By March of the following year the *Rundbriefe*, that marvelous epistolary legacy conceived by Otto Fenichel, united the scattered members of the Children's Seminar group to track their evolving body of social and political theory. They used psychoanalysis as a virtual metaphor to examine life in and around Germany of the mid-1930s, at times yielding to the smallest details of Marxist speculation and at times striving to render objective critiques of new theory.

"Psychoanalysis [as] the germ of the dialectical-materialist psychology of the future"

1934

"WE ARE ALL convinced," Otto Fenichel wrote from Oslo in March of 1934, "that we recognize in Freud's Psychoanalysis the germ of the dialectical-materialist psychology of the future, and therefore we desperately need to protect and extend this knowledge."[1] So begins the extraordinary series of 119 letters written between 1934 and 1945 and circulated between and among a core group of activist psychoanalysts who had met at the Berlin Poliklinik in the 1920s, fled the Nazis, and remained close friends and political allies in exile. Otto Fenichel, principal author of the *Rundbriefe*, or circular letters, embodied that core's spirit and the *Rundbriefe* tell the story of the psychoanalysts' evolution from 1934 to 1945, the activities of its participants, and their larger ideological struggles in Europe and America. When nine-tenths of the psychoanalysts were forced to flee Berlin and Vienna between 1933 and 1938, they took with them a particular humanitarian ideology forged in a curious time. On the one hand, the new nation states had traded monarchy for participatory democracy, the Hapsburg Empire had dissolved, and women had gained the right to vote; on the other hand, there was boundless anti-Semitism, encroaching fascism, and intellectual persecution. Though classified since then as politically left wing, or even radical, a designation Fenichel's Marxist group would have actually welcomed, they hardly represented a disaffected "left opposition" in psychoanalysis. For one, all psychoanalysts were at the least social democratic. Second, as Fenichel recognized, the exiled group's ideology stemmed from the same progressive impulse that had guided psychoanalysis after World War I. Third, this group stayed true to Freud, while the IPA and its branch societies, increasingly oppressed and factionalized, had become unhappily rigid and more conservative. The *Rundbriefe* thus document the actual history of psychoanalysis, as classical in its own way as Fenichel's major psychoanalytic text, *The Psychoanalytic Theory of Neurosis.*

Of the *Rundbriefe*'s 119 confidential letters, about half were written from within Europe until 1938; from 1938 until 1945, from the United States. The core group—Edith Jacobson, Otto Fenichel, Annie Reich, Wilhelm Reich, Barbara Lantos, Edyth (Glück) Gyömröi, George Gerö, and Frances Deri— had convened exactly ten years earlier in 1924 at the Poliklinik's Children's Seminar. These psychoanalytic "children" of the movement, now mostly scattered into exile around Scandinavia and Europe and eventually the United States, on the whole welcomed Fenichel's intellectual and political leadership. The *Rundbriefe* consisted of ideological arguments, organizational reports from branch societies on three continents, psychoanalytic wranglings, a long meticulously theoretical public disagreement with Reich and shorter barbs aimed at the purported neo-Freudians, analyses of scientific meetings, position papers, book and article reviews, political opinions, and gossipy chatter. Over three thousand pages were exchanged, mostly typed on thin white paper, double-spaced, carbon copies or mimeographs, each page hand corrected. Some of the longer letters are really loosely bound packages of information containing facsimiles of letters between analysts outside the *Rundbriefe* circle, newspaper and journal clippings, programs, some with fragments of earlier circular letters attached. Generally, the letters are long and laboriously detailed, averaging twenty-three pages and ranging from ten pages to eighty pages, carefully numbered and serialized, and written in an inelegant executive style.

Fenichel's first Rundbrief (figure 35) was dated March 1934 from Oslo; the one-hundredth issue was issued in July 1943; the last letter was dated July 14, 1945, from Los Angeles. To the initial planners the letters may have been secret or clandestine. But as the young Martin Grotjahn, then still in Berlin, later remembered, he somehow knew that his friend Fenichel was writing and organizing them. He "was a prolific writer who put together drafts of very long letters, up to 30 pages, sent the manuscripts to his friends who added their comments, sent the package on, until the letter found its way back to Otto."[2] Some of these were shared solely with the core group absorbed in working out the theoretical issues of psychoanalysis and Marxism. Other letters had a far wider readership and were directed toward an outer circle, a

35 Manuscript of Otto Fenichel's first *Rundbriefe*, March 10, 1934 (Austen Riggs Center, Stockbridge, Massachusetts)

secondary group of politically engaged analysts who had not belonged to the Berlin Children's Seminars. Anything was open to critique. At different times Fenichel critiqued biologism, culturalism, sentimentality, and romantic historicism. The second letter from Oslo is dated April 1934 and is circulated to Erich Fromm, Frances Deri, George Gerö, Edith Glück (Gyömröi), Nic Hoel, Edith Jacobson, Käthe Misch-Frankl, Wilhelm Reich, Annie Reich, Vera Schmidt, and Barbara Schneider-Lantos. Still more members of the outer circle, who received occasional and less urgent letters, were Alice Bálint, Michael Bálint, Therese Benedek, Martin Grotjahn, René Spitz, Abram Kardiner, Angel Garma, and Sándor Radó.

This single-minded writing style of Otto Fenichel, who detested the hypocrisy of preserving some sort of expedient, sanitized version of psychoanalysis when its very existence was under attack, merely held back his political passion. Like Reich and Simmel, he believed in sociological work or social work, where the rightful use of psychoanalysis lay in its practical accomplishments, in giving ordinary people access to the privilege of insight. Throughout the narrative of the *Rundbriefe*, a dialectical subtext aims to show that abiding by a wholly Marxist sociology is a precondition to practicing psychoanalysis from an equally spotless Freudian point of view. The contributors' anecdotes, comments, and polemics told the story of a group working out this theoretical struggle while fighting on multiple fronts at once, both within and outside the confines of the psychoanalytic world. In the *Rundbriefe* the analysts sought to hold onto their original political mission while their own professional association (the IPA) under Ernest Jones's policy of appeasement was apparently granting concessions to the very people (the Nazis) who had condemned them to exile. To survive as exiles in host or hostile countries with little prospect of returning to Berlin, even those already accustomed to an "outsider" status craved the personal closeness of friends. Of utmost importance, therefore, Fenichel's plans to gather the group together for a summer 1934 meeting in Oslo developed rapidly. To drive the scattered analysts to attend this caucus, Fenichel described what was happening at their old institute in Berlin: the recently founded German Medical Society for Psychotherapy had given Carl Jung a prominent role in the new society.

Carl Jung's name had sounded alarms for Freudian analysts ever since Jung's official break with the IPA just before the onset of the First World War. Character and relationships aside, Freud and Jung's differing worldviews appeared in stark contrast after 1918. While Freud was elaborating his firmly secular social democratic platform and exploring the unconscious permutations of human sexuality, his old friend and bitter rival was forging a spiritually linked system of psychological archetypes. Desexualizing human motivation and behavior had always angered Freud—it had caused his break with Adler and Stekel—who had constructed psychoanalysis precisely to undo individual damage cause by society's repression of unacceptable sexuality. Freud had also long suspected Jung of anti-Semitism. And, indeed, in February of 1933 Jung had accepted Heinrich Mathias Göring's invitation to participate in the direction of the Allgemeine Ärztliche Gesellschaft für Psychotherapie, the new society of psychiatrists and psychotherapists working out of the Wichmanstrasse headquarters of the former Poliklinik. Göring made his clinic's mission clear. In his closing speech to the General Medical Congress for Psychotherapy, he exhorted his audience to abide by Hitler's *Mein Kampf* and, in this official capacity, referred to Carl Jung as interpreter of the Hitlerian ideal.

> We National Socialist doctors, National Socialist academics, stand up absolutely for our idea, for love of our people. . . . I take it for granted that all members of the Society have worked through this book in all scientific seriousness and recognize it as the basis for their thought. I require all of you to study in detail Adolf

Hitler's book and speeches. Whoever reads the Führer's book and speeches and studies his essential nature will observe that he has something which most of us lack: Jung calls it intuition. Heil Hitler![3]

Suddenly the ideological quarrels between inner circle members, especially Fenichel and Reich, seemed less important. Quoting Lenin's famous "What is to be done?" (Simmel's motto as well), Edith Glück suggested forging a compromise between Fenichel's wish to bring about organizational change from within the IPA and Reich's insistence on producing an entirely new theoretical platform. The *Rundbriefe* group agreed to stay united, to tolerate their colleagues' increasingly reactionary attitudes, and to argue for tolerance and constitutional reforms at the forthcoming eighteenth IPA Congress in Lucerne. They would abide by the IPA's "bourgeois-liberal ideology," though they found the organization undemocratic and hoped to mobilize it toward more committed antifascist political action. "All the reasons that Ferenczi originally gave for founding the I. P. A. still exist today, it seems to us, in concentrated form," Fenichel wrote to reassure his friends. "For though Psychoanalysis thoroughly permeates the public sphere, in psychiatric and educational theory, this does not inevitably mean, as Freud has emphasized, the triumph of Psychoanalysis. If [Psychoanalysis] must constantly abandon its autonomy, change its language and moderate itself time and again in order to receive universal approval, this only strikes a keener death knell."[4] Thus emboldened, the *Rundbriefe* group arrived at the Lucerne meetings only to confront, to their dismay, the behavior of their post-1933 colleagues. Those who could still remain in Austria and Germany (twenty-four of the thirty-six Berlin analysts had fled), as well as the traveling Americans, had started to remake Freudian theory into bland counterrevolutionary dogma. And according to Anna Freud, even Teresa Benedek and the few still left in Berlin found "their 'paradise' in the last year not quite as ideal as Boehm described it."[5] Ernest Jones's role as president of the IPA was far too ambiguous, they thought, given his insistence on achieving a settlement with the Nazis, on the one hand, and, at the same time, his tremendous efforts to physically rescue analysts from the Nazi grip in Berlin. Ultimately, Reich's contention that the IPA was actively stifling dissent proved true: in a plan that Anna Freud and Jones had been hatching for a year, Reich was expelled from membership in the IPA in August, just at the end of the Thirteenth International Psychoanalytic Congress held in Lucerne. And it turned out that Jones's strategy for rescuing his colleagues expelled from the Berlin society masked his continued collusion with Boehm and Müller-Braunschweig. But, unlike Jones and many of his IPA colleagues, Reich could never sidestep inquiry nor put distance between himself and either the more conservative or the more Marxist psychoanalysts. Anna Freud blamed Reich's insistence on locating socialist potential within psychoanalytic theory, and starting a concurrent movement and a journal, above his allegiance to her father or to the Communist Party. Reich, on the other hand, claimed to have been victimized for his highly visible anti-Nazi mobilization just when Jones, Anna Freud, and Freud were negotiating to maintain more or less viable psychoanalytic activity in Germany under Hitler. In truth, Anna Freud was quite skilled when the nature of her work had more to do with clinical evaluation than with raw politics. In perhaps the most perceptive assessment of Reich to date, Anna Freud described his personality to Jones. "I have quite a long Reich experience behind me and I could always get along with him a little longer than the others," she wrote to Jones,

> because I tried to treat him well instead of offending him. It helps a little way and would help more if he were a sane person which he is not. . . . There is a wall somewhere where he stops to understand the other person's point of view and flies off into a world of his own. . . . I always thought that he is honest as far as he himself knows, which most of the others do not believe of him. But, of course, he is not consistent or logic[al] in his actions, which one could expect if he were honest *and* sane. I think he had quite a deep understanding of psycho-analysis and is taking it in places now where it does not go together with his much less complicated beliefs. He is an unhappy person . . . and I am afraid this will end in sickness. But since he is our world still, I am sure the way you dealt with him is the best possible way. He is near Vienna in the mountains just now to see his wife and children.[6]

When Fenichel and Reich reasoned that their stance on politics and sexuality, and on the totality of theory and praxis, was closer to the original Freud, they were correct. Psychoanalysis could only reach its full potential in a socialist society. Fenichel was neither isolationist nor sectarian, since he merely elaborated on Freud's own postwar social democratic thinking. On the personal level, however, the arguments between Fenichel and Reich escalated and the two men, friends and coworkers since medical school in 1919, separated at the end of 1934. Reich, tired of the bickering, turned to his work in Oslo, while Fenichel, who loved to write, kept up his essays for the Sex-Pol journal. Even to an outsider like Martin Grotjahn, Fenichel's differences with Reich had become obvious. Anna Freud noticed it too. "Somebody told me privately," she wrote to Jones, "that now Fenichel's troubles with Reich have begun."[7] Reich still identified with Communism, while Fenichel held to his social democratic roots in Red Vienna. Second, Reich, considered as much a deviant in institutional psychoanalysis as in institutional Communism, had been rejected by both establishments whereas Fenichel embraced organizational affiliations at almost any cost. Ever since medical school, Fenichel had seemed to push his friends too hard, but he also stayed extremely loyal. In letters, essays, papers, and speeches he continued to argue that Marxism should accept psychoanalysis and that his friend Wilhelm Reich had understood that best. "The materialist's distrust of psychology [is] understandable [but] . . . is not justified," he wrote. "The [Marxists'] unawareness of the details of dynamic interactions can become a great impediment to their cause. . . . Reich placed these factors[8] in their proper light."[9]

In a barely disguised whitewashing of the Nazi takeover, the *IJP* editors announced that "according to information received [the Berlin society and Poliklinik] resumed work in January 1934. Lecture courses for practitioners of psychoanalysis and for teachers are being given on approximately the same lines as before, the Institute having new regulations for admission." Presumably it was Jones who found just the right euphemisms for masking the facts, but he was worried. "Have you found any reason to suppose," he asked Eitingon, "that the Society will depart from our work in either theory or practice?"[10] Obviously Eitingon had, or he would still be in Berlin. Jones's failure to comprehend what he called the "riddle" of why Eitingon "left Germany for good" was nothing new. In all the early years of the psychoanalysis, Jones had tried to put the movement's needs ahead of his own and generally succeeded, if only for lack of imagination. But his devotion had been painfully tested recently, and the seemingly sudden resolve of so many colleagues (all Jews) to safeguard themselves instead of the "cause" unnerved him. He concluded that Ernst Simmel had "got in with a rather bad lot" when he drew up plans for an experimental, and no doubt politically activist, institute in Los Angeles.[11] And, instead of conceding that the mass relocation of traumatized colleagues might justifiably destabilize their institutions, Jones suggested narrowly that "the old Berlin Society has transferred its interminable personal quarrels to other countries."[12] Fortunately Jones made other public announcements as well. "A Psycho-Analytical Institute and a Treatment Centre will be opened shortly in Jerusalem under the direction of Dr. Eitingon" and a few former associates from Berlin.[13] Actually both Jones and Anna Freud were genuinely delighted that Eitingon had petitioned the chancellor of Jerusalem's Hebrew University to organize a "department of psychoanalysis."[14] In the midst of the destruction all around them, new academic activity would be "splendid."

Meanwhile what was left of the Poliklinik was now reluctantly codirected by Martin Grotjahn, one of the *Rundbriefe* outer circle members, just then winding up his own analysis with Felix Boehm. For the first few months of the year, Grotjahn treated a handful of "orphaned" patients remaining at the clinic when their analysts fled the country. Though he came up with various justifications for this work, he felt so anxious that Magnus Hirschfeld's invitation to leave the Poliklinik in order to direct the Institute for Sexual Science came as a welcome relief. One day after Grotjahn started the new job, the building was surrounded, raided, and burned by Nazi stormtroopers. Since 1919 Hirschfeld's institute had housed four clinical departments (psychotherapy, somatic sexual medicine, forensic sexology, and gynecology and marriage counseling) as well as a library and the offices of the World League for Sexual Reform and Scientific Humanitarian Committee, the first homosexual organization. Like the Poliklinik, it had emerged in the context of the Weimar Republic's progressive reform movement and, after 1933, was denounced as immoral, Jewish, and social democratic. Also like the Poliklinik, the institute was closed and reopened as a Nazi office building just three months after Hitler's takeover. By late fall, as the half-hearted investigation into Edith Jacobson's recent arrest by the Gestapo continued, an anxious cynicism set in with Grotjahn and other members of the *Rundbriefe* group. By the next year Jacobson would be in jail. Many analysts had been threatened or harassed, but until then no others had been taken into custody. Grotjahn himself had managed to fend off the government for a while simply by ignoring it: the official paperwork asking about his racial purity and political affiliations lay unanswered on his desk, gathering dust. But his denial and momentary good luck had to be confronted, and his half-Jewish wife's dismissal from her job as a physician signaled that the moment of decision had arrived. They too ran for their lives.

Red Vienna fell on February 12. Though the Nazis' attempted takeover failed, Engelbert Dolfuss was assassinated and Kurt von Schuschnigg became Austria's new chancellor. Fifteen years of a worker's regime in an urban environment had attempted to show that a new social structure could survive based on equitable housing, employment, and welfare services. It could survive market forces but not armed ones. With the fascist desolation spreading over Europe, Alfred Adler and Wilhelm Reich, two analysts rarely linked in the annals of psychoanalysis, emigrated to the United States. Within an overall socialist municipal policy, these two had militated for the practical application of psychoanalysis, Adler pedagogically and Reich in mental hygiene. Interestingly, separated from the workers movements of Red Vienna, their theories became markedly more removed from social factors. Adler's educational theories were championed by America's overvaluation of individualism, while Reich's bioenergic research and theories of sexual liberation were taken up by later countercultural and radical therapies.

The Ambulatorium, however, seemed to have great staying power even when Red Vienna's outlook was at its lowest. Otto Isakower, a psychiatrist who had worked in Wagner-Jauregg's clinic with Paul Schilder and Heinz Hartmann during the late 1920s, joined Hitschmann and was installed as deputy director of the Ambulatorium in 1934. During his psychiatric rounds at the public hospital, Isakower met and hired Betty Grünspan, one of those extraordinary veteran nurses who labored on the front lines of disease as vigorously against syphilis and tuberculosis in the local hospital as against the cholera and spotted fever on the Serbian front in World War I. Like many of her friends among the modern Viennese New Women, she was constantly seeking out fresh challenges and decided to become a physician and specialize in surgery. In the mid-1920s Grünspan followed Tandler into leadership of the public health offices and chartered a continuing education school for graduate nurses. In addition to her teaching, she directed surgery and aftercare at the Am Steinhof Hospital and so habitually observed the mental processes of psychiatric patients. The effects of training notwithstanding, psychotic suffering is particularly vivid to clinicians who watch closely, and Betty Grünspan resolved to study psychoanalysis in order to develop treatments for psychosis. She attended the institute's training seminars on Pelikangasse, analyzed adults and children, and, in one of those curious twists of fate, lost her post as municipal physician but remained a psychoanalyst at the Ambulatorium, exactly the opposite of the earlier governmental decree of "physicians only" for the Ambulatorium. There Grünspan's combination of skills and independence attracted the attention of the American pediatrician and child analyst Edith Jackson who would found, license, and finance the Jackson Nursery.[15] Only a woman with Grünspan's personality would have the strength to take over as assistant at the Ambulatorium in 1937, the clinic's last intrepid year before the Anschluss.

"A written Children's Seminar of Marxist psychoanalysis"

1935

LIKE MOST Nazis in 1935, Felix Boehm did not hesitate to expose the estranged psychoanalysts to betrayal and even death if he thought it would benefit the aryanized Poliklinik. As president of the new DPG, he informed Jones that the exiled Jewish analysts had lost their membership status in the society and were now consigned to the rank of "guest." Despite Müller-Braunschweig's urgent interventions with the Kampfbund, Boehm reported, not even Teresa Benedek and the few others left in Berlin were safe. Jones was not fooled. "It looks as if the German Society will soon be forced to expel all its Jewish members," he wrote to Brill with a touch of irony. "The situation for Jews in Germany is a great deal worse than any of the newspaper reports admit."[1] The remaining Aryans were hardly better off: they were forced to delete "Berlin" from their institute's name and to change the clinic's title from *Poliklinik* to *Ambulatorium*. The name change would indicate that the current clinic was totally separate from the government.[2] Nevertheless, Boehm brazenly asked all analysts, exiles and residents alike, for written congratulations on the fifteenth anniversary of their organization. The *Rundbriefe* group heard of this and felt that Boehm was trying to corner them into unspoken collusion (or forgiveness) by hinting at Freud's flattering tenth anniversary endorsement of the Poliklinik in 1930. Even so, Edith Gyömröi decided to cable a response. "On the occasion of the fifteenth anniversary," she wrote, "former members think fondly of the old administration of free research and wish further prospering under the old flag."[3] Gyömröi was really trying to say that, even in 1935, she remained committed to Freud's 1918 principle of free treatment and research and that her comrades stood by her in their struggle against its corruption. Unless the German government formally altered its position on the management of the Poliklinik, activists who wanted to practice psychoanalysis should stay far away. Her friend Fenichel understood this, but he also believed that Gyömröi and the rest of the *Rundbriefe* group would be less vulnerable if they focused on their strength, a unified psychological and political theory.

Otto Fenichel had just moved from Oslo to Prague and resumed his rhythmic production of the *Rundbriefe*. Every three to six weeks he offered his readers a virtual smoke-filled political meeting by correspondence, with a fantastic range of new opportunities to critique, comment, analyze, or condemn their colleagues' ideas. His meticulous style of gathering and shaping data into a readable document was to make his later textbook of classical psychoanalysis one of the most widely adopted worldwide. Until they were published, the letters survived in loosely collated carbon copies, typed and hand corrected, held together in dog-eared batches with rusting paperclips. "Despite all obstacles," he wrote, "these *Rundbriefe* are necessary for the union of analysts of our orientation . . . a written Children's Seminar of Marxist psychoanalysis."[4] In this he depended on colleagues throughout Europe, the United States, and Latin America to maintain the open flow of news, information, theories, conference and book reports, and commentaries. But unlike the Children's Seminar at the Poliklinik, the *Rundbriefe* members had to agree to secrecy. Fenichel lamented the fact, but his belief in the project and his love of psychoanalytic thinking never wore out. He saw no contradiction between Marxism and psychoanalysis, and he encouraged his scattered colleagues to apply political theory to clinical practice case by case, and fee free if necessary. The analysts' task, he insisted, was to provide direct help for individuals suffering from mental distress, not to give bourgeois moral uplift. This was neither charity nor "therapy for the masses," as Fenichel and Simmel had repeated over the years to the analytic and political communities, both of whom regularly misunderstood the *Rundbriefe* group's primary purpose. Marxists lacked a sense of individual reality, while most analysts missed the significance of the larger social reality, and Fenichel tried to correct both sets of misperceptions concurrently.

The *Rundbriefe* group's pledge to sustain ongoing and open discussions of theory and political psychoanalysis meant that controversy would continue to dominate the circular letters well into the next few years. There were controversies about Wilhelm Reich, about Marxism versus socialism, about

Freudian versus neo-Freudian analysts, about internal versus external life, about the impact of culture on the psyche, patients, societies, and more. For the moment debate between colleagues lessened the isolative pain of exile. Do nationalities have specific character structures? Weighing in from Copenhagen, George Gerö imagined that the human unconscious was "international" but that "character form" was unique to each country and was based largely on the superego. As the child develops into an adult, this character form (or "national character") becomes stronger along with the expanding power of the superego, the mind's unconscious place for safekeeping cultural norms. According to this argument, each country's population would have an overriding political character as well. Fenichel liked the basic idea, but warned Gerö of the intellectual hazards of reductionism. Historical conditions, Fenichel reminded the group, determine national character for all citizens, and a country's historical development parallels the course of a neurosis among individuals and their society.[5] Most of the refugee psychoanalysts coped with their rejection by advancing explanatory theory, but Fenichel, who loved the argument more than the resolution, refused to reduce anything to a single linear explanation.

Not long after Gerö's theory appeared in the *Rundbriefe*, Michael Bálint sent Fenichel a manuscript that reinterpreted the stages of the libido with particular emphasis on education and culture. Bálint, who had taken over direction of the Budapest clinic at Ferenczi's death in 1933, had been at the Berlin Poliklinik in the 1920s, a member of the clinical faculty at the Charité, and lecturer at the Institute of Organic Chemistry at the Berlin Royal Academy. Now writing from Budapest, Bálint ostensibly refuted his former neglect of social factors and his fondness for biologism, another reductionist approach that Fenichel abhorred. In spite of that, Fenichel responded with a fifteen-page critique, which brought out the ultra-Freudian tone he used to criticize analysts he called "neo-Freudians," those who placed the impact of culture above instinct. He reprimanded Bálint's wife, Alice, for yielding to single-minded culturalism. Whatever its actual contribution to technique, he said, the Bálints's disregard for the instinctual base of psychic life ignored reality. Of course he closed with a friendly, "Send me an anti-critique!"[6] The friends continued to exchange caustic threats, and their rounds of letters traveled with a never-ending fund of commentaries interspersed with news reports from the German front.

A few months after Edith Jacobson's imprisonment for high treason by the Gestapo on October 24, Jones expressed his confusion to his friend Marie Bonaparte in Paris. "The situation in Germany is one of extraordinary terrorism," he wrote, "not least within the ranks of the Nazi party itself. An enormous amount of energy is taken up with constant espionage and counter-espionage."[7] Jacobson had been arrested in Berlin the moment she returned from visiting Reich in Scandinavia in view of resuming her resistance work with the New Beginning group. It was exciting, heart-felt work. "*Neu Beginnen* was a small political organization," recalled Jacobson's colleague Gerhard Bry, "a radical socialist group that had developed out of a predominantly communist tradition, but turned gradually in the direction of social-democratic convictions and policies."[8] In Germany and elsewhere the political left had broken up into competing, partisan factions. As a result, much of the activist collaboration against the main Nazi threat was exhausted, and what little remained after January 1933 disappeared. Nevertheless, the planners of the Neu Beginnen secretly organized some of the most critical members from the remnants of these political groups. They met in tiny private clusters, collected and distributed information, and smuggled people and money across borders. "We were young, optimistic, and we fully expected that much of the future would be ours," Bry said. Edith Jacobson (figure 36) was apparently the only psychoanalyst among the new exiles to risk going back to Germany, and did so despite the DPG's explicit order prohibiting analysts from treating patients opposing the Nazis. With a code name of "John," the accusers said, she had opened her home to political meetings, contributed five marks per month to clothe and feed political prisoners, and had even treated Miles-Gruppe members in her psychoanalytic office. Rumor had it that Jacobson's treatment of a young Communist woman, subsequently killed by the Gestapo, particularly angered the police, who hungered for confidential information from her analysis. "They first arrested some of her patients and murdered one of them," Jones wrote to Brill, "and we have been very much afraid of her being tortured to give information."[9] Jones was so shaken he resolved to visit Berlin immediately, even though the government seemed content, for the moment, to let Jacobson stay in prison without a trial. But he was also careful. "It would be evidently wrong to try to use any influence in a case as yet undecided," he cautioned Anna Freud, "in the hands of the proper judicial authorities."[10] The decision to hire a Nazi lawyer for Edith was an odd but apparently deliberate decision to use Nazi paranoia against itself. Both Jones and Fenichel (who rarely agreed on anything) calculated that, if she were freed too soon from the local prison, the Gestapo would place her in *Schutzhaft* (protective custody) and dispatch her to a concentration camp or *Schulungslager* (re-education camp),[11] the notorious euphemistic term taken up Felix Boehm. Jones then reinterpreted the account

36 Edith Jacobson (Special Collections,
A. A. Brill Library, New York Psychoanalytic
Society and Institute)

for Brill's sake. Jacobson's lawyer was "in with the other side," he suspected, "and is arranging to keep her in longer than is necessary so as to increase his already exorbitant fees."[12]

The same week Ernest Jones returned to London, Felix Boehm dashed off an odd and urgent telegram warning him to stop the fund-raising campaign planned to help Edith Jacobson out of prison. Though her lawyer suggested that foreign pressure might speed her release, Boehm objected to any gesture that would publicly connect the DPG to her case. He was particularly afraid of angering his friends in government with the news that Jacobson had hosted anti-Nazi resistance meetings in her home while working as an analyst at the Poliklinik. Was she really a menace to psychoanalysis? Within the small circle of key psychoanalytic players in 1935, it was possible not only for Felix Boehm to think so in the midst of Nazi Berlin but also for Anna Freud to agree. "Edith had been very uncautious and had put the analytic movement in danger," Anna told their Scandinavian colleague Nic Hoel. "How should Boehm be able to go to the minister of culture," Anna continued, "and talk with him about the conformity of analysis with the German meanings?"[13] Anna Freud, naively impressed with what she had learned about Felix Boehm, blamed Edith Jacobson for her own imprisonment. Anna's deeply internalized fear of anti-Semitism had blinded her to the Nazi's inappropriate confiscation of psychoanalysis and caused her to hold Jacobson responsible for the verdict. Perhaps more to the point, Anna Freud had now sided with Boehm and the police regime against political activism, the historical core of the psychoanalytic movement. Meanwhile, Ernest Jones, as dedicated to the psychoanalytic cause as Anna Freud, was quite comfortable with political contradictions and enjoyed, most of all, competing for attention inside the distinctive subculture of Freud's own guards. "I am at present engaged in seeing what can be done by way of appealing to the German Government for a *Gnadenact* [pardon]," Jones wrote to Eitingon after he tried contacting Hitler's personal representative in London. "I cannot say that I think the prospects very rosy. . . . Edith Jacobson was sentenced to two and a quarter years *Zuchthaus* [penitentiary], six months of which were deducted on account of her previous imprisonment."[14] The actual case was postponed for another year, but the flurry of visits and internal correspondence converging on Jacobson's story points to the IPA's quandary at the end 1935. They were caught between condemning the German analysts for collaborating with the Nazis and denouncing the analysts for participating in active political resistance. The Nazis won.

"Social psychoanalysis"

1936

THE POLIKLINIK'S premises at 10 Wichmannstrasse were taken over by the German Institute for Psychological Research and Psychotherapy on October 15, 1936. Headed by Matthias Heinrich Göring, protected by Reichsmarschall Hermann Göring, and assisted by Carl C. Jung, the newly configured Göring Institute was the Nazi regime's center for racialized psychotherapy training and treatment at least until the end of World War II. Through a set of complex and often ethically compromised maneuvers, Felix Boehm and Carl Müller-Braunschweig managed to retain their society's membership in the IPA. Boehm and Müller-Braunschweig apparently felt they could count on the support of Anna Freud and IPA president Ernest Jones in complying with Matthias Göring's wishes to cleanse the Berlin society and the DPG of all its Jewish members.

Jones believed that organizational duty required from him an agreement with Matthias Göring to maintain the DPG, now absorbed into the German Institute for Psychological Research and Psychotherapy, as a component society of the IPA. "Personally, I am favorably inclined to the possibility of the German Society remaining with us," he wrote to Anna Freud, with the caveat that it might not "prove to be possible on both sides."[1] When he met with Müller-Braunschweig, Boehm, and Göring, Göring disingenuously assured Jones that psychoanalysis would retain its independence within the new institute. In exchange, Jones agreed to make possible the relocation of all Jewish members who had "voluntarily resigned" from the Berlin society. Jones collaborated, remained friendly with Müller-Brauschweig, and watched the shattered Poliklinik mutate from a progressive institution committed to social intervention to a reprehensible hub for Nazi activity. Throughout the Göring administration and after World War II, Jones and Anna Freud insisted that they were simply preserving psychoanalysis at any cost.

At first glance, the Göring Institute still seemed like a conventional outpatient mental health clinic. The premises were those of the former Poliklinik. A staff of fifty-two psychotherapists treated patients, supervised students, consulted with the public schools, and defined their mission as an institution for paupers (*Anstalt für mittellose Volksgenossen*, literally a "Foundation for Racial Comrades without Means"). Some patients were transferred from the old Poliklinik, and doctors at the Charité referred others for the treatment of psychosis, alcoholism, depression, and the full range of mental disorders. The institute's affiliation with the Ministry of the Interior and the *Reichsärzteführer* (director of the state medical board) gave them federal protection. But neither Boehm nor Herbert Linden, the psychiatrist appointed as chief administrative officer of the Göring Institute, believed that the former Poliklinik's psychoanalytic approach could (or even should) be coordinated with the New German Psychotherapy. The new German psychotherapy was a vague but indicative set of standards—most of them overtly propagandist—that reflected the fascists' aim to strengthen their patients' belief in core values, life, and the greatness of the German people. "Müller-Braunschweig is combining a philosophy of Psychoanalysis with a quasi-theological conception of National-Socialistic ideology," Jones, who had recently met the new leaders in Berlin, wrote to Anna Freud.[2] Ultimately, the *Seelenheilkunde* placed mental health patients in danger of euthanasia if the treatment failed. The dual principles of "healing and extermination" would be codified by von Hattinberg (based on Carl Jung's outlines) and implemented by Herbert Linden in 1938.[3]

Once Göring and Boehm had secured the right to run the institute as they wished, they decided to support their decisions by keeping a statistical record similar to Eitingon's. The former Poliklinik's old record-keeping forms were probably still filed away in a desk drawer (the Göring Institute had appropriated all the Ernst Freud furniture), but Boehm, who enjoying producing regular statistics and medical reports, inadvertently portrayed a very new kind of clinic. In contrast to the earlier Poliklinik's focus on poor and lower classes, almost 80 percent of the Göring Institute patients were middle class, 10 percent were working class, and the remaining 10 percent were upper class.[4] The new demographic majority represented just the kind of patient who is tagged as a classic bourgeois consumer of psychoanalysis, rarely seen in the 1920s but still commonly attributed to Freudian practice. Free treatment was abandoned. All patients paid for their analysis, and the institute compensated therapists if the fees fell below six marks per hour. At least half the cases were prescribed a specific type of focused short-term treatment (*Fokaltherapie*) designed for its efficient elimination of neurosis and improvement of public health. Concentrated treatment also guaranteed the clinicians would not be wasting their time on adults who were considered incurable or "children emotionally torn by state demands to inform on their parents" or anyone defined by the Nazis as "hereditarily damaged."[5] As Göring had explained the year before,

> We know that there are still party members—and colleagues—who deny the necessity of psychotherapy, who assert that heredity is the only thing that matters and that education is unnecessary. Like the Führer, we claim that character can be developed and because of that psychotherapy is of the greatest importance. For psychotherapy, as Jung has emphasized over and over, is not just about curing people, but about making fit people who lack the correct attitude toward life.[6]

Wilhelm Reich's ominous descriptions of the dangers and historical course of fascism had been all too accurate. Reich has been considered an alarmist, a political fanatic, sexually obsessed, and paranoid, but his Sex-Pol work was curiously optimistic. He postulated that the human core, though biological, is innately social, sexual, and feeling. It was only authoritarian political regimes, replicated in the patriarchal family structure and in the push to accumulate money and status, that repressed the true goodness of the human being and created individual and societal neuroses. In an uncanny repetition of history, Wilhelm Reich, who emigrated to the United States to escape Nazi persecution in 1935, would see his work burned and banned by the government of the United States and die in prison in 1957. Yet, in the intervening years when he lectured at the New School for Social Research in New York and at his own school and laboratory in Maine, Reich had a profound effect on American clinicians. Therapists of the 1960s and early 1970s saw Reich as a leading mental health practitioner and reformist, known for his compassionate interest in the problems of youth. All the while, Reich championed Freud as the revolutionary who transformed bourgeois culture. He believed that Freud was as aware of cultural and environmental factors in human development as Harry Stack Sullivan and Karen Horney. His former supporters from the *Rundbriefe* would have agreed.

The *Rundbriefe* group met in person one last time, without Reich, at the fourteenth IPA congress held in Marienbad, Czechoslovakia in 1936. Communication by mail became more difficult as censorship encroached on Europe, even as the exiles' need to stay in touch became more acute. Their colleague Edith Jacobson had just been arrested and plans had to be made to obtain her release. At Marienbad the friends decided to continue producing the circular letters despite what Fenichel called "profound differences of opinion in the realm of economic Marxism," specifically, to keep on exchanging information on psychoanalytic events and publications.[7] Inevitably, though, no one was as diligent a writer as Fenichel (figure 37), who refused to submit, as a writer or an activist, to complacency. He stayed the heart of the *Rundbriefe*, which, until 1945, chronicled the exceptional story of a Marxist's struggle to report on history, accept its contradictions, and fight as much for the "correct application of psychoanalysis to sociology" as for "the very existence of Freudian psychoanalysis."[8]

Erich Fromm, a member of the *Rundbriefe*'s outer circle, had settled in New York. Back in 1929, when Fromm had joined the Frankfurt School and practiced in its allied free clinic, a reunion in New York might have seemed like an interesting but extravagant trip to the land of florid capitalism. Since then the explosion of Nazi violence, along with the growing influence of American intellectuals interested in Critical Theory, had made that prospect look serious and welcoming. By 1934, when Nicholas Murray Butler issued an

37 Otto Fenichel, 1934 (Photo by Eduard Bibring; Archives of the Boston Psychoanalytic Society and Institute)

invitation to house Horkheimer, Marcuse, and their institute at Columbia University in a building of their own (429 West 117 Street), the possibility was irresistible. The Frankfurt School refugees arrived in New York over the course of the year and found resettlement less disturbing than many of their fellow expatriates, partly because of their relative financial independence and partly because they chose to work on so many challenging and relevant subjects. By the time his colleagues reached New York, Fromm had already separated from the group, having arrived two years earlier to lecture with Franz Alexander at the Chicago Institute for Psychoanalysis. Even in exile, Fromm's relationship with psychoanalysis was strained, since it fell somewhere between the culturalist "neo-Freudians" and the purist establishment analysts in New York. His contentious *Rundbriefe* friend Otto Fenichel occupied a unique place at the forefront of this conflict. After Fromm published an article on the social bases of psychoanalysis, Fenichel sought to renew their "interrupted connection" and connect all supporters of "social psychoanalysis."[9] At one point in the *Rundbriefe* he assailed Fromm's praise of Ferenczi as a "revolutionary artist who overcame liberalism."[10] Liberalism represented precisely the flaw of the neo-Freudians, who, Fenichel thought, believed in social reform without depth (not Marxist) and in the biological nature of psychic life. But social psychoanalysis postulated that these two separate elements (culture and instinct) existed dialectically and could be merged only in practice, as at the free clinics. Even Wilhelm Reich had it wrong, Fenichel believed, while Freud understood this in principle and agreed with it. To today's readers, the *Rundbriefe* may be a history of psychoanalysis, politics, and new publications. But to those who wrote them, day after day, the letters stood as tingling reminders of late-night arguments in smoky rooms of their old café world. Some had even maintained their dues-paying membership in the Berlin society.

While the exiles endured most news from Germany with stoicism, they were shocked to hear that all Jews had been expelled from the Poliklinik. "That you should have done this without even telling me (quite apart from the justification of this step, about which I do not want to speak here) seems to me so incredible," Fromm wrote to Müller-Braunschweig, "that I am first asking you to enlighten me as to whether this rumour corresponds with the facts."[11] It did. The mass departure had started shortly after the passage of Hitler's frightful Enabling Act and had accelerated throughout the past two years. What was at stake in the psychoanalytic community in 1936, and brought into stark relief by Fromm's letter to Müller-Braunschweig, was the anti-Semitic nature of Jones's view that the Jewish members had resigned "voluntarily." True, the few analysts still in Berlin had decided not to dissolve their society and not to resign from the IPA. But either gesture, they told Jones, would have been tantamount to conceding they had disregarded Nazi protocol. The Jewish members were politically sophisticated and their ultimate response to Müller-Braunschweig's demand for immediate resignation is unclear to this day. Whether or not the Jewish members actually agreed to resign, or resigned "voluntarily" under duress, or would resign later though they had first said they would leave immediately, or had asked Jones to announce they had resigned without actually doing so—is unresolved. In some ways the question is moot since they were driven out under threat of death anyway, and Jones, ambivalent as always, probably indicated that some relocation assistance was available. Nevertheless, it was also to Jones that Müller-Braunschweig turned after receiving Fromm's troubling letter. "The enclosed letter from Dr. Fromm raises the doubt whether you have informed all the Jewish members living abroad and asked them to resign," he wrote to Jones.[12] Even if illusory, Müller-Braunschweig thought, Jones's defense of the Jewish members would make him and Boehm seem like traitors to the German state. But, in fact, Jones, who thought little about foreign policy beyond its effects on psychoanalysis, always placed the "cause" ahead of individual psychoanalysts' welfare. The cumulative experience of Ernest Jones's small but continual series of compromises with people who signed their letters "Heil Hitler!" adding ambiguity to terror, made an indelible imprint on the history of the psychoanalytic movement. "It is not literally true that they have been excluded," he answered Fromm with a characteristic measure of self-protection, "but . . . [the Jewish members] decided it would be in everyone's interest for them to send in their resignation."[13]

Ernest Jones was not just politically craftier than he seemed at first. He was also administratively quite adept. By 1936 Jones was the highest-ranking psychoanalyst in the IPA, and his lifelong fondness for the conservative end of all things Freudian seemed fully formed. But, for the last ten years since 1926, he had proved to be as profoundly in favor free treatment as Fenichel or Reich. Of all the free psychoanalytic clinics in Europe, London's was the most economically viable at the moment. Jones knew that its budget was strained, however, and proposed electing Pryns Hopkins to associate membership. Once it became evident that the clinic's new educational and treatment programs could not survive without financial assistance, Hopkins stood out as the patron to help them—and do so generously. "I remember very clearly all the time," Donald Winnicott wrote later to John Bowlby, "that it is due to Pryns Hopkins that we have a clinic at all."[14] Founder of two progressive schools for boys and a left-wing magazine, Hopkins had issued a pamphlet entitled "Is Opinion a Crime?" at the end of World War I. His association with New York anarchists led him to found the League for the Amnesty of Political Prisoners with Margaret Sanger and Lincoln Steffens in the early 1920s. In January 1936 Pryns Hopkins became Honorary Almoner to the clinic more or less in the tradition of von Freund, Max Eitingon, and Marie Bonaparte, though he did not intend to "take up therapeutic treatment" as they had.[15] Instead of investing directly in the building's upkeep, Hopkins decided to strengthen a relief program of grants-in-aid for clinic patients. He was concerned with the "external circumstances of the patients under treatment," knowing full well that psychotherapy is an empty gesture when the patient is too poor to eat. Meanwhile, Jones especially wanted to build up a separate children's department for Melanie Klein, whose play therapy required ample space and special furniture. But Klein's estranged daughter, Dr. Melita Schmideberg (also a member of the British society), took the occasion to critique Jones and pose some of the more controversial questions raised by the clinic's expansion. At a meeting of the board, Schmideberg asked if the society was ready to handle an increased number of cases, to retract their demand for complete analyses, and to leave unresolved the question of diagnosis—all issues occasioned by enlarging the clinic's capacity. The dispute proved to be just quarrelsome and meddling since, as Jones said, the clinic staff was discussing the treatment of acute conditions just then and would soon develop more formal criteria. As to the expansion, the clinic had appropriated almost the entire building at 36 Gloucester Place[16] over the last four years, including the two upper floors previously rented out for income.[17] The number of staff and students and patients had also increased considerably. Hopkins was convinced of the clinic's merit and was to support this and other psychoanalytic funds on both sides of the Atlantic intermittently until 1956.

Where the London clinic seemed full of strife but was actually flourishing, and the Berlin clinic was an acrimonious opposite of its original self, the spirit of the Vienna Ambulatorium of 1936 is harder to describe. Fenichel thought the Viennese analysts were simply blind to the city's increasing anti-Semitism and found it maddening. "Although it is now three years since Freud's books were burned in Berlin," he wrote in the news section of the *Rundbriefe*, "the International Psychoanalytic Press left the bulk of its book stock in Leipzig.[18] Now on the order of the regime the stock has been seized and ordered destroyed. The Press . . . plans to lodge a complaint—in German courts!"[19] Less skeptical (or more contrary) Viennese analysts chose to remain at Freud's side despite the alarming news of the Jews' expulsion from Berlin and Edith Jacobson's recent arrest. Anything else, they felt, would have meant abandoning faith in psychoanalysis itself. A few months after their decision to stay in Vienna, the analysts could feel vindicated because the city's health department offered to celebrate Freud's eightieth birthday by financing a suite of large new offices for the Ambulatorium and institute. "A piece of good news," Anna Freud had written to Jones at the end of 1935. "We have really taken the apartment in Berggasse 7. . . . Ernst will come after the New Year to advise us about . . . our various institutions and the furnishing. It will all have to be very simple but I am extremely happy about is and so is the Society."[20]

The Viennese psychoanalysts' new accommodations were located just one block and a few doors down from Freud's home and office at 19 Berggasse. The Ambulatorium could now move from the cramped quarters it still shared with the cardiology department at the hospital; the institute would have its own lecture and meeting rooms; and the Verlag would have office space plus, presumably, room to store the books and move them from Leipzig to Vienna. By May Ernst had remade the 7 Berggasse quarters. The new facilities, Richard Sterba recalled, included "a beautiful meeting room for [up to] fifty people . . . treatment rooms, a kitchen and a library. The Bordeaux-red drapes and upholstered chairs were well-proportioned and comfortable."[21] Everything was finished in time to coincide with Freud's eightieth birthday. Once Jones realized that 7 Berggasse would really happen, he urged all IPA analysts to support the kind of grand opening they had enjoyed in the early 1920s. As president of the IPA and director of the London clinic, Jones (who loved rituals and found the prospect of an opening irresistible) announced that he would personally inaugurate the new building. Meanwhile, Freud expected that the May inaugural would preempt other annoying eightieth birthday celebrations. "I am *very* [22] pleased to hear that you will be in Vienna for the housewarming of our new home," he wrote to Jones.[23] In a note to Ludwig Binswanger, an analyst and old friend living in Switzerland, Freud repeated the same sentiment. "The opening of our new home for the Vienna Society," he said, "will be the worthiest substitute for festivities. We regard the other festivities coldly."[24] Whether he liked it or not, both the observance of Freud's birthday and the housewarming party went forward much as the 1920 opening celebrations for the Poliklinik. Karl Landauer attended from Frankfurt and the novelist Thomas Mann read his lyrical paper on "Freud and the Future" to an international audience at the Academic Society for Medical Psychology. Jones went to Vienna for the party as well, but he preceded his trip with an unusually ambivalent and rather patronizing letter to Anna Freud. "It is a significant sign of honorable poverty that the Vienna Psychoanalytic Society, the mother of all others, has suffered," Jones wrote, "that it took more than thirty years until it found a decent home of its own."[25] Ultimately, Freud's physical weakness prevented him from attending the opening ceremony or even visiting the new premises until a month later, on June 5. In the past the purpose of such a convocation had been as much to enhance the public visibility of psychoanalysis as to fete the movement's progress. Now Freud, though flattered by the government's attention, was wary. The Vienna society seemed to have survived, not only unimpeded but actually invigorated by the Dollfuss regime. Even if Dollfuss was a boor, did the government's gesture mean that the Freuds would be protected? Freud, who had no desire to leave Vienna, hoped to maintain a fairly good relationship with the new government; his absence from the opening suggests a delicate deference to the political officials.

The Ambulatorium's move to 7 Berggasse would place the clinic in a strong position to demonstrate the value and benefits of psychoanalysis to the public. Freud knew what was at stake. Since 1918 his deliberate effort to propel psychoanalysis into the public purview had produced some of the most compelling clinical services of the twentieth century and had released it from the stagnant isolation of exclusive private practice. "Out of their own funds," he wrote in the 1935 addition to his brief autobiography, "the local [psychoanalytic] societies support . . . out-patient clinics in which experienced analysts as well as students give free treatment to patients of limited means."[26] The clinics ranged from very small—in Zahgreb the grouping hardly constituted a clinic at all—to the large organization in Berlin. But as Imre Hermann from Budapest pointed out to Anna Freud and Eduard Bibring, only a serious study by the IPA (as Eitingon had conducted for the Poliklinik) would gather enough empirical data to bring out the larger socioeconomic purpose for supporting the clinics. Members of the Training Commission agreed and sent out a six-page questionnaire on their own letterhead, asking all local society directors to concentrate on "Part II above all else," part 2 being the section entitled "Bericht der Klinik Ambulatoriums" (Report on the Outpatient Clinic) in their reports. The three-part survey revisited Fenichel's charts but produced an unfocused set of questions regarding numbers of male and female registered patients, their ages (adult or child), their treatment status, and their overall diagnoses subdivided by gender. Presumably all clinics maintained these records, and like-minded clinic directors easily tabulated their data. Conspicuously absent from these forms were any questions with regard to fees, income, or patient eligibility. Since this same questionnaire went to Göring as head of the Berlin institute, one

wonders to what extent senior leaders of the IPA were relying on these numerical data to avoid revealing the extent of their compromises. With so
many of their colleagues forced into exile, the remaining analysts wanted to
prevent any external investigation of their clinics. One result was the simple
article of faith, that the number of patients registered at the clinic was the
number treated at no cost.

The themes of the Vienna Ambulatorium in its last year—public access,
personal privacy, treatment expertise—had not changed since its first year.
Since 1918 Freud had associated himself solidly with people like Max Eitingon,
Ernst Simmel, and Sándor Ferenczi who placed their faith in the clinics. When
Joseph Wortis, then a skeptical young American analysand, questioned Freud,
the old man held to the standard, unfailing defense of the clinics.

"An acquaintance of mine," I said, "a rich American woman, is now in her fifth
year of analysis."

"She must be rich to afford it. . . . It is a question of medical ethics," said
Freud. "Abuses are possible in analysis as in other branches of medicine."

"Except," I said, "for the special weapon of the positive transference. At any
rate, it raises the whole question of the importance of money to patients in
analysis."

"Now that we have free clinics and the psychoanalytic institutes, the question
no longer arises. Anybody can now be analyzed; they may have to wait a little,
but everybody has the privilege. Besides, every analyst undertakes to treat two
free patients. When one considers that an active analyst can at best treat seven or
eight patients at a time, then you must appreciate that it means a considerable
sacrifice."

"I spoke of the place of psychoanalysis in socialized medicine, but Freud did
not like the notion."

"It is not suited to state supervision and has found no place in the social insurance schemes here; the present system seems best, and there is no occasion to
worry about it."[27]

Except for the cautious last passage concerning socialized practice (now
defunct along with Red Vienna), this was, to the letter, the Budapest speech
of 1918. Few had predicted then exactly the impression Freud's speech would
make or how his project would unfold. Edith Jackson (figure 38), presumably
the "rich American woman" Freud mentioned to Wortis, was a candidate at
the Vienna institute who understood implicitly that the charge of the Budapest speech had stayed valid for almost two decades. Over the years, she

38 Edith Jackson (*left*) with Michael Bálint and a colleague, Paris 1938
(Photo by Eduard Bibring; Archives of the Boston Psychoanalytic
Society and Institute)

had visited Schloss Tegel, amply financed the Verlag, and, in Vienna and later in London, funded an experimental nursery school. Like Freud, she was
proud of Vienna's extensive network of services and the formal presence of
psychoanalysis within them. Many years later she remembered that "the
mothers and infants were more close together in the nursing homes there [in
Austria], where mothers were taken care of, than they were in our own country".[28] She had seen it firsthand at the Ambulatorium and also at Anna Freud
and Dorothy Burlingham's experimental nursery school for the "poorest of
the poor," work they were to take up later at the Hampstead War Nurseries
in London.[29] Edith financed the little school on Rudolfplatz. She paid the
rent, bought food and furniture, and underwrote many of Anna and
Dorothy's early childhood research projects.

In a later context Erik Erikson, Edith Jackson's contemporary in Vienna of
the 1920s and then in mid-century New England, praised her "Rooming-In
Unit" at the Yale–New Haven Hospital. He also acknowledged how unusual
she was. Jackson was "able to fulfill one of Sigmund Freud's greatest hopes,"
he said. She could "glean out of what we know of psychopathology gains for

normal psychology; to take what we have learned from sick lives and apply it to the very beginning of what we hope will be healthy lives."[30] Erikson had been one of the first analysts to leave Vienna in 1933 and had emigrated with his family to Boston after some difficult months in Copenhagen. Like Edith Jackson, Erikson was distrusted by American physicians, who could have undermined his career but never really did. When he met up with Edith again, he was impressed that she had translated her Vienna experience into everyday practice. Her hospital staff met from five to six-thirty every evening to review and critique activities of the day, exactly like Anna Freud's seminar, and, interestingly, at the same hour as Jackson's daily analysis with Freud several decades earlier. Nothing exactly like the rooming-in concept had been discussed during her time in Vienna, either among the analysts or within the trainees' group.

Similarly, Karen Horney and Teresa Benedek sought to infuse their American work with aspects of their free clinic experience, but they found it difficult. Horney did return to Berlin briefly to give one lecture at the new German Institute. But she never sided with Felix Boehm, the same Boehm who had signed her lecture invitation "Heil Hitler!" and returned quickly to her state of exile.[31] Back in the United States, Horney soon left Chicago for New York, and Benedek took over her position as staff and training analyst. Obviously unable to stay in Germany, Teresa Benedek had thought of moving to South Africa, then to China, but settled in Chicago to replace Horney and work with Franz Alexander, their old friend from the Poliklinik.[32] Benedek easily recognized aspects of the Chicago institute's clinic that Alexander carried over from Berlin days. "It happens that patients, due to economic reverses, are unable to continue to maintain the fee which they originally started to pay" wrote Bill Harrison to the Rockefeller Foundation's comptroller, to answer a few questions concerning gaps in their estimated income. Just as they had in Berlin, "the doctors, as well as the Institute, have a moral obligation to complete the treatment."[33]

"These were traumatic times and we talked little about them later"

1937

A NEW daycare center was Edith Jackson's answer to several problems. First, Jackson knew that Anna Freud craved a true research environment in which to test out her theories on early childhood development, and a clinical setting in which to conduct long-term observations of one and two year olds would suit this ideally. As the Nazis closed in more and more oppressively on the Freuds, and with her father still refusing to leave the homeland, Anna's need for new work was palpable. Second, Jackson was immensely grateful to Freud for her own analysis and wanted to repay him with a gesture beyond the standard fee. From the meetings of the Kinderseminar she had attended at the Ambulatorium, she knew that Freud still supported the idea of free clinics. Even with expanded facilities at 7 Berggasse, the analysts' clinic had become seriously overcrowded. And, third, with the Social Democrats out of office and Red Vienna's welfare infrastructure scrapped, the few resources still granted to poor people had now been taken away. And so, to paraphrase Alfred Adler in 1919, why not start a new clinic?

Edith Jackson decided that her no-fee day care center (*Krippe*) for very small children from Vienna's poorest families would open shortly. Anna Freud and Dorothy Burlingham tracked down a suitable working space for a community-based nursery school or pre-kindergarten. They located a Montessori kindergarten in Vienna's first district, just then short on money and looking to rent out a few of its rooms. The little school, about half of which now went to the analysts, was built on the pleasant sunny side of Rudolfsplatz. Anna threw herself into designing the research protocols and redecorating at the same time and lent her Austrian countryside look to everything from the child-sized painted chairs to little tablecloths. Edith Jackson agreed to pay for the rent and rebuilding the furniture as well as for the government licensing fees, the upkeep, and the new furniture and toys. This frenetic activity, born as much by the desire to help others as to deny impinging fascism, permitted the doors to the renovated "Jackson *Krippe*" to open several weeks later. Like the Heitzing School, Rudolfsplatz was an intimate, all-day program that joined education to pediatric and psychiatric care. And like the crowd in the first days of the Poliklinik, at least twenty young mothers living in the second district, in families described by Dorothy as "beyond the dole," brought their children to the new daycare center.

At the Krippe the toddlers were fed, bathed, freshly clothed, and entertained. They had free medical and dental exams and were generally well attended during the parents' workday.[1] Most of the children were from one to six years old, and the scope of their parents' work, from laundry maids to street beggars, was wide-ranging and underpaid. Edith Jackson asked Josephine Stross, a lively analytically trained pediatrician, to work there; she was assisted by Julia Deming (another American) and a few local volunteers who oversaw meals, naps, and playtime. The child analysts observed and treated onsite most mental health disorders they saw in the school-aged children. Meanwhile, Anna and Dorothy set up the centerpiece of the program, a threefold research agenda to collect data on the eating, sleeping, and toilet training habits of the toddlers. In the years since the Heitzing School had closed, evidence of children's vulnerability in the face of danger or abandonment during their formative years had mounted. At the same time, Anna and Dorothy were increasingly persuaded of a personal mission, to alleviate childhood suffering through psychoanalysis. Child analysis, however, required a new kind of in-depth knowledge of human growth and development. Anna and Dorothy were able to see at close hand how Stross's team was trying to guide the children, and they laid out a timeline for their own experiments as soon as Edith Jackson agreed to fund their research. First they explored their concept of children's innate self-regulation by watching how toddlers fed themselves. They set up individual "baby buffets" (figure 39) on child-sized tables and watched the children crawl around and select food without adult interference. How the children ate! Many years later the Viennese psychoanalyst Eva Laible laughed fondly about the buffet and Josephine Stross's stories. "The children had never seen many of the foods on the buffet. First they ate everything for three days. Then they turned back to bread

39 The "Baby Buffet" at the Jackson Nursery, Vienna 1937 (Photo by Willi Hoffer; Freud Museum, London)

and butter."[2] At first, of course, the toddlers all gorged on chocolate, but the children started feeding themselves a balanced diet surprisingly fast. Had the children and their families not actually benefited from this study—which they did—it might suggest charitable condescension. Instead, the project succeeded in several ways. With the municipal welfare system virtually gone in 1937, the Krippe stretched Red Vienna's vanquished model of direct assistance for one more year and, with the help of Edith Jackson and Betty Grünspan, offset the Ambulatorium's curtailed capacity to treat children.[3] In 1938, once Anna and Dorothy had moved to London under pressure, the Krippe's basic plan provided them with an effective blueprint for developing the celebrated Hamsptead War Nurseries. Though the meticulous clinical notes vanished in the Anschluss, the Rudolfsplatz project promised a humane formula for analyzing child development. By observing how toddlers of very poor families determine their personal needs for sleep and food independently, the analysts began to formulate the concepts of "child time" and resilience that pervade today's child welfare services. The Krippe stayed open until Anna Freud's very last days in Vienna and was soon reconstructed in London complete with the original baby furniture[4].

Meanwhile, in Germany the director of the German Medical Society for Psychotherapy had opened talks with Carl Jung as part of an ambitious plan to develop a form of psychotherapy blended with a mystical belief in the curative power of the fascist nation. Jung despised not only Freud himself but everything his work stood for. From the start, Jung had advised the Göring Institute in Berlin to offer two psychotherapy tracks simultaneously. One was an aryanized, or non-Jewish, non-Freudian, version of classical psychoanalysis with an added element of spirituality. The other favored traditional medical psychiatry augmented by an increasingly ruthless biological program of sterilization and euthanasia for a broadly defined group of "incurably insane." The Reich's Department of the Interior had authorized Göring to set up the institute as a practice arena for Jungian, Adlerian, and independent psychotherapists, provided he closed down the "Jewish" psychoanalytic institute. In sifting through the patient demographics maintained by the Göring administration, neither track is clear. In 1937 Boehm and Göring evaluated 259 patients for treatment, rejected 110 as unsuitable, handed 43 to private practitioners, and continued 58 at the clinic.[5] The Göring Institute and its branches now engaged 128 members including 60 doctors (10 of them female), plus 25 members with university degrees and 43 (including 39 females) without.[6] The institute was generally short of funds and relied on its teachers and administrators to work without pay. The Wichmanstrasse facilities were so expensive to maintain that even the Berlin Jungians, as Göring wrote to Carl, were reluctant to join.[7] Nevertheless, the institute also staffed subsidiary branches in Düsseldorf, Munich, Stuttgart, and Wuppertal. The Munich affiliate (near Dachau) was particularly active. Its director Leonhard Seif, who had founded the first local individual psychology group outside of Vienna in 1920 and hosted the First International Congress of Individual Psychology in 1922, coined the term *psychagogy* to describe his work preventing child and family neurosis. His efforts apparently required collaboration with the Hitler Youth and the League of German Girls. Seif's work in Munich made very clear the dissonance between Adler and Freud's ideas of community. In Freud's view, human beings are embedded in the community but do not lose their individual selves and, in fact, keep up a constant unconscious struggle between the two. In Adler's view the relationship between person and community is paramount, with community gaining the upper hand. Aside from Freud and Adler, the idea of "community" rule can, but need not, be confused with totalitarianism and is subject to swings in ideological interpretation. Red Vienna, for example, attempted to provide its citizens with centralized "cradle to grave" services, including mental health, infused with the idea of community yet all the while reinforcing individual autonomy. In contrast, the Third Reich's partiality to total "care and control" (including professional psychotherapy at the Göring Institute) of the German *Volk* was fascistic because it deliberately eliminated individual volition. The success of mental health experts associated with the Göring Institute reflected not only the collusion with state racism among large numbers of German mental health professionals. But also, and in the same manner, this racism unified psychotherapists in their own aspirations to professionalize their discipline under Nazi rule.[8] "These were traumatic times," Martin Grotjahn recalled, "and we talked little about them later."[9]

"The fate of psychoanalysis depends on the fate of the world"

1938

THE END of the free psychoanalytic clinics came on March 12, 1938, as thousands of bayoneted German Wehrmacht troops marched the conquering Nazi flag into Vienna. "The whole city," wrote Sterba, "changed overnight."[1] Schuschnigg had capitulated to Hitler, and so, the Göring Institute believed, Freud should surrender the Ambulatorium to the Nazi analysts. Matthias Göring urged Müller-Braunschweig to seize the moment. "The provisional directorship of the [Vienna] Clinic had best be taken by a therapist from outside the various analytic trends," he wrote to his colleague on March 20. "Besides, I should not like to have a one-sided clique in Vienna. Best wishes and Heil Hitler!"[2] With Hitler's acquiescence, Göring appointed Dr. Anton Sauerwald, a Nazi chemist, as interim administrator of the clinic, the publishing company, and the Vienna Psychoanalytic Society. Sauerwald and Müller-Braunschweig met with leaders of the Vienna society the same day. Jones attended the meeting as president of the IPA, along with Anna Freud, Martin Freud, Paul Federn, Eduard Hitschmann, Willi Hoffer, Ernst Kris, Robert Waelder, and Herta Steiner. The debate on the fate of the society was forcibly short and resulted in the expected decision to delegate trusteeship of the Vienna group to Göring's DPG. The Vienna institute would become a component of the DPG and, of course, all "non-Aryan" members would be expelled immediately. The few remaining analysts resigned before they could be excluded, and the only 2 left of the original 102 were Wilhelm Sölms and August Aichorn. Meanwhile, Sauerwald's team had already swept down on 7 Berggasse, destroyed the Ambulatorium's clinical records, looted all the books, and draped 19 Berggasse with a swastika. "The Ambulatorium, Bibliothek . . . the Verlag and everything else ha[s] been confiscated," Jones wrote to Edith Jackson at the end of March.[3] The Nazis had moved into Vienna swiftly. Whatever resistance the vanquished Social Democrats had planned folded fast, and the Wehrmacht laid waste to much of the city not only unimpeded but with ample enthusiasm from anti-Semitic Viennese citizens in a jubilant frame of mind. An early April plebiscite affirmed their wishes.

Because Müller-Braunschweig believed the recent annexation of Austria would entitle him to superintend all of Freud's psychoanalytic activity, a post even more prestigious than Göring's in Berlin, he wasted little time in starting to aryanise the Ambulatorium. "As trustee of the Vienna Psychoanalytical Association and Clinic," he wrote to the new district leader Josef Bürckel, Hitler's representative for the plebiscite in Austria, "I urge the authorization, as rapidly as possible, of reform[s]. Delay would harm not only the patients of the Polyclinic, but also financing of the institutions which is based essentially on the fees of the patients of the Polyclinic and on income from lectures and training. Heil Hitler."[4] As acting head of the Nazi party in Vienna (and Heinrich Himmler's future chief of staff), Bürckel had been assigned the task of integrating Austria politically, economically, and culturally into the German Reich. Tall and blonde, with smooth skin and soft, slightly droopy eyes, Bürckel was, by Nazi standards, the purist kind of Aryan man. Josef Bürckel understood that Nazi "reform" meant expelling all Jews and replacing Freudian psychoanalysis with an alternative, civic-minded psychotherapy. Unfortunately for him and Müller-Braunschweig, most Jewish analysts were already gone and the few Gentiles who remained, like Richard Sterba, were on their way. The Nazi's effort to aryanize the Ambulatorium was already seen as precarious because, unlike Berlin, the psychoanalysts had already decided to fold and to relocate wherever Freud moved. As for the publishing company, Müller-Braunschweig figured on issuing a new journal "on a purely Aryan basis, and in the spirit of the cultural and political guidelines in force . . . a German journal for psychoanalysis, firmly grounded in the soil of the Third Reich."[5] This effort failed as well. Within a month Müller-Braunschweig admitted defeat and turned over his brief trusteeship of the Vienna society to the general medical directorship (*Landesärzteführer*) for Germany-Austria. He did not withdraw from his post, however, without asking the new government to repay his expenses "after the release of liquid assets, at present blocked, of the former Vienna Psychoanalytical Association and the Vienna Psychoanalytical Clinic. Heil Hitler."[6]

In the weeks before the Freuds finally fled to England in June 1938, Muriel Gardiner and Edith Jackson were still carrying out psychoanalysts' commitment for a better world as perhaps only these American women could. Using the code name "Mary," Muriel Gardiner funded resistance groups and helped manufacture and distribute passports to escaping colleagues. Meanwhile, Edith Jackson, according to the psychoanalyst Edith Buxbaum, "drove people who were in danger, into Czechoslovakia by breaking through the border barriers with her car."[7] Jackson spent the better part of her final year in Vienna helping her social democratic friends fend off the Nazis with the use of her car or with money. The experimental Krippe on Rudolfsplatz that she had financed was either "kept up until the 1rst of April,"[8] as Dorothy Burlingham said, or was "closed with the seal of the American Embassy on it," per Ernest Jones.[9] Evidently the project itself held on after she left Vienna, and the psychoanalytic community generally wanted to see it last longer. "When I realize that the F[reud]'s are still in Vienna," came Dorothy's curious mix of despair and artifice, "I feel quite sick and find it premature to talk of plans."[10] In contrast, Jones's more objective letters urged her to start preparing immediately for the Freud's life in London. He charged Edith (now back in Boston) to keep Anna's plans for settling in England secret and, at the same time, pressed her to transfer money and continue supporting the cause. "Naturally [Anna] wishes to build up something of her former activities," he wrote from London, coincidentally the same day Müller-Braunschweig petitioned for the aryanization of the Ambulatorium. "Her heart is specially set on the Day Nursery which you showed so much foresight in endowing."[11] Edith did remind him of her five-thousand-dollar donation to the Krippe in 1936 and 1937 but, at Jones's insistence, decided to commit about the same amount again this year. She then forecast that Anna and Dorothy would set up an early childhood research center in England and resolved to support it, "provided the original plans and intentions can be carried on under its present direction."[12] Six weeks later Anna Freud was still in Vienna. Her letter of May 18, penned a few days before she was detained by the Gestapo, was almost comic in its defensiveness. "Your gift of the nursery," she wrote to Edith, "has made the last Vienna year for me the best that I have ever had here."[13]

Muriel Gardiner's emphasis on underground work, as distinct from Jackson's more visible projects like the Krippe, was not surprising. Since 1934 Gardiner had immersed herself in the anti-Nazi efforts of the socialists and, using the code name "Mary," had taken secret actions against the Dolfuss regime. By 1938 she had formed a fruitful connection with Red Vienna's great

Social Democrats of the 1920s, Otto Bauer, now exiled in Brno, and Viktor Adler in Paris. After March 11, and for the next ten months, Muriel's increasingly urgent assignments took her to the same Herzstation where, incidentally, so many activist analysts had carried out the social obligations of psychoanalysis. Now that the analysts had moved to 7 Berggasse, the Herzstation physicians had resumed their daily rounds of X rays, medical examinations, and trauma care. The lines of patients waiting for help were long, and Muriel found that she could blend into the banal space quite easily by reading a book or just looking around. In fact she was locating her contacts. The next step— the task of determining who should get the passports and how to transport them—belonged to her clandestine friends. Gardiner said that she felt "suddenly moved, as by some great work of art" one rainy day and took twelve new "legal" Czech passports in hand to the Herzstation—the same Herzstation that housed the Ambulatorium. She "was able to distribute these passports safely either directly or through intermediaries" to the imperiled psychoanalysts and socialist colleagues like the Austro-Marxist leader of Red Vienna, Otto Bauer, and his family.[14] Muriel was to shelter Bauer again after he escaped to the United States. Following her marriage to Joseph Buttinger, former head of the Austrian Social Democratic Party, Bauer lived with them as librarian in residence.

For the first time since 1902, when Freud had convened a few friends for Wednesday evening discussions, the entire apparatus of progressive psychoanalytic activity in Vienna had been eliminated. From Prague to Berlin and beyond, increasingly apprehensive psychoanalysts were preparing to leave Europe. At the moment, even Fenichel abandoned his criticism of the finer points of psychoanalysis. Faced with barbarism and "raw stupidity," he urged psychoanalysts not to isolate themselves but to continue fighting for the cause, even in new and foreign countries. "Where there is still truth," he wrote in the *Rundbriefe*, "it will be preserved, even if it must flee far. . . . The fate of psychoanalysis depends on the fate of the world."[15]

Meanwhile, in Berlin, Matthias Göring was celebrating the two-year anniversary of the German Institute for Psychological Research and Psychotherapy on Wichmanstrasse. Much as the 1922 Freudians had impressed their colleagues at the Seventh International Psychoanalytic Congress in Berlin, so Göring and Boehm now used the former Poliklinik as a showcase for their Nazi friends invited to the 1938 conference of the Allgemeine Ärztliche Gesellschaft für Psychotherapie. The obeisance to Hitler was astounding. The Göring group, even though it was proud of its offerings in treatment and training, regarded Hitler as the omnipotent judge to whom they owed not only their institute's existence but also its very meaning. To the *Reichsärztefürhrer* and the minister of the interior they telegrammed assurances of "our complete commitment to the cause of National Socialism." Their work, they said, "rests on the foundations given to us by our National Socialist State, our Führer. We have him[16] to thank that science and our work can develop undisturbed." Boehm sent another telegram directly to Hitler:

I offer you, my Führer, a vow of eternal fidelity. [Our] Institute's supreme task is to work for the mental and physical health of our people in the spirit of National Socialism.[17]

To which Hitler replied:

I thank the German Medical Society for Psychotherapy for their vow of eternal fidelity, and for the announcement of the establishment of a German Institute for Psychological Research and Psychotherapy. I wish you great success in your work.[18]

Now that the new regime had secured the Poliklinik' s psychoanalytic library for themselves (along with Ernst Freud's bookcases and his other furniture), they could restock the shelves with titles more to their liking. Freud's publications were locked up in a "poison cupboard" and replaced with hand-picked authors including, as Göring exclaimed, "to our joy also C. G. Jung."[19] The books ranged from dream symbolism and racial heredity to abnormality and child psychology. Göring had a vested interest in portraying his institute as a mental health center for children and families as well as individual adults. To be part of the national effort to secure genetic purity for future Aryan generations, the institute called up its most valuable assets: abundant access to high government officials, an authorized Jungian practice ideology, and a group of psychotherapists who believed in curing psychological impediments to human procreation. Psychoanalytic terminology was replaced with desexualized, pre-Freudian words: *Oedipus* was changed to *family,* and the term *psychoanalysis* itself became *developmental psychology.*[20] With the augmentation of the Nuremberg Race Laws, patients who were identified as homosexual, non-Aryan, or diagnosed with impotence came under particular scrutiny. At the same time, racially desirable women (for whom abortion was banned) were provided with psychological support for bearing children and fertile Aryan men were compensated and treated for psychogenic illness. Göring insisted that the new psychotherapy could transform Germany into a wealthy nation of happy, successful workers by eliminating the mentally impaired and adjusting distressed people with "bad habits." The *Neue Deutsche Seelenheilkunde* would replace insight-oriented treatment with a psychology of pragmatic resilience and civic fitness. On a larger scale the Nazis used the Poliklinik itself to rid Germany of social influences they considered degenerate, modern, Jewish, democratic, and communist.

By the time the Freuds had settled in London in the summer of 1938, safe from their enemies in Germany and Austria (figure 40), their old activist friend Ernst Simmel had relocated to Los Angeles. He made Fenichel's move to join him there possible as well, and together they decided to build a psychoanalytic sanatorium like Schloss Tegel and to name this one after Simmel's mentor. "Your Sanatorium is not yet completed," Freud wrote to Simmel on January 9, 1939, along with New Year's greetings. "If at the time of its opening I am no longer alive you can do as you please anyway. If contrary to expectations I am still here, a cable from you will make a quick decision possible."[21]

Freud always believed that psychoanalysis would release the reasoning abilities in oppressed individuals and that personal insight (combined with critical thinking) naturally led to psychological independence. In *Civilization*

40 Anna Freud and Melanie Klein side by side, with Ernest Jones and Marie Bonaparte, Paris 1938 (Photo by Eduard Bibring; Archives of the Boston Psychoanalytic Society and Institute)

and Its Discontents, arguably his most overt discussion of political thought, Freud outlines the way in which the human quest for instinctual satisfaction is constantly frustrated by—and yet requires—the external constraints of culture. Far from proving that Freud's view of human nature was negative or pessimistic, the little volume, written a few years before Hitler's ascent to power, asserts precisely that human survival does not lie solely in individual strength or free will. "The replacement of the power of the individual by the power of a community constitutes the decisive step of civilization."[22] Suggesting that social life should be regulated only if it benefits the *collective*, Freud states that the "first requisite of civilization is that of justice—that is, the assurance that a law will not be broken in favor of an individual." He has prefaced this with a contention about human nature, that "human life in common is only made possible when a majority comes together which is stronger than any separate individual and which remains united against all separate individuals." The autonomous ego exists, but it is mutable and driven to reach out to others in order to survive. In his wide-ranging speculations on the relationship between individuals and culture, he affirms interdependency, attachment, and collectivity as the appropriate—and most effective—vehicles for human emancipation. As Freud had said in 1918, "the poor man should have just as much right to assistance for his mind as he now has to the life-saving help offered by surgery . . . and can be left as little as the latter to the impotent care of individual members of the community." Until 1938, at least, the community had cared.

NOTES

The Conscience of Society—Introduction

1. Sigmund Freud, "Lines of Advance in Psychoanalytic Psychotherapy" (1918), in *The Standard Edition* 17:167.
2. Ibid.
3. Sigmund Freud, "Postcript to an Autobiographical Study" (1935), in *The Standard Edition* 20:73.
4. Deutsch, *Confrontations*, 84.
5. See Hale, *Freud and the Americans*.
6. Reich, "The Living Productive Power," 75.
7. See Sigmund Freud, "Further Recommendations on the Technique of Psychoanalysis: On Beginning the Treatment, the Question of the First Communications, the Dynamics of the Cure" (1913), in *The Standard Edition* 12:123–156.
8. Freud, "Lines of Advance."
9. French and Smith, *The Commonwealth Fund*, 121.
10. See Gruber, *Red Vienna*.
11. Else Pappenheim, "Politics and Psychoanalysis in Vienna Before 1938," paper presented to the 1984 Oral History Workshop of the American Psychoanalytic Association.
12. For in-depth research arguing the top-heavy application of "high culture" privileges to the lower classes, see Gruber, *Red Vienna*.
13. Bluma Swerdloff, interview with Sándor Radó (1965), in "History of the Psychoanalytic Movement," Oral History Collection, Columbia University Libraries, New York.
14. Norman W. Lyon, letter, August 5, 1929, to "Secretary, Psycho-analytic Institute, Berlin, Germany," Archives of the Berlin Poliklinik, Koblenz, Germany.

15. For the progressive civic spirit of the Berlin society, see Ludwig M. Hermanns, "Karl Abraham und die anfänge der Berliner Psychoanalytischen Vereinigung," pp. 30–40, and Rotraut De Clerck, "Der Traum von einer bess'ren Welt": Psychoanalyse und kulture in der mitte der zwanziger jahre," 41–70, both in *Luzifer*.

1918

1. Eitingon, "Report on the Berlin Psycho-Analytical Institute, May 1924–August 1925."
2. Even in that discussion of setting the fee Freud mentions that "for ten years or so I set aside one hour a day, and sometimes two, for gratuitous treatments."
3. Freud, "Further Recommendations" 12:131.
4. Freud, letter no. 1079, September 19, 1926, to Ferenczi, in Falzeder and Brabant, *Correspondence* 3:278.
5. McGrath, *Freud's Discovery of Psychoanalysis*. See Gay, *Freud*, 14–21.
6. Sigmund Freud, "An Autobiographical Study," in *The Standard Edition* 20:8.
7. Ibid., 9.
8. Anna Freud Bernays, "My Brother, Sigmund Freud" (1940), in Hendrik M. Ruitenbeek, ed., *Freud as We Knew Him* (Detroit: Wayne State University Press, 1973).
9. Goldmann. *Living My Life*, 173.
10. Ferenczi, letter no. 124, March 22, 1910, to Freud, in Brabant, Falzeder, and Giampieri-Deutsch, *Correspondence* 1:153.
11. *Internationale Zeitschrift für Ärztliche Psychoanalyse* 5(1919): 228.
12. Freud, letter no. 542, April 8, 1915, to Ferenczi, in Falzeder and Brabant, *Correspondence* 2:55.
13. Freud, letter no. 646, January 28, 1917, to Ferenczi, in Falzeder and Brabant, *Correspondence* 2:179.
14. Freud, letter no. 762, October 11, 1918, to Ferenczi, ibid. 2:299.
15. Similarly, Freud later scolded Wilhelm Reich for *reading* a paper to the society in 1921. Reich never did again, and Ilse Reich recalled the vivid image of Freud comparing a lecturer reading a paper to a train engineer driving his locomotive at great speed while the passengers run beside it, trying to latch on. Freud likened a read document to a resolute position paper, a fiat and not a discussion. Jones may have misunderstood the disturbance caused by this choice in Budapest or simply tried to ignore the paper's political implications.
16. Jones, *Life and Work* 1:198.
17. Freud, "Lines of Advance," 166.
18. Ibid., 167.
19. Here referring to terms coined by C. Wright Mills in *The Sociological Imagination*.
20. Freud, "Lines of Advance," 166.
21. Ibid.
22. Freud, "Further Recommendations," 139.
23. Freud, "Lines of Advance," 166.
24. Ibid., 167.

25. Bluma Swerdloff, interview with Sándor Radó (1965), in "History of the Psycho-analytic Movement," Oral History Collection, Columbia University Libraries, New York.

26. Melanie Klein in Grosskurth, *Melanie Klein*, 71.

27. Freud to Abraham, August 27, 1918, in Ernst Falzeder, *The Complete Correspondence of Sigmund Freud and Karl Abraham, 1907–1925* (London and New York: Karnac, 2002), 381.

28. With a contribution by Ernest Jones, *Zur Psychoanalyse der Kriegs-Neurosen*, (Leipzig, 1919); Simmel, Ferenczi, Abraham, and Jones, *Psychoanalysis and the War Neuroses*.

29. Sigmund Freud, "Dr. Anton von Freund: Obituary" (1920), in *The Standard Edition* 18:267–268.

30. Sigmund Freud, "Memorandum on the Electrical Treatment of War Neurotics" (1920), in *The Standard Edition* 17:215.

31. Jones, letter to van Emden, November 14, 1920, document no. CVA/F03/02, Archives of the British Psychoanalytical Society.

32. Karl Abraham, in *Zur Psychoanalyse der Kriegs-Neurosen*, cited in Brunner, "Psychiatry, Psychoanalysis, and Politics," 357.

33. Forms of electric shock therapy used by Julius Wagner-Jauregg on psychiatric patients and opposed by Sigmund Freud and the Social Democrats (see 1920).

34. Ernst Simmel, in *Zur Psychoanalyse der Kriegs-Neurosen*. Kaufmann, "Science as Cultural Practice," 140.

35. Ernst Simmel, *Psycho-Analysis and the War Neuroses*, intro. Sigmund Freud (London: International Psycho-Analytical, 1921). Originally published as *Kriegs-Neurosen und Psychisches Trauma;* see note 18, introduction.

36. Freud, "Memorandum on the Electrical Treatment of War Neurotics," 215.

37. Ferenczi to Freud, letter no. 556, July 24, 1915, in Falzeder and Brabant, *Correspondence* 2:71.

38. Ferenczi to Freud, letter no. 767, October 8, 1918, ibid. 2:298.

39. Sigmund Freud, "Introduction to 'Psychoanalysis and War Neuroses'" (1919), in *The Standard Edition* 17:209.

40. Simmel, "War Neuroses and 'Psychic Trauma,'" in Kaes, Jay, and Dimendberg, *The Weimar Republic Sourcebook*, 7.

41. Abraham to Freud, October 27, 1918, in Falzeder, *Complete Correspondence of Freud and Abraham*, 383.

42. Freud to Jones, letters no. 222 and 306, November 10, 1918, in Paskauskas, *Complete Correspondence of Freud and Jones*, 325.

43. Freud to Ferenczi, letter no. 772, November 17, 1918, in Falzeder and Brabant, *Correspondence* 2:311.

44. See McGrath, *Dionysian Art*.

45. Ibid.

46. See Boyer, *Culture and Political Crisis in Vienna*.

47. Michael Molnar, ed. and trans., *The Diary of Sigmund Freud, 1929–1939: A Record of the Final Decade* (New York: Scribner's, 1992), 202.

48. Freud, "An Autobiographical Study," 7.

49. Freud to Julie Braun-Vogelstein, 1927, in Martin Grotjahn, "A Letter by Sigmund Freud with Recollections of His Adolescence," *Journal of the American Psychoanalytic Association* 4 (1956): 644–652.

50. Freud to Silberstein, March 7, 1875, in Boehlich, *Complete Letters of Freud to Silberstein,* 97.

51. Pappenheim, interview with the author, November 22, 1995.

52. French and Smith, *The Commonwealth Fund,* 109.

53. Ibid., 103.

54. Sterba, *Reminiscences of a Viennese Psychoanalyst,* 21–22.

55. Jahoda, "Emergence of Social Psychology," 343.

56. An ardent socialist revolutionary and cofounder of the Spartacus League, Luxemburg was arrested with Karl Liebknecht and shot by the Freikorps troops in Berlin the next year.

57. Reich, *Passion of Youth,* 74.

58. Ibid., 136.

59. Bettelheim, "Last Thoughts on Therapy," 65.

60. Gustav Landauer, a colleague of Martin Buber, Thomas Mann, and Walter Benjamin, was influenced by the anarchist Max Stirner's 1844 book "The Ego and Its Own." Landauer had served as education minister of the short-lived Bavarian Workers' Republic and was assassinated in 1919 by the reactionary Freikorps. His most popular book, the 1911 *Aufruf zum Sozialismus* (Call to Socialism) combined anarchist and spiritual theories with Stirner's more individualistic form of social democracy. Wilhelm Reich's later theories draw heavily on both Stirner and Landauer.

61. Bettelheim, *Freud's Vienna,* 25.

62. Rudolf Ekstein, "Foreword" (1991), in Gardner and Stevens, *Red Vienna.*

63. Freud to Eitingon, October 25, 1918, in Gay, *Freud.*

1919

1. Kramer, "First Child Guidance Center," 34.

2. See Pollak, "Psychanalyse et Austromarxisme," 83.

3. Sterba, *Reminiscences,* 81.

4. Federn et al., "Thirty-Five Years with Freud," 38.

5. Report on "Reconstruction Work in Europe," 1919, from conferences held at the Red Cross, Washington DC, October 29–31, box 25, folder 223, Barry C. Smith series 2, subseries 4, Commonwealth Fund Collection, Rockefeller Foundation Archives.

6. Walter Gropius, "First Proclamation of the Weimar Bauhaus" (1919), in Bayer, Gropius, and Gropius, *Bauhaus,* 16.

7. CV of Dr. Felix Tietze, box 24, folder 206, R. G. Barry Smith series 2, subseries 4, Commonwealth Fund Collection, Rockefeller Foundation Archives.

8. Gruber, *Red Vienna.* 66.

9. Sanford Gifford, transcribed interview with Clare Fenichel, May 1, 1984, Archives of the Boston Psychoanalytic Society, 10–11.

10. A highly influential educational reformer of the Wandervogel movement, Wyneken founded a *freie schulgemeinde* (free school community) in the Taunus mountains. Josephine Dellisch, a friend of Anna Freud and Alix Strachey and a patient at the Berlin Poliklinik, taught in a Wyneken school in the mid-1920s. Walter Benjamin, later a star of the Frankfurt School, which integrated psychoanalysis into Marxism, was a pupil of Wyneken's.

11. Gifford, interview with Fenichel, 21.

12. Deutsch, *Confrontations,* 161.

13. Young-Bruehl, *Anna Freud,* 100.

14. Anna Freud, "A Short History of Child Analysis," *Psychoanalytic Study of the Child* 21(1966): 7–14.

15. See "Siegfried Bernfeld," in Roudinesco and Plon, *Dictionaire de la Psychanalyse,* 109.

16. Sanford Gifford, "Grete Bibring, 1899–1977," obituary in the *Harvard Medical Alumni Bulletin,* December 1977.

17. See Roudinesco and Plon, "Siegfried Bernfeld."

18. Franz Alexander, "Recollections of Berggasse 19," *Psychoanalytic Quarterly* 9 (1940): 196.

19. Deutsch, *Confrontations,* 148.

20. Levine, "Interview with Erik H. Erikson," 5.

21. Sterba, *Reminiscences,* 81.

22. Freud's 1908 Christmas card to Karl Abraham depicted a scene at the Café Riedl and "awakened many memories" of his early visits to Vienna. Karl Abraham to Sigmund Freud, January 13, 1909, in Falzeder, *Complete Correspondence of Freud and Abraham,* p. 75.

23. See Reich, *Zeitschrift für Sexualwissenchaft,* vol. 10, no. 23, and *Early Writing.*

24. Reich, *Passion,* p. 80.

25. Helene Deutsch, "Freud, and His Pupils: A Footnote to the History of the Psychoanalytic Movement, 1940,"in H. M. Ruitenbeek, ed., *Freud as We Knew Him* (Detroit: Wayne State University Press, 1973).

26. Karen Horney. "The Establishment of a Training Program: On Its Organization," in Eitingon et al., *Zehn Jahre.*

27. Freud, "Lines of Advance," 167.

28. Abraham to Freud, August 21, 1908, in Falzeder, *Complete Correspondence of Freud and Abraham,* 56.

29. Brecht et al., *Here Life Goes On,* 80.

30. Freud to Abraham, January 2, 1912, in Falzeder, *Complete Correspondence of Freud and Abraham,* 145.

31. Abraham to Freud, October 19 and November 23, 1919, ibid., 405, 407.

32. Korrespondenzblatt, *Internationale Zeitschrift für Psychoanalyse* 6(1920): 100.

33. In Berlin, as in Vienna and all European hubs of psychoanalysis, the analysts set up first the free outpatient clinic and then the training institute. Karl Abraham to Sigmund Freud, August 3, 1919, in Falzeder, *Complete Correspondence of Freud and Abraham.* 402..

34. Abraham to Freud, December 7, 1919, ibid., 410.

35. This was the influential Secret Committee, proposed by Ernest Jones in 1912 and composed of Freud's six leading supporters (Karl Abraham, Hanns Sachs, Otto Rank, Sándor Ferenczi, and Anton von Freund, now replaced by Eitingon) who vowed to preserve psychoanalytic doctrine and promote IPA policy. Freud gave each man an elegant gold ring. Sigmund Freud to Karl Abraham, October 3, 1919, ibid., 404.

1920

1. Freud, letter no. 837, to Ferenczi, March 15, 1920, in Falzeder, Brabant, and Giampieri-Deutsch, *Correspondence* 3:12.

2. Jones to van Emden, November 14, 1920, document no. CVA/F03/02, Archives of the British Psychoanalytical Society.

3. Abraham to Freud, March 13, 1920, in Falzeder, *Complete Correspondence of Freud and Abraham,* 418.

4. See Worbs, "Ernst Ludwig Freud in Berlin."

5. Benton, *A Different World,* 156.

6. Ibid.

7. Abraham to Freud, March 13, 1920, in Falzeder, *Complete Correspondence of Freud and Abraham,* 418.

8. Brecht et al., *Here Life Goes On,* 32.

9. Ernst Simmel, "On the History and Social Significance of the Berlin Psychoanalytic Institute," in Eitingon et al., *Zehn Jahre.*

10. Gay, *Weimar Culture,* 35.

11. Abraham to Freud, December 29, 1919, in Falzeder, *Complete Correspondence of Freud and Abraham,* 413.

12. Abraham to Freud, May 1, 1920, ibid., 421.

13. Abraham to Freud, March 13, 1920, ibid., 418.

14. Deutsch, *Confrontations,* 136.

15. Ibid.

16. Eitingon, "Report on the Berlin Psycho-Analytical Institute, May 1924–August 1925."

17. Writers like Brody, "Freud's Case-load," have tried to show that psychoanalytic theory and practice were predicated exclusively on the basis of a sample of affluent, nonworking female patients. In contrast, data from the clinic show that that gender distribution was equal for both consultation and treatment over ten years. As for social class (defined by occupation), the all-female category of "married with no occupation" denoted a mere *7 percent* of the entire service population over two years, 1923–1925. The largest category of patients (± 40 percent) was "professionals," followed closely by artisans and clerks.

18. Bluma Swerdloff, interview with Sándor Radó (1965), in "History of the Psychoanalytic Movement," Oral History Collection, Columbia University Libraries, New York, 84.

19. Abraham to Freud , June 6, 1920, Abraham and Freud, *A Psycho-Analytic Dialogue,* 314.

20. Abraham, *Rundbrief* no. 11, December 12, 1920, series 1, subseries 2, Otto Rank Papers, Columbia University Libraries.

21. Freud to Abraham, November 28, 1920, in Falzeder, *Complete Correspondence of Freud and Abraham,* 434.

22. Edith Jacobson, "Fenichel-Simmel Memorial Lecture, 1966," in Mühlleitner and Reichmayr, "Otto Fenichel," 162.

23. Fenichel, "Psychoanalysis as the Nucleus," 307.

24. Simmel, "On the history of the Berlin Psychoanalytic Institute."

25. Eitingon, "Report of the Berlin Psycho-Analytical Policlinic, March 1920–June 1922."

26. Oberndorf, "The Berlin Psychoanalytic Policlinic."

27. Benedek, "A Psychoanalytic Career Begins," 4–5.

28. Freud to Jones, letter no.275, May 13, 1920, in Paskauskas, *Complete Correspondence of Freud and Jones,* 379.

29. Jones to van Emden, November 14, 1920.

30. Jones to Eitingon and Freud (or Rank?), *Rundbrief* L6 (1920), Archives of the British Psychoanalytical Society.

31. Jones to Eitingon, September 27, 1928, document no. CEC/F01/28, Archives of the British Psychoanalytical Society.

32. Minutes of the British Psycho-Analytical Society, meeting of May 27, 1920, document no. FAA/01, Archives of the British Psychoanalytical Society.

33. Paul Federn, "Sixtieth Birthday of Eduard Hitschmann: July 28, 1931," *International Journal of Psychoanalysis* 13(1932): 263–264.

34. Else Pappenheim, interview with author, November 22, 1995.

35. Young-Bruehl, *Anna Freud,* 157.

36. Freud to Ferenczi, letter no. 855, October 31, 1920, Falzeder, Brabant, with Giampieri-Deutsch, *Correspondence* 3:37.

37. Freud to Abraham, July 4, 1920, in Falzeder, *Complete Correspondence of Freud and Abraham,* 430.

38. Sanford Gifford, "Interview with Grete Bibring," May 11, 1973, 15, Archives of the Boston Psychoanalytic Society.

39. Even around the psychoanalyst's dinner table, Ernest Jones said, the saying went that "poor immigrants from Galicia arrive in Palestine with no clothes but with Marx' *Das Kapital* in hand and *Traumdeutung* under the arm." Dr. Heimann's witticism might not have been just a casual joke. Jones to Budapest and Berlin, *Rundbrief* no. 10, December 7, 1920, Archives of the British Psychoanalytical Society.

40. Gifford, "Interview with Grete Bibring."

41. For a comprehensive overview of both the positive and negative reception to Freud's ideas in the U.S., see Hale, *Freud and the Americans.*

42. Putnam to Freud, letter no.10, November 17, 1909, in Hale, *James Jackson Putnam and Psychoanalysis,* 86.

43. Max Eastman, "Differing with Freud," in Eastman, *Great Companions,* 178.

44. Freud to Ferenczi, letter no. 841, April 22, 1920, in Falzeder, Brabant, and Giampieri-Deutsch, *Correspondence* 3:17.

45. Eversole to Pearce, "Conditions In Austria." July 9, 1924.p. 3, Sub-series A, Series 705, RG 1.1, Rockefeller Foundation Archives.

46. Pearce to Gregg, "Alan Gregg Diary Jan. 28–Feb 2, 1926," subseries A, series 705, RG 1.1, Rockefeller Foundation Archives.

47. Jones, *Sigmund Freud* 3:5.

48. See Kaufmann, "Science as Cultural Practice," 141.

49. See "Nevrose de Guerre," in Roudinesco and Plon, *Dictionaire,* 731–732.

50. Freud, letter no. 853, October 11, 1920, in Falzeder, Brabant, and Giampieri-Deutsch, *Correspondence* 3: 35.

51. Mühlleitner, *Biographisches Lexikon der Psychoanalyse,* 161.

52. Jones, *Sigmund Freud* 3:157.

53. Holzknecht to Hitschmann, June 16, 1920, *Archiv des Psychoanalytischen Ambulatoriums Wien,* Archives of the Freud Museum, London.

54. Eduard Hitschmann, in Fallend, *Sonderlinge,* 114.

55. Holzknecht to Hitschmann, June 23,1920, in Fallend, *Sonderlinge,* 114.

56. Julius Tandler, *Krieg und Bevölkerung* (Berlin, 1917), p. 555, cited in Reinhard Sieder, "Housing Policy, Social Welfare and Family Life in 'Red Vienna,' 1919–1934," *Oral History: Journal of the Oral History Society* 13/2(1985): 41.

57. Ibid., 43.

58. French and Smith, *The Commonwealth Fund,* 21.

59. Ibid., 24–25.

60. Seidler, "School Guidance Clinics in Vienna," 75.

61. Reich, *Passion.*110.

62. Among his tumultuous relationships with women, this one was to haunt Reich. Freud reprimanded him personally but also absolved him. The event "happened four years ago," as Freud wrote to Ferenczi, well before Reich's installation into the Vienna Society. See letter no. 922, March 19, 1923, in Falzeder and Brabant, *Correspondence* 3:97.

63. Deutsch, *Confrontations,* 110.

64. See Reich, *Early Writings.*

65. Reich, *Passion,* 129.

66. Freud and Rank, *Rundbrief,* no. CFC/FO5/15, Archives of the British Psychoanalytical Society.

1921

1. Freud to Jones, letters nos. 304 and 306, March 18 and April 12, 1921, in Paskauskas, *Freud and Jones,* 416, 419.

2. Michael Molnar, ed. and trans., *The Diary of Sigmund Freud, 1929–1939: A Record of the Final Decade* (New York: Scribner's, 1992), 96.

3. Julius Wagner-Jauregg, in Fallend, *Sonderlinge,* 114.

4. Else Pappenheim, interview with author, November 22, 1995.

5. H. Orgler, *Alfred Adler: The Man and His Work* (New York: Liveright, 1963).

6. Italics in original, Reich, *Passion*,147.

7. Ibid, 161.

8. Eitingon to his colleagues, November 3, 1921, folder 168, series 1, subseries 2, Otto Rank Papers, Columbia University.

9. These monetary conversions use Clarence Oberndorf's 1926 equivalency of seventy-five marks to eighteen dollars (U.S.) and depict the widespread inflation and weakening currency that plagued the Poliklinik—and the Weimar Republic.

10. Alix to James Strachey, Tuesday afternoon [December 16, 1924], in Meisel and Kendrick, *Bloomsbury/Freud*, 147.

11. Franz Alexander, "Psychoanalytic Training in the Past, the Present, and the Future: A Historical View," address to the Association of Candidates of the Chicago Institute for Psychoanalysis, October 26, 1951, archives of the Chicago Institute for Psychoanalysis.

12. Observation made by Grosskurth, in *Melanie Klein*.

13. Melanie Klein's case material, "Heinrich 1921," box 6, file B-5, series PP/KLE, Contemporary Medical Archives Center, Wellcome Institute for the History of Medicine.

14. See Eric J. Engstrom, "Social Prophylaxis: Psychiatric Policlinics," in "The Birth of Clinical Psychiatry: Power, Knowledge, and Professionalization in Germany, 1867–1914," PhD diss., University of North Carolina at Chapel Hill, 1997.

15. Pearl King, interview with the author, July 5, 2000.

16. Minutes of the British Psycho-Analytical Society, October 19, 1921, Archives of the British Psychoanalytical Society.

17. Lewis, "Red Vienna," 343.

18. Robert Danneberg, *Kampf Gegen,* cited in Collotti, "Socialdemocrazia e Amministrazione Municipale," 454.

19. Guerrand, "Vienne-La-Rouge," 84.

20. Adolf Loos, "Die Modern Siedlung," in Blau, *The Architecture of Red Vienna*, 101.

1922

1. The Herzstation of the General Hospital reappears periodically in the history of psychoanalysis. In March of 1938, for example, Muriel Gardiner arranged to meet Otto Bauer, now exiled in Brno, at this clinic to retrieve the life-saving passports that would allow Jews and Socialists to escape post-Anschluss Austria..

2. Schick to the International Health Board of the Rockefeller Foundation. April 25, 1922, subseries A, series 705, RG 1.1, Rockefeller Foundation Archives.

3. Gruber, *Red Vienna*, 106–107.

4. Faye Sawyier, interview with Helen Ross, Portraits in Psychoanalysis videotape series, Gitelson Film Library, Chicago Institute for Psychoanalysis.

5. Hitschmann, "A Ten Years' Report," 246.

6. Ferenczi and Radó to Freud, May 24, 1922, Archiv des Psychoanalytischen Ambulatoriums Wien, Archives of the Freud Museum, London.

7. Eitingon to Freud, May 30, 1922, ibid.

8. Sigmund Freud, "Preface to Max Eitingon's 'Report on the Berlin Psycho-Analytic Policlinic'" (1922), in *The Standard Edition* 19:285.

9. Possibly the American William B. Parker, editor of *Psychotherapy: A Course of Reading in Sound Psychology, Sound Medicine, and Sound Religion* (New York: Centre, 1909); personal communication, November 15, 2000, from Michael Molnar.

10. Franz Alexander, "Recollections of Berggasse 19," *Psychoanalytic Quarterly* 9(1940): 195.

11. "A Psychoanalytic Ambulatorium in Vienna," *Ärztliche Reform-Zeitung* 9/10(May 1922): 49, Archiv des Psychoanalytischen Ambulatoriums Wien, Archives of the Freud Museum, London.

12. See Freud, "Further Recommendations" 12:139.

13. Else Pappenheim, "Remarks on Training at the Vienna Psychoanalytic Institute" (transcribed and expanded), Oral History Workshop of the American Psychoanalytic Association Meeting, December 1981.

14. See Hitschmann, *A Ten Years' Report.*

15. Hitschmann, in Lobner, "Discussions on Therapeutic Technique," 30.

16. Pappenheim, "Remarks on Training."

17. Anna Freud, "The Ideal Psychoanalytic Institute," in Freud, *The Writings of Anna Freud* 7:80.

18. Gifford, "Interview with Grete Bibring," 1–2.

19. R. Grayson, unpublished interview with Dr. Marianne Kris (1972), A. A. Brill Archives and Special Collections of the New York Psychoanalytic Society.

20. Sterba. *Reminiscences,* 41.

21. Gifford, "Interview with Grete Bibring," 5.

22. Ibid., 4.

23. Freud to Kata Levy, cited in Gay, *Freud,* 388.

24. Gröger et al., *On the History of Psychiatry in Vienna,* 49.

25. Fallend, *Sonderlinge,* 115.

26. Federn, "Sixtieth Birthday of Eduard Hitschmann, 263–264.

27. Kardiner, *My Analysis with Freud,* 83.

28. Freud to Abraham, September 22, 1914, in Falzeder, *Complete Correspondence of Freud and Abraham,* 279.

29. Menaker, *Appointment in Vienna.*

30. French and Smith, *The Commonwealth Fund,* 27.

31. Else Pappenheim, interview with author, November 22, 1995.

32. Beth Noveck. "Hugo Bettauer and the Political Culture of the First Republic." *Contemporary Austrian Studies* 3(1995):143.

33. Paul Tillich, cited in Gay, *Weimar Culture,* 36.

34. Jones, *Sigmund Freud* 3:88.

35. "Report of the General Meeting of the Vienna Psycho-Analytical Society, October 18, 1922," *International Journal of Psychoanalysis* 4(1923): 252.

36. Freud, "Preface to Max Eitingon's 'Report'" 19:285.

37. Bluma Swerdloff, interview with Sándor Radó (1965), in "History of the Psycho-

analytic Movement," Oral History Collection, Columbia University Libraries, New York., 24.

38. Weber and Engstrom, "Kraepelin's Diagnostic Cards," 382.

39. "Report of the Berlin Psychoanalytic Society," *International Journal of Psychoanalysis* 3(1922): 261.

40. Benedek, "A Psychoanalytic Career Begins," 8–9.

41. Abraham to Sigmund Freud, December 3, 1924, in Falzeder, *Complete Correspondence of Freud and Abraham,* 526.

42. Franz Alexander, "Psychoanalytic Training in the Past, the Present, and the Future: A Historical View," address to the Association of Candidates of the Chicago Institute for Psychoanalysis, October 26, 1951, Archives of the Chicago Institute for Psychoanalysis.

43. Ibid.

44. Quinn, *A Mind of Her Own*, 197.

45. The standard police guard assigned to such meetings.

46. Reich, "This Is Politics!" 99.

47. Sharaf, *Fury on Earth*, 136.

48. Reich, "This Is Politics!" 110.

49. Ibid., 109.

50. See Friedrich Engels, *The Origin of the Family, Private Property, and the State* (New York: International, 1945 [1845]).

51. Reich, *The Sexual Revolution*, 69–70.

52. Reich, "This Is Politics!" 111.

53. Reich, *The Sexual Revolution,* 68–69.

54. Gruber, *Red Vienna*, 159.

1923

1. Paul Federn, December 5, 1923, meeting of the Technical Seminar originally published in the *Jahrbuch der Psychoanalyse*. Hans Lobner and Louis Rose, *Discussions* (Brno, Stuttgart, Vienna: Hans Huber, 1978), 23.

2. Ferenczi to Freud, letter no. 961, May 14, 1924, in Falzeder, Brabant, and Giampieri-Deutsch, *Correspondence* 3:149.

3. Franz Alexander, "Recollections of Berggasse 19," *Psychoanalytic Quarterly* 9(1940): 203.

4. Sterba, *Reminiscences*, 24, 27.

5. Robert Stewart, interview with author, October 6, 1995.

6. Sigmund Freud to Franz Alexander. May 13, 1928, in Jones, *Life and Work*, 3:447–448.

7. Else Pappenheim, interview with author, November 22, 1995.

8. Ibid.

9. The New York Psychoanalytic Society had just drafted their proposal for the New York Psycho-Analytic Clinic and agreed to petition the state for authorization. The charter was denied by the New York State Board of Charities.

10. "Report of the Berlin Psycho-Analytical Society," *International Journal of Psychoanalysis* 4(1923): 510.
11. Ibid., 511.
12. Abraham to Sigmund Freud, January 7, 1923, in Falzeder, *Complete Correspondence of Freud and Abraham,* 464.
13. The Central Institute for Education and Instruction.
14. Abraham to Sigmund Freud, October 16 and November 26, 1923, in Falzeder, *Complete Correspondence of Freud and Abraham,* 473 and 476.
15. Roazen, *Helene Deutsch,* 223.
16. Freud to Abraham, November 28, 1924, in Falzeder, *Complete Correspondence of Freud and Abraham,* 524.
17. Joan Fleming, "A Tribute to Therese Benedek," 1977, archives of the Chicago Institute for Psychoanalysis.
18. Standard practice in the nineteenth century and, many would argue, still today.
19. Horkheimer, "Ernst Simmel and Freudian Philosophy," 113.
20. Freud, "Preface to Max Eitingon's 'Report,'" in *The Standard Edition* 19:285.
21. Richardson to Smith, December 11, 1922, box 24, folder 206, R. G. Barry Smith series 2, subseries 4, Commonwealth Fund Collection, Rockefeller Foundation Archives.
22. Richardson to Smith, June 4, 1923, ibid.
23. "History of the Rockefeller Foundation," 14:3426–3427, Rockefeller Foundation Archives.
24. Julius Tandler, *Ehe und Bevölkerungspolitik* (Vienna, Leipzig, 1924), 15, in Sieder, "Housing Policy," 42.
25. Ibid., 36.
26. Anna Müller, interview no. 18, ibid., 38.
27. Schütte-Lihotzsky, "Vienne-Francfort," 129.
28. Blau, *The Architecture of Red Vienna,* 189.

1924

1. Federn, "Thirty-five Years with Freud," 24–25.
2. Sigmund Freud to Ernest Jones, letter no. 469, December 13, 1925, in Paskauskas, *Freud and Jones,* 586.
3. In a succinct explanation for Ernest Jones's evasion of this event in his biography of Freud, Federn said that Jones "paid little attention to the political and social climate of Vienna and having been himself a political conservative, could not care less about the Social Democrats."
4. Freud to Abraham, May 4, 1924, in Falzeder, *Complete Correspondence of Freud and Abraham,* 501.
5. Freud to Oliver and Henny Freud, May 7, 1924, papers of Sigmud Freud, Collections of the Manuscript Division, U.S. Library of Congress, and Falzeder, Brabant, with Giampieri-Deutsch, *Correspondence* 3:152, note 1.
6. Federn, "Thirty-Five Yars with Freud," 26.

7. Wilhelm Reich, "Politicizing the sexual problem of youth" (1932), in Baxandall, *Sex-Pol.*

8. Reich, "This Is Politics!"

9. Reich, *Wilhelm Reich,* 13.

10. Grete Bibring [Bibring-Lehner], "Seminar for the Discussion of Therapeutic Technique," *International Journal of Psychoanalysis* 13(1932): 259.

11. Else Pappenheim, interview with author, November 22, 1995.

12. Hans Lobner and Louis Rose, *Discussions* (Brno, Stuttgart, Vienna: Hans Huber, 1978).

13. Uncatalogued newspaper clipping in the Archiv des Psychoanalytischen Ambulatoriums Wien, Archives of the Freud Museum, London.

14. Eversole to Pearce, "Conditions in Austria," July 9, 1924, series 705, subseries A, RG 1.1, Rockefeller Foundation Archives.

15. Deutsch, *Confrontations,* 111–112.

16. Sterba, *Reminiscences,* 32.

17. Noveck, "Hugo Bettauer," 145.

18. Ibid., 147.

19. Kraus, *Half-Truths,* 77.

20. Pappenheim, interview.

21. Lobner and Rose, *Discussions,* 23.

22. Sanford Gifford, "Interview with Helene Deutsch," June 28, 1965, Archives of the Boston Psychoanalytic Society, 6.

23. Sanford Gifford, "Interview with Grete Bibring," May 11, 1973, 16, Archives of the Boston Psychoanalytic Society.

24. Pappenheim, "Politik und psychoanalyse."

25. "4% tax," in Lobner and Rose, *Discussions.*

26. Freud to Ferenczi, letter no. 963, May 28, 1924, Falzeder, Brabant, with Giampieri-Deutsch, *Correspondence* 3:153; see also Grosskurth, *The Secret Ring,* 158.

27. Freud to Abraham, letter dated October 17, 1924, in Falzeder, *Complete Correspondence of Freud and Abraham,* 518.

28. Ferenczi to Freud, letter no. 962, May 25, 1924, Falzeder, Brabant, with Giampieri-Deutsch, *Correspondence* 3:152.

29. Ferenczi to Rank, letter of May 25, 1924, box 3, series 1, subseries 2, Otto Rank Papers, Columbia University.

30. Gay, *Freud,* 498–499, and Sándor Ferenczi letter no. 1005, March 15, 1925, to the committee, note 6. Falzeder, Brabant, with Giampieri-Deutsch, *Correspondence* 3:208.

31. Freud to Ferenczi, letter no. 863, February 6, 1921, Falzeder, Brabant, with Giampieri-Deutsch, *Correspondence* 3:46.

32. Letter from Alix to James Strachey, "Sat. aft. December 6th" (1924), in Meisel and Kendrick, *Bloomsbury/Freud,* 138–139.

33. Report of the Berlin Psycho-Analytical Society," *International Journal of Psychoanalysis* 5(1924): 118.

34. Ford to Ruml, February 23, 1924, box 52, folder 558, RG 3.6, LSRM (Laura Spellman Rockefeller Memorial) Collection, Rockefeller Foundation Archives.

35. Eversole to Pearce, "Conditions in Austria, " July 9, 1924, series 707, subseries A, RG 1.1, Rockefeller Foundation Archives.

36. Letter from Alix to James Strachey, "Oct. 22nd" (1924), in Meisel and Kendrick, *Bloomsbury/Freud*, 94.

37. Roazen, *Helene Deutsch*, 223.

38. Alix to James Strachey, "Sunday, December 7th" (1924), in Meisel and Kendrick, *Bloomsbury/Freud*, 141.

39. The story of Max Eitingon's family relationship to Naum (or Leonid) Eitingon (or Ettingon), a high-ranking official under Stalin and responsible for several assassinations including hiring his lover's son to kill Trotsky in Mexico City, is dubious but persistent. The historical evidence is unclear concerning Max's alleged involvement in political conspiracies, then or in Israel after 1933.

40. Alix to James Strachey, "Thursday, December 11th" (1924), in Meisel and Kendrick, *Bloomsbury/Freud*, 144.

41. Harold Nicolson, "The Charm of Berlin," in Kaes, Jay, and Dimendberg, *The Weimar Republic Sourcebook*, 425–426.

42. Jacoby, *Repression*, 67; see also Hermanns, "Conditions et Limites," 81.

43. Deutsch, *Confrontations*, 91.

44. See Deutsch's comments in her report, *International Journal of Psychoanalysis* 7(1926): 138–139.

1925

1. James to Alix Strachey. "Saturday afternoon. Jan. 24th" (192), in Meisel and Kendrick, *Bloomsbury/Freud*, 187.

2. *International Journal of Psychoanalysis*, 7(1925): 136.

3. James to Alix Strachey, "Saturday afternoon. Jan. 24th (192) in Meisel and Kendrick, *Bloomsbury/Freud*, 187.

4. Minutes of the meeting of January 7, 1925, Archives of the British Psychoanalytical Society.

5. Ibid.

6. Alix to James Strachey, "Saturday May 16th" (1925), in Meisel andr Kendrick, *Bloomsbury/Freud*, 267.

7. Quinn, *A Mind of Her Own*, 199.

8. Bluma Swerdloff, interview with Sándor Radó (1965), in "History of the Psychoanalytic Movement," Oral History Collection, Columbia University Libraries, New York, 84.

9. Brecht et al., *Here Life Goes On*, 152.

10. Michael Molnar, ed. and trans., *The Diary of Sigmund Freud, 1929–1939: A Record of the Final Decade* (New York: Scribner's, 1992), 81.

11. "Report of the Berlin Psycho-Analytical Society," *International Journal of Psychoanalysis* 6(1925): 523.

12. Ernst Simmel, *Der Sozialistische Arzt* 1/1(March 1925).

13. "Report of the New York Psycho-Analytical Society," *International Journal of Psychoanalysis* 7(1926): 293.

14. Smith to Scoville, January 16, 1925, frontmatter, box 1, folder 7, series 6, R. G., Austria Program, Commonwealth Fund Collection, Rockefeller Foundation Archive.

15. Hitschmann, "A Ten Years' Report," 249.

16. Deutsch, *Confrontations,* 155.

17. Anna Freud, "Indications for Child Analysis" (1945), in Freud, *The Writings of Anna Freud* 4:5.

18. "Frst Quarterly Report of the Vienna Psycho-Analytical Society," *International Journal of Psychoanalysis* 6(1925): 528.

19. See Eitingon's views in the "Preliminary Discussion of the Question of Analytical Training," *International Journal of Psychoanalysis* 7(1926): 123.

20. Jackson to Irmarita Putnam, April 22, 1932, box 5, folder 102, series 3, Edith Banfield Jackson Papers, Schlesinger Library, Radcliffe Center for Advanced Study, Harvard University.

21. Jahoda, "Emergence of Social Psychology in Vienna," 346.

22. Eduard Hitschmann, "Report of the Out-Patient Clinic of the Vienna Psycho-Analytical Society," *International Journal of Psychoanalysis* 7(1926): 137–138.

23. Lynn and Vaillant, "Anonymity," 165.

24. Abraham to Freud, October 28, 1914, in Falzeder, *Complete Correspondence of Freud and Abraham,* 284.

25. Hitschmann, "Report of the Out-Patient Clinic," 137.

26. Jahoda, "Emergence of Social Psychology in Vienna," 344.

27. Sándor Ferenczi, quoted in Ben Shephard, *A War of Nerves – Soldiers and Psychiatrists in the Twentieth Century* (Cambridge, Mass: Harvard University Press, 2001): 148 and 425 (see note #18).

28. See illustration in Gruber, *Red Vienna,* 149.

29. Noveck, "Hugo Bettauer," 147.

30. Jahoda, "Emergence of Social Psychology in Vienna," 347.

31. Sigmund Freud, "Preface to Aichhorn's 'Wayward Youth'" (1925), in *The Standard Edition* 19:273.

32. Freud, "August Aichorn," 53.

33. Franz Alexander, "Recollections of Berggasse 19," *Psychoanalytic Quarterly* 9 (1940): 199.

1926

1. Jones to Freud, letter no. 471, December 18, 1925, in Paskauskas, *Freud and Jones,* 588.

2. Jones, "The London Clinic of Psycho-Analysis Decennial Report," 7.

3. Freud to Jones, letter no. 473, December 21, 1925, in Paskauskas, *Freud and Jones,* 589.

4. Freud to Jones, letter no. 491, September 27, 1926, ibid., 606.

5. Minutes of the Education Committee, November 3, 1926, Archives of the British Psychoanalytical Society.

6. Klein to Jones, October 24, 1926, box 2, file A-12, series PP/KLE, Contemporary Medical Archives Center, Wellcome Institute for the History of Medicine.

7. Minutes of the board meeting of November 17, 1926, Archives of the British Psychoanalytical Society.

8. Klein, "Diary," 1924, box 2, file A-20, series PP/KLE, Contemporary Medical Archives Center, Wellcome Institute for the History of Medicine.

9. "Reports," *International Journal of Psychoanalysis* 9(1928): 147.

10. Interview with Helen Ross by Faye Sawyier, "Portraits in Psychoanalysis" videotape series, Gitelson Film Library, Chicago Institute for Psychoanalysis.

11. Waelder-Hall, "Structure of a Case of Pavor Nocturnis," 267.

12. Sanford Gifford, "Interview with Jenny Waelder-Hall," August 19, 1982, Archives of the Boston Psychoanalytic Society, 6–7.

13. Dorothy Burlingham, in Burlingham, *The Last Tiffany*, 177.

14. Gifford, "Interview with Jenny Waelder-Hall," 5.

15. *Leipziger Volkszeitung*, Sunday, November 25, 1926, folder "Psychoanalysis & Socialism, 1926–29–1937," container 7, papers of Siegfried Bernfeld, Collections of the Manuscript Division, U.S. Library of Congress.

16. Feuilleton from the *Leipziger Volkszeitung*, Wedneday, October 13, 1926, "Die Entwicklung der Psychoanalyse," ibid.

17. Freud to his colleagues, May 20, 1926, in the Freud Museum (Vienna) Archives, and letter no. 1059, in Falzeder, Brabant, with Giampieri-Deutsch, *Correspondence* 3:257.

18. Gardiner, *Code Name "Mary,"* 35.

19. Ibid., 36.

20. Bettelheim, *Freud's Vienna and Other Essays*, 29.

21. Gardiner, *Code Name "Mary,"* 81.

22. Goetz, "Some Memories."

23. Jones to Freud, letter no. 476, February 25, 1926, in Paskauskas, *Correspondence*, 592.

24. With comments by Ernst Simmel, *Der Sozialistiche Arzt*, vol. 2, 1926.

25. Brecht et al., *Here Life Goes On*, 40.

26. Ferenczi to Freud, letter no. 1045, January 14, 1926, in Falzeder, Brabant, with Giampieri-Deutsch, *Correspondence* 3:244.

27. Max Eitingon, "Memorial Meeting for Karl Abraham, Report of the Berlin Psycho-Analytical Society," *International Journal of Psychoanalysis* 7(1926): 287.

28. Sándor Ferenczi, Circular letter to "Liebe Freunde," January 31, 1926, document no. CFC/F01/77, Archives of the British Psychoanalytical Society.

29. "Report," *International Journal of Psychoanalysis* 9(1928): 148.

30. Ibid., 148–149.

31. Franz Alexander, "Psychoanalytic Training in the Past, the Present, and the Future: A Historical View," address to the Association of Candidates of the Chicago Institute for Psychoanalysis, October 26, 1951, Archives of the Chicago Institute for Psychoanalysis.

32. Alix to James Strachey, "Dec 3d" (1924), in Meisel and Kendrick, *Bloomsbury/Freud*, 134.

33. Interview with Franz Alexander by Francesca Alexander, "The Man Who Brought Freud Here," *Chicago* (October 1956): 27 .

34. Comment by Alain de Mijolla during the July 2000 meeting of the International Association for the History of Psychoanalysis, Versailles, France.

35. Carol Tosone, "Sándor Ferenczi: Forerunner of Modern Short-Term Psychotherapy," *Journal of Analytic Social Work* 4/3(1997): 23–41.

1927

1. Reich, "This Is Politics!"

2. Freud to Jones, October 11, 1928, in Paskauskas, *Freud and Jones,* 649.

3. Freud to Simmel, April 1, 1927, in Deri and Brunswick, "Freud's Letters to Ernst Simmel," 102.

4. Simmel to Freud, March 29, 1927, ibid., 101.

5. Simmel, "Psycho-Analytic Treatment," 74.

6. Ibid., 78.

7. Ibid., 86.

8. Ernst Simmel, "Erstes Korreferat," in *Zur Psychoanalyse der Kriegs-Neurosen* (1918), in Doris Kaufmann, "Science as Cultural Practice: Psychiatry in the First World War and Weimer Germany," *Journal of Contemporary History* 34(1999): 140.

9. Freud to Simmel, July 1, 1927, in Deri and Brunswick, "Freud's Letters to Ernst Simmel," 102–103.

10. Eva Rosenfeld memoir, unpublished, cited in Victor Ross's biographic essay in Heller, *Anna Freud's Letters to Eva Rosenfeld,* 27.

11. Lawrence J. Friedman, *Identity's Architect: A Biography of Erik H. Erikson,* (New York: Scribner's, 1999), 60.

12. Erik Erikson, "Anna Freud: Reflections" (1983), in *A Way of Looking at Things – Selected Papers from 1930–1980* (New York: Norton, 1987), 73.

13. Huber, *Psychoanalyse in Osterreich Seit 1933* (Vienna, Salzburg: Geyer, 1977), 27.

14. Sigmund Freud, telegram of September 2, 1927, at the business meeting of the 10th Congress, *International Journal of Psychoanalysis* 9(1928): 141.

15. *Stuttgart Tagblatt,* 1927, clipping in folder "Psychoanalysis & Socialism, 1926–29–1937," container 7, papers of Siegfried Bernfeld, Collections of the Manuscript Division, U.S. Library of Congress.

16. "Statutes of the International Psycho-Analytical Association," *International Journal of Psychoanalysis* 9(1928): 156.

17. Eduard Hitschmann, document, January 1927, in the Archiv des Psychoanalytischen Ambulatoriums Wien. Archives of the Freud Museum, London.

18. Paul Federn, "Sixtieth Birthday of Eduard Hitschmann: July 28, 1931," *International Journal of Psychoanalysis* 13(1932): 263–264.

19. French and Smith, *The Commonwealth Fund,* 103.

20. Interview no. 6 in Sieder, "Housing Policy," 41.

21. Gruber, *Red Vienna,* 69.

22. Hans Paradeiser, "Ausschnitte aus dem System der Wiener Jugendfürsorge," in *Blätter für das Wohlfahrtweser* 28/271(1929): 76, in Sieder, "Housing Policy," 43.

23. See statistical tables of "Reasons for Admission of Children to the Municipal Child Observation Centre, in Sieder, "Housing Policy," 43.

24. Report of the British Psychoanalytic Society, second quarter, 1927, *International Journal of Psychoanalysis* 8/2(1927): 558–559.

25. Ferenczi to Freud, letter no. 1090, February 26, 1927, Falzeder, Brabant, with Giampieri, *Correspondence* 3:301.

26. Ferenczi to Freud, letter no. 1108, October 2, 1927, ibid. 3:325.

1928

1. Reich, "The Living Productive Power," 74.

2. Reich, "This Is Politics!" 111.

3. Gardner and Stevens, *Red Vienna*, 72.

4. Sigmund Freud, "The Question of Lay Analysis" (1927), in *The Standard Edition* 20:249–250.

5. K. R. Eissler, "The Interview" [with Wilhelm Reich] (1952), in M. Higgins and C. M. Raphael, "Editors' Preface," *Reich Speaks of Freud.*.

6. French and Smith, *The Commonwealth Fund*, 107.

7. *Die Stunde*, September 16, 1928, in folder "Psychoanalysis & Socialism, 1926–29–1937," container 7, papers of Siegfried Bernfeld, Collections of the Manuscript Division, U.S. Library of Congress.

8. *Der Tag*, September 14, 1928, clipping, folder "Professional File—Europe: 1858–1942", container 5, papers of Siegfried Bernfeld, Collections of the Manuscript Division, U.S. Library of Congress.

9. Brecht et al., *Here Life Goes On*, 57.

10. Felix Boehm, "Report of August 21, 1934, " in Brecht et al., *Here Life Goes On*,118.

11. Fromm, *Sigmund Freud's Mission*, 105.

12. Ernst Simmel and Ewald Fabian, *Der Sozialistiche Arzt* 4/3/4(December 1928).

13. Clark to Eitingon, October 10, 1928, Archives of the Berlin Poliklinik, Koblenz.

14. Eitingon to Clark, October 14, 1928, document no. CEC/F02/77, Archives of the British Psychoanalytical Society.

15. Carter to Eitingon, June 9, 1928, Archives of the Berlin Poliklinik, Koblenz.

16. Dollard to Eitingon, n.d., Archives of the Berlin Poliklinik, Koblenz.

17. Mary C. Jarrett to "Members of the Training Committee," March 23, 1928, Archives of the Berlin Poliklinik, Koblenz, Germany.

18. White, *The Autobiography of a Purpose*, 106, 198.

19. Stanley Davies, letter dated March 12, 1928 and addressed to "Training Committee," Archives of the Berlin Poliklinik, Koblenz, Germany.

1929

1. Reich, "This Is Politics!" 108.

2. Sharaf, *Fury on Earth*, 133.
3. English, "Some Recollections," 240.
4. Ibid.
5. *Arbeiter Zeitung*, December 15 1929, clipping in folder "Psychoanalysis & Socialism, 1926–29–1937," container 7, papers of Siegfried Bernfeld, Collections of the Manuscript Division, U.S. Library of Congress.
6. Reich, "Dialectical Materialism and Psychoanalysis."
7. Brecht et al., *Here Life Goes On*, 152.
8. Simmel, "Psycho-Analytic Treatment," 81.
9. Simmel, "The Psychoanalytic Sanitorium," 142.
10. Brecht et al., *Here Life Goes On*, 55.
11. Schultz and Hermanns, "Das Sanatorium Schloss Tegel," 61.
12. Freud to Simmel, September 5, 1929, in Deri and Brunswick, "Freud's Letters to Ernst Simmel," 105.
13. Jones to Eitingon, March 9, 1929, document no. CEC/FO1/30, and March 15, 1929, document no. CEC/Fo1/31, Archives of the British Psychoanalytical Society.
14. Anna Freud to Rosenfeld, September 18, 1929, in Heller, *Anna Freud's Letters to Eva Rosenfeld*, 122.
15. Anna Freud to Rosenfeld, September 29, 1929, ibid., 125.
16. Minutes of the board meeting of January 15, 1930, FSA/4, Archives of the British Psychoanalytical Society.
17. Anna Freud to Rosenfeld, October 14, 1929, in Heller, *Anna Freud's Letters to Eva Rosenfeld*, 129.
18. "Report of the Frankfurt Psychoanalytic Institute," *International Journal of Psychoanalysis* 11(1930): 246–247.
19. Cited in Wiggershaus, *The Frankfurt School*, 34.
20. Minutes of the Ordinary Meeting of February 20, 1929, Archives of the British Psychoanalytical Society.
21. Brecht et al., *Here Life Goes On*, 57.
22. Ibid., 60.
23. *Der Volkslehrer*, July 7 1929, clipping in folder "Psychoanalysis & Socialism, 1926–29–1937," container 7, papers of Siegfried Bernfeld, Collections of the Manuscript Division, U.S. Library of Congress.
24. Anna Freud to Eitingon, April 17, 1928, in Peter Heller, "Introduction," in Heller, *Anna Freud's Letters to Eva Rosenfeld*, 80.
25. Jones to Eitingon, January 5, 1929, document no. CEC/Fo1/20, Archives of the British Psychoanalytical Society.
26. Heinrich Meng's autobiography cited in Wiggershaus, *The Frankfurt School*, 55.
27. Jones to Eitingon, November 18, 1929, document no. CEC/Fo1/41, Archives of the British Psychoanalytical Society.
28. "Report of the British Psychoanalytic Society, fourth quarter, 1929," *International Journal of Psychoanalysis* 11(1930): 119; also see minutes of October 2, 1929, of the board of the British Psycho-Analytic Society, Archives of the British Psychoanalytical Society.

29. Jones to Freud, no. 546, October 14, 1929, in Paskauskas, *Sigmund Freud and Ernest Jones,* 665; also see Jones to Eitingon, October 18, 1929, document no. CEC/F01/40, Archives of the British Psychoanalytical Society.

30. Friedman, *Identity's Architect,* 221.

31. Not to be confused with the Berlin group bearing the same name but with a very different function.

32. French and Smith, *The Commonwealth Fund,* 1.

33. Hermann, "Sándor Ferenczi," 116.

34. Sándor Ferenczi, "Aus der Kindheit eines Proletarmädchen," *Zeitschrift für Psychoanalytische Pädagogik,* year 3, part 5/6 (February-March 1929).

1930

1. Sigmund Freud. "Preface to Ten Years of the Berlin Psycho-Analytic Institute" (1930), in *The Standard Edition* 21:257.

2. Robert Graves, quoted in Shephard, *A War of Nerves,* 164.

3. Edith B. Jackson to Helen Jackson, February 1, 1929, box 1, folder 3, series 1, Edith Banfield Jackson papers, Schlesinger Library, Radcliffe Center for Advanced Study, Harvard University.

4. Underlined in the original.

5. Edith B. Jackson to Helen Jackson, May 11, 1930, box 1, folder 3, series 1, Edith Banfield Jackson papers, Schlesinger Library, Radcliffe Center for Advanced Study, Harvard University.

6. In 1939, with the Nazis consuming Europe like an uncontrollable forest fire almost a decade later, Reich compared the social atmosphere of New York City, where he then lived, to Berlin in 1930.

6. Hermanns, "Conditions et limites," 81.

7. Sharaf, *Fury,* 136.

8. Reich, *Wilhelm Reich,* 21.

9. Freud to Ferenczi, letter no. 1199, November 5, 1930, Falzeder, Brabant, and Giampieri-Deutsch, *Correspondence* 3:402.

10. Freud to Zweig, November 26, 1930, in Ernst Freud, ed., *The Letters of Sigmund Freud and Arnold Zweig* (New York: New York University Press, 1970), 21.

11. Organized by Albert Moll in 1926 in association with Magnus Hirschfeld's Berlin Institute for Sexology (Institut für Sexualwissenschaft), precursor to the Kinsey Institute.

12. World League for Sexual Reform, an unequivocally left-wing organization; Jones to Eitingon, July 22, 1930, document no. CEC/F01/48, Archives of the British Psychoanalytical Society.

14. Landauer to Eitingon, September 15, 1930, in Brecht et al., *Here Life Goes On,* 64.

15. Jay, *The Dialectical Imagination,* 88.

16. Frankfurt Psychoanalytic Institute, "Second Report on Activities," *Internationale Zeitschrift für Psychoanalyse,* 1933, 276–278, in Brecht et al., *Here Life Goes On,* 58.

17. Jay, *The Dialectical Imagination,* 101.

18. Horkheimer, "Ernst Simmel and Freudian Philosophy," 110–111.
19. "Reports," *International Journal of Psychoanalysis* 11(1930): 518.
20. Annual Business Meeting of the British Psychoanalytic Society, July 16, 1930, Archives of the British Psychoanalytical Society.
21. In April, Robert Hutchins, president of the University of Chicago, and Franklin McLean, head of the university clinics, offered Alexander a one-year visiting post in psychiatry after hearing his paper on "criminality" at the Second International Congress of Mental Health in Washington DC. Alexander sought the more controversial title of "professor of *psychoanalysis*."
22. Sándor Ferenczi, *Rundbrief*, letter no. 1201, November 30, 1930, in Falzeder, Brabant, with Giampieri-Deutsch, *Correspondence* 3:404.
23. "Reports," *International Journal of Psychoanalysis* 11(1930): 354.
24. Sándor Ferenczi, postscript to letter no. 1182, February 4, 1930, to Sigmund Freud and note 5, in Falzeder, Brabant, and Giampieri-Deutsch, *Correspondence* 3:389.

1931

1. Grotjahn, *My Favorite Patient*, 31.
2. "Fourth Quarter 1931 Report of the German Psycho-Analytical Society," *International Journal of Psychoanalysis* 13(1932): 267.
3. "Report of the British Psychoanalytic Society, Second Quarter, 1931," *International Journal of Psychoanalysis* 12(1931): 511.
4. Otto Fenichel, cited in Mühlleitner and Reichmayr, "Otto Fenichel," 163.
5. "Fourth Quarter 1931 Report of the Hungarian Psycho-Analytical Society," *International Journal of Psychoanalysis* 13(1932): 268.
6. Ferenczi to Sigmund Freud, letter no. 1206 of May 31, 1931, and copy of letter to Eitingon, same date, Falzeder, Brabant, and Giampieri-Deutsch, *Correspondence* 3:411.
7. Imre Hermann, "Report of the Hungarian Psychoanalytic Society, Second Quarter 1931." *International Journal of Psychoanalysis* 12(1931): 520–521.
8. Judith Dupont, interview with the author, January 28, 2000.
9. Sándor Ferenczi, *Rundbrief*, November 30, 1930, in Falzeder, Brabant, with Giampieri-Deutsch, *Correspondence* 3:403.
10. Ferenczi to Sigmund Freud, letter no. 1206 of May 31, 1931, ibid. 3:410.
11. Eduard Hitschmann, "Sixtieth Birthday of Josef K. Friedjung: May 6, 1931," *International Journal of Psychoanalysis* 13(1932): 260.
12. Paul Federn, "Sixtieth Birthday of Eduard Hitschmann: July 28, 1931," *International Journal of Psychoanalysis* 13(1932): 263–264.
13. Michael Molnar, ed. and trans., *The Diary of Sigmund Freud, 1929–1939: A Record of the Final Decade* (New York: Scribner's, 1992), 284.
14. Ibid., 113–114.
15. Freud to Paul Federn, November 1, 1931, in Federn et al., "Thirty-Five Years with Freud," 20.
16. Edith B. Jackson to Helen Jackson, February 6, 1931, box 1, unprocessed, Edith

Banfield Jackson papers, Schlesinger Library, Radcliffe Center for Advanced Studies, Harvard University.

17. Anna Freud to Rosenfeld, August 1931, in Heller, *Anna Freud's Letters to Eva Rosenfeld*, 162.

18. Ibid., 165.

19. From Eva Rosenfeld's memoirs, in Heller, *Anna Freud's Letters to Eva Rosenfeld*, 39.

20. Simmel, "Psycho-Analytic Treatment in a Sanatorium," 89.

21. Freud to Jones, September 30, 1929, in Paskauskas, *Complete Correspondence of Freud and Jones*, 664.

1932

1. Hitschmann, "A Ten Years' Report," 255.

2. Helen Schur, interview with the author, November 8, 1995.

3. Table illustrating the elections of the community of Vienna in Collotti, "Social-democrazia," 438.

4. Cited in Goggin and Goggin, *Death of a "Jewish Science,"* 50.

5. G. F. Mohr, "August Aichorn: Friend of Wayward Youth," in Alexander, Eisenstein, and Grotjahn, *Psychoanalytic Pioneers*, 348–359.

6. Anna Freud to Rosenfeld, March 25–26,1932, in Heller, *Anna Freud's Letters to Eva Rosenfeld*, 170.

7. Jackson to Irmarita Putnam, January 11, 1932, box 5, folder 102, series 3, Edith Banfield Jackson papers, Schlesinger Library, Radcliffe Center for Advanced Study, Harvard University.

8. Not until 1973 did Bernfeld's campaign for the universal recognition of child neglect finally prevail in the U.S., when the National Center for the Prevention of Child Abuse and Neglect dedicated the Edith Banfield Jackson Family Development Center in her honor.

9. Jackson to Irmarita Putnam, January 12, 1932, box 5, folder 102, series 3, Edith Banfield Jackson papers, Schlesinger Library, Radcliffe Center for Advanced Study, Harvard University.

10. Sigmund Freud quoted in Edith B. Jackson letter to Irmarita Putnam, January 11, 1932, ibid.

11. Ernst Simmel, *Der Sozialistische Arzt*, vol. 8, September 1932.

12. Eva Rosenfeld memoir, unpublished, cited in Victor Ross's biographic essay in Heller, *Anna Freud's Letters to Eva Rosenfeld*, 39.

13. Anna Freud to Rosenfeld, August 27, 1931, in Heller, *Anna Freud's Letters to Eva Rosenfeld*, 167.

14. Rosenfeld to Glover, June 14, 1939, document no. CGA/F30/18, Archives of the British Psychoanalytical Society.

15. Michael Molnar, ed. and trans., *The Diary of Sigmund Freud, 1929–1939: A Record of the Final Decade* (New York: Scribner's, 1992), 119.

16. Interview with Franz Alexander by Francesca Alexander, Archives of the Chicago Institute for Psychoanalysis, 27.
17. Brill to Jones, November 17, 1933, document no. CBO/FO4/27, Archives of the British Psychoanalytical Society.
18. Ibid.
19. Crowley, "Psychiatry, Psychiatrists, and Psychoanalysts," 558.
20. Franz Alexander, "Psychoanalytic Training in the Past, the Present, and the Future: A Historical View," address to the Association of Candidates of the Chicago Institute for Psychoanalysis, October 26, 1951, Archives of the Chicago Institute for Psychoanalysis, 6.
21. Minutes of the board meetings of April 6 and June 15, 1932, Archives of the British Psychoanalytical Society.
22. Ferenczi to Freud, letter no. 1218, January 21, 1932, in Falzeder, Brabant, with Giampieri-Deutsch, *Correspondence* 3:425.
23. Ferenczi to Freud, letter no. 1221, April 21, 1932, ibid. 3:428.

1933

1. Max Eitingon, "Memo of April 7, 1933," in Brecht et al., *Here Life Goes On,* 113.
1. Jones to Anna Freud, June 13, 1933, document no. CFA/FO1/17, Archives of the British Psychoanalytical Society.
2. Felix Boehm, "Report of August 21, 1934," in Brecht et al., *Here Life Goes On,* 119.
3. Ibid., 120.
4. Otto Fenichel, *Rundbriefe,* May 1937, in Jacoby, *The Repression of Psychoanalysis,* 100.
5. Roudinesco and Plon, "Felix Boehm," in *Dictionaire de la Psychanalyse,* 136–137.
6. John Rickman, Report on visits to Berlin to interview psychoanalysts, in Pearl King, "Sur les Activités et l'Influence des Psychoanalystes Britanniques durant la Deuxième Guerre Mondiale," *Revue Internationale d'Histoire e la Psychanalyse* 1(1988): 154.
7. Jones to Brill, September 25, 1933, document no. CBO/FO4/25s, Archives of the British Psychoanalytical Society.
8. Goggin and Goggin, *Death of a "Jewish Science,"* 57.
9. Jones to Brill, December 2, 1933, document no. CBO/FO4/28, Archives of the British Psychoanalytical Society.
10. Jones to Eitingon, March 11, 1933, document no. CEC/Fo1/63A, ibid.
11. Van Ophuijsen to Jones, Brecht et al., *Here Life Goes On,* 114.
12. Hildegard Brenner, quoted in Hochman, *Architects of Fortune,* 74.
13. Boehm, "Report of August 21, 1934," 120.
14. Carl Müller-Braunschweig, "Memorandum of September 29, 1933," in Brecht et al., *Here Life Goes On,* 115.
15. Boehm, "Report of August 21, 1934," 122.
16. Künkel to Göring, December 12, 1933, in Brecht et al., *Here Life Goes On,* 114.

17. Jones to Anna Freud, October 3, 1933, in Goggin and Goggin, *Death of a "Jewish Science,"* 21.
18. Boehm, "Report of August 21, 1934," 122.
19. Minutes of April 5, 1933, of the board of the British Psycho-Analytic Society, document no. FSA/54, Archives of the British Psychoanalytical Society.
20. Minutes of June 13, 1933, of the board of the British Psycho-Analytic Society, document no. FSA/57, ibid.
21. Jones to Anna Freud, June 13, 1933, document no. CFA/Fo1/36, ibid.
22. Jones to Brill, June 20, 1933, document no. CBO/Fo4/22, ibid.
23. R. H. Jokl, "Fourth Quarter Report of the Vienna Psycho-Analytical Society," *International Journal of Psychoanalysis* 15(1934): 383–384.
24. Roudinesco and Plon, "Matthias Heinrich Göring," in *Dictionaire de la Psychanalyse,* 402.
25. Goggin and Goggin, *Death of a "Jewish Science,"* 23, 92–93.
26. Brecht et al., *Here Life Goes On,* 111.
27. Edith L. Gyömröi, "Recollections of Otto Fenichel" (unpublished manuscript) cited in Jacoby, *The Repression of Psychoanalysis,* 82.
28. Edith B. Jackson to Helen Jackson, May 14, 1933, box 1, folder 5, series 1, Edith Banfield Jackson papers, Schlesinger Library, Radcliffe Center for Advanced Study, Harvard University.
29. Edith B. Jackson to Helen Jackson, November 12, 1933, ibid.
30. "Fourth Quarter Report of the Vienna Psycho-Analytical Society," *International Journal of Psychoanalysis* 14(1933): 280.
31. "Annual Report 1931–1933 of the Institute of Psycho-Analysis, London," *International Journal of Psychoanalysis* 15(1934): 113.

1934

1. Fenichel to Edith Jacobsen, Annie Reich, Barbara Lantos, Edith Gyömröi, George Gero, and Frances Deri, *Rundbriefe* no.1, March 1934, box 1, folder 1, Austen Riggs Library.
2. Grotjahn, *My Favorite Patient,* 77.
3. M. H. Göring, "Concluding Speech," in Brecht et al., *Here Life Goes On,* 148.
4. Grotjahn, *My Favorite Patient,* 77.
5. Anna Freud to Jones (n.d.), 1934, document no. CFA/Fo2/59, Archives of the British Psychoanalytical Society.
6. Anna Freud to Jones, January 1, 1934, document no. CFA/FO1/59, ibid.
7. Anna Freud to Jones, November 24, 1934, document no. CFA/FO2/17, ibid.
7. "Mills of ideology" such as the family and the social repression of sexuality.
8. Fenichel, "Psychoanalysis as the Nucleus," 298.
9. Jones to Eitingon, January 24, 1934, document no. CBO/FO2/10, Archives of the British Psychoanalytical Society.
10. Jones to Anna Freud, March 7, 1934, document no. CFA/FO1/75, ibid.

11. Jones to Anna Freud, July 2, 1934, document no. CFA/FO1/78, ibid.

12. R. H. Jokl, "Fourth Quarter Report of the Vienna Psycho-Analytical Society," *International Journal of Psychoanalysis* 15(1934): 383–384.

13. Jones to Anna Freud, November 3, 1933, document no. CFA/FO1/50, Archives of the British Psychoanalytical Society.

14. C. V. of Dr. med Betty Grünspan, box 1, folder 6, Edith Banfield Jackson papers, Schlesinger Library, Radcliffe Center for Advanced Study, Harvard University.

1935

1. Jones to Brill, November 13, 1935, document no. CBO/FO4/43, Archives of the British Psychoanalytical Society.

2. Cocks, *Psychotherapy in the Third Reich,* 117.

3. Edith Gyömröi, *Rundbriefe* no. 7, 1935, in Jacoby, *The Repression of Psychoanalysis,* 99.

4. Otto Fenichel, *Rundbriefe* no. 11, 1935, ibid., 87.

5. Otto Fenichel and George Gero, *Rundbriefe* no. 12, 1935, ibid., 102.

6. Ibid., 103.

7. Jones to Marie Bonaparte, December 4, 1935, document no. G07/BC/FO2/01, Archives of the British Psychoanalytical Society.

8. Gerhard Bry, "Resistance: Recollections from the Nazi Years, 1930–1948," memoir collection; microfilm, Archives of the Leo Baeck Institute, 5–8.

9. Brill to Jones, November 13, 1935, document no. CBO/FO4/43, Archives of the British Psychoanalytical Society.

10. Jones to Anna Freud, December 2, 1935, in Brecht et al., *Here Life Goes On,* 130.

11. Technically, there was a retrospective distinction between extermination (Auschwitz) and reeducation (Buchenwald) camps.

12. Jones to Brill, December 24, 1935, document no. CBO/FO4/49, Archives of the British Psychoanalytical Society.

13. Hoel to Jones, January 4, 1935, in Brecht et al., *Here Life Goes On,* 129.

14. Jones to Eitingon, October 2, 1935, document no. CBO/FO2/59, Archives of the British Psychoanalytical Society.

1936

1. Jones to Anna Freud, July 11, 1936, document no. CFA/FO2/77, Archives of the British Psychoanalytical Society.

2. Jones to Anna Freud, February 12, 1935, Brecht et al., *Here Life Goes On,* 131.

3. Brecht et al., *Here Life Goes On,* 156 and 162.

4. Cocks, *Psychotherapy in the Third Reich,*181.

5. Ibid., 184.

6. Ibid., 116.

7. Otto Fenichel, in Mühlleitner and Reichmayr, "Otto Fenichel," 166.

8. Ibid., 171.

9. Otto Fenichel, *Rundbriefe* no. 13, 1936, in Jacoby, *The Repression of Psychoanalysis,* 108.

10. Ibid., 109.

11. Fromm to Müller-Braunschweig, March 11, 1936, in Brecht et al., *Here Life Goes On,* 139.

12. Müller-Braunschweig to Jones, March 22, 1936, ibid. 139.

13. Jones to Fromm, March 25, 1936, ibid., 138.

14. Winnicott to Bowlby, December 10, 1927, document no. GO3/BA/F09/84, Archives of the British Psychoanalytical Society.

15. Minutes of the business meeting of January 15, 1936, ibid.

16. Documents from the Vienna clinic were buried there for at least twenty years. Anna Freud went "through the house from top to bottom now [and finally] found . . . material concerning the Ambulatorium." Anna Freud to Jones, July 14, 1953, document no. CFF/F02/28, ibid.

17. Ernest Jones, "The London Clinic of Psycho-Analysis Decennial Report," ibid., 8.

18. Martin Freud, as director of the Verlag, pursued very complicated negotiations with the German and Austrian foreign ministries and did succeed in retrieving roughly half the banned books. The Verlag survived until 1941.

15. Otto Fenichel, *Rundbriefe* no. 16, 1936, in Jacoby, *The Repression of Psychoanalysis,* 100.

16. Anna Freud to Jones, December 28, 1935, document no. CFA/FO2/61, Archives of the British Psychoanalytical Society.

17. Sterba, *Reminiscences,* 153.

18. Italics in original.

19. Freud to Jones, no.645, March 3, 1936, in Paskauskas, *Complete Correspondence of Freud and Jones,* 751.

20. Michael Molnar, ed. and trans., *The Diary of Sigmund Freud, 1929–1939: A Record of the Final Decade* (New York: Scribner's, 1992), 202.

21. Jones to Anna Freud. April 3, 1936, document no. CFA/FO2/70, Archives of the British Psychoanalytical Society.

22. Sigmund Freud, "Postcript to an Autobiographical Study"(1935), in *The Standard Edition* 20:73.

23. Wortis, *Fragments of an Analysis with Freud,* 151.

24. Interview with Edith Jackson by Dr. Milton Senn, folder AJ119—Oral History; original in the National Library of Medicine Oral History Collection.

25. Eva Laible, interview with the author, July 25, 2000.

26. Wessel and Blodgett, "Edith B. Jackson," 438.

27. Invitation, December 22, 1937, in Brecht et al., *Here Life Goes On,* 159.

28. Jones to Anna Freud, September 19, 1933, document no. CFA/FO1/40, Archives of the British Psychoanalytical Society.

29. Harrison to Beale, April 4, 1936, box 3, folder 30, series 216A, RG 1.1, Rockefeller Foundation Archives

1937

1. Burlingham, *The Last Tiffany*, 228.
2. Eva Laible, interview with the author, July 25, 2000.
3. C. V. of Dr. med Betty Grünspan, box 1, folder 6, Edith Banfield Jackson papers, Schlesinger Library, Radcliffe Center for Advanced Study, Harvard University.
4. This stellar program of research and direct assistance is now the Hampstead Child Therapy Course and Clinic and the Anna Freud Center.
5. Cocks, *Psychotherapy in the Third Reich*, 181.
6. Ibid., 178.
7. Ibid., 160.
8. For a thorough discussion of this argument, see Cocks and Jarausch, *German Professions*.
9. Grotjahn, *My Favorite Patient*, 54.

1938

1. Sterba, *Reminiscences*, 159.
2. Göring to Carl Müller-Braunschweig, March 20, 1938, in Brecht et al., *Here Life Goes On*, 144.
3. Jones to Edith Jackson, March 30, 1938, box 1, folder 7, series 1, Edith Banfield Jackson papers, Schlesinger Library, Radcliffe Center for Advanced Study, Harvard University.
4. Müller-Braunschweig to Brückel, March 30, 1938, in Brecht et al., *Here Life Goes On*, 145.
5. Müller-Braunschweig to Wirz, April 1, 1938, ibid., 144–145.
6. Müller-Braunschweig to Kaufmann, April 11, 1938, ibid., 144.
7. Buxbaum to Steele, January 25, 1979, Edith Banfield Jackson papers, Schlesinger Library, Radcliffe Center for Advanced Study, Harvard University.
8. Burlingham to Edith Jackson, April 8, 1938, ibid.
9. Jones to Edith Jackson, March 30, 1938, box 1, folder 7, series 1, ibid.
10. Burlingham to Edith Jackson, April 8, 1938, ibid.
11. Jones to Edith Jackson, March 30, 1938, ibid.
12. Edith Jackson to Jones. March 24, 1938, ibid.
13. Anna Freud to Edith Jackson. May 18, 1938, box 1, folder 6, series 1, ibid.
14. Gardiner, *Code Name "Mary,"* 109–110.
15. Otto Fenichel, *Rundbriefe* no. 18, 1938, in Jacoby, *The Repression of Psychoanalysis*, 116–117.
16. Note that "state" and "him" are merged into a single sovereign unit.
17. Boehm to Hitler, 1938, in Brecht et al., *Here Life Goes On*, 146.
18. Hitler to Boehm, ibid.
19. Cocks, *Psychotherapy in the Third Reich*, 179.
20. Ibid., 201.

21. Freud to Simmel, January 9, 1939, in Deri and Brunswick, "Freud's Letters to Ernst Simmel," 108.

22. Sigmund Freud, *Civilization and Its Discontents* (1930), in *The Standard Edition* 21:96.

BIBLIOGRAPHY

Abraham, Hilda C., and Ernst L. Freud. *A Psycho-Analytic Dialogue: The Letters of Sigmund Freud and Karl Abraham, 1907–1926.* New York: Basic, 1965.

Alexander, Franz, Samuel Eisenstein, and Martin Grotjahn, eds. *Psychoanalytic Pioneers.* New York: Basic, 1966.

Aron, Lewis, and Adrienne Harris, eds. *The Legacy of Sándor Ferenczi.* Hillsdale, NJ: Analytic, 1993.

Bayer, Herbert, Walter Gropius, and Isa Gropius. *Bauhaus, 1919–1928.* New York: Museum of Modern Art, 1990 [1938].

Benedek, Thomas G. "A Psychoanalytic Career Begins: Therese F. Benedek, M.D.: A Documentary Biography," 3–15. *Annual of Psychoanalysis,* vol. 7 (New York: International Universities Press, 1979).

Benton, Charlotte A. *Different World: Emigre Architects in Britain, 1928–1958.* London: RIBA Heinz Gallery, 1995.

Bergmann, Martin, "Reflections on the History of Psychoanalysis." *Journal of the American Psychoanalytic Association* 41/4(1993): 929–955.

Berner, Peter et al. *Zur Geschchte der Psychiatrie in Wien: Eine Bilddokumentation.* Vienna: Christian Brandstätter, 1995.

Bettelheim, Bruno. *Freud's Vienna and Other Essays.* New York: Knopf, 1990.

—— "Last Thoughts on Therapy: An Interview with David James Fisher." *Society* 28/3(1991): 62–69.

Bion, W. R. *The British Psycho-Analytical Society Fiftieth Anniversary.* Privately printed. London, 1963.

Birnbaum, Ferdinand. "The Individual Psychological Experimental School in Vienna." *International Journal of Individual Psychology* no. 2(1935): 118–124.

Blau, Eve. *The Architecture of Red Vienna.* Cambridge: MIT Press, 1998.

Boehlich, Walter, ed. *The Complete Letters of Sigmund Freud to Eduard Silberstein,*

1871–1881. Trans. Arnold J. Pomerans. Cambridge: Belknap Press of Harvard University Press, 1990.

Boyer, John W. *Culture and Political Crisis in Vienna: Christian Socialism in Power, 1897–1918*. Chicago: University of Chicago Press, 1995.

Brabant, Eva, Ernst Falzeder, and Patrizia Giampieri-Deutsch, eds. *The Correspondence of Sigmund Freud and Sándor Ferenczi: Volume 1, 1908–1914*. Trans. Peter T. Hoffer. Cambridge: Belknap Press of Harvard University Press, 1994.

Brabant-Gerö, Eva. *Ferenczi et l'école hongroise de psychanalyse*. Paris: Harmattan, 1977.

Brecht, Karen, Volker Friedrich, Ludger M. Hermanns, Isidor J. Kaminer, and Dierk H. Juelich, eds. *Here Life Goes On in a Most Peculiar Way: Psychoanalysis Before and After 1933*. Ed. Hella Ehlers, trans. Christine Trollope. Hamburg: Kellner, 1990.

—— "La Psychanalyse sous l'Allemagne nazie: Adaptation à l'institution, relations entre psychoanalystes juifs and non juifs." *Revue Internationale d'Histoire de la Psychanalyse* 1(1988): 95–108.

Brinkschulte, Eva. "Stationär oder Ambulant: Die orthopädische Poliklinik zwischen klinischer Rekrutierung und allgemeiner Krankenversorgung." *Jahrbuch für Universitätsgeschichte* 3:181–194. Stuttgart: Steiner, 2000.

Brody, Benjamin. "Freud's Case-load." *Psychotherapy: Theory, Research, and Practice* 7(1970): 8–12.

Brunner, José. "Psychiatry, Psychoanalysis, and Politics During the First World War." *Journal of the History of the Behavioral Sciences* 27(1991): 352–365.

Burlingham, Michael John. *The Last Tiffany: A Biography of Dorothy Tiffany Burlingham*. New York: Atheneum, 1989.

Burnham, John Chynoweth. "Psychiatry, Psychology, and the Progressive Movement." *American Quarterly* 12(1960): 457–465.

Carsten, F. L. *The First Austrian Republic, 1918–1938*. London: Gower/Maurice Temple Smith, 1986.

Cocks, Geoffrey. *Psychotherapy in the Third Reich: The Göring Institute*. 2d ed. New Brunswick: Transaction, 1997.

Cocks, Geoffrey, and Konrad H. Jarausch, eds. *German Professions, 1800–1950*. New York: Oxford University Press, 1990.

Colby, Kenneth Mark. "On the Disagreement Between Freud and Adler." *American Imago* 8/3(1951): 229–238.

Collotti, Enzo. "Socialdemocrazia e Amministrazione Municipale: Il Caso della 'Vienna Rossa.'" *Annali del'Istituto Giangiacomo Feltrinelli* (1984): 431–474.

Crowley, Ralph M. "Psychiatry, Psychiatrists, and Psychoanalysts: Reminiscences of Madison, Chicago, and Washington-Baltimore in the 1930s." *Journal of the American Academy of Psychoanalysis* 6/4(1978): 557–567.

Deri, Frances, and David Brunswick. "Freud's Letters to Ernst Simmel." *Journal of the American Psychoanalytic Association* 12/1(1964): 93–109.

Deutsch, Helene. *Confrontations with Myself: An Epilogue*. New York: Norton, 1973.

Drell, Martin J. "Hermine Hug-Hellmuth: A Pioneer in Child Analysis." *Bulletin of the Menninger Clinic* 46/2(1982): 139–150.

Eastman, Max. *Great Companions: Critical Memoirs of Some Famous Friends*. NewYork: Farrar, Straus and Cudahy, 1942.

Eissler, K. R. *Freud as an Expert Witness: The Discussion of War Neuroses Between Freud and Wagner-Jauregg*. Trans. Christine Trollope. Madison, CT: International Universities Press, 1986.

——— "On Some Theoretical and Technical Problems Regarding the Payment of Fees for Psychoanalytic Treatment." *International Review of Psychoanalysis* 1(1974): 73–101.

Eitingon, Max. "Report of the Berlin Psycho-Analytical Policlinic, March 1920–June 1922." *International Journal of Psychoanalysis* 4(1923):254–269.

——— "Report on the Berlin Psycho-Analytical Institute, May 1924–August 1925." *International Journal of Psychoanalysis* 7(1926): 139–141.

Eitingon, Max, Ernst Simmel, Otto Fenichel, and Karen Horney. *Zehn Jahre Berliner Psychoanalytisches Institut, 1920–1930*; rev. ed., foreword by Anna Freud, *Berliner Psychoanalytisches Institut der Deutschen Psychoanalytischen Vereinigung*. Meisenheim: Hain, 1970 [1930].

English, O. Spurgeon. "Some Recollections of a Psychoanalysis with Wilhelm Reich: September 1929–April 1932." *Journal of the American Academy of Psychoanalysis* 5/2(1977): 239–253.

Engstrom, Eric J. "Emil Kraepelin: Psychiatry and Public Affairs in Wilhelmine Germany." *History of Psychiatry* 2(1991): 111–132.

——— "The Birth of Clinical Psychiatry: Power, Knowledge, and Professionalization in Germany, 1867–1914." Ph.D. dissertation, University of North Carolina at Chapel Hill, 1997.

Etkind, Alexander. *Eros of the Impossible: The History of Psychoanalysis in Russia*. Trans. Noah and Maria Rubins. New York: Westview, 1997.

Fallend, Karl. *Sonderlinge, Träumer Sensitive: Psychoanalyse auf den Weg zur Institution und Profession*. Vienna: Jugend and Volk, 1995.

——— *Wilhelm Reich in Wien. Psychoanalyse und Politik*. Vol. 17. Vienna: Ludwig Boltzmann Institute, 1988.

Falzeder, Ernst, ed. *The Complete Correspondence of Sigmund Freud and Karl Abraham, 1907–1925*. London and New York: Karnac, 2002.

Falzeder, Ernst, and Eva Brabant, with Patrizia Giampieri-Deutsch, eds. *The Correspondence of Sigmund Freud and Sándor Ferenczi: Volume 2, 1914–1919*. Trans. Peter Hoffer. Cambridge: Belknap Press of Harvard University Press, 1996.

——— *The Correspondence of Sigmund Freud and Sándor Ferenczi: Volume 3, 1908–1914*. Trans. Peter Hoffer. Cambridge: Belknap Press of Harvard University Press, 2000.

Federn, Ernst et al. "Thirty-Five Years with Freud: In Honor of the Hundredth Anniversary of Paul Federn, MD." *Journal of the History of the Behavioral Sciences* 8/1(1972): 3–55.

Fenichel, Otto. *119 Rundbriefe, 1934–1945*. 2 vols. Ed. Elke Mühlleitner and Johannes Reichmayr. Frankfurt: Stroemfeld, 1998.

——— "Psychoanalysis as the Nucleus of a Future Dialectical-Materialistic Psychology." *American Imago* 24(1967): 290–311.

French, William J., and Geddes Smith. *The Commonwealth Fund Activities in Austria, 1923–1929.* New York: Commonwealth Fund Division of Publications, 1930.

Freud, Anna. "August Aichorn: July 27, 1878–October 17, 1949." *International Journal of Psychoanalysis* 32(1951): 51–56.

—— *The Writings of Anna Freud.* Vols. 1–8. New York: International Universities Press, 1974.

Freud, Sigmund. *The Standard Edition of the Complete Psychological Works of Sigmund Freud.* 24 vols. Ed. and trans. James Strachey, with Alix Strachey. London: Hogarth, 1953–74.

Friedman, Lawrence J. *Identity's Architect: A Biography of Erik H. Erikson.* New York: Scribner's, 1999.

Fromm, Erich. *Sigmund Freud's Mission: An Analysis of His Personality and Influence.* New York: Harper, 1959.

Gardiner, Muriel. *Code Name "Mary": Memoirs of an American Woman in the Austrian Underground.* New Haven: Yale University Press, 1983.

Gardner, Sheldon, and Gwendolyn Stevens. *Red Vienna and the Golden Age of Psychology, 1918–1938.* New York: Praeger, 1992.

Gay, Peter. *Freud: A Life for Our Time.* Rev. ed. New York: Norton, 1999.

—— *Freud for Historians.* New York: Oxford University Press, 1985.

—— *Freud, Jews, and Other Germans: Masters and Victims in Modernist Culture.* New York: Oxford University Press, 1978.

—— *Weimar Culture: The Outsider as Insider.* New York: Harper and Row, 1968.

Gifford, Sanford. "'Repression' or Sea-Change: Fenichel's *Rundbriefe* and the 'Political Analysts' of the 1930s." *International Journal of Psychoanalysis* 66(1985): 265–271.

Gifford, Sanford, and Ann Menashi. *In Memoriam: Edward Bibring and Grete L. Bibring.* Privately printed for the library of the Boston Psychoanalytic Society and Institute, 1979.

Goetz, Bruno. "Some Memories of Sigmund Freud" [1952]. In Hendrik M. Ruitenbeek, ed., *Freud as We Knew Him.* Detroit: Wayne State University Press, 1973.

Goggin, James E., and Eileen Brockman Goggin. *Death of a "Jewish Science": Psychoanalysis in the Third Reich.* West Lafayette, IN: Purdue University Press, 2001.

Goldmann, Emma. *Living My Life.* New York: New American Library, 1977.

Gröger, Helmut. "Zur Gründungsgeschichte des Wiener Psychoanalytichen Ambulatoriums." *Sigmund Freud House Bulletin* 18/1B(1994): 3–22.

Gröger, Helmut, Eberhard Gabriel, and Siegfried Kasper, eds. *On the History of Psychiatry in Vienna.* Vienna: Brandstätter, 1997.

Grosskurth, Phyllis. *Melanie Klein: Her World and Her Work.* Harvard University Press, 1987.

—— *The Secret Ring: Freud's Inner Circle and the Politics of Psychoanalysis.* New York: Addison-Wesley, 1991.

Grotjahn, Martin. *My Favorite Patient: The Memoirs of a Psychoanalyst.* Frankfurt and New York: Lang, 1987.

Gruber, Helmut. *Red Vienna: Experiment in Working-Class Culture, 1919–1934.* New York: Oxford University Press, 1991.

Guerrand, Roger-Henri. "Vienne-La-Rouge." *Histoire* no. 88(1986): 3–6.

Guttman, Samuel A. "In Memoriam Muriel M. Gardiner, MD." *Psychoanalytic Study of the Child* 40(1985): 1–7.

Hale, Nathan G, Jr. *Freud and the Americans: The Beginnings of Psychoanalysis in the United States, 1876–1917.* New York: Oxford University Press, 1971.

——— "From Bergasse XIX to Central Park West: The Americanization of Psychoanalysis, 1919–1940." *Journal of the History of the Behavioral Sciences* 14(1978): 299–315.

——— *The Rise and Crisis of Psychoanalysis in the United States: Freud and the Americans, 1917–1985.* New York: Oxford University Press, 1995.

Hale, Nathan G., Jr., ed. *James Jackson Putnam and Psychoanalysis.* Cambridge: Harvard University Press, 1971.

Hall, Murray G. "The Fate of the Internationaler Psychoanalytischer Verlag." In Edward Timms and Naomi Segal, eds., *Freud in Exile: Psychoanalysis and Its Vicissitudes*, pp. 90–108. New Haven: Yake University Press, 1988.

Harmat, Paul. "Die zwanziger Jahre: Die Blütezeit der Budapester psychoanalytischen Schule." *Medezinhistorisches Journal* 23/3–4(1988): 359–366.

Harris, Benjamin, and Adrian Brock. "Freudian Psychopolitics: The Rivalry of Wilhelm Reich and Otto Fenichel, 1930–1935." *Bulletin of the History of Medicine* 66/4(1992): 578–612.

——— "Otto Fenichel and the Left Opposition in Psychoanalysis." *Journal of the History of the Behavioral Sciences* 27(1991): 157–165.

Heller, Peter. *Anna Freud's Letters to Eva Rosenfeld.* Trans. Mary Weigand. Madison, Conn: International Universities Press.

Hermann, Imre. "Sándor Ferenczi: The Man." *New Hungarian Quarterly* 25/9(1984): 115–118.

Hermanns, Ludger M. "Conditions et limites de la productivité scientifique des psychanalystes en Allemagne de 1933 à 1945: Un premier tableau d'ensemble et un essai à titre d'exemple sur Alexander Mette (1897–1985) et son projet sur Novalis." *Revue Internationale d'Histoire de la Psychanalyse* 1(1988): 71–93.

Hitschmann, Eduard. "A Ten Years' Report of the Vienna Psycho-Analytic Clinic." *International Journal of Psychoanalysis* 13:245–255.

Hochman, Elaine S. *Architects of Fortune: Mies van der Rohe and the Third Reich.* New York: Weidenfeld and Nicolson, 1989.

Hoffman, Louise E. "War, Revolution, and Psychoanalysis: Freudian Thought Begins to Grapple with Social Reality." *Journal of the History of the Behavioral Sciences* 17(1981): 251–269.

Horkheimer, Max. "Ernst Simmel and Freudian Philosophy." *International Journal of Psychoanalysis* 29(1948): 110–113.

Huber, Wolfgang. *Psychoanalyse in Osterreich Seit 1933.* Vienna: Geyer, 1977.

Hug-Hellmuth, Hermine (Grete Lainer). *A Young Girl's Diary.* Ed. Daniel Gunn and Patrick Guyomar. London: Unwin Hyman, 1990 [1919].

Jacoby, Russell. *The Repression of Psychoanalysis: Otto Fenichel and the Political Freudians.* Chicago: University of Chicago Press, 1986.

Jahoda, Marie. "The Emergence of Social Psychology in Vienna: An Exercise in Long-Term Memory." *British Journal of Social Psychology* 22(1983): 343–349.

Jay, Martin. *The Dialectical Imagination: A History of the Frankfurt School and the Institute of Social Research, 1923–1950.* Berkeley: University of California Press, 1973.

Jones, Ernest. *Glossary for the Use of Translators of Psycho-Analytical Works.* London: Baillière, Tindall and Cox, 1926; supplement no. 1 to the *International Journal of Psychoanalysis,* vol. 7, 1926.

—— *The Life and Work of Sigmund Freud.* 3 vols. New York: Basic, 1955.

—— "The London Clinic of Psychoanalysis Decennial Report." London: Institute of Psychoanalysis, 1936.

Jurji, David. "The Significance of Freud for Radical Theory and Practice." *Issues in Radical Therapy* 10/2(1982): 23–55.

Kaes, Anton, Martin Jay, and Edward Dimendberg. *The Weimar Republic Sourcebook.* Berkeley: University of California Press, 1994.

Kardiner, Abram. *My Analysis with Freud.* New York: Norton, 1977.

Kaufmann, Doris. "Science as Cultural Practice: Psychiatry in the First World War and Weimer Germany." *Journal of Contemporary History* 34/1(1999): 125–144.

Keibl, Ernst. "Zur Geschite der Herzstation." *Osterreischische Arztezeitung* 11(June 1972): 701–703.

King, Pearl. "Sur les activités et l'influence des psychoanalystes britanniques durant la Deuxième Guerre Mondiale." *Revue Internationale d'Histoire et la Psychanalyse* 1(1988): 133–165.

Kirsch, Thomas B. *The Jungians: A Comparative and Historical Perspective.* London: Routledge, 2000.

Kohler, Robert E. "A Policy for the Advancement of Science: The Rockefeller Foundation, 1924–1929." *Minerva* 16(1978): 480–515.

Kramer, Hilde C. "The First Child Guidance Clinic and Its First Patient." *Individual Psychology Bulletin* no. 2(1942): 32–37.

Kramer, Rita. *Maria Montessori: A Biography.* New York: Putnam's, 1976.

Kraus, Karl. *Half-Truths and One and a Half Truths: Selected Aphorisms.* Ed. and trans. Harry Zohn. Montreal: Egendra, 1976.

Kurzweil, Edith. *The Freudians: A Comparative Perspective.* New Haven: Yale University Press, 1989.

Landauer, Gustav. *For Socialism.* Trans. David J. Parent. St. Louis: Telos, 1978.

Laqueur, Walter. *Weimar: A Cultural History, 1918–1933.* London: Weidenfeld and Nicolson, 1974.

Levine, Howard. "Interview with Erik H. Erikson." *Boston Psychoanalytic Society and Institute Newsletter* 1/2(1985): 1–3.

Lewis, Jill. "Red Vienna: Socialism in One City, 1918–1927." *European Studies Review* 13(1983): 335–355.

Lobner, Hans. "Discussions on Therapeutic Technique in the Vienna Psycho-Analytic Society (1923–1924)." *Sigmund Freud House Bulletin* 2/2(1978): 15–32.

Lomax, Elizabeth. "The Laura Spelman Rockefeller Memorial: Some of Its Contributions to Early Research in Child Development." *Journal of the History of the Behavioral Sciences* 13(1977): 283–293.

Lynn, David J., and George E Vaillant. "Anonymity, Neutrality, and Confidentiality in the Actual Methods of Sigmund Freud: A Review of Forty-three Cases, 1907–1939." *American Journal of Psychiatry* 155/2(February 1998): 163–171.

McGrath, William J. *Dionysian Art and Populist Politics in Austria.* New Haven: Yale University Press, 1974.

────── *Freud's Discovery of Psychoanalysis: The Politics of Hysteria.* Ithaca: Cornell University Press, 1986.

McLynn, Frank. *Carl Gustav Jung.* New York: St. Martin's, 1997.

Menaker, Esther. *Appointment in Vienna: An American Psychoanalyst Recalls Her Student Days in Pre-War Austria.* New York: St. Martin's, 1989.

Meisel, Perry, and Walter Kendrick, eds. *Bloomsbury/Freud: The Letters of James and Alix Strachey, 1924–1925.* New York: Norton, 1990.

Mészáros, Judit. "Entretien avec un patient d'Alice Balint au cours des années trente." *Coq-Héron* no. 153(1998): 101–115.

Molnar, Michael, ed. and trans. *The Diary of Sigmund Freud, 1929–1939: A Record of the Final Decade.* New York: Scribner's, 1992.

Mühlleitner, Elke. *Biographisches Lexikon der Psychoanalyse: Die Mitglieder der Psychologischen Mittwoch-Gesellchaft und der Wiener Psychoanalytischen Vereinigung von 1902–1938.* Tübingen: Diskord, 1992.

Mühlleitner, Elke, and Johannes Reichmayr. "Otto Fenichel: Historian of the Psychoanalytic Movement." *Psychohistory Review* 26/2(1998): 159–174.

Neiser, E. M. J. "Max Eitingon, Leben und Werk." Unpublished medical dissertation, University of Mainz, 1978.

Noveck, Beth. "Hugo Bettauer and the Political Culture of the First Republic." *Contemporary Austrian Studies* 3(1995): 138–170.

Nunberg, Hermann, and Ernst Federn, eds. *Minutes of the Vienna Psychoanalytic Society.* 3 vols. New York: International Universities Press, 1962.

Oberborbeck, K. W. "Kinderanalyse im umfeld des Berliner Psychoanalytischen Instituts 1920 bis 1933." *Luzifer-Amor* 13(1994): 71–120.

Oberndorf, C. P. "The Berlin Psychoanalytic Policlinic." *International Journal of Psycho-Analysis* 7(1926): 318–322.

Pappenheim, Else. "Politik und psychoanalyse in Wien vor 1938." *Psyche* 43/2 (1989): 120–141.

Paskauskas, R. Andrew, ed. *The Complete Correspondence of Sigmund Freud and Ernest Jones, 1908–1939.* Cambridge: Belknap Press of Harvard University Press, 1993.

Pollak, Michael. "Psychanalyse et Austromarxisme." *Austriaca* 21/2(1985): 83–88.

Quinn, Susan. *A Mind of Her Own: The Life of Karen Horney.* Reading, MA: Addison-Wesley, 1987.

Reich, Ilse O. *Wilhelm Reich: A Personal Biography.* New York: St. Martin's, 1969.

Reich, Peter. *A Book of Dreams: A Memoir of Wilhem Reich.* New York: Harper and Row, 1989.

Reich, Wilhelm. "Dialectical Materialism and Psychoanalysis" (1929). In Lee Baxandall, ed., *Sex-Pol: Essays 1929–1934.* New York: Random House, 1972.

────── *Early Writings,* vol. 1 (New York: Farrar, Straus and Giroux, 1975).

———— *The Mass Psychology of Fascism.* Trans. Vincent Carfagno. New York: Noonday, 1970 [1942].

———— *Passion of Youth: An Autobiography, 1897–1922.* New York: Paragon House, 1990.

———— "The Living Productive Power, 'Work-Power,' of Karl Marx" (1936). In Mary B. Higgins and Philip Schmitz, eds. and trans., *People in Trouble,* vol. 2: *The Emotional Plague of Mankind.* New York: Farrar, Strauss and Giroux, 1976.

———— *The Sexual Revolution: Toward a Self-Governing Character Structure.* New York: Farrar, Straus and Giroux, 1945.

———— "This Is Politics!" (1937). In Mary B. Higgins and Philip Schmitz, eds. and trans., *People in Trouble,* vol. 2: *The Emotional Plague of Mankind,* 77–117. New York: Farrar, Strauss and Giroux, 1976.

———— *Zeitschrift für Sexualwissenchaft,* vol. 10, no. 23.

Reichmayr, Johannes. "Rudolf von Urbantschitsch [Rudolf von Urban] (1879–1964)." *Revue Internationale d'Histoire de la Psychanalyse* 4(1991): 647–658.

Reppé, Susanne. *Der Karl Marx Hof: Geschichte Eines Gemeindebaus und Seiner Bewohner,* Vienna: Picus, 1993.

Roazen, Paul. *Freud and His Followers.* New York: Knopf, 1971.

———— *Helene Deutsch: A Psychoanalyst's Life.* Garden City, NY: Doubleday, 1985.

Robinson, Paul A. *The Freudian Left: Wilhelm Reich, Geza Roheim, Herbert Marcuse.* New York: Harper and Row, 1969.

Roudinesco, Elisabeth, and Michel Plon, *Dictionaire de la Psychanalyse.* Rev. ed. Paris: Fayard, 2000.

Sablik, Karl. "Sigmund Freud und Julius Tandler: Eine rätselhafte Beziehung." *Sigmund Freud House Bulletin* 9/2(1985): 12–19.

Schorske, Carl. *Fin-de-Siècle Vienna.* New York: Random House, 1981.

Schröter, Michael. "Max Eitingon and the Struggle to Establish an International Standard for Psychoanalytic Training (1925–1929)." *International Journal of Psychoanalysis* 83(2002): 875–893

Schultz, U., and Ludwig M. Hermanns. "Das Sanatorium Schloss Tegel Ernst Simmels: Zur Geschichte und Konzeption der Ersten Psychoanalytischen Klinik." *Psychotherapie. Psychosomatik. Medizinische Psychologie* 37/2(1987): 58–67.

Schütte-Lihotzky, Margarete. "Vienne-Francfort: Construction de logements et rationalisation des travaux domestiques: Coup d'oeil sur les années vingt." *Austriaca* 12(1981): 129–138.

Sieder, Reinhard. "Housing Policy, Social Welfare, and Family Life in 'Red Vienna,' 1919–1934." *Oral History: Journal of the Oral History Society* 13/2(1985): 35–48.

Seidler, Regine. "School Guidance Clinics in Vienna." *International Journal of Individual Psychology* 2/4(1936): 75–78.

Sharaf, Martin. *Fury on Earth: A Biography of Wilhelm Reich.* New York: St. Martin's/Marek, 1993.

Shephard, Ben. *A War of Nerves: Soldiers and Psychiatrists in the Twentieth Century.* Cambridge: Harvard University Press, 2001.

Shorter, Edward. "Private Clinics in Central Europe, 1850–1933." *Social History of Medicine* 3(1990): 159–195.

Simmel, Ernst. "Psycho-Analytic Treatment in a Sanatorium." *International Journal of Psycho-Analysis* 10/4(1929): 70–89.

———— "The 'Doctor-Game': Illness and the Profession of Medicine." *International Journal of Psychoanalysis* 7(1926): 470–483.

———— "The Psychoanalytic Sanatorium and the Psychoanalytic Movement." *Bulletin of the Menninger Clinic* 1(1937): 133–143.

Steiner, Riccardo. "It Is a New Kind of Diaspora . . . " *International Review of Psycho-Analysis* 16(1989): 35–78.

Stepansky, Paul. *In Freud's Shadow: Adler in Context.* Hillsdale, NJ: Analytic, 1983.

Sterba, Richard. *Reminiscences of a Viennese Psychoanalyst.* Detroit: Wayne State University Press, 1982.

Stern, Fritz. *The Failure of Illiberalism: Essays on the Political Culture of Modern Germany,* Chicago: University of Chicago Press, 1975.

Taylor, Seth. *Left-Wing Nietzscheans: The Politics of German Expressionism, 1910–1920.* Berlin and New York: de Gruyter, 1990.

Tennant, F. S., and C. M. Day. "Survival Potential and Quality of Care Among Free Clinics." *Public Health Reports* 89/6(1974): 558–562.

Thomä, Helmut. "Some Remarks on Psychoanalysis in Germany, Past and Present." *International Journal of Psychoanalysis* 50(1969): 683–691.

Timms, Edward, and Naomi Segal, eds. *Freud in Exile: Psychoanalysis and Its Vicissitudes.* New Haven: Yale University Press, 1988.

Waelder-Hall, Jenny. "Structure of a Case of Pavor Nocturnis." *Bulletin of the Philadelphia Association for Psychoanalysis* 20(1971): 267–274.

Watson, John B. "Psychology as the Behaviorist Views It." *Psychological Review* 20(1913): 158–177.

Weber, Matthias M., and Eric J. Engstrom. "Kraepelin's Diagnostic Cards: The Confluence of Clinical Research and Preconceived Categories." *History of Psychiatry* 8(1997): 382–385.

Wegs, J. Robert. "Working Class Respectability: The Viennese Experience." *Journal of Social History* 15(1982): 621–635.

Wessel, Morris, and Frederic Blodgett. "Edith B. Jackson and Yale Pediatrics." *Connecticut Medicine* 26(1962): 438.

White, William Alanson. *The Autobiography of a Purpose.* New York: Doubleday, 1938.

Wiggershaus, Rolf. *The Frankfurt School: Its History, Theories, and Political Significance.* Cambridge: MIT Press, 1993.

Willett, John. *The Weimar Years: A Culture Cut Short.* New York: Abbeville, 1984.

Worbs, Dietrich. "Ernst Ludwig Freud in Berlin." *Bauwelt* 88/42(November 1997): 2398–2403.

Wortis, Joseph, *Fragments of an Analysis with Freud.* New York: Aronson, 1984.

Wright, John H., and Jack M. Hicks. "Construction and Validation of a Thurstone Scale of Liberalism-Conservatism." *Journal of Applied Psychology* 50/1(1966): 9–12.

Young-Bruehl, Elisabeth. *Anna Freud: A Biography.* New York: Summit, 1988.

INDEX